Morality, Ethics, and Gifted Minds

Don Ambrose · Tracy Cross
Editors

Morality, Ethics, and Gifted Minds

 Springer

Editors

Dr. Don Ambrose
Rider University
Graduate Education, Leadership,
   & Counseling
2083 Lawrenceville Road
Lawrenceville NJ 08648-3099
USA
ambrose@rider.edu

Dr. Tracy Cross
Ball State University
Teachers College
Muncie IN 47306
USA
tcross@bsu.edu

ISBN: 978-0-387-89367-9   e-ISBN: 978-0-387-89368-6
DOI: 10.1007/978-0-387-89368-6
Springer Dordrecht Heidelberg London New York

Library of Congress Control Number: 2008944288

Printed on acid-free paper

Springer is part of Springer Science+Business Media (www.springer.com)

Contents

Contents

Author Bios

Don Ambrose, Ph.D. is Professor of Graduate Education and Coordinator of the Center for Innovative Instruction at Rider University in Lawrenceville, NJ, editor of the *Roeper Review*, a journal on high ability, and past chair of the Conceptual Foundations Division of the National Association for Gifted Children. Most of his scholarship consists of theoretical syntheses and philosophical analyses driven by a wide-ranging, interdisciplinary search for theories, philosophical perspectives, and research findings that challenge, refine, and expand thinking about the development of creative intelligence. Other books include *Expanding Visions of Creative Intelligence: Interdisciplinary Perspectives, Creative Intelligence: Toward Theoretic Integration*, and *Imagitronics*.

Laurence F. Bove, Ph.D. is professor of Philosophy and Provost at Walsh University in North Canton, Ohio. He received his B.A. and Ph.D. in Philosophy from St. John's University, New York. His presentations and publications examine issues concerning ethics, bio-ethics, social and political philosophy, and peace studies. He has written extensively on the nature and ethics of revenge. He co-edited *From the Eye of the Storm: Regional Conflicts and the Philosophy of Peace*, 1995 and *Philosophical Perspectives on Power and Domination*, 1997. Dr. Bove is a past president of Concerned Philosophers for Peace.

Yuanshan Cheng, Ph.D. (BA Beijing Normal University, China; MA Beijing Normal University, China, Ph.D. University of Ottawa, Canada) has extensive expertise in research methodology and statistics. Currently a member of the department of Psychological Studies at the National Institute of Education, Nanyang Technological University in Singapore, he also worked at Beijing Normal University and the University of Ottawa. As an experimental cognitive psychologist, he is interested in how people make their judgments under different contingencies. He has conducted many educational studies in educational assessment and students' discipline problems.

Tracy L. Cross, Ph.D. George and Frances Ball Distinguished Professor of Gifted Studies, is the Associate Dean for Graduate Studies, Research and Assessment for Teachers College at Ball State University. For 9 years he served as the Executive Director of the Indiana Academy for Science, Mathematics and Humanities, a public residential school for academically gifted adolescents. Dr. Cross has published 100+ articles and book chapters, and a coauthored textbook *Being Gifted in School: An Introduction to Development, Guidance and Teaching*. He is the editor of the *Journal for the Education of the Gifted* and editor emeritus of the *Roeper Review, Gifted Child Quarterly*, and the *Journal of Secondary Gifted Education*.

Meir Dan-Cohen, J.S.D. received his law degree from the Hebrew University in Jerusalem, and his LL.M. and J.S.D. from the Yale Law School. Since 1977 he has taught at the University of California at Berkeley, where he holds the Milo Reese Robbins Chair in Legal Ethics, and is an Affiliate of the Philosophy Department. He has also served on the law faculties at Columbia University and Tel-Aviv University. He is the author of *Rights, Persons, and Organizations: A Legal Theory for Bureaucratic Society* (1986), *Harmful Thoughts: Essays on Law, Self, and Morality* (2002), and articles in legal theory and moral philosophy.

Katie Davis is a doctoral student and research assistant at the Harvard Graduate School of Education. Her research focuses on adolescents' psychosocial development.

Linda Elder, Ph.D. is an educational psychologist and a prominent authority on critical thinking. She is President of the Foundation for Critical Thinking and Executive Director of the Center for Critical Thinking. Dr. Elder has co-authored four books, including *Critical Thinking: Tools for Taking Charge of Your Learning and Your Life, Critical Thinking: Tools for Taking Charge of Your Professional and Personal Life* and *Twenty-Five Days to Better Thinking and Better Living*. She has co-authored 18 thinker's guides on critical thinking and co-authors a quarterly column on critical thinking in the Journal of Developmental Education. Her writings have been translated into French, Spanish, Polish, Japanese, Chinese, Korean, Turkish, German, and other languages.

Christy Folsom, Ph.D. is an associate professor in Early Childhood and Childhood Education at Lehman College, CUNY where she teaches curriculum development and supervises student teachers. She developed the TIEL model during her doctoral work at Teachers College, Columbia University. She uses the model in preparing inservice and preservice teachers to design curriculum that integrates the teaching of thinking and social emotional processes within content. Her background includes preschool, deaf, gifted, and general education. She also directs the TIEL Institute through which she works with gifted children and consults with schools.

Howard Gardner, Ph.D. is Hobbs Professor of Cognition and Education at the Harvard Graduate School of Education. The author of many books in psychology and education, he has co-directed the Good Work Project since 1995.

Kay L. Gibson, Ph.D. is Associate Professor in Gifted Education at Wichita State University. Kay's research focuses primarily on the identification and development of appropriate curriculum for gifted students, particularly students who are culturally and linguistically diverse; and on the integration of global learning into K-20 programs. She has published articles related to her research and presented about the importance of global learning in curriculum for gifted students at state, national and international conferences. Kay helped to pioneer global learning at WSU and received a Global Learning Course Redevelopment Team Excellence Award in 2002. Marjorie Landwehr-Brown and Kay created the Global Learning Curriculum Development Model, which is now being used by numerous teachers in several states.

Amit Goswami, Ph.D. is professor emeritus of physics at the University of Oregon. As a pioneer of a new paradigm of science (science within consciousness) he explained the implications of this paradigm and solved the quantum measurement problem elucidating the famous observer effect in his seminal book, *The Self-Aware Universe*. He has written six other popular books based on his research on quantum physics and consciousness. These include *The Visionary Window*, *Physics of the Soul*, *Quantum Creativity*, *The Quantum Doctor*, *Creative Evolution*, and *God Is Not Dead*. Goswami also was featured in the films *What the Bleep Do We Know?* its sequel *Down the Rabbit Hole* and in the documentary *Dalai Lama Renaissance*.

Barry Grant, Ph.D. has published in the areas of gifted education, moral development, and counseling. He is especially interested in examining the moral bases of gifted education and in exploring alternatives to compulsory education.

Tom L. Green is an ecological economist who studied briefly with Herman Daly, earned his masters in ecological economics from the University of Victoria and is now at the University of British Columbia, Canada, working on an interdisciplinary Ph.D. focused on greening undergraduate economics education. From 2003–2007, he was the director of socio-economics for a coalition of environmental groups working to protect human and ecosystem wellbeing in British Columbia's Great Bear Rainforest. He remains hopeful that mainstream economics education will come to terms with the fact that humanity is constrained by ecological limits and that human wellbeing is not enhanced by ever increasing consumption.

Mary-Elaine Jacobsen, Ph.D. is a clinical psychologist, assistant professor of psychology at Salem College, adjunct professor at the Wake Forest University Medical School, author, speaker, and talent psychology specialist. She is co-Director of a new U.S.A. and U.K. partnership, Leadership Gifted International, a global consultancy specializing in organizational talent development and high-potential leadership. Her first book, *The Gifted Adult*, is read worldwide, and remains the only comprehensive book on the psychology and life issues of gifted adults.

Mark Johnson, Ph.D. is professor of philosophy and Knight Professor of Liberal Arts and Sciences at the University of Oregon. His research has focused on the philosophical implications of the role of human embodiment in meaning, conceptualization, reasoning, and values. He is co-author, with George Lakoff, of *Metaphors We Live By* (1980) and *Philosophy in the Flesh: The Embodied Mind and Its Challenge to Western Thought* (1999) and author of *The Body in the Mind: The Bodily Basis of Meaning, Imagination, and Reason* (1987), *Moral Imagination: Implications of Cognitive Science for Ethics* (1993), and *The Meaning of the Body: Aesthetics of Human Understanding* (2007).

Marjorie Landwehr-Brown is the Gifted Facilitator and the Global Learning Director in the Douglass public schools in Kansas. Her Education degree is from Southwestern College, Winfield, Kansas and she earned a Political Science degree and her Master's of Gifted Education from Wichita State University. She earned the

2004 Global Learning Student, the 2006 Freeman Foundation China/Korea Field Experience, a 2007 Fulbright Memorial Fund Scholarship, and a Korean Workshop Studies award. Marjorie has presented on global learning at New Orleans and Warwick World Gifted Conferences, Kansas Gifted and Talented Conferences, and Wichita State University Global Learning Conferences.

Deirdre V. Lovecky, Ph.D. is a clinical psychologist at the Gifted Resource Center of New England in Providence RI. She has worked for more than 25 years specializing in assessment, psychotherapy and consultation for gifted children and their families. She has written many articles and book chapters on gifted children, and is the author of *Different Minds: Gifted Children with AD/HD, Asperger Syndrome and Other Learning Deficits*. She can be reached through GRCNE02940@aol.com.

Adam Martin is a graduate student in the Department of Political Science at the University of California Irvine, where he works at the intersection of political psychology, religion, ethics, and international politics. Newly-admitted to candidacy, Martin is writing a thesis on forgiveness and the neuroscientific and political psychological aspects surrounding individual forgiveness, reconciliation and recovery from traumatic events, such as wars, genocide, and political conflict.

Kristen Renwick Monroe, Ph.D. is professor of political science and philosophy and Director of University of California Irvine's Interdisciplinary Center for the Scientific Study of Ethics and Morality. Author or editor of 12 books, Monroe is best known for two prize-winning books on altruism. *The Heart of Altruism*, a Pulitzer Prize nominee, won the 1997 Best Book Award from the APSA's Section on Political Psychology. *The Hand of Compassion* was a National Book Award nominee, won honorable mention for the APSA's Sartori Award and won the Robert Lane Award. Her most recent co-edited works are *Fundamentals of the Stem Cell Debate*, favorably reviewed in *Nature* and *The New England Journal of Medicine*, and a forthcoming volume (Oxford) on benevolence in a global age. A new book on gender equality in academia builds on her 2008 article in *Perspectives on Politics*.

Maureen Neihart, Psy.D. is a licensed clinical child psychologist with more than 25 years' experience working with high ability children. She is author of *Peak Performance for Smart Kids* and co-editor of the text, *The Social and Emotional Development of Gifted Children: What Do We Know?* Dr. Neihart is former member of the board of directors of the National Association for Gifted Children (US) and serves on the editorial boards of *Gifted Child Quarterly*, *Roeper Review*, and *Journal of Education for the Gifted*. She is associate professor and deputy head of Psychological Studies at the National Institute of Education, Singapore.

Richard Paul, Ph.D. is a major leader in the international critical thinking movement. He is Director of Research at the Center for Critical Thinking, and the Chair of the National Council for Excellence in Critical Thinking, author of more than 200 articles and seven books on critical thinking. Dr. Paul has given hundreds of workshops on critical thinking and made a series of eight critical thinking video programs for PBS. His views on critical thinking have been canvassed in *New York Times*, *Education Week*, *The Chronicle of Higher Education*, *American Teacher*, *Educational Leadership*, *Newsweek*, *U.S. News and World Report*, and *Reader's Digest*.

Michael M. Piechowski, Ph.D. holds doctorates in molecular biology and counseling psychology, both from the University of Wisconsin. A Senior Fellow of the Institute for Educational Advancement, he has worked and lectured throughout North America, New Zealand, Australia, Belgium, and Poland. Since 2002 he has been involved with the Yunasa summer camp for highly gifted youth. He has published over 40 papers and chapters, is a contributor to the *Handbook of Gifted Education* and the *Encyclopedia of Creativity*, and is the author of *"Mellow Out," They Say. If I Only Could. Intensities and Sensitivites of the Young and Bright.*

Jane Piirto, Ph.D. is Trustees' Distinguished Professor at Ashland University in Ohio. A Mensa Lifetime Achievement Award winner, she has written 16 books. The most recent is a book of poems titled *Saunas*. Her textbook on giftedness is *Talented Children and Adults: Their Development and Education*. Her books on creativity include *Understanding Creativity* and *My Teeming Brain: Understanding Creative Writers*. The chapter in this volume is the third piece she has co-authored with F.C. Reynolds presenting a view of giftedness and depth psychology.

F. Christopher Reynolds is a teacher, singer/songwriter and healer. He teaches French for the Berea City School District in Ohio and creativity studies at Ashland University. He is a facilitator of Earth-based ceremonies such as the sweat lodge. He is the curriculum leader in World Languages and is currently developing a world leadership program for the Berea district. He has released 15 original CDs and cassettes and is the founder of the Urrealist Art Movement.

Annemarie Roeper, Ed.D. is a consultant with 60 years of experience entering the inner worlds of gifted children. Co-founder of The Roeper School and the journal *The Roeper Review*, her wisdom has guided several generations. She developed the Annemarie Roeper Qualitative Method of Qualitative Assessment, training practitioners globally. In addition to numerous articles and chapters, she published *Educating Children for Life: The Modern Learning Community, My Life Experiences with Children, The "I" of the Beholder*, and four books for young gifted children. At the age of 90, she continues to see children and adults at the Roeper Consultation Service in El Cerrito, California.

Deborah Ruf, Ph.D. Minneapolis, private consultant and specialist in gifted assessment, test interpretation, and guidance for the gifted, maintains an overarching interest in educational policy, particularly how schools are set up to meet not only academic but also social and emotional needs of children, through grouping with true peers. Experienced as a parent, teacher and administrator in elementary through graduate education, she writes and speaks about school issues and social and emotional adjustment of gifted children and adults. Her book, *Losing Our Minds: Gifted Children Left Behind* (July 2005), summarizes "levels of intelligence" and highlights highly to profoundly gifted children.

Mark A. Runco earned his Ph.D. from the Claremont Graduate School. He is Past President of the American Psychological Association's Division 10. Currently he is the E. Paul Torrance Professor of Creativity and Gifted Education at the University of Georgia, Athens and Professor at the Norwegian School of Economics and Business Administration. He has edited the *Creativity Research Journal* since 1989.

Scott Seider, Ed.D. is an assistant professor at Boston University. His research focuses on the development of social responsibility in adolescence and emerging adulthood. Thus far, his work has been published in the *Journal of Adolescent Research, Journal of Civic Commitment, Journal of College & Character,* and *Journal of Research in Character Education.*

Linda Kreger Silverman, Ph.D. is a licensed psychologist who has studied the gifted since 1961 and contributed over 300 publications to the field, including *Counseling the Gifted & Talented* and *Upside-Down Brilliance: The Visual-Spatial Learner.* She founded and directs the Institute for the Study of Advanced Development (ISAD), which publishes *Advanced Development,* a journal on the moral development of gifted adults. She also founded ISAD's subsidiaries, the Gifted Development Center (www.gifteddevelopment.com), which has assessed over 5,600 children in the last 30 years, and Visual-Spatial Resource (www.visualspatial.org). For 9 years, she served the University of Denver in counseling psychology and gifted education.

Robert J. Sternberg, Ph.D. is Dean of the School of Arts and Sciences and Professor of Psychology at Tufts University. He is also Honorary Professor of Psychology at the University of Heidelberg, Germany. Sternberg received his Ph.D. from Stanford and also holds ten honorary doctorates from ten countries. He is a former president of the American Psychological Association and the Eastern Psychological Association. He has won the E. Paul Torrance and Distinguished Scholar Awards from the National Association for Gifted Children.

Chua Tee Teo, Ph.D. With advanced training in gifted education and special education from universities in Singapore and Australia, Dr. Teo has trained teachers in China, India, Indonesia, and Thailand, and has been an invited keynote speaker in Beijing, China and Seoul, Korea. She received scholarships for her postgraduate studies and is currently teaching at the department of Psychological Studies at the National Institute of Education of the Nanyang Technological University in Singapore. Her areas of research include self-knowledge of gifted pupils; volitional and ego studies; creative and critical thinking; virtues and character development; gifted leadership studies; happiness studies and teacher education.

David A. White, Ph.D. (University of Toronto) has published over 50 articles and nine books in ancient philosophy, continental philosophy, and literary criticism. Dr. White taught at Northwestern's Center for Talent Development for 14 years, and has taught primary-source philosophy in gifted programs for the Chicago Public Schools since 1991. This teaching served as background for *Philosophy for Kids* (Prufrock Press, 2001), which has been translated into Korean, German, and Chinese, as well as *The Examined Life: Advanced Philosophy for Kids* (Prufrock Press, 2005). Dr. White currently teaches philosophy at DePaul University.

Part I
Launching the Exploration

Chapter 1
Connecting Ethics with High Ability:
An Interdisciplinary Approach

Don Ambrose and Tracy L. Cross

Abstract This book builds interdisciplinary bridges between two very broad inquiry domains: ethics and high ability. Studies of ethics delve into conceptions of right conduct and the nuances of moral behavior. Studies of high ability scrutinize the nature and dynamics of giftedness, talent development, creativity, and intelligence. First, this chapter provides some justification for connecting these very complex, divergent bodies of knowledge. Second, it employs a variety of theories and research findings to illustrate the complexity, longevity, and interdisciplinary nature of the body of inquiry pertaining to ethics and morality. Third, it outlines a set of questions that underlie most of the work of the contributing authors. Finally, it provides an overview of the chapters in the volume.

Those of extraordinary ability can use their gifts and talents for good or ill (Tannenbaum 2000) so exceptional intelligence, talents, and creativity represent opportunities for both improvement and corrosion of the human condition. In recognition of these opportunities and dangers, prominent thinkers frequently have been attracted to explorations of the nature and nuances of morality. This book is an attempt to expand and clarify our conceptions of morality and ethics while connecting them with high ability (i.e., any blend of intelligence, giftedness, talent, and creativity) by bringing together varying insights from leading minds in diverse disciplines. Some contributors are from high-ability fields (e.g., gifted education; creative studies). Others contribute insights from "outside" disciplines in the social sciences, humanities, and natural sciences. Bringing the ideas of outsiders

D. Ambrose (✉)
Editor, Roeper Review, Graduate Department, School of Education, College of Liberal Arts, Education, and Sciences, Rider University, 2083 Lawrenceville Road, Lawrenceville, NJ, 08648-3099, USA
e-mail: ambrose@rider.edu

T.L. Cross
Editor, Journal for the Education of the Gifted, Dean's Office, Teachers College, Room 1008, Ball State University, Muncie, IN 47306, USA
e-mail: tcross@bsu.edu

D. Ambrose, T. Cross (eds.), *Morality, Ethics, and Gifted Minds*,
DOI: 10.1007/978-0-387-89368-6_1,

together with the work in high-ability fields generates some rich, creative, idea combinations. It also augments some important theoretical, philosophical, and research-based insights with practical ideas about how to nurture the development of positive ethical dispositions in those of high ability.

Such a collaborative, interdisciplinary effort is particularly important in today's world because current trends and issues bring forth considerable immoral behavior on the part of many gifted leaders and innovators. Educators, counselors, and mentors who work closely with today's brightest young minds must be aware of the ethical dimensions of high ability because they should be nudging the development of impressive talent toward positive purposes. If they are unaware of the ethical influences they exert, they could be pushing their bright protégés toward morally reprehensible future actions.

While the twentieth century arguably was the most brutal in human history featuring numerous mass genocides and the creation and use of weapons of mass destruction (Glover 2000), the twenty-first century seems to be starting out not much different. Ethical problems abound, including the following:

> The persistence of ethnic and religious conflicts based on warped, superficial understanding of others (see Chirot and McCauley 2006; Madsen and Strong 2003).
> The serious erosion of democracy in some developed, Western nations once thought to epitomize the most just and participatory forms of governance (see Hacker and Pierson 2005; Wolin 2008).
> Deterioration of the media, which generates excessive ideological spin and mind-numbing entertainment while abdicating its responsibility for providing objective, investigative journalism – the lifeblood of democracy (Belsey 1998; Gans 2003; Lance et al. 2007).
> Hegemonic globalized capitalism, which has degenerated from its original ideal of providing opportunity for all to become a large-scale system for concentrating wealth and power in the hands of a few while exploiting the deprived (McMurtry 1999, 2002; Wolin 2008).

These are a few of many large-scale problems that derive from the misapplication of gifted minds. Fortunately, there are many examples of gifted people traveling along more positive ethical paths. For example, members of the nongovernmental organization, Doctors Without Borders, selflessly serve the powerless and downtrodden in some of the most dangerous regions of the world (Leyton 1998); the heroic activist, Aung San Su Kyi, provides inspiration to millions around the world through her leadership of nonviolent resistance to the totalitarian regime in Myanmar (Victor, 1998); and journalist, Amy Goodman, tenaciously digs into the essence of complex news stories and societal issues to reveal hidden corruption (see Holbrook 2006). These impressive altruists follow the lead of their historical antecedents such as William Wilberforce, the activist who worked diligently to eradicate the British slave trade in the late eighteenth and early nineteenth centuries (Metaxas 2007); and Mahatma Gandhi who catalyzed the nonviolent overthrow of British colonial oppression in early-mid-twentieth century India (Gardner 1997; Wolpert 2002).

These examples of issues, groups, and individuals, both positive and pernicious, accentuate the importance of blending ethics with high ability. For the purposes of this introduction, we distinguish between ethics and morality as similar to distinctions between theory and practice. The term ethics denotes theories of right conduct whereas the term morality denotes the actual practice of right conduct (see Sahakian and Sahakian 1966).

Keywords Altruism · Cognitive diversity · Creativity · Doctors without borders · Giftedness · Intelligence · Interdisciplinary · Metaphor · Morality · Religion · Self-interest

1.1 Sampling the Breadth and Complexity of Morality and Ethics

Contemplation of ethics and morality has a long and distinguished history, which is too rich to describe here in depth. Nevertheless, the following limited and over-simplified set of examples suggests the remarkable range and diversity of this exploration.

1.1.1 The Golden Mean

Stretching back well over two millennia, we come to Aristotle's (350 B.C.E./1908) notion of the golden mean, which identified virtuous action as artful navigation between behavioral extremes. A specific sample from his framework is a portrayal of righteous indignation as a virtuous midpoint between maliciousness, the vice of deficiency, and envy, the vice of excess.

1.1.2 Moral Intuition and the Categorical Imperative

Immanuel Kant (1781/1988) argued that people are more prone to wickedness if they are unimaginative. In order to become more ethical we must have the capacity to imagine what would happen if our decision rules became universal requiring everyone to follow them.

1.1.3 Stages of Moral Development

Some scholars discerned stages of moral development ranging from low-level egocentrism to levels at which the individual reflexively follows the dictates of external authority, to the highest levels of universal altruism (e.g., Kohlberg 1984). Development to higher levels is not guaranteed because large numbers of people remain stunted at the low levels of moral functioning.

1.1.4 Particularist and Universalist Morality

Other investigators delved into the interesting phenomenon of moral particularism in which an individual or group confines altruistic actions within the borders of a particular, favored, ethnic, religious, or regional identity group while feeling little or no compunction about denigrating or even seriously harming outsiders (e.g., Gewirth 1998; Koonz 2003; Moore 2000; Pérez 2006). In contrast, universalist morality denotes the tendency of some individuals to transcend self and ethnicity, launching themselves into altruistic action in service of those far outside their identity group because their senses of selfhood force them to view themselves as inextricably intertwined with the whole of humanity (see Gewirth 1998; Martin 1997; Monroe 1996, 2004).

1.1.5 Religious Perspectives and Their Influences on Ethics

Moore (2000) and Stark (2003) showed how monotheistic religion can provide strong bases for the establishment of group identity and positive, altruistic action; however, it also can portray outsiders as impure and deserving of punishment because they do not follow the teachings of the one true God. Consequently, vicious mass persecutions can occur when a monotheistic religion generates a perceived monopoly on virtue among its insiders and labels outsiders as immoral heretics. In addition, major religious traditions show some intriguing, deep-seated commonalties while also representing widely divergent teachings on particular rules for action (see Banner 2002; Hanafi 2002; Madsen 2002; Stone 2002). Based on these analyses we can suggest that surface-level religious beliefs can lead to both good and evil action while deeper spirituality, where the altruistic commonalties reside, more often leads to positive, moral effects.

1.1.6 Cognition as Metaphorical

Contrary to assumptions that our minds are amenable to our own rational-analytic scrutiny, developments in cognitive science reveal that the mind is much deeper and more complex: a Gordian knot resistant to logical scrutiny such as that attempted by analytic philosophy and much of psychology. The abstractions commonly dealt with by intelligent minds are mostly metaphorical and deeply rooted in our bodily experiences (Lakoff 1993, 2002; Lakoff and Johnson 1980, 1999). Considerations of morality and ethics rely on such deep, metaphorical abstractions.

1.1.7 Large-Scale Sociocontextual Influences on Morality

Some investigators have attempted to reveal various dimensions of the large-scale, sociopolitical, economic, or cultural contexts that influence moral behavior. Lakoff (2002) revealed metaphorical cognitive processes underpinning some extreme behaviors that emerge from dynamic tensions between right- and left-wing ideologies. Ambrose (2002, 2003, 2008) discussed the influences of deprivation and privilege on the moral aspects of high ability, and revealed the ethical dangers of widespread utopian thinking (2008).

1.1.8 Altruism as a Product of Genetics and Evolutionary Processes

Sociobiology and related fields highlight biological and evolutionary bases for human nature including its moral dimensions (see Dawkins 2006; Wilson 1975, 1978). De Waal (2006) argued that primate behaviors reveal evolutionary continuity between animals and humans, which highlight altruism as an aspect of our essential natures. He attacked veneer theory, which portrays altruism as a thin, culturally induced layer of civilization over our baser, brutish natures.

1.1.9 Resisting Self-Interest as a Basis for Morality

Some have been challenging the dominance of evolutionary psychology as well as rational choice theory in the social sciences, which portray self-interest as dominant in the motivational aspects of human behavior. These challenges make moral behavior seem less self-centered (see Mansbridge 1990; Martin 1997; McKinnon 2005; Monroe 1996, 2004).

1.1.10 Postmodern Skepticism About Grand Explanations

Postmodern theorists add even more uncertainty to arguments about ethics by warning that prominent theories of human behavior often are excessively ambitious, overarching explanations prone to oversimplification and overgeneralization (see Cahoone 1996). They argue that exploitation and evil can come from too much trust in modernist grand narratives.

1.1.11 Ethical Absences or Opposites

Some thinkers have sought to reveal dimensions of morality by exploring the ways in which moral vacuums or serious moral transgressions occur in human experience. For example, the seventeenth-century philosopher Thomas Hobbes, (1651/1985) argued that we need a strong social contract entailing legal agreements that impose order. Without such a system our rational but wicked essential nature would doom us to solitary, poor, nasty, brutish, and short lives. Midgley (1988) reinforced this idea that vile actions are ubiquitous in the human experience. McLaren (1993, 1999) described the great harm done by some creative people. Hare (1963) argued that psychopathology is more widespread and pernicious than commonly believed. Consequently, we must be wary of people who seem normal on the surface but are self-centered, cunning, exploitative, and remorseless in many of their interactions with others.

1.2 Driving Questions for This Interdisciplinary Exploration

As with any vigorous inquiry into a complex, multidimensional issue, the search for deeper and broader understanding of morality and ethics springs from a set of key questions. The following are some questions that underpin the chapters in this volume:

What key concepts should we consider in explorations of morality and ethics (e.g., selfishness, generosity, greed, exploitation, identity, dogmatism, among others)?

Which concepts, issues, or concerns reside at the core of conflicts over ethics?

What dynamic tensions exist between moral principles and the laws established in particular societal contexts?

How far can ethical frameworks extend toward either absolutist sets of incontrovertible laws for behavior or relativistic acceptance of widely divergent practices?

Who, if anyone, has the right to impose a set of moral principles on others in a society, and how far does this right extend?

Are there aspects of human nature that predispose us toward certain moral behaviors? If yes, are some of these aspects rooted in our biology?

Which moral behaviors are most conducive to shaping, magnification, or suppression by our socioeconomic, political, and cultural contexts?

Is moral behavior responsive to algorithmic, rule-bound thinking or does it require more nuanced, nonalgorithmic, intuitive cognitive processing?

What roles do spirituality and religion play in moral thought and action? What are the differences between spirituality and religion and what are the ethical implications of these differences?

If an individual is highly intelligent, talented, or creative, does he or she carry additional, or different, moral responsibility than less-gifted peers?

Are certain kinds of intelligence, giftedness, talent, or creativity more bound up in ethical concerns than other kinds of high ability?

Is it possible to teach young people to behave in morally responsible ways? If so, what are the most effective strategies for instruction and mentorship?

Of course this list is not exhaustive. Although it emerges from a very broad, interdisciplinary project encompassing a collection of scholars from very diverse fields, a collaborative brainstorming by knowledgeable investigators beyond this volume likely would extend the list somewhat. Including ideas from other major thinkers from the past, and from diverse cultures, might expand it even more. Suffice it to say that these questions hint at the enormous breadth and deep complexity of the topic.

1.3 Exploiting Interdisciplinary Cognitive Diversity

Complex human issues often require interdisciplinary collaboration because their multiple dimensions usually stretch beyond the borders of a single discipline (Ambrose 2005; Nicolescu 1996). Ethics and high ability are two very complex areas of study, and each entails many, diverse subcategories. Bringing them together into a common forum adds even more complexity because the combination of remotely associated ideas can produce unpredictable, creative insights (Koestler 1964; Mednick 1976). In addition, according to analyses of *cognitive diversity*, diverse groups of thinkers bring varied conceptual frameworks and problem-solving heuristics into play, and the resulting idea mixtures produce better results in complex problem solving than would the collective contributions of a homogenous group (Page 2007). The nuances and benefits of our cognitive diversity are explored in more detail in Chapter 25.

For all of these reasons, we thought it wise to assemble a diverse, interdisciplinary group of leading minds for this large-scale attempt to bridge ethics and high ability. Our authors include scholars of high ability who spend their time researching aspects of giftedness, talent, intelligence, or creativity. Some study the theoretical or philosophical dimensions of high ability. Others attend to practical applications such as mentoring and instructional methodologies. But our group extends beyond high-ability scholars to include investigators from the social sciences, the humanities, and the natural sciences whose work pertains to ethics but has not before been applied to giftedness, talent development, intelligence, or creativity in systematic ways. In short, they are outsiders to high-ability disciplines, and they enrich our cognitive diversity considerably. Our outsiders include representatives of psychology, ethical philosophy, peace studies, political philosophy, neuroscience, biology, economics, legal theory, critical thinking, and theoretical physics.

1.4 Perspectives on Morality, Ethics, and High Ability in This Volume

The contributions of our authors fit into some interesting patterns represented generally in the structure of the sections to come, which align as follows: ethical leadership; a diverse collection of insights from the outside disciplines; a set of probings into the ethical aspects of the inner experience of bright, young people; a collection of advice about how to guide the behavior and moral development of the gifted and creative; and finally we address other promising cross-disciplinary connections in our final chapter while inviting you to look for more.

In Part II, experts from creative-intelligence fields provide key ideas about leadership and its fit with high ability and ethics. Starting the discussion of leadership, Robert Sternberg illustrates why behaving ethically often is a difficult path to follow. In Chapter 2, he develops a multi-step model for ethical behavior, which reveals a number of pitfalls that can subvert ethical decision making. Deviating from notions of moral giftedness, he suggests his model can help virtually all individuals develop stronger moral fiber.

In Chapter 3, Mary-Elaine Jacobsen looks into what it takes to become an effective, ethical leader while recognizing a worldwide shortage of leadership talent, especially a lack of ethical leadership in view of proliferating scandals in private-sector and governmental organizations, Significant parallels exist between intellectual ability and leadership. With suitable opportunities for learning, intellectual gifts can be aligned with effective leadership skills and moral principles.

The interdisciplinary insights in Part III begin with a big-picture framework. In Chapter 4, Don Ambrose develops a theoretic model of moral impact to assist thinking about the connection between ethics and high ability. Suggesting that bright individuals navigate a metaphorical landscape that undulates between the extremes of several continua (high to low influence and ability; benevolence to malevolence, high to low impact on the world) the model provides a lens for analysis of other conceptions of ethics and giftedness, talent, or creativity.

In Chapter 5, Adam Martin and Kristen Renwick Monroe synthesize insights from moral psychology and neuroscience and delve deeply into identity formation, connecting it with the moral imagination. They also employ findings about the morally admirable behavior of altruistic rescuers – those who risk themselves to help others, their analysis reveals how identity serves as a cognitive menu constraining the moral choices individuals make, and inclining them toward or away from self-transcending, altruistic behavior.

Tom Green investigates an important paradox in Chapter 6. He analyzes a globe-spanning incongruity that influences moral behavior throughout modern societies. Asking why intelligent economists can be so thickheaded, he concludes that economics education derives from short-sighted models with narrow perceptual frames. Such education encourages otherwise bright people to act in morally vacuous, or even morally pernicious, and environmentally destructive ways.

In Chapter 7, Mark Runco connects creativity with giftedness and ethics, showing how these important elements of human thought and action interact, constrain, and support one another. Creativity is an interesting ingredient here because it gives the individual a larger range of options for moral action. Thoughts and actions must be original and useful to be creative but creativity does not necessarily dovetail with morality. Runco argues that restructuring our thought to make room for creative options can improve our chances for morally positive outcomes.

Richard Paul and Lauren Elder look at the ethical opportunities that effective thinking can generate as well as some serious problems often produced by ineffective thinking. In Chapter 8, they build bridges connecting critical thinking, creative thinking, and ethical reasoning, which are commonly and errantly portrayed as separate. While illuminating these important connections, they explore a variety of intellectual virtues along with pernicious thought processes that counterfeit for ethical reasoning. Their analysis ranges broadly, addressing religious beliefs, social conventions, ideology, law, and other aspects of the human experience.

Amit Goswami takes us in a different direction in Chapter 9. He employs some insights from a new philosophy of science, which derives from the strange paradoxes of quantum physics, to posit a grand opportunity for turning business models toward morally positive, environmentally sustainable, more spiritually attuned processes. Overall, this opportunity represents a logical outcome of a global shift in consciousness away from the mechanistic, technocratic thinking of the past.

Contributors from outside disciplines had the option of providing brief synopses of key ideas from their work or longer analyses, and our next three authors in this interdisciplinary subsection chose mini-chapters as the appropriate venues for their contributions. Mark Johnson provides an overview of some cognitive science research and theory in Chapter 10. Illustrating how abstract moral concepts are grounded metaphorically and viscerally in our bodily experiences and emotions, he portrays moral reasoning as a problem-solving process amenable to imaginative thought. Such a process seems ideally suited to the creative propensities of gifted individuals. Meier Dan-Cohen, in Chapter 11, argues that the nature of individual identity in a society has great bearing on ethical issues. The values and legal frameworks that dominate a society influence the development of personal identity. Consequently, the socially constructed self is at the core of moral action in the world because inner motivation and external, societal compulsions are inextricably intertwined in considerations of ethics. In Chapter 12, Laurence Bove provides some insights from ethical philosophy and the interdisciplinary field of peace studies by revealing some ethical aspects of power and domination in societies. He suggests ways in which intelligent individuals can employ conceptual framing and storytelling to move us toward peace through nonviolence. There are strong implications for gifted young people who must grapple with the complexities of an unjust world.

Part IV includes works that study the inner experiences of the individual. In Chapter 13, Deirdre Lovecky explores pathways to the precocious development of empathy and compassion in young people while additionally delving into the more rule-based structures of moral reasoning. In addition, she analyses some of the substantial problems that early awareness of moral difficulties often brings to gifted young people. Environmental, familial, and personal factors that affect the self-actualization and moral development of the highly gifted are scrutinized. The effects of intensity and sensitivity are considered within the framework of a type of asynchrony between what the young child feels and what he or she is able to do.

In Chapter 14, Michael Piechowski highlights the inner, emotional lives of the gifted as crucial to their advanced development, and to their moral behavior. Portraying giftedness as deriving from higher levels of energy, emotional tension, overexcitability, and sensitivity, among other phenomena, he also shows how Dabrowski's theory of positive disintegration can illuminate the phenomenon of positive maladjustment as well as connections between morality and emotional development.

Christopher Reynolds and Jane Piirto give us a glimpse of the emerging field of depth psychology in Chapter 15. They note that this field focuses on the psyche, emphasizing the unconscious rather than ego consciousness, which is an area of study that they believe has received too much attention. They include topics that are uncommon to the literature in the field of gifted studies such as the collective unconscious, the presence and importance of archetypes, and the darker side of human nature.

While still generating some important theoretical and philosophical insights, Part V also moves us toward practical implications. In Chapter 16, Scott Seider, Katie Davis, and Howard Gardner question the prevalent assumption that high ability equates with moral awareness and posit that intelligence and reasoning ability are neither moral nor immoral. Based on research from the Good Work Project, they share several key findings that have emerged regarding the ethical dilemmas and pitfalls often faced by adolescents and young adults as well as some of the supports that increase the likelihood of young people doing good work.

David White employs philosophical analysis in Chapter 17 to grapple with the nettlesome ethical problem of cultural and personal values. He articulates differences between facts and values, while delineating variations in the latter, and then clarifies the nebulous nature of cultures. He also provides a framework for dealing with cross-cultural differences in values.

Chua Tee Teo and Yuanshan Cheng provide an international, comparative perspective to the discussion of moral education. In Chapter 18, they use empirical evidence to examine the philosophical underpinnings and practical interventions that characterize moral education for bright young people in Singapore, China, Indonesia, South Korea, and Thailand. The patterns of similarity and difference between nations, and between East and West, are informative.

In Chapter 19, Annemarie Roeper and Linda Silverman detail the great cognitive ability, powers of observation, sensitivity, and intuitive capacities that enable gifted youth to develop an unerring sense of morality and justice. At the same time, they note that experiential and cognitive distortions can lead them astray. Roeper and Silverman employ positive and negative examples such as Adolf Hitler and Nelson Mandela to illustrate the dynamics of these developmental processes.

In Chapter 20, Deborah Ruf addresses the question, "Does being smart necessarily lead to being emotionally mature and wise?" Through analyses of the self-actualization of highly gifted individuals, she reveals great diversity in their moral development. They spread over the entire range of a moral-development continuum rather than clustering at the highly virtuous end. She explores environmental effects and considers how family, school, and social background may contribute to self-actualization and advanced moral reasoning among people with gifts and talents.

Recognizing that many gifted individuals possess high degrees of ethical sensibility while others use their intellectual ability to override ethical behavior for selfish purposes, Christy Folsom presents and explains a curriculum model that brings together the intellectual and ethical aspects of learning in Chapter 21. The Teaching for Intellectual and Emotional Learning (TIEL) model helps young people advance both intellectually and ethically from an early age by developing a balance of intellectual skills and strong qualities of character. Folsom claims that the TIEL model successfully connects cognitive and affective components of learning for teaching students about moral-ethical issues.

Kay Gibson and Marjorie Landwehr-Brown argue that gifted young people have the potential to become the leaders of the world. Consequently, adults in positions of influence are responsible for helping them develop into ethical and moral leaders. In Chapter 22, based on the fact that the world is both interconnected and interdependent, they examine ways that global learning in schools will prepare the gifted to display high ethical standards and moral behavior.

In one of the most provocative arguments, Maureen Neihart describes ways in which bright minds can devolve toward criminality. In Chapter 23, she draws on syllogism, research, and other forms of analysis to illustrate a pattern of thinking that she describes as criminal logic. Prior research revealing common characteristics of students with high abilities are considered in light of the characteristics of those who engage in unethical acts. The chapter shows the critical need to help those prone to criminal thinking to develop more positive ethical patterns of thought and behavior.

In Chapter 24, Barry Grant critiques character-education (CE) initiatives, showing how they can derive from superficial thinking. While analyzing various values frameworks, he illustrates inconsistencies between the moral values often established as goals for CE programs and the values actually taught in compulsory schooling. Finally, he urges educators to pry deeper into justifications for CE programs, and to question assumptions underpinning compulsory education per se.

Finally, Part VI returns to the large-scale patterns in the book. In Chapter 25, Don Ambrose attempts an embryonic synthesis of the contributions in the volume. Employing the concept of cognitive diversity; which reveals the benefits of combining diverse, interdisciplinary insights in complex problem solving; he calls for more interdisciplinary bridging between ethics and high ability while drawing some interconnections among the chapters in this collection. He also points out some areas of disagreement, which may represent some opportunities for unforeseen progress.

We hope the varied insights provided here will prompt you to generate your own inquiries into the nature of morality and ethics. If the perspectives represented in this volume induce you to think beyond current wisdom about morality and its manifestations in the most creatively intelligent minds, this exploration will have been well worthwhile.

References

Ambrose, D. (2002). Socioeconomic stratification and its influences on talent development: Some interdisciplinary perspectives. *Gifted Child Quarterly, 46*, 170–180.

Ambrose, D. (2003). Barriers to aspiration development and self-fulfillment: Interdisciplinary insights for talent discovery. *Gifted Child Quarterly, 47*, 282–294.

Ambrose, D. (2005). Interdisciplinary expansion of conceptual foundations: Insights from beyond our field. *Roeper Review, 27*, 137–143.

Ambrose, D. (2008). Utopian visions: Promise and pitfalls in the global awareness of the gifted. *Roeper Review, 30*, 52–60.

Aristotle. (1908). *The Nicomachean ethics* (W. D. Ross, Trans.). Oxford, UK: Clarendon. (Original work published 350 B.C.E.)

Banner, M. (2002). Christianity and civil society. In S. Chambers & W. Kymlicka (Eds.), *Alternative conceptions of civil society* (pp. 114–130). Princeton, NJ: Princeton University Press.

Belsey, A. (1998). Journalism and ethics: Can they co-exist? In M. Kieran (Ed.), *Media ethics* (pp. 1–14). London: Routledge.

Cahoone, L. (Ed.). (1996). *From modernism to postmodernism: An anthology.* Oxford, UK: Blackwell.

Chirot, D., & McCauley, C. (2006). *Why not kill them all? The logic and prevention of mass political murder.* Princeton, NJ: Princeton University Press.

Dawkins, R. (2006). *The selfish gene* (3rd ed.). New York: Oxford University Press.

de Waal, F. B. M. (2006). *Primates and philosophers: How morality evolved.* Princeton, NJ: Princeton University Press.

Gans, H. J. (2003). *Democracy and the news: Restoring the ideals of a free press.* New York: Oxford University Press.

Gardner, H. (1997). *Extraordinary minds.* New York: Basic Books.

Gewirth, A. (1998). *Self-fulfillment.* Princeton, NJ: Princeton University Press.

Glover, J. (2000). *Humanity: A moral history of the twentieth century.* New Haven, CT: Yale University Press.

Hacker, J. S., & Pierson, P. (2005). *Off center: The Republican revolution and the erosion of American democracy.* New Haven, CT: Yale University Press.

Hanafi, H. (2002). Alternative conceptions of civil society: A reflective Islamic approach. In S. Chambers & W. Kymlicka (Eds.), *Alternative conceptions of civil society* (pp. 171–189). Princeton, NJ: Princeton University Press.

Hare, R. M. (1963). *The language of morals.* Oxford, UK: Oxford University Press.

Hobbes, T. (1985). *Leviathan.* New York: Penguin. (Original work published 1651)

Holbrook, K. (2006). *Global values 101.* Boston, MA: Beacon Press.

Kant, I. (1988). *Critique of judgment* (J. C. Meredith., Trans.). Oxford, UK: Clarendon. (Original work published 1781)

Koestler, A. (1964). *The act of creation.* New York: Macmillan.

Kohlberg, L. (1984). *The psychology of moral development* (Vol. II). San Francisco, CA: Harper & Row.

Koonz, C. (2003). *The Nazi conscience.* Cambridge, MA: Harvard University Press.

Lakoff, G. (1993). The contemporary theory of metaphor. In A. Ortony (Ed.), *Metaphor and thought* (2nd ed., pp. 202–251). New York: Cambridge University Press.

Lakoff, G. (2002). *Moral politics: How liberals and conservatives think* (2nd ed.). Chicago, IL: University of Chicago Press.

Lakoff, G., & Johnson, M. (1980). *Metaphors we live by.* Chicago, IL: University of Chicago Press.

Lakoff, G., & Johnson, M. (1999). *Philosophy in the flesh: The embodied mind and its challenge to Western thought.* New York: Basic Books.

Lance, B. W., Lawrence, R. G., & Livingston, S. (2007). *When the press fails: Political power and the news media from Iraq to Katrina.* Chicago, IL: University of Chicago Press.

Leyton, E. (1998). *Touched by fire: Doctors without borders in a third world crisis.* Toronto: McClelland & Stewart.

Madsen, R. (2002). Confucian conceptions of a civil society. In S. Chambers & W. Kymlicka (Eds.), *Alternative conceptions of civil society* (pp. 190–204). Princeton, NJ: Princeton University Press.

Madsen, R., & Strong, T. B. (Eds.). (2003). *The many and the one: Religious and secular perspectives on ethical pluralism in the modern world.* Princeton, NJ: Princeton University Press.

Mansbridge, J. J. (Ed.). (1990). *Beyond self-interest.* Chicago, IL: University of Chicago Press.

Martin, G. T. (1997). Eschatological ethics and positive peace: Western contributions to the critique of the self-centered ego and its social manifestations. In L. Duhan-Kaplan & L. F. Bove (Eds.), *Philosophical perspectives on power and domination* (pp. 79–92). Amsterdam: Rodopi.

McKinnon, S. (2005). *Neo-liberal genetics: The myths and moral tales of evolutionary psychology.* Chicago, IL: Prickly Paradigm Press.

McLaren, R. (1993). The dark side of creativity. *Creativity Research Journal, 6,* 137–144.

McLaren, R. (1999). Dark side of creativity. In M. A. Runco & S. R. Pritzker (Eds.), *Encyclopedia of creativity* (Vol. 1, pp. 483–491). New York: Academic.

McMurtry, J. (1999). *The cancer stage of capitalism.* London: Pluto Press.

McMurtry, J. (2002). *Value wars: The global market versus the life economy.* London: Pluto Press.

Mednick, S. A. (1976). The associative basis of the creative process. In A. Rothenberg & C. Hausman (Eds.), *The creativity question* (pp. 227–237). Durham, NC: Duke University Press.

Metaxas, E. (2007). *William Wilberforce.* New York: HarperCollins.

Midgley, M. (1988). The reality of human wickedness. In D. M. Rosenthal & F. Shehadi (Eds.), *Applied ethics and ethical theory* (pp. 306–321). Salt Lake City, UT: University of Utah Press.

Monroe, K. R. (1996). *The heart of altruism.* Princeton, NJ: Princeton University Press.

Monroe, K. R. (2004). *The hand of compassion: Portraits of moral choice during the Holocaust.* Princeton, NJ: Princeton University Press.

Moore, B., Jr. (2000). *Moral purity and persecution in history.* Princeton, NJ: Princeton University Press.

Nicolescu, B. (1996). Levels of complexity and levels of reality: Nature as trans-nature. In B. Pullman (Ed.), *The emergence of complexity in mathematics, physics, chemistry, and biology* (pp. 393–417). Vatican City: Pontifical Academy of Sciences.

Page, S. E. (2007). *The difference: How the power of diversity creates better groups, firms, schools, and societies.* Princeton, NJ: Princeton University Press.

Pérez, J. (2006). *The Spanish Inquisition: A history* (J. Lloyd, Trans.). New Haven, CT: Yale University Press.

Sahakian, W. S., & Sahakian, M. L. (1966). *Ideas of the great philosophers.* New York: Barnes & Noble.

Stark, R. (2003). *For the glory of God: How monotheism led to reformations, science, witch-hunts, and the end of slavery.* Princeton, NJ: Princeton University Press.

Stone, S. L. (2002). The Jewish tradition and civil society. In S. Chambers & W. Kymlicka (Eds.), *Alternative conceptions of civil society* (pp. 152–170). Princeton, NJ: Princeton University Press.

Tannenbaum, A. J. (2000). Giftedness: The ultimate instrument for good and evil. In K. A. Heller, F. J. Mönks, R. J. Sternberg & R. Subotnik (Eds.), *International handbook of giftedness and talent* (2nd ed., pp. 447–465). Oxford, UK: Pergamon.

Victor, B. (1998). *The lady: Aung San Suu Kyi, Nobel laureate and Burma's prisoner.* New York: Faber & Faber.

Wilson, E. O. (1975). *Sociobiology: The new synthesis.* Cambridge, MA: Harvard University Press.

Wilson, E. O. (1978). *On human nature.* Cambridge, MA: Harvard University Press.

Wolin, S. S. (2008). *Democracy incorporated: Managed democracy and the specter of inverted totalitarianism.* Princeton, NJ: Princeton University Press.

Wolpert, S. (2002). *Gandhi's passion.* New York: Oxford University Press.

Part II
Ethical Leadership

Chapter 2
Reflections on Ethical Leadership

Robert J. Sternberg

Abstract This chapter discusses why ethical behavior is more of a challenge than it would first appear to be. In particular, ethical behavior requires a person to (1) recognize that there is an event to which to react; (2) define the event as having an ethical dimension; (3) decide that the ethical dimension is significant; (4) take responsibility for generating an ethical solution to the problem; (5) figure out what abstract ethical rule(s) might apply to the problem; (6) decide how these abstract ethical rules actually apply to the problem so as to suggest a concrete solution; (7) enact the ethical solution, meanwhile possibly counteracting contextual forces that might lead one not to act in an ethical manner; (8) deal with possible repercussions of having acted in what one considers an ethical manner. In some ways, therefore, behaving ethically is nontrivial in the same ways as is bystander intervention, itself an ethical challenge. The challenges are put in the context of a theory of ethical leadership.

"I am very proud of myself," I told the 17 students in my seminar, Psychology 60, The Nature of Leadership. I had just returned from a trip and was about to fill out the reimbursement forms when I discovered that I could actually get reimbursed twice. The first reimbursement would come from the organization that had invited me, and required me merely to fill out a form listing my expenses. The second reimbursement would come from my university, Tufts, upon my submitting the receipts from the trip. I explained to the class that I had worked really hard on the trip speaking about ethical leadership, and so I was pleased that by getting reimbursed twice, I could justify to myself the amount of work I had put into the trip.

I waited for the firestorm. Would the class – which had already studied leadership for several months – rise up in a mass protest against what I had done? Or would only a half-dozen brave souls raise their hands and roundly criticize me for what was obviously patently unethical behavior? I waited, and waited, and waited.

R.J. Sternberg
Dean Arts & Sciences, Office of the Dean of Arts and Sciences, Ballou Hall, 3rd Floor, Tufts University, Medford, MA 02155, USA
e-mail: Robert.Sternberg@tufts.edu

D. Ambrose, T. Cross (eds.), *Morality, Ethics, and Gifted Minds*,
DOI: 10.1007/978-0-387-89368-6_2,

Nothing happened. I then decided to move on to the main topic of the day – I do not even remember what it was. All the time I was speaking about that main topic, I expected some of the students to raise their hands and demand to return to the topic of my double reimbursement. It didn't happen.

Finally, I stopped talking about whatever the topic was, and flat-out asked the class why no one had challenged me. I figured that they would, to a person, be embarrassed for not having challenged me. Quite a few of them were embarrassed. Others thought I must be kidding. What I did not expect, though – especially after having taught them for several months about ethical leadership – was that some of the students would commend me on my clever idea and argue that, if I could get away with it, I was entitled to receive the money.

This experience reminded me of how hard it is to translate theories of ethics, and even case studies, into one's own practice. The students had read about ethics in leadership, heard about ethics in leadership from a variety of real-world leaders, discussed ethics in leadership, and then apparently totally failed to recognize unethical behavior when it stared them in the face. (Full disclosure: I did *not* really seek double reimbursement!) Why is it so hard to translate theory into practice, even after one has studied ethical leadership for several months?

I was reminded of the work of Latané and Darley (1970), which showed that divinity students who were about to lecture on the parable of *The Good Samaritan* were no more likely than other bystanders to help a person in distress who was in need of – a good Samaritan! Drawing upon their model of bystander intervention, I here propose a model of ethical behavior that would seem to apply to a variety of ethical problems.

The model is also grounded in a theory I have proposed of good and effective leadership, called WICS. WICS is an acronym for wisdom, intelligence, and creativity, synthesized (Sternberg 2003a, b, 2005, 2008). The basic idea is that gifted leaders excel in having a creative vision for where they wish to lead people; in being able to analyze whether the vision is a good one (analytical intelligence); in being able practically to implement the vision and persuade others of its value (practical intelligence); and in ensuring that the vision wisely helps lead stakeholders toward a common good.

Keywords Balance · Common good · Ethics · Extrapersonal interests · Intrapersonal interests · Interpersonal interests · WICS · Wisdom

2.1 A Model for Ethical Behavior

According to the proposed model, enacting ethical behavior is much harder than it would appear to be because it involves multiple, largely sequential, steps. To behave ethically, the individual has to:

Recognize that there is an event to which to react.
Define the event as having an ethical dimension.
Decide that the ethical dimension is significant.

Take responsibility for generating an ethical solution to the problem.

Figure out what abstract ethical rule(s) might apply to the problem.

Decide how these abstract ethical rules actually apply to the problem so as to suggest a concrete solution.

Enact the ethical solution, meanwhile possibly counteracting contextual forces that might lead one not to act in an ethical manner.

Deal with possible repercussions of having acted in what one considers an ethical manner.

Seen from this standpoint, it is rather challenging to respond to problems in an ethical manner. Consider the example of the supposed double reimbursement.

2.1.1 Recognize That There Is an Event to Which To React

The students were sitting in a class on leadership, expecting to be educated by an expert on leadership about leadership. In this case, I did not present the problem as one to which I expected them to react. I was simply telling them about something I had done. They had no a priori reason to expect that this was something for which an authority figure would require any particular kind of reaction, perhaps, except for taking notes. So for some students, the whole narrative may have been a nonevent.

This, of course, is a problem that extends beyond this mere classroom situation. When people hear their political, educational, or religious leaders talk, they may not believe there is any reason to question what they hear. After all, they are listening to authority figures. In this way, leaders, including cynical and corrupt leaders, may lead their flocks to accept and even commit unethical acts.

2.1.2 Define the Event as Having an Ethical Dimension

Not all students in the class defined the problem as an ethical one. It became clear in the discussion that some students saw the problem as utilitarian: I had worked hard, had been underpaid, and was trying to figure out a way to attain adequate compensation for my hard work. In this definition of the problem, I had come up with a clever way to make the compensation better fit the work I had done.

Cynical leaders may flaunt their unethical behavior – one is reminded today of Robert Mugabe, but there are other world leaders who might equally be relevant here. When Mugabe and his henchmen seized the farms of white farmers, the seizure was presented as one of compensating alleged war heroes for their accomplishments. Why should it be unethical to compensate war heroes?

As I write, the Chinese government is attempting to manipulate media to downplay the dimensions of an event with a huge ethical component (Atlas 2008). On May 12, 2008, an earthquake in Sichuan province killed an estimated ten thousand school children. But there was an irregularity in the buildings that imploded during the earthquake. Schools for children of well-connected party leaders, as well as government buildings, withstood the earthquake with no problem. In contrast, schools housing poor children crumbled to dust. It turned out that the schools had been built in ways that could only poorly withstand an earthquake. Presumably, the money that was supposed to have supported better construction went to line the pockets of Party functionaries (Atlas). The government has done what it can to suppress these basic facts.

Lest one believe that only other governments engage in such attempts to lead people to believe that events do not hold ethical dimensions, McClellan (2008), even by the most charitable interpretation, makes clear that the administration of George W. Bush engaged in such a constant barrage of half-truths and outright lies that it is unclear whether all its members were even able to distinguish their lies from the truth, or cared.

2.1.3 Decide That the Ethical Dimension Is Significant

In the case of my having sought double reimbursement, some of the students may have felt it was sketchy or dubious, but not sufficiently so to make an issue of it. Perhaps they had themselves asked for money twice for the same cause. Or perhaps they had sometimes taken what was not theirs – say, something small like a newspaper or even money they found on the ground – and saw what I was doing as no more serious than what they had done. So they may recognize an ethical dimension, but not see it as sufficiently significant to create a fuss.

Politicians seem to specialize in trying to downplay the ethical dimension of their behavior. The shenanigans and subsequent lies of Bill Clinton regarding his behavior are well known. On the day I write this chapter (June 5, 2008), a state senator in Massachusetts was arrested the day before for attempting to grope a woman on the street (Senator faces list of assault allegations 2008). He apparently has a record of harassing other women over a period of years. What is more amazing than his pleading innocent after being caught red-handed is that, when asked his name, he gave the name of a colleague in the state senate as his own name! He thereby sought to duck responsibility for his own unethical behavior.

2.1.4 Take Responsibility for Generating an Ethical Solution to the Problem

The students may have felt that they are, after all, merely students. Is it their responsibility, or even their right, to tell a professor in a course on leadership how to act, especially if the professor is a dean? From their point of view, it was perhaps my responsibility to determine the ethical dimensions of the situation, if any.

Similarly, people may allow leaders to commit wretched acts because they figure it is the leaders' responsibility to determine the ethical dimensions of their actions. Isn't that why they are leaders in the first place? Or people may assume that the leaders, especially if they are religious leaders, are in a uniquely good position to determine what is ethical. If a religious leader encourages someone to become a suicide bomber, that "someone" may feel that being such a bomber must be ethical. Why else would a religious leader suggest it?

2.1.5   Figure Out What Abstract Ethical Rule(s) Might Apply to the Problem

Perhaps some of the students recognized the problem I created for them as an ethical one. But what rule applies? Have they ever had to figure out reimbursements? Perhaps not. So it may not be obvious what rule would apply. Or even if they have, might there be some circumstances in which it is ethical to be dually reimbursed? Maybe the university supplements outside reimbursements, as they sometimes do fellowships? Or maybe the university does not care who else pays, so long as they get original receipts. Or maybe what I meant to say was that I had some expenses paid by the university and others by the sponsoring organization, and I had actually misspoken. Especially in new kinds of situations with which one has little familiarity, it may not be clear what constitutes ethical behavior.

Most of us have learned, in one way or another, ethical rules that we are supposed to apply to our lives. For example, we are supposed to be honest. But who among us can say he or she has not lied at some time, perhaps with the excuse that we were protecting someone else's feelings? By doing so, we insulate ourselves from the effects of our behavior. Perhaps, we can argue that the principle that we should not hurt someone else's feelings takes precedence over not lying. Of course, as the lies grow larger, we can continue to use the same excuse. Or politicians may argue that they should provide generous tax cuts to the ultra-wealthy on the theory that the benefits will "trickle down" to the rest of the population. So perhaps one is treating all people well, as we learn to do – just some people are treated better than others with the rationalization that eventually the effects will reach all the others.

2.1.6   Decide How These Abstract Ethical Rules Actually Apply to the Problem so as to Suggest a Concrete Solution

Perhaps the students had ethical rules available and even accessible to them, but did not see how to apply them. Suppose they have the rule that one should only expect from others what one deserves. Well, what did I deserve? Maybe, in application, they saw me as deserving more because I said I did. Or suppose they had the rule that one should not expect something for nothing. Well, I did something, so I was only trying to get something back that adequately reflected my work. In the end, they may have had trouble translating abstract principles into concrete behavior.

This kind of translation is, I believe, nontrivial. In our work on practical intelligence, some of which was summarized in Sternberg et al. (2000), we found that there is, at best, a modest correlation between the more academic and abstract aspects of intelligence and its more practical and concrete aspects. Both aspects, though, predicted behavior in everyday life. People may have skills that shine brightly in a classroom, but that they are unable to translate into real-world consequential behavior. For example, someone may be able to pass a written drivers' test with flying colors, but not be able to drive. Or someone may be able to get an A in a French class, but not speak French to passers-by in Paris. Or a teacher may get an A in a classroom management course, but be unable to manage a classroom. Translation of abstracted skills into concrete ones is difficult, and may leave people knowing a lot of ethical rules that they are nevertheless unable to translate into their everyday lives.

If one follows reports in the media, there are any number of instances in which pastors who are highly trained in religion and ethics act in unethical and unscrupulous ways. They may be able to teach classes on ethics, but they fail to translate what they teach into their own behavior. One may tend to be quick to blame them, but as a psychologist I know that there are many competent psychologists who are unable to apply what they do in therapy to their own lives. Being a psychologist is no protection against personal strife, any more than being an ethicist is protection against unethical behavior.

2.1.7 Enact the Ethical Solution, Meanwhile Possibly Counteracting Contextual Forces That Might Lead One Not to Act in an Ethical Manner

You sit in a classroom and hear your teacher brag about what you perhaps consider to be unethical behavior. You look around. No one else is saying anything. As far as you can tell, no one else has even been fazed. Perhaps you are simply out of line. In the Latané and Darley (1970) work, the more bystanders there were, the less likely one was to take action to intervene. Why? Because one figured that, if something is really wrong, then someone among all the others witnessing the event will take responsibility. You are better off having a breakdown on a somewhat lonely country road than on a busy highway, because a driver passing by on the country road may feel that he or she is your only hope.

Sometimes, the problem is not that other people seem oblivious to the ethical implications of the situation, but that they actively encourage you to behave in ways you define as unethical. In the Rwandan genocides, Hutus were encouraged to hate Tutsis and to kill them, even if they were within their own family (see discussion in Sternberg and Sternberg 2008). Those who were not willing to participate in the massacres risked becoming victims themselves (Gourevitch 1998). The same applied in Hitler's Germany. Those who tried to save Jews from concentration camps themselves risked going to such camps (Monroe 1996, 2004; Totten et al. 2004).

2.1.8   Deal with Possible Repercussions of Having Acted in What One Considers an Ethical Manner

One may hesitate to act because of possible repercussions. Perhaps students in my class saw me as grossly unethical, but did not want to risk challenging me openly and thereby potentially lowering their grade. In genocides, opposing the perpetrators may make one a victim. Or one may look foolish acting in an ethical way when others are taking advantage of a situation in a way to foster their personal good. Even before one acts, one may be hesitant because of the aftermath one anticipates, whether real or merely imagined.

We would like to think that the pressure to behave ethically will lead people to resist internal temptations to act poorly. But often, exactly the opposite is the case. In the Enron case, when Sherron Watkins blew the whistle on unethical behavior, she was punished and made to feel like an "outcast" (Person of the Week: Enron Whistleblower Sherron Watkins 2002). In general, whistleblowers are treated poorly, despite the protections they are supposed to receive.

2.2   Is There an Ethical Giftedness?

Gardner (1999) has wrestled with the question of whether there is some kind of existential or even spiritual intelligence that guides people through challenging life dilemmas. Coles (1998) is one of many who have argued for a moral intelligence in children as well as adults. Is there some kind of moral or spiritual intelligence in which some children are inherently superior to others? Kohlberg (1984) believed that there are stages of moral reasoning, and that as children grow older, they advance in these stages. Some will advance faster and further than others, creating individual differences in levels of moral development.

The perspective of this chapter is perhaps a bit different. People can certainly differ in their moral reasoning and moral development, but we can teach children as well as adults to enhance their ethical reasoning and behavior simply by instructing them regarding the challenges of thinking and acting in an ethical way. It is not enough to teach religion or values or ethics. One needs to teach children about the steps leading to ethical behavior. In this way, they will be able to recognize the challenges involved in behaving ethically. They need education and they need inoculation against the forces that are likely to lead them to fail to behave ethically because they do not make it through all eight of the steps as described above.

From this point of view, ethical giftedness is not some kind of inherent characteristic, but something we can develop in virtually all children (assuming they are not psychopathic). But such development is difficult because, as we have seen, thinking and acting ethically is more of a challenge than would appear. Merely going to religion or ethics classes will not, in and of itself, produce ethical behavior.

2.2.1 Foolishness as the Opposite of Ethical Giftedness

In speaking of the challenges of leadership, and particularly of leaders who become foolish, I have spoken of the risk of ethical disengagement (Sternberg 2008). Ethical disengagement (based on Bandura 1999) is the dissociation of oneself from ethical values. One may believe that ethical values should apply to the actions of others, but one becomes disengaged from them as they apply to oneself. One may believe that one is above or beyond ethics, or simply not see its relevance to one's own life.

There are other fallacies that lead people to be foolish (Sternberg 2008). They include.

2.2.1.1 Egocentrism

The person comes to believe that his or her leadership or power is for purposes of self-aggrandizement. Tyco CEO Dennis Kozlowski, currently in prison for tax evasion, ran the company as though it was his own personal piggybank (Timeline of the Tyco International Scandal 2005). Ethics took the back seat to Kozlowski's desire to enrich himself and his family.

2.2.1.2 False Omniscience

Some people come to believe themselves as all-knowing. The surprising thing about the behavior of a Bill Clinton or a George W. Bush, in quite different domains, is not that they made mistakes, but rather, that they kept making the same mistakes over and over again. Clinton correctly viewed himself as very intelligent, and perhaps thought that his intelligence and excellent education gave him levels of knowledge that he did not have. George W. Bush appears to have believed that he could trust his gut. He was wrong, over and over again, but was so lacking in intrapersonal intelligence (Gardner 1983) and self-reflection, that he learned little, if anything, from his mistakes.

2.2.1.3 False Omnipotence

Napoleon's failed invasion of Russia stands as one of the great historical monuments to false feelings of power. Napoleon believed himself to be extremely powerful. His invasion of Russia was politically pointless and strategically flawed; but he wanted the prize nevertheless. The invasion was the beginning of the end for Napoleon. Like so many other powerful leaders, he over-reached, and his feelings of omnipotence led to his doom.

2.2.1.4   False Invulnerability

Perhaps Eliot Spitzer, as governor of New York State, felt himself not only extremely powerful, but invulnerable. He must have felt pretty close to invulnerable, because as a former prosecutor, he must have known that police agencies had multiple ways of tracking patrons of prostitutes. He nevertheless engaged in a pattern of repeated reckless behavior (Spitzer is linked to prostitution ring 2008), which eventually cost him the governorship.

2.3   Conclusion

People may differ in their ability to behave ethically, but, to my knowledge, there is no evidence of intrinsic differences in "ethical giftedness" or "moral intelligence." The difference in people's behavior appears rather to be in their skill in completing a set of eight steps that, conjointly, produce ethical behavior. Failure of an earlier step is likely to lead to failure to execute the later steps. Teaching children abstract principles of ethical behavior or ethical rules is unlikely, in itself, to produce ethical behavior. Rather, children need to be taught the sequence of processes leading to ethical thinking, and to inoculate themselves against pressures – both external and internal – to behave in unethical ways. If we want to produce ethical giftedness, we have to develop it, not hope it will be a given in some group of intrinsically gifted children.

References

Atlas, T. (2008). The cost of corruption. *US News & World Report*, June 9, 144, 8–9.
Bandura, A. (1999). Moral disengagement in the perpetration of inhumanities. *Personality and Social Psychology Review, 3*, 193–209.
Coles, R. (1998). *The moral intelligence of children: How to raise a moral child.* New York: Plume.
Gardner, H. (1983). Frames of mind: The theory of multiple intelligences. New York: Basic.
Gardner, H. (1999). Are there additional intelligences? The case for naturalist, spiritual, and existential intelligences. In J. Kane (Ed.), *Education, information, and transformation* (pp. 111–131). Upper Saddle River, NJ: Prentice-Hall.
Gourevitch, P. (1998). *We wish to inform you that tomorrow we will be killed with our families: Stories from Rwanda.* New York: Farrar, Straus & Giroux.
Kohlberg, L. (1984). *The psychology of moral development: The nature and validity of moral stages.* New York: HarperCollins.

Latané, B., & Darley, J. M. (1970). *Unresponsive bystander: Why doesn't he help?* Englewood Cliffs, NJ: Prentice-Hall.

McClellan, S. (2008). *What happened: Inside the Bush White House and Washington's culture of deception.* New York: Public Affairs.

Monroe, K. R. (1996). *The heart of altruism.* Princeton, NJ: Princeton University Press.

Monroe, K. R. (2004). *The hand of compassion: Portraits of moral choice during the Holocaust.* Princeton, NJ: Princeton University Press.

"Person of the Week: 'Enron Whistleblower' Sherron Wilson" (2002). http://www.time.com/time/pow/article/0,8599,194927,00.html, retrieved June 5, 2008.

"Senator faces list of assault allegations" (2008). http://www.boston.com/news/local/massachusetts/articles/2008/06/05/senator_faces_list_of_assault_allegations/, retrieved June 5, 2008.

"Spitzer is linked to prostitution ring" (2008). http://www.nytimes.com/2008/03/10/nyregion/10cnd-spitzer.html?_r = 1&oref = slogin, retrieved June 5, 2008.

Sternberg, R. J. (2003a). WICS: A model for leadership in organizations. *Academy of Management Learning & Education, 2,* 386–401.

Sternberg, R. J. (2003b). WICS as a model of giftedness. *High Ability Studies, 14,* 109–137.

Sternberg, R. J. (2005). WICS: A model of giftedness in leadership. *Roeper Review, 28,* 37–44.

Sternberg, R. J. (2008). The WICS approach to leadership: Stories of leadership and the structures and processes that support them. *The Leadership Quarterly, 19,* 360–371.

Sternberg, R. J., & Sternberg, K. (2008). *The nature of hate.* New York: Cambridge University Press.

Sternberg, R. J., Forsythe, G. B., Hedlund, J., Horvath, J., Snook, S., Williams, W. M., Wagner, R. K., & Grigorenko, E. L. (2000). *Practical intelligence in everyday life.* New York: Cambridge University Press.

"Timeline of the Tyco International Scandal" (2005). http://www.usatoday.com/money/industries/manufacturing/2005–06–17-tyco-timeline_x.htm, retrieved June 5, 2008.

Totten, S., Parsons, W. S., & Charny, I. W. (Eds.). (2004). *Century of genocide: Critical essays and eyewitness accounts.* New York: Routledge.

Chapter 3
Moral Leadership, Effective Leadership, and Intellectual Giftedness: Problems, Parallels, and Possibilities

Mary-Elaine Jacobsen

Abstract Leadership is one of the most studied aspects of human behavior, resulting in numerous models and thousands of books. The current literature is replete with alarms about leadership problems, including a worldwide shortage of competent leaders and leadership talent. Moreover, scandalous catastrophes set in motion by unethical leaders have aimed the spotlight on the critical need for moral leadership. Though the debate persists over definitions of leadership excellence, informative parallels can be drawn between and among moral leadership, leadership effectiveness, and cognitive ability, with implications for gifted education and organizational talent development.

Keywords Effective leaders · Effective leader traits · Ethical leadership · Gifted leadership · Gifted traits · High potential · Leader(s) · Leadership · Leadership ability · Moral leadership · Talent assessment · Talent psychology

3.1 Conceptualizing Moral Leadership

Leadership is one of the most studied aspects of human behavior, resulting in numerous theoretical models and thousands of books. One does not need to look far to find copious sources of information on organizational ethics. In a 2007 Google and Yahoo search, Yetmar (2008) identified nearly 300 websites dedicated to professional and business ethics associations and institutes, ethics journals, US and internationally based university ethics centers, business and professional codes of conduct, and ethics cases and studies. A 2006 Yahoo search by Fuqua and Newman

M.-E. Jacobsen
4220 Redwing Circle, Winston-Salem, NC 27106, USA
e-mail: mjacobsen@isgaa.org

D. Ambrose, T. Cross (eds.), *Morality, Ethics, and Gifted Minds*,
DOI: 10.1007/978-0-387-89368-6_3,

resulted in 3,280,000 hits on "business ethics," plainly reflecting widespread interest and concern. As of 2005, the number of international leadership training programs numbered in the thousands, with new ones surfacing all the time (Ciulla).

Current news reports and the organizational research literature are replete with alarms about a worldwide shortage of leadership talent. Coincidentally, once the corruption within Enron, WorldCom, Tranz Rail, and other organizations was exposed, the elephant in the room could no longer be ignored: leadership without morality is a recipe for disaster. Yet ethical and moral leadership problems are not exclusive to the corporate arena. An April 2008 Reuters report exposed a scandal linking Colombian President Alvaro Uribe's closest political allies to far-right death squads (Bronstein). In 2007 representatives of a French charity involved in international adoptions were charged with kidnapping Chadian children claiming they were orphans from Darfur (Schwarz 2007). And the long history (1950–2002) of accusations of sexual abuse of children by more than 4,000 Roman Catholic priests and deacons is infamous (Terry et al. 2004). Events such as these shocked the public and knocked the wind out of those who trusted their leaders, having had no idea they were being double-crossed behind closed doors. Certainly, years of leadership experience means little when lessons are learned too late or not at all and the cost is ruinous. All told, the corruption in the first part of the twenty-first century has had a stunning effect on society's views of leadership. Two questions have been heard in conversations everywhere: "What is wrong with our leaders?" and "What can we do to keep this from happening again?"

To begin to address these problems we must wrestle with the fundamental question of what we mean by "moral leadership." In many ways moral behavior falls into that category of indescribable constructs where we find ourselves saying things like, "You just know it when you see it." It is unlikely that we will ever reach complete agreement on what constitutes moral leadership (which is conceivably a good thing in that debate and disagreement keep attention focused on the subject). Perhaps it is the complexity of the matter that is both the catch and the allure. In a course on moral leadership at Harvard Graduate School of Business Administration, Joseph Badarracco, Jr. summarizes the predicament:

> From time to time, one hears that "moral leadership is basically simple – it's just a matter of X." Sometimes X is defined as doing the right thing, sometimes as having a moral compass, sometimes – for managers – as serving the interest of the shareholders.... if moral leadership could be defined as X, someone would have put X on laminated cards and given them to leaders, who could pull the cards out when they faced serious ethical challenges. In reality, moral leadership is multi-faceted and complex. It defies simple definition. (2001, p. 4)

A review of the literature was conducted to establish an understanding of current definitions of moral leadership. For purposes of clarification, "moral leadership" and "ethical leadership" are used interchangeably herein because of their overlapping meanings involving judgments about human beliefs and behavior in terms of good/bad and right/wrong (Payne and Joyner 2006; Remley and Herlihy 2006). A meta-analytical investigation of the meaning of ethical leadership as a construct (Treviño et al. 2000, 2003; Brown et al. 2005; Brown and Treviño 2006) resulted in a definition of ethical leadership founded in social learning theory (Bandura 1977): "the demonstration of normatively appropriate conduct through personal actions and interpersonal relationships, and the promotion of such conduct to followers through two-way communication, reinforcement, and decision-making" (Brown et al. 2005, p. 120).

In a 2007 interview published in the *Harvard Business Review*, Howard Gardner discusses his views on what he terms the *ethical mind*:

> An ethical mind broadens respect for others into something more abstract. A person with an ethical mind asks herself, "What kind of person, worker, and citizen do I want to be?" … ethical conceptions and behaviors demand a certain capacity to go beyond your own experience as an individual person. Once you have developed an ethical mind, you become more like an impartial spectator of the team, the organization, the citizenry, the world. (p. 52)

According to Ciulla (2005), two primary questions are to be asked about a leader's ethics: (1) "Does a leader do the right thing, the right way and for the right reason?" and (2) "What standards do we use for determining these things?" (p. 331). She also reminds us of the critical role of followers in the consideration of ethical leadership: "If you accept the proposition that leadership is a relationship, then you cannot study the ethics of leaders without including the ethics of followers. … All too often, people forget that followers have power and hence responsibility. After all, without followers, leaders simply do not exist" (p. 329).

Sama and Shoaf (2008) discuss ethical leadership in the professions, arguing ethical leadership is based on a vision of "achieving moral good" and built upon principles of "integrity, trust, and moral rectitude" (p. 41). They contend that ethical leaders serve as moral models whose behaviors motivate others to behave ethically while promoting moral change on a larger scale. Their definition of moral leadership corresponds with Kohlberg's (1969) theoretical stage of moral development wherein an individual considers morality as part of something above and beyond minimal rules and laws. In essence, such a person would consistently look beyond the current bottom line and conventional practices to discern the difference between right according to rules or norms, and right based on moral responsibility for their decisions and the resulting consequences.

3.2 What Do We know about Leaders?

Personal characteristics such as honesty and reliability have long been considered important features of moral leadership, and studies bear this out (Brown and Treviño 2006; Den Hartog et al. 1999; Dirks and Ferrin 2002; Kirkpatrick and Locke 1991; Posner and Schmidt 1992). Trait investigators consider, "who is likely to make a good leader, and why?" Galton (1869) and others embarked on studies to predict who might be capable of effective leadership. At the beginning of the twentieth century, Thomas Carlyle's (1907) investigation of "great men" led him to conclude that human progress and the annals of history are largely fashioned by exceptional leaders. Following his point of view, an interest in the qualities of leaders captured the focus of researchers.

In 1948, Stogdill determined that a set of five traits (intelligence, dominance, self-confidence, energy/activity level, and task-specific knowledge) separated leaders from non-leaders. On the other hand, he concluded that "mere possession of some combination of traits" is insufficient in explaining leadership, noting that many people who possessed such traits were content to be followers. His explanation for this discrepancy was based on situational factors. As a result, theories that suggested a universal leadership trait were by and large set aside.

Much of the leadership literature from 1950s into the 1980s followed this line of inquiry focusing predominantly on situational perspectives (Katz et al. 1950, 1951). The research was influenced by Lewin's argument in the late 1930s that human behavior is the result of a combination of person and environmental factors (Lewin et al. 1939). However, many researchers found that studies of discrete leadership behaviors were limited and limiting in that such narrow and fragmented foci often led to conclusions about leadership that were too situation specific and ungeneralizable (Carroll and Gillen 1987; Pratch and Jacobowitz' 1997; Skinner and Sasser 1977; Whitley 1989).

Throughout this period of emphasis on situational factors, organizational psychologists never lost sight of the importance of individual differences. Their work provided considerable empirical support for trait-based explanations of leadership effectiveness (Bentz 1967; Boyatzis 1982; Bray et al. 1974; McCall and Lombardo 1983). Several models of leadership excellence have emerged since the early 1990s (Antonakis et al. 2004; Borman et al. 1993; Davis et al. 1992; Mumford et al. 2000b, c; Yukl et al. 1990). Because certain traits appeared in leaders again and again, and with many of the earlier assessment problems solved, interest in leadership characteristics was revived and advanced by the introduction of the Five-Factor Model of personality (Tupes and Cristal 1961).

Trait theories of leadership continue to hold sway, though generally acknowledging the fact that situational dynamics must also be taken into account because no leader operates in a vacuum. Jim Collins's popular book, *Good to Great* (2001) reports the results of a study of Fortune 1000 companies, investigating 11 organizations with 15 years of below-average performance followed by 15 years of above-average performance. Collins concluded the primary reason for the turnaround was a change in CEOs. An analysis of these CEOs demonstrated two shared traits: (a) they were modest and humble and (b) they were extraordinarily persistent. These findings were stunning at a time when self-promoting, dramatic styles of "charismatic leadership" were all the rage. This unexpected and bewildering discovery accentuates the value of personality research in leadership studies.

Pratch and Jacobowitz' (1997) findings indicate:

> effective executive leadership depends on the ability to respond in an adaptive manner to emergent, dynamic, and complex situations. This ability, in turn, requires the readiness to continually develop new skills and knowledge for coping with complexity and change. ... Effective executive leaders demonstrate three tendencies that reflect active coping: (a) a relative autonomy from group values and attitudes, (b) the openness to synthesize complexity, and (c) the readiness to overcome obstacles in striving for long-term goals. ... They reflect the structural psychological conditions for the many specific, sometimes seemingly contradictory, qualities that give rise to outstanding leadership (p. 56).

Fleming's (2004) research on predicting leadership effectiveness supported the important contribution of certain characteristics. The study included application of the *Hogan Personality Inventory*, the HPI (Hogan and Hogan 1995), an assessment based on the Big-Five model of personality (McCrae and John 1992; Tupes and Cristal 1961; Wiggins 1996) specifically designed to "predict performance in real world settings" (p. 4). Results indicated effective leaders are: "stress tolerant (Adjustment), driven (Ambition), and task focused (lower Sociability). ... maintaining composure (lower Excitable) and being responsive to others' needs (i.e., lower Leisurely) contributed to higher Leadership performance ratings. Contrary to expected relations, possessing exceptionally high standards and seeming meticulous (i.e., Diligent) was generally helpful across performance dimensions" (p. 6).

Contemporary theories have resulted in three primary models with overlapping traits at the heart of their theoretical underpinnings: *authentic leadership, spiritual leadership, and transformational leadership* (Avolio and Gardner 2005). Likewise, these three models share many of the key characteristics of ethical leadership: concern for others, integrity, ethical decision making, and role modeling (Brown and Treviño 2006). Following on the assumptions of social learning theory (Bandura 1977), Kohlberg (1969) observed that most people look beyond themselves for guidance with ethical concerns. Hence, it is important to consider the dynamic nature of the traits that comprise moral leadership:

> In a corporate environment where ethics messages can get lost amidst messages about the bottom line and the immediate tasks at hand, ethical leaders also focus attention on ethics by frequently communicating about ethics and making the ethics message salient. They set clear and high ethical standards for others and follow these standards themselves. They also use rewards and punishments to influence followers' ethical behavior. (Brown and Treviño 2006, p. 598)

3.3   Parallels Between Leadership and Cognitive Ability

To expand the concept of moral leadership it is also important to consider leadership effectiveness. Leaders' effectiveness and morality are both critical factors in organizational success and survival, and moreover of great import in the lives of their constituents. Hogan and Kaiser (2005) established, "First, leadership solves the problems of how to organize collective effort; consequently, it is the key to organizational effectiveness. ... Second, and important from a moral perspective, bad leaders perpetrate terrible misery on those subject to their domain" (p. 169).

It may seem obvious that competence is the bedrock leadership effectiveness. Regrettably, the track record of many organizations for selecting and developing competent leaders has been anything but stellar. As far back as 1987, corporate failures in America were on the rise, with at least 57,000 failures reflecting a combination of leadership incompetence and changes in the market that leaders neglected to adequately anticipate or address (Ropp). By 2003, DeVries and Kaiser discovered the failure rate among senior executives in America was at least 50%. Worse yet, the failures were primarily due to *managerial incompetence*. In other words, scores of senior-level leaders have been sinking their own organizations primarily because they lack the ability to do otherwise. It is easy to see the link between leader competence and effectiveness, but far more difficult to grasp the connection between leader competence and ethical leadership. Yet the argument can be made that if competence is an integral part of effective leadership it is likewise a major aspect of moral leadership. Cuilla (2005) offers a compelling line of reasoning:

> Ethics and effectiveness converge around this question: What does it mean for a person to do something the right way? For example, what would we say about an incompetent surgeon who continues to practice surgery, despite the fact that he keeps killing his patients? Is such a person behaving ethically? …. Unethical behavior is sometimes the result of incompetence and vice versa. If a person knows how to do something well, he or she is less likely to cheat at doing it. But leaders also behave unethically when they are very competent and successful. As mentioned earlier, in some cases successful leaders start to believe that they are Gods or exceptions to the rules. In these cases, we might say that leaders are morally incompetent at being successful. (p. 333)

Against this backdrop, recent trait-centered models of effective leadership have tended to focus on two primary areas: ability and personality (Ilies et al. 2004). A review of these models suggests effective leadership depends on a cluster of traits and/or abilities rather than one primary characteristic. However, cognitive ability is nearly always identified as an essential factor in the effective leadership equation (Ghiselli 1971; Guzzo and Salas 1995; Heslin 1964; Lord and Hall 1992; Schmidt and Hunter 1998). For example, Robert Sternberg's (2007) WICS model of effective leadership proposes a synthesis of "wisdom, creativity, and intelligence", arguing that intelligence "as traditionally defined is definitely related to leadership effectiveness". Specifically:

> analytical "skills and dispositions matter for leadership. Leaders need to be able to retrieve information that is relevant to leadership decisions (memory) and to analyze and evaluate different courses of action, whether proposed by themselves or by others (analysis) (p. 37). … No one, no matter how creative, always has good ideas. Analytical intelligence is essential to distinguish the wheat from the chaff." (p. 39)

Mumford et al. (2000a) confirmed that "general cognitive ability is perhaps the individual characteristic that has most consistently been associated with leadership success" (p. 21). Smith (1998) study demonstrated that cognitive ability, persuasiveness, and general self-efficacy were positively associated with leader emergence. It is also clear that the relationship between general cognitive ability and leadership reaches beyond high achievement in academic settings. In fact, cognitive ability has been shown to be one of the best predictors of occupational advancement and job performance in any organizational setting (Schmidt and Hunter 1998, 2004). In a 2002 journal article titled *The Role of General Cognitive Ability and Job Performance: Why There Cannot Be a Debate*, business and social scientist Frank Schmidt provided a convincing meta-analysis:

> Research in differential psychology has shown that GCA [general cognitive ability] is related to performances and outcomes in so many areas of life–more than any other variable measured in the social sciences–that it would not be possible for job performance to be an exception to the rule that GCA impacts the entire life–space of individuals. (p. 199)

Especially significant for today's leaders are findings that indicate as job complexity increases so does the importance of cognitive ability. A study by Kuncel et al. (2004) substantiates previous evidence (Borman et al. 1993; McCloy et al. 1994; Schmidt and Outerbridge 1986) that cognitive ability is significantly related to success in multiple domains and is related to learning and complexity: "general cognitive ability predicts job performance because it predicts learning and acquisition of job knowledge. Job knowledge requirements and the complexity of jobs tend to go hand in hand" (p. 149). This relationship between cognitive ability and complexity is particularly pertinent for organizations that must rely on knowledge workers and inventiveness. The global economy is changing so rapidly that jobs that entail complex tacit interactions, requiring a high level of judgment, have grown three times as fast as employment in general (*Economist* 2006, p. 5). In other words, the greater the complexity in a leadership role, the greater the dependence on higher cognitive ability.

More and more, leadership challenges are dilemmas that have no single correct answer, which means the days of ordinary problems and puzzles being the bread and butter of a leadership agenda are long past. The unavoidable rise in complexity in today's organizations is tied to rising uncertainty and ambiguity. The result is a shift from everyday problem-solving to dilemmas with unclear resolutions or multiple options, all of which require advanced reasoning abilities and discerning judgment (Jacobsen and Ward 2007). As such, organizations require leaders who can apply their intellect to emerging multifaceted issues.

It has been long established that general intelligence can empower performance on all mental tasks (Foti and Hauenstein 2007; Jensen 1988; Judge et al. 2002; Lord et al. 1986; Schmidt and Hunter 1998, 2000, 2004; Spearman 1904). Even when taking into account different approaches to leadership, the importance of cognitive ability outweighs leadership style (Zaccaro et al. 2000). Zaccaro et al. (2000) discovered three primary cognitive characteristics known to be associated with leadership effectiveness with which scholars and professionals in the field of intellectual giftedness are quite familiar:

1. Strong ability and desire to learn
2. Ability to efficiently solve novel and ill-defined problems
3. Divergent/creative thinking

More recently, self-monitoring and self-efficacy have also been found to reliably predict leader emergence and effectiveness (Day et al. 2002; Foti and Hauenstein 2007). Self-monitoring is considered to be a facet of social awareness and flexibility (cf. Zaccaro et al. 1991b) significantly related to leadership emergence across situations (Hall et al. 1998; Zaccaro et al. 1991a). Individuals with well-developed self-monitoring grasp interpersonal cues and pay attention to the suitability and effect of their behavior for purposes of self regulation (Snyder 1974). They have also been more often rated high as leaders (Dobbins et al. 1990; Ellis and Cronshaw 1992).

According to Bandura (1982), self-efficacy is one's belief that he or she is capable of successful performance toward a specific goal. Shelton (1990) considered self-efficacy to be a fairly stable "global trait" that can shift over time depending on experiences of success and failure. In a similar vein, self-confidence and achievement have been repeatedly found to be related to leader effectiveness (Atwater et al. 1999; Bentz 1990; Judge et al. 2002).

Dominance has also been identified as a central trait of transformational leaders (House 1977). However, for those unfamiliar with the personality research literature, it must be noted that this term does not mean domineering, pushy, aggressive, or controlling. In personality psychology "dominance" describes someone who takes the initiative, is involved, interesting, stimulating and humorous (House and Howell 1992). In support of these findings, in their 9-month study of emerging leaders, Foti and Hauenstein (2007) found the integrated pattern of high intelligence, high dominance, high self-efficacy, and high self-monitoring to be significantly related to both leadership emergence and effectiveness. Moreover, they found that subjects scoring high on this pattern of variables did indeed "emerge as leaders, were promoted to leadership positions, and were rated by their superiors as effective leaders" (p. 353).

Thus, it appears that there is consistent evidence that certain identifiable and measurable traits – perhaps especially in the particular pattern of high intelligence, self-efficacy, self-monitoring, and dominance – are reliable predictors of leadership emergence and effectiveness.

3.4 Intersection of Giftedness, Leadership, and Morality

For those familiar with the literature on giftedness, many of the characteristics noted above are consistent with the findings on gifted traits. Leadership has long been considered a distinct feature of giftedness in many (approximately 40%) state definitions (Matthews 2004), and following the Marland Report (1972) was included in the U.S. federal definition of giftedness to help identify gifted and talented children as those with demonstrated achievement and/or potential ability [identified by professionally qualified persons] in general intellectual ability, specific academic aptitude, creative or productive thinking, leadership ability, visual and performing arts, and/or psychomotor ability. It is generally agreed that application of these criteria for the identification of the gifted and talented will result in the inclusion of approximately 3–5% of the population.

Scholars who investigate giftedness and work directly with gifted individuals have proposed a variety of characteristics in their definitions of leadership, including influence and self-management (Gonsalves et al. 1981; Huckaby and Sperling 1981; Oakland et al. 1996; Plowman 1981). Sisk (1993) proposed the inclusion of "setting goals, responding to the future, developing a success syntax, gaining self-knowledge, becoming interpersonally competent, and coping with value differences" (as cited in Lee and Olszewski-Kubilius 2006, p. 33).

When considering a potential link with gifted leadership characteristics and potential for moral leadership, several investigators and experts have found that from an early age many gifted children demonstrate exceptional sensitivity to issues of justice and morality, particularly in their capacity for empathizing with others, showing compassion, and advanced interest in world affairs, matters of justice, and overall right and wrong, and strong sense of responsibility. (Galbraith 1985; Gross 1993; Hollingworth 1942; Janos and Robinson 1985; Lovecky 1997; Roeper 1988, 1995; Silverman 1993, 1994; Terman 1925). Piechowski (1991), noted that gifted youth, like gifted adults, feel a deep longing for ideals in life, such as justice, fairness, honesty, and responsibility (as cited in Lovecky 1997).

Throughout her years of direct work with gifted adults in leadership positions, Jacobsen (1999a–c, 2000a–d, 2003, 2004, 2008) has observed that the key traits of gifted children noted above do not simply vanish in adulthood. The manifestation of gifted traits is likely to be different, as should be expected. For example, perfectionism in a 5-year-old may result in a tantrum while in a gifted adult perfectionism may be the force that leads to excellence and the perpetuation of high ideals. Likewise, the need to "do something that really matters" seems to grow stronger in many gifted adults (Jacobsen 2008). Time and again they report feeling internally driven to take on projects that truly challenge their intellectual abilities and require them to wrestle with ethical issues in order to contribute positive change in the world. Such daring breaks with the status quo call for comprehensive leadership – of self and other – rooted in morality, fueled by exceptional ability, and propelled by effectiveness.

Nevertheless, despite the fact that leadership development is often included in gifted programs and curricula, Lee and Olszewski-Kubilius (2006) have argued, "the relationship between leadership and intellectual giftedness is not clear and is not necessarily linear" (p. 34). Results of their 2006 study of leadership, moral judgment, and emotional intelligence in gifted students indicated:

> the independence of these various domains, as higher levels of moral reasoning or emotional intelligence were not associated with higher levels of leadership ... One might have expected, for example, that students high in leadership would also evidence advanced levels of moral reasoning. These do not necessarily go together. ... while academically gifted students appear to have some propensity for reaching higher levels of moral development and demonstrating leadership, special and specific programs and interventions are also needed to optimize the development of these attributes. Advanced cognitive reasoning abilities may help an individual understand the nuances of a moral dilemma or a political situation, but they do not propel gifted students to take the right actions. (pp. 59–60)

3.5 Possibilities for Leadership Development

For purposes of leadership development, it seems we must endeavor to discern the essential qualities of effective leaders and to determine which skills can be improved through learning. Indeed, a meta-analysis of 78 studies by Ilies et al. (2004) supported the conclusion that the combination of high intelligence and leadership traits is strongly associated with leadership emergence, underscoring the implications for well thought-out talent assessment and selection procedures. Important leadership competencies such as attitudes, specialized proficiencies, sound judgment, and social intelligence can be taught and improved, given well-designed learning opportunities (Ward 2008). The following comparison chart (Jacobsen 2008;

Jacobsen and Ward 2007) presents a summary of the similarities between and among characteristics often found in intellectually gifted individuals and those of effective leaders and moral leaders (Table 3.1):

Table 3.1 Comparison of intellectually gifted individuals, effective leaders, and moral leaders

Traits often found in intellectually gifted individuals	Traits often found in effective leaders	Traits often found in ethical/moral leaders
Exceptional cognitive ability	√	Undetermined
Natural potential for leadership	√	Undetermined
Ability to absorb information and learn quickly and thoroughly; retain and apply what is learned	√	Undetermined
Exceptional memory, large storehouse of information, mind works on multiple tracks at once	√	Undetermined
Highly perceptive; effective problem-finder and problem-solver; quick to see more than one way to reach a goal	√	Undetermined
√	√	Internal locus of control; self-motivated and self-directed; penchant for excellence; willing to strive for important goals
Enjoys complexity, uncertainty and change; resilient; does well with the unexpected; highly adaptable	√	Undetermined
Visionary; sees the "big picture"; anticipatory; recognizes trends early; synthesizer; readily grasps connections; emphasizes vision and intellectual stimulation	Visionary; sees the "big picture"; anticipatory; recognizes trends early; synthesizer; readily grasps connections	√
Concerned about fairness, justice, and morality; exceptional capacity for principled reasoning	Sometimes	Concerned about fairness, justice, and morality; exceptional capacity for principled reasoning and ethical decision-making
√	Confident; willing to take a stand; able to arouse enthusiasm in others; brings people onboard; action-oriented	Confident; willing to take a stand; able to arouse enthusiasm in others; brings people onboard; action-oriented; prosocial model
√	Original thinker; inventive; designs new strategies and products; creative producer	Undetermined

(continued)

Table 3.1 (continued)

Traits often found in intellectually gifted individuals	Traits often found in effective leaders	Traits often found in ethical/moral leaders
Sensitive, empathic, compassionate, concerned about others and society	Sensitive, empathic, compassionate, concerned about others and society	Sensitive, empathic, compassionate, concerned about others and society; supportive and nurturing
√	Persuasive, influential; creates enthusiasm; inspires others; models excellence and values	Persuasive, influential; creates enthusiasm; inspires others; models excellence and values; uses power to benefit others
√	√	Seeks out alternate views, uses advanced judgment, considers outcomes carefully and thoroughly; weighs out long- and short-term consequences
Has a repertoire of skills	Demonstrates flexibility; adaptable; can appropriately respond from a repertoire of skills	√
√	√	Organized; sets clear priorities based on principles and standards; applies principles to self and others; conscientious; reliable
Authenticity often important	√	Authentic; self-aware without being a chameleon to please others; consistent across situations
Undetermined	√	Able to maintain positive relationships; grasps situational dynamics; builds effective teams; manages diversity well
Undetermined	√	Adept at providing support and direction for others; shares the limelight; serves as a mentor
Unclear; some evidence of pre-adult problems with stress management and impulse control	Emotionally stable; turns setbacks into opportunities; successfully manages stress; competent under pressure;	Emotionally stable; turns setbacks into opportunities
Makes connections others do not; capable of seeing many sides of an issue	Good listener, communicator and negotiator; bridge-builder, brings people together	Brings people together around ethical standards; emphasizes moral management

Despite the obvious overlaps of characteristics between and among intellectually gifted individuals, effective leaders, and moral leaders, organizations will necessarily require different kinds of talent and individuals with a variety of skill sets and bases of knowledge. Nevertheless, the importance of cognitive ability for leadership effectiveness is unquestionable, especially in organizational settings that depend on innovation and are confronted with intense complexity and demands for change. Nor, given the unforgettable spate of tragedies set in motion by unethical leaders, can we assume that leadership alone implies effectiveness and/or morality.

As we have seen, certain characteristics play a significant role in effective leadership, exceptional cognitive ability amongst them. To be effective in today's complex organizations and to promote ethical standards along the way, leaders must be able to "interact almost simultaneously with a variety of stakeholders in multiple and rapidly changing settings covering a virtually endless list of contingencies" (Hooijberg et al. 1997, p. 376). It quickly becomes obvious that such an advanced level of complexity must be matched by a leader's ability to work proficiently in multifaceted environments, and to do so in the face of rapid change, increasing diversity, inescapable unforeseen events, and a variety of ethical dilemmas.

The recognizable link between features of exceptional intelligence, effective leadership and moral leadership provides some compelling reasons to provide appropriate early learning opportunities for the gifted that are founded in both the childhood and adult literature to increase the likelihood that programs are aimed in the right direction. For curriculum developers and educators of the gifted, it appears that a thorough understanding of the current leadership literature is essential, and perhaps ongoing collaboration with those directly involved in the study of leadership in adulthood as well. Additionally, we must not overrate the strong evidence of leadership characteristics and abilities in gifted youngsters or inclusion of leadership traits in the U.S. federal definition of giftedness, mistakenly concluding that effective moral leadership is the automatic result. Lee and Olszewski-Kubilius (2006) argued,

> This addition, however, has minimally affected the instruction of gifted and talented students, as few schools address this dimension. ... If educational directives for the gifted ignore the need for leadership development, the leadership potential of gifted children may not become actualized, or, at worst, may become misdirected (p. 42). ... while academically gifted students appear to have some propensity for reaching higher levels of moral development and demonstrating leadership, special and specific programs and interventions are also needed to optimize the development of these attributes. Advanced cognitive reasoning abilities may help and individual understand the nuances of a moral dilemma or a political situation, but they do not propel gifted students to take the right actions. (p. 60)

For organizations intent on successfully attracting, developing, and retaining those individuals equipped with much of what is known to be necessary for leadership effectiveness and ethical leadership, staying abreast of the leadership research appears necessary, as does a more far-reaching understanding of the psychology of leadership effectiveness and morality. This is certainly not intended to imply that exceptional cognitive ability and leadership traits are sufficient for excellence in ethical leadership. Well thought out programs can help high-potential individuals develop many of the skills necessary for the more advanced forms of leadership (e.g., transformational, authentic, ethical) can be learned and polished. By providing them the proper coaching and opportunities to improve in any areas of relative weakness, far more of them may become exemplars of moral leadership so clearly needed in our global societies.

References

Antonakis, J., Ciancolo, A., & Sternberg, R. J. (Eds.). (2004). *Handbook of leadership*. Thousand Oaks, CA: Sage.

Atwater, L. E., Dionne, S. D., Avolio, B., Camobreco, F. E., & Lau, A. W. (1999). A longitudinal study of the leadership development process: Individual differences predicting leadership effectiveness. *Human Relations, 52*, 1543–1562.

Avolio, B. J., & Gardner, W. L. (2005). Authentic leadership development: Getting to the root of positive forms of leadership. *Leadership Quarterly, 16*, 315–338.

Badarracco, Jr., J. L. (2001, Fall). *The Moral Leader*. Graduate School of Business Administration course overview, George F. Baker Foundation, Harvard University, Boston, MA.

Bandura, A. (1977). *Social learning theory*. Englewood, NJ: Prentice-Hall.

Bandura, A. (1982). Self-efficacy mechanism in human agency. *American Psychologist, 37*, 122–147.

Bentz, V. J. (1967). The Sears experience in the investigation, description, and prediction of executive behavior. In F. R. Wickert & D. E. McFarland (Eds.), *Measuring executive effectiveness* (pp. 147–206). New York: Appleton-Century-Crofts.

Bentz, V. J. (1990). Contextual issues in predicting high-level leadership performance: Contextual richness as a criterion consideration in personality research with executives. In K. E. Clark & M. B. Clark (Eds.), *Measures of leadership* (pp. 131–143). West Orange, NJ: Leadership Library of America.

Borman, W. C., Hanson, M. A., Oppler, S. H., & Pulakos, E. D. (1993). The role of early supervisory experience in supervisor performance. *Journal of Applied Psychology, 78* (3), 443–449.

Boyatzis, R. R. (1982). *The competent manager: A model for effective performance*. New York: Wiley.

Bray, D. W., Campbell, R. J., & Grant, D. L. (1974). *Formative years in business: A long term AT&T study of managerial lives*. New York: Wiley.

Bronstein, H. (2008, April 21). Colombia's Uribe hit by another political scandal. *Reuters Online*. Retrieved Jun 1, 2008 from http://www.reuters.com/article/worldNews/idUSN2141899520080421

Brown, M., & Trevino, L. K. (2006). Ethical leadership: A review and future directions. *Leadership Quarterly, 17* (6), 595–616.

Brown, M., Trevino, L. K., & Harrrison, D. (2005). Ethical leadership: A social learning perspective for construct development and testing. *Organizational Behavior and Human Decision Processes, 97*, 117–134.

Carlyle, T. (1907). *On heroes, hero-worship, and the heroic in history*. Boston, MA: Houghton-Mifflin.

Carroll, S., & Gillen, D. (1987). Are the classical management functions useful in describing managerial work? *Academy of Management Review, 12* (1), 38–51.

Collins, J. (2001). *Good to great*. New York: HarperCollins.

Ciulla, J. B. (2005). The state of leadership ethics and the work that lies before us. *Business Ethics: A European Review, 14* (4), 323–335.

Davis, B. L., Hellervik, L. W., Sheard, J. L., & Skube, C. J., Gebelein, S. H. (1992). *Successful manager's handbook: Development suggestions for today's managers* (5th ed.). Minneapolis, MN: Personnel Decisions.

Day, D. V., Schleicher, D. J., Unckless, A. L., & Hiller, N. J. (2002). Self-monitoring personality at work: A meta-analytic investigation of construct validity. *Journal of Applied Psychology, 87* (2), 390–401.

Den Hartog, D. N., House, R. J., Hanges, P. J. Ruiz-Quintilla, S. A., Dorfman, P. W., et al. (1999). Culturally specific and cross-culturally generalizable implicit leadership theories: Are attributes of charismatic/transformational leadership universally endorsed? *Leadership Quarterly, 10* (2), 219–256.

DeVries, D. L., & Kaiser, R. G. (2003, November). Going sour in the suite: What you can do about executive derailment. Presented in S. Steckler, D. Sethi & R.K. Prescott (coordinators) *Maximizing Executive Effectiveness: Developing Your Senior Leadership* workshop hosted by the Human Resources Planning Society, Miami, FL.

Dirks, K. T., & Ferrin, D. L. (2002). Trust in leadership: Meta-analytic findings and implications for research and practice. *Journal of Applied Psychology, 87*, 611–628.

Dobbins, J. H., Long, W. S., Dedrick, E. J., & Clemons, T. C. (1990). The role of self-monitoring and gender on leader emergence: A laboratory and field study. *Journal of Management, 16*, 493–502.

Economist (2006, October 7). Everybody's doing it. *381*, 5–8.

Ellis, R. J., & Cronshaw, S. F. (1992). Self-monitoring and leader emergence: A test of moderator effects. *Small Group Research, 23*, 113–129.

Foti, R. J., & Hauenstein, N. M. L. (2007). Pattern and variable approaches in leader effectiveness and emergence. *Journal of Applied Psychology, 92* (2), 347–355.

Fuqua, D. R., & Newman, J. L. (2006). Moral and ethical issues in human systems. *Consulting Psychology Journal: Practice and Research, 58* (4), 206–215.

Fleming, W. D. (2004). *Predicting leadership effectiveness: Contributions of critical thinking, personality and derailers.* Paper presented at the 19th Annual Conference of the Society for Industrial and Organizational Psychology, Chicago, IL.

Galbraith, J. (1985). The eight great gripes of gifted kids: Responding to special needs. *Roeper Review, 8*, 15–18.

Galton, F. (1869). *Hereditary genius.* New York: Appleton.

Ghiselli, E. E. (1971). *Exploration in managerial talent.* Pacific Palisades: Goodyear Publishing.

Gonsalves, W. C., Grimm, J., & Welsh, J. M. (1981). Leadership training: A lesson in living. *Roeper Review, 3*, 16–19.

Gross, M. U. M. (1993). *Exceptionally gifted children.* New York: Routledge.

Guzzo, R. A., & Salas, E. S. (1995). *Team effectiveness and decision making in organizations.* San Francisco, CA: Jossey-Bass.

Hall, R. J., Workman, J. W., & Marchioro, C. A. (1998). Sex, task and behavioral flexibility: Effects on leadership perceptions. *Organizational Behavior and Human Decision Processes, 74* (1), 1–32.

Heslin, R. (1964). Predicting group task effectiveness from member characteristics. *Psychological Bulletin, 62*, 248–256.

Hogan, R., & Hogan, J. (1995). The Hogan Personality Inventory (1995). Retrieved on June 10, 2008, from http://www.hoganassessments.com/products_services/hpi.aspx, Hogan Assessments.

Hogan, R., & Kaiser, R. B. (2005). What we know about leadership. *Review of General Psychology, 9* (2), 169–180.

Hollingworth, L. S. (1942). *Children above 180 IQ Stanford-Binet: Origin and development.* Yonkers, NY: World Book.

Hooijberg, R., Hunt, J. G., & Dodge, G. E. (1997). Leadership complexity and development of the leaderplex model. *Journal of Management, 23* (3), 375–408.

House, R. J. (1977). A 1976 theory of charismatic leadership. In J. G. Hunt & L. L. Larson (Eds.), *Leadership: The cutting edge* (pp. 189–207). Carbondale, IL: Southern Illinois University Press.

House, R. J., & Howell, J. M. (1992). Personality and charismatic leadership. *Leadership Quarterly, 3*, 81–108.

Huckaby, W., & Sperling, H. B. (1981). Leadership giftedness: An idea whose time has not yet come. *Roeper Review, 3*, 19–22.

Ilies, R. Gerhardt, M. W., & Le, H. (2004). Individual differences in leadership emergence: Integrating meta-analytic findings and behavioral genetics estimates. *International Journal of Selection and Assessment, 12* (3), 207–219.

Jacobsen, M. E. (1999a). *Liberating everyday genius®: A revolutionary guide for identifying and mastering your exceptional gifts (hardcover version of The Gifted Adult)*. New York: Ballantine.

Jacobsen, M. E. (1999b). Arousing the sleeping giant: Giftedness in adult psychotherapy. *Roeper Review, 22* (1), 36–41. MI: Bloomfield Hills.

Jacobsen, M. E. (1999c). The brilliant mind and the path of excellence, *New England Journal of Finance*, special edition, published interview.

Jacobsen, M. E. (2000a). *The gifted adult: A revolutionary guide for liberating everyday genuis®*. New York: Ballantine.

Jacobsen, M. E. (2000b). Being smart is never enough: Creating *cooperative autonomy©*, comprehensive team-building workshop for gifted government scientists, the MITRE Corporation, Bedford, MA.

Jacobsen, M. E. (2000c). Giftedness in the workplace: Can the bright mind thrive in today's organizations? Fifth Biennial Wallace National Research Symposium on Talent Development, invited address; *Proceedings of the Fifth Biennial Wallace National Research Symposium on Talent Development*, University of Iowa, Iowa City, IA.

Jacobsen, M. E. (2000d). The roots of integrity: Gifted traits, gifted truths. *The California Communicator, 31* (3), 19–35.

Jacobsen, M. E. (2003). If only I had known: Lessons from gifted adults. *Duke Gifted Letter*, Durham, NC: Duke University Talent Identification Program.

Jacobsen, M. E. (2004). Perfectionism vs. the urge to perfect in gifted adults: Foundations of excellence. Biennial Wallace National Research Symposium on Talent Development, Iowa City, IA: University of Iowa.

Jacobsen, M. E. (2008). Giftedness in the workplace: Can the bright mind thrive in today's organizations? *MENSA Research Journal, 39* (2), 15–20.

Jacobsen, M. E., & Ward, K. (2007, August). *The leadership gifted: Embrace your stars or the competition will*. Training program for the British Ministry and Department of Work and Pensions, London, UK.

Janos, P. M., & Robinson, N. M. (1985). Psychosocial development in intellectually gifted children. In F. D. Horowitz & M. O'Brien (Eds.), *The gifted and talented: Developmental perspectives* (pp. 149–195). Washington, DC: American Psychological Association.

Jensen, A. R. (1988). *The g factor: The science of mental ability*. Westport, CT: Pareger/ Greenwood.

John Jay College of Criminal Justice (Washington, DC: USCCB (2004). The ethical mind: A conversation with psychologist Howard Gardner. (2007, March). *Harvard Business Review, 85* (3), 51–56.

Judge, T. A., Bono, J. E., Ilies, T., & Gerhardt, M. W. (2002). Personality and leadership: A qualitative and quantitative review. *Journal of Applied Psychology, 87*, 765–780.

Katz, D., Maccoby, N., & Morse, N. (1950). *Productivity, supervision, and morale in an office situation*. Ann Arbor, MI: Institute for Social Research.

Katz, D., Maccoby, N., Gurin, G., & Floor, L. (1951). *Productivity, supervision, and morale among railroad workers*. Ann Arbor, MI: Institute for Social Research.

Kirkpatrick, S. A., & Locke, E. A. (1991). Leadership: Do traits matter? *Academy of Management Executive, 5* (2), 48–60.

Kohlberg, L. (1969). Stage and sequence: The cognitive-developmental approach to socialization. In D. A. Goslin (Ed.), *Handbook of socialization theory and research* (pp. 347–480). Chicago, IL: Rand McNally.

Kuncel, N. R., Hezlett, S. A., & Ones, D. S. (2004). Academic performance, career potential, creativity, and job performance: Can one construct predict them all? *Journal of Personality and Social Psychology, 86* (1), 148–161.

Lee, S.-Y., & Olszewski-Kubilius, P. (2006). The emotional intelligence, moral judgment, and leadership of academically gifted adolescents. *Journal for the Education of the Gifted, 30* (1), 29–67.

Lewin, K., Lippitt, R., & White, R., K. (1939). Patterns of aggressive behavior in experimentally created social climates. *Journal of Social Psychology, 10*, 271–299.

Lord, R. G., & Hall, R. J. (1992). Contemporary views of leadership and individual differences. *Leadership Quarterly, 3*, 137–157.

Lord, R. G., De Vader, C. L., & Alliger, G. M. (1986). A meta-analysis of the relation between personality traits and leadership perceptions: An application of validity generalization procedures. *Journal of Applied Psychology, 71*, 402–410.

Lovecky, D. (1997). Identity development in gifted children: Moral sensitivity. *Roeper Review, 20* (2), 90–94.

Matthews, M. S. (2004). Leadership education for gifted and talented youth: A review of the literature. *Journal for the Education of the Gifted, 28* (1), 77–113.

Marland, S. P., Jr. (1972). Education of the gifted and talented: Report to the Congress of the United States by the U.S. Commissioner of Education and background papers submitted to the U.S. Office of Education, 2 vols. Washington, DC: U.S. Government Printing Office. (Government Documents Y4.L 11/2: G36)

McCall, M. W. Jr., & Lombardo, M. M. (1983). *Off the track: Why and how successful executives get derailed*. Greensboro, NC: Center for Creative Leadership.

McCloy, R. A., Campbell, J. P., & Cudeck, R. R. (1994). A confirmatory test of a model of performance determinants. *Journal of Applied Psychology, 79*, 493–505.

McCrae, R. R., & John, O. P. (1992). An introduction to the five-factor model and its applications. *Journal of Personality, 60* (2), 175–215.

Mumford, M. D., Zacarro, Harding, S. J., Jacobs, T. O., & Fleishman, E. A. (2000a). Leadership skills for a changing world: Solving complex social problems. *Leadership Quarterly, 11*, 11–35.

Mumford, M. D., Zacarro, S. J., Harding, F. D., Fleishman, E. A., & Reiter-Palmon, R. (2000b). Cognitive and temperament predictors of executive ability: Principles for developing leadership capacity. Alexandria, VA: U.S. Army Research Institute for the Behavioral and Social Sciences.

Mumford, M., D., Zaccaro, S. J., Johnson, J. R., Diana, M., Gilbert, J. A., & Threlfall, K. V. (2000c). Patterns of leader characteristics: Implications for performance and development. *Leadership Quarterly, 11*, 115–133.

Oakland, T., Falkenberg, B. A., & Oakland, C. (1996). Assessment of leadership in children, youth, and adults. *Gifted Child Quarterly, 40*, 138–146.

Payne, D., & Joyner, B. E. (2006). Successful U.S. entrepreneurs: Identifying ethical decision-making and social responsibility behaviors. *Journal of Business Ethics, 65*, 203–217.

Piechowski, M. M. (1991). Emotional development and emotional giftedness. In N. Colangelo & G. Davis (Eds.), *Handbook of gifted education* (pp. 285–306). Boston, MA: Allyn & Bacon.

Plowman, P. D. (1981). Training extraordinary leaders. *Roeper Review, 3* (3), 13–16.

Posner, B. Z., & Schmidt, W. H. (1992). Values and the American manager: An update updated. *California Management Review, 34*, 80–94.

Pratch, L., & Jacobowitz, J. (1997). The psychology of leadership in rapidly changing conditions: A structural psychological approach. *Genetic, Social, and General Psychology* Monographs, *123* (2), 169–196.

Remley, T. P. Jr., & Herlihy, B. (2006). *Ethical, legal, and professional issues in counseling*. Upper Saddle River, NJ: Prentice Hall.

Roeper, A. (1988). Should educators of the gifted and talented be more concerned with world issues? *Roeper Review, 11*, 12–13.

Roeper, A. (1995). Global awareness and the young child. In A. Roeper. *Selected writings and speeches* (pp. 179–182). Minneapolis, MN: Free Spirit.

Ropp, K. (1987, February). Restructuring: Survival of the fittest. *Personnel Administrator*, 45–47.

Sama, L. M., & Shoaf, V. (2008). Ethical leadership for the professions: Fostering a moral community. *Journal of Business Ethics, 78*, 39–46.

Schmidt, F. L. (2002). The role of general cognitive ability and job performance: Why there cannot be a debate. *Human Performance, 15*, 187–210.

Schmidt, F. L., & Hunter, J. E. (1998). The validity and utility of selection methods in personnel psychology: Practical and theoretical implications of 85 years of research findings. *Psychological Bulletin, 124*, 262–274.

Schmidt, F. L., & Hunter, J. E. (2000). Select on intelligence. In E. A. Locke (Ed.), *The handbook of organizational principles* (pp. 3–14). Oxford: Blackwell.

Schmidt, F. L., & Hunter, J. E. (2004). General mental ability in the world of work: Occupational attainment and job performance. *Journal of Personality and Social Psychology, 86* (1), 162–173.

Schmidt, F. L., & Outerbridge, A. H. (1986). Impact of job experience and ability on job knowledge, work sample performance, and supervisory ratings of job performance. *Journal of Applied Psychology, 71*, 432–439.

Schwarz, N. (2007, November 11). Scandal in Chad raises adoption debate. *Voice of America News Online.* Retrieved March 11, 2008 from http://www.voanews.com/english/archive/2007–11/2007–11–08voa74.cfm?CFID = 8973314&CFTOKEN = 10024638

Shelton, S. H. (1990). Developing the construct of general self-efficacy. *Psychological Reports, 66*, 987–994.

Silverman, L. K. (1993). Social development, leadership, and gender issues. In L. K. Silverman (Ed.), *Counseling the gifted and talented* (pp. 291–327). Denver: Love.

Silverman, L. K. (1994). The moral sensitivity of gifted children and the evolution of society. *Roeper Review, 17*, 110–116.

Sisk, D. A. (1993). Leadership education for the gifted. In K. A. Heller, F. J. Mönks, & A. H. Passow (Eds.), *International handbook of research and development of giftedness and talent.* New York: Pergamon.

Skinner, W., & Sasser, W. E. (1977). Managers with impact: Versatile and inconsistent. *Harvard Business Review, 55* (6), 140–148.

Smith, A., & Foti, R. J. (1998). A pattern approach to the study of leader emergence. *Leadership Quarterly, 9*, 147–151.

Snyder, M. (1974). Self-monitoring of expressive behavior. *Journal of Personality and Social Psychology, 30*, 526–537.

Spearman, C. (1904). General intelligence, objectively determined and measured. *American Journal of Psychology, 15*, 201–293.

Sternberg, R. J. (2007). A systems model of leadership: WICS. *American Psychologist, 62*, 34–42.

Stogdill, R. M. (1948). Personal factors associated with leadership: A survey of the literature. *Journal of Psychology, 25*, 35–71.

Terman, L. M. (1925). *Genetic studies of genius: Vol. I. Mental and physical traits of a thousand gifted children.* Stanford, CA: Stanford University Press.

Terry, K., Galieta, M., O'Connor, M., Penrod, S., & Schlesinger, L. (2004). The nature and scope of the problem of sexual abuse of minors by priests and deacons. Report commissioned by the U.S. Conference of Catholic Bishops. John Jay College of Criminal Justice (Washington, DC: USCCB, 2004).

Treviño, L. K., Hartman, L. P, & Brown, M. (2000). Moral person and moral manager: How executives develop a reputation for ethical leadership. *California Management Review, 42*, 128–142.

Treviño, L. K., Brown, M., & Hartman, L. P. (2003). A qualitative investigation of perceived executive ethical leadership: Perceptions from inside and outside the executive suite. *Human Relations, 55*, 5–37.

Tupes, E. C., & Cristal, R. E. (1961). Recurrent personality factors based on trait ratings (Tech. Rep. ASD-TR-61–97). Lackland Air Force Base, TX: U.S. Air Force.

Ward, K. Z. (2008). Creating value through people: The role of talent management in creating sustainable organizational performance. MBA training program, Ashridge Business School, Berkhamsted, Hertfordshire, UK.

Whitley, R. (1989). On the nature of managerial tasks and skills: Their distinguishing characteristics and organisation. *Journal of Management Studies, 26* (3), 209–224.

Wiggins, J. S. (1996). *The five-factor model of personality*. New York: Guilford.

Yetmar, S. (2008). Business ethics resources on the internet. *Journal of Business Ethics, 80* (2), 281–288.

Yukl, G., Wall, S., & Lepsinger, R. (1990). Preliminary report on validation of the Managerial Practices Survey. In K. E. Clark & M. B. Clark (Eds.), *Measures of leadership* (pp. 223–237). West Orange, NJ: Leadership Library of America.

Zaccaro, S. J., Foti, R. J., & Kenny, D. A. (1991a). Self-monitoring and trait-based variance in leadership: An investigation of leader flexibility across multiple group rotations. *Journal of Applied Psychology, 76*, 308–315.

Zaccaro, S. J., Gilbert, J. A., Thor, K. K., & Mumford, J. D. (1991b). Leadership and social intelligence: Linking social perceptiveness and behavioral flexibility to leader effectiveness. *Leadership Quarterly, 2*, 317–342.

Zaccaro, S. J., Mumford, M. D., Connelly, M. S., Marks, M., A., & Gilbert, J. A. (2000). Assessment of leader problem-solving capabilities. *Leadership Quarterly, 11*, 37–64.

Part III
Interdisciplinary Perspectives on Ethics

Chapter 4
Morality and High Ability: Navigating a Landscape of Altruism and Malevolence

Don Ambrose

Abstract This wide-ranging exploration of theory and research from ethical philosophy, political science, economics, psychology, primatology, and other disciplines extends beyond current perspectives on morality and giftedness in high-ability fields such as gifted education and creative studies. Morality largely derives from identity formation and maps along three dimensions on a new theoretic model of moral-ethical impact: from pure altruism through malevolence, from local to global impact, and from minimal to exceptional ability and influence. Providing a framework for synthesis of diverse conceptions of morality, the model incorporates various forms of moral behavior such as universalist and particularist morality, amorality, quasi-altruism, immorality, moral atomism, and reciprocal altruism. The nature and dynamics of these and other forms of morality are explored along with some important sociocontextual influences on individuals' identity formation and actions in the world. The influence of globalized, neoliberal ideology provides a specific example of the model's dynamics. Implications for the moral development of bright young people are discussed.

Keywords Altruism · Creativity · Ethics · Giftedness · Identity formation · Interdisciplinary · Morality · Neoliberal ideology · Rational choice theory · Self-interest · Veneer theory

When individuals of high ability (broadly defined here as any combination of giftedness, talent, creativity, and intelligence) follow their aspirations and exercise their talents in the world their actions can have considerable moral impact. Understanding this impact requires an interdisciplinary search for insights because the nuances of high ability are too complex to be captured within the confines of one

D. Ambrose
Editor, Roeper Review, Graduate Department, School of Education, College of Liberal Arts, Education, and Sciences, Rider University, 2083 Lawrenceville Road, Lawrenceville, NJ, 08648-3099, USA
e-mail: ambrose@rider.edu

D. Ambrose, T. Cross (eds.), *Morality, Ethics, and Gifted Minds*,
DOI: 10.1007/978-0-387-89368-6_4,
© Springer Science+Business Media LLC 2009

or a few disciplines (Ambrose 2005a, in press). The wide-ranging analysis in this chapter draws from multiple disciplines and generates a new conceptual model of moral-ethical impact.

Many of the research studies and theories in the analysis are little known in fields such as gifted education and creative studies, yet they have strong relevance to high ability. For example, much current theorizing about morality emerges from rational-choice theory in the social sciences and similar theory in evolutionary biology. These theories often imply that moral behavior derives from reciprocal altruism – doing something for others with the expectation of payback in the future. These explanations can elucidate cases of low-level altruism but they do not explain the more impressive acts of relational-altruistic, universalist morality, which come from perceptions of self as integrated with humanity as a whole as opposed to self as atomistic individual, or as part of an insular group (for elaboration, see Gewirth 1998; Monroe 1996, 2004). Considered together, discoveries from multiple disciplines provide more complete explanations of the more remarkable forms of altruism.

4.1   Global Conditions Magnify the Importance of the Ethics-Giftedness Nexus

As of this writing, America was embroiled in chaotic, disastrous Middle-Eastern wars. Meanwhile, the Intergovernmental Panel on Climate Intergovernmental Panel on Climate Change (2007), representing an overwhelming consensus of climate scientists, was announcing the latest strong confirmation of human responsibility for the looming catastrophe of global warming. Both of these enormous, nettlesome macroproblems have been aggravated by an elemental lack of ethical wisdom on the part of many influential leaders and citizens. Magnification of the moral-ethical dimensions of high ability has never been more important or urgent.

Not that we've been without forewarning. Scholars in the fields of creative studies and gifted education often highlight the nature and importance of the moral dimensions of high ability (see Ambrose 2000, 2008, in press; Csikszentmihalyi 1993; Csikszentmihalyi and Nakamura 2007; Derryberry et al. 2005; Dabrowski 1964; Dabrowski and Piechowski 1977; Damon 2008; Damon and Colby 1996; Folsom 1998; Gardner 1991, 2007; Gibson et al. 2008; Gardner et al. 2001; Grant 1995; Gruber 1989, 1993; Hague 1998; Lee and Olszewski-Kubilius 2006; Lovecky 1997; Michaelson 2001; Piechowski 2003; Piirto 2005; Runco and Nemiro 2003; Roeper 2008; Silverman 1993; Spreacker 2001; Sriraman and Adrian 2005; Sternberg 2001, 2005; Tannenbaum 2000; Tirri and Nokelainen 2007; Tolan 1998). For example, Gruber (1993) urged us to apply creativity to moral issues in the late twentieth century, which was rocked by rapid social and technological change and multiple global crises. World civilization as presently constituted is committed to policies entailing unregulated economic growth and the amoral or immoral exploitation of resources and populations. Such conditions affect moral issues of fairness, justice, caring for others, and even truth.

Early in the twenty-first century our socioeconomic, political, and cultural contexts demand ever more attention to the moral dimensions of human experience. The unpredictable, nebulous, and rapidly evolving phenomenon of economic and cultural globalization is threatening international stability by making political and economic boundaries more porous (Rosenau 2003; Singer 2002; Xiang 2007). Enhanced global interconnections bring diverse economic and cultural groups into tighter juxtaposition and magnify their differences, thus creating dynamic tensions between desires to maintain local traditions and the wish to capitalize on foreign ideas (Rosenau). Such dynamic tensions can generate serious conflicts requiring wise, ethical leadership for their mitigation. Instability makes more room for creative and clever but morally hollow people to engage in unethical behavior such as economic exploitation and political-military conquest. Moreover, the rapid pace of technological progress in today's world spawns high-impact, rapid-fire innovations in burgeoning domains such as biotechnology and information technology, which generate novel prospects for substantial progress along with opportunities for the immoral exploitation of others and possibilities for environmental disasters (Launis et al. 1999). The problem of global warming may be the most prominent, widespread, and potentially devastating result of our technological progress unfettered by ethical guidance (see Flannery 2006; Hansen 2005).

4.2 Human Nature and Identity as Key Aspects of Morality and Ethics

Although many perspectives on human nature and morality are worthy of note, I have selected several here for special attention. First, de Waal's (2006) employment of primate observation and evolutionary analysis to deconstruct veneer theory enables some escape from the amoral rational-choice theory that dominates the social sciences, not to mention the ideological context of the globalized sociopolitical environment. Second, Monroe's work (1996, 2004), which includes analyses of altruistic rescuers who put their own lives on the line to help strangers, reveals the powerful influence of identity on moral behavior while contributing to the escape from rational-choice theory.

4.2.1 Breaking Down Veneer Theory

According to psychologist/primatologist Frans de Waal (2006), some prominent moral theorists have headed down the wrong path in their beliefs that humans are innately asocial or antisocial and brutish (e.g., philosopher Thomas Hobbes 1651/1985) or extremely selfish (e.g., evolutionary biologists such as Trivers 1971; Wilson 1978). According to Hobbes, our brutish, predatory nature forced us to develop strong legal systems to keep us from each other's throats. Evolutionary biologists and evolutionary psychologists posit selfish genetic influences that make us victims of evolutionary processes leading to self-centered behavior.

De Waal (2006) argued that veneer theory emerges from these flawed positions and encourages us to assume that we cannot expect much good from human nature. According to veneer theory, morality is but a thin veneer covering an immoral or at best amoral core human nature. When all is calm the veneer keeps us from exploiting and abusing one another, but scratching this surface, as occurs in crises such as tragedies or resource shortages, reveals our unsavory core dispositions that give rise to evil behavior. Undoubtedly, evil does emerge under such conditions but veneer theory magnifies it while obscuring our altruistic inclinations.

Instead, de Waal (2006) based his opposing, more optimistic vision of human nature on many years of observing primates, concluding that evolutionary processes favor collaborative, altruistic behavior. His findings revealed that altruism is common among primates and it derives from their emotional responses to the plight of others. Furthermore, contrary to the arguments of some evolutionary biologists and psychologists, such emotion-driven, altruistic responses are adaptive from an evolutionary viewpoint because they promote group cohesion and groups survive better than scatterings of atomistic individuals. The altruism that typically emerges is genuine, not the tit for tat reciprocal altruism in which the altruist expects some form of payback from the beneficiary. While reciprocal altruism does occur in some cases, it does not dominate such actions.

4.2.2   Identity as an Atomistic Individual or Intertwined with Humanity?

Monroe (1996, 2004) revealed some flaws of rational-choice theory, which promotes the idea that individuals develop as self-encapsulated, atomistic egos whose identities are defined by highly competitive pursuit of domination, control, and materialistic accumulation. The dehumanizing use of others as means to individual gain is an intrinsic element of societies built on rational-choice assumptions (see Beckert 2002).

Running counter to rational choice constructs, Monroe discovered identity dynamics defined by a collaborative connectedness with others and an accompanying sense of self-transcendence. In studies of altruistic behavior she investigated the experiences, reflections, and motivations of moral exemplars, focusing on those who compromised their own safety and well being to rescue strangers who were in serious danger. She discovered that the dynamics of personal identity formation are crucial in the positioning of individuals along a continuum ranging from egoistic self-interest to altruism. The altruistic rescuers were not driven by self-centered, rational, utilitarian, cost-benefit calculation but by an emotional sense of connectedness with others. Rescuing behavior happened reflexively, without much thought.

In contrast, less altruistic individuals tend to engage in some kind acts toward others but in so doing are more inclined to employ rational, cost-benefit calculation. Those far less altruistic can exhibit cruelty because they insulate their identities from the cognitive dissonance that normally would ensue from their wicked actions.

They can maintain a positive self-perception by detaching themselves from those they intend to abuse. For example:

> Genocidalists appeared to psychologically distance themselves from neighbors once considered friends, relegating them to the subhuman category in order to justify mistreating them. Reclassification and recategorization seem to be critical parts of the psychological process by which other human beings are declared "unworthy of life." (Monroe 2004, p. 256)

Chirot and McCauley (2006) concurred with the importance of these identity dynamics and illustrated how those wanting to advance the interests of their own identity groups often portray other racial, ethnic, or religious minorities as polluting influences, thereby justifying extreme acts of aggression against them up to and including genocide:

> Mass murders or deportations that are ethnically, religiously, ideologically, or class based can be caused by fear of pollution. This is at once the most intense, but also the psychologically most difficult cause to understand for those who do not share the sentiment that a particular group is so polluting that its very presence creates a mortal danger. (p. 36)

These insights magnify the importance of self-perception and identity formation in the development of gifted individuals. To the extent that we enable them to view themselves in highly individualistic terms, as atomistic entities, or as members of a preferred superior group, we may be aggravating the erosion of their ethical fiber over the long term. We may be creating very clever but potentially diabolical agents in the world.

4.3 Confounding Legality with Morality

Societies built on flawed ethical assumptions, such as an overreliance on rational-choice theory, must follow Hobbes' (1651/1985) advice and create strong legal frameworks to keep humans from excessively harming one another. A strong legal system can make a society stable and just (Habermas 1996) but if a society's laws condone some degree of degradation or exploitation of some people by others, the fact that these actions are legal does not make them ethical. The dominance of rational-choice theory might lead us to confuse morality and legality on the large scale. If a morally questionable act is deemed legal by society, bright but morally hollow people can consider its legality a green light for action regardless of the ethical implications. Actions with moral dimensions can be legal but immoral, moral but illegal, both moral and legal, both immoral and illegal, or they can fall into gray areas between morality and immorality, or between legality and illegality. While we can posit a correlation between morality and legality with some degree of confidence, there is plenty of room for immoral, even monstrous actions that a culture or society deems perfectly legal. Twentieth-century South African apartheid and racial segregation in the American South were two prominent examples.

Dangers arising from confusing legality with morality are most prominent in sociopolitical systems that trust their legal systems as proxies for moral guidance.

Neoliberal, capitalist nations rely heavily on their legal systems because governmental power in the lives of citizens is restricted to refereeing disputes among self-interested rational actors in a laissez-faire marketplace (Wolin 2008). Such refereeing is to be as hands-off as possible.

These systems can sustain morality and ethics, at least to some extent, as long as the legal frameworks stay transparent, fair, and free of corruption, but that is a seldom-realized ideal. A socioeconomic system based on the lionization of the self-loving, atomistic, materialistic, self-aggrandizing individual allocates considerable freedom to those who would apply their creativity and talents to the exploitation of others. It makes room for creative manipulation of the legal system itself so that the most selfish, ruthless, and cunning make laws and loopholes that favor their own unsavory, manipulative actions over those of their more virtuous peers. Neoliberal, laissez-faire socioeconomic systems make the most room for such manipulation because they lionize the individual, rational actor more than any other system (for examples see Hacker and Pierson 2005).

4.4   A Model of Moral-Ethical Impact in the World

The foregoing analyses of ethics, morality, and sociopolitical contexts represent an incomplete but highly complex picture because they derive from very diverse theories and research findings from multiple disciplines. The cube-shaped moral-ethical impact model in Fig. 4.1 represents an attempt to capture and simplify much of this complexity within its three dimensions and on the undulating surface within. Imagine the cube as gargantuan, half-filled with earthen material representing a landscape upon which individuals and societies locate themselves according to the ethical or unethical nature of their actions. The surface of the landscape is rather flat and gently sloping on the left side and on the right side it has a steep hill at the back and deep valley at the front.

The model includes three continua that represent three different dimensions of ethics. The depth dimension, moving from back to front, represents a continuum of *moral disposition and action* ranging from highly admirable, altruistic moral action at the back of the model to despicable, immoral, evil action at the front. The midpoint in the back-to-front dimension represents amoral or morally neutral behavior.

The vertical dimension represents the *moral impact* of one's actions in the world. Listed here are characterizations of these impacts ranging from top to bottom on the model:

Lofty position at or near the top of the hill in the back-right corner of the earthen landscape. Far-reaching, positive, altruistic global impact on large swaths of humanity. (e.g., transforming the institutions or ideology of a society to create a more humane context for human development; inspiring large masses of people to become more altruistic over the long term).

Just above the neutral, mid-level. Small-scale moral actions ranging from high to low impact on one or a few individuals, or having minor impact on many, but

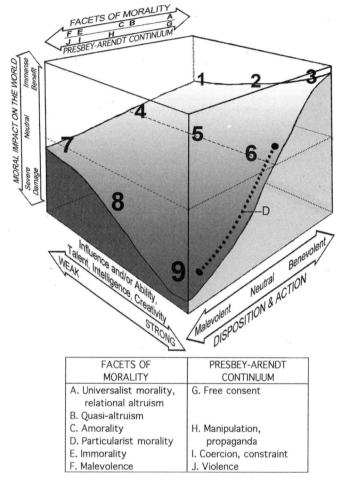

FACETS OF MORALITY	PRESBEY-ARENDT CONTINUUM
A. Universalist morality, relational altruism	G. Free consent
B. Quasi-altruism	
C. Amorality	H. Manipulation, propaganda
D. Particularist morality	
E. Immorality	I. Coercion, constraint
F. Malevolence	J. Violence

Fig. 4.1 Model of moral–ethical impact

ultimately generating little impact on the world. (e.g., being a good Samaritan to a lost or injured individual; giving a modest sum to a worthy charity).

Neutral position at the middle. Actions that have no noticeable moral impact on the world. Many of our everyday actions fit here.

Just below the neutral mid-level. Small-scale immoral actions ranging from high to low impact on one or a few individuals, or having minor impact on many, but ultimately generating little impact on the world (e.g., stealing a car; abusing a child).

At or near the bottom of the valley in the front-right corner of the earthen landscape. High-impact immoral or evil effects on large swaths of humanity (e.g., transforming the institutions or ideology of a society to benefit oneself and a favored identity group while oppressing or doing violence to many others; starting wars for vainglorious purposes).

The distinctions here are not meant to diminish the importance of small-scale altruism or the gravity of small-scale immoral acts. Helping an endangered individual may be the epitome of heroism. In fact, the actions of Monroe's (1996, 2004) subjects in her studies of altruism often were extremely heroic but would not rise high on this model, only because they had small impact on the world. Similarly, abusing a child is a horrific, evil act. Such small-scale evil actions do not extend very low on the model simply because they do not individually impact the word in significant ways. Nevertheless, small actions can become global if, for instance, the single beneficiary of an altruistic act is inspired by that act to do great, altruistic things later in life. In addition, many small, positive actions done by many individuals can additively generate very large global impact while many small, immoral actions can accumulate into collective depravity and generate widespread misery in the world. For the sake of this analysis, however, these collective influences are set aside in order to focus on the actions of individuals.

The left-to-right dimension of the model represents *the power an individual exercises in the world*. Those with little power and influence act on the left side where the impact of their actions on the world is minimal, as signified by the very low rise in elevation toward the back of the model and the very shallow valley toward the front. Those with enormous power and influence act on the right side where their actions can have immense influence on the world, as signified by the tall peak of altruism at the back of the model and the very deep valley of malevolence at the front. In general, those born into deprivation have little power to influence the world as individuals, so most of them operate at the left side of the model. Conversely, those born into privilege have more opportunities to develop their talents, and have more ready access to important resources and influential support networks, so they find it easier to gain access to the levers of power; hence, they tend to operate on the right side. Gifted, talented, creative, or intelligent individuals have capacities that can magnify their influence in the world so they are more likely to move rightward on the model as they mature, operating closer to the right side of the model when they become adults.

The surface of the model shows how individuals and groups can locate themselves as ethical, or unethical, actors in the world. They can spend most of their lives operating at one specific location on the surface. Alternatively, they can evolve over time as ethical agents, moving (a) from left to right as they develop their talents and gain more power and influence; (b) from front to back if they become more altruistic, (c) from back to front if their ethical sensibilities erode; (d) from lower slopes on the undulating surface to higher levels as they impact the world positively; or (e) from higher levels to lower if their impact is harmful.

Figure 4.1 also maps some major theorists' categorizations of ethical behavior (see de Waal 2006; Gewirth 1998; Monroe 1996, 2004) onto the surface of the model. While amorality resides in the morally neutral territory midway between front and back on the model, and immorality and malevolence are situated at the front, universalist morality and relational altruism extend to the higher elevations and the most benevolent region at the back (see the Facets of Morality arrow in Fig. 4.1). Relational altruism entails behavior intended to benefit others, even when it may bring harm to the altruist (Gewirth 1998; Monroe 1996). Some forms of benevolent behavior are called quasi-altruistic because they don't rise to the high level of pure altruism seeing that they do not entail risk to self, or they are done largely for selfish purposes. For example, people are quasi-altruistic if they give to a charity to assuage their own guilt, to look good in the eyes of others, or to magnify their own senses of self-importance. Particularist morality is represented by a dashed line (labeled "D" on the model) stretching from mild positive influence in the world all the way down to the depths of widespread, devastating, evil effects, because people who confine their altruism to those who are most like them can do good for insiders while seriously harming outsiders (Chirot and McCauley 2006). The Presbey-Arendt continuum is explained in a later subsection.

4.4.1 Individuals' Locations and Life Trajectories on the Landscape of the Model

The locations shown by numbers one through nine on the surface of the model in Fig.4.1 represent the moral locales in which people can spend their lives. They also represent locations individuals can move toward during moral development. Such movement can be from less to more benevolent behavior, or the reverse; from less to more personal ability and/or influence in the world, or the reverse; and toward either less or more benefit or damage to the world.

Individuals' locations or developmental movements largely depend (metaphorically speaking) on magnetic attraction or repulsion from the right-side panel on the model, which represents the location of strongest power and influence. The right-side panel attracts individuals who possess high ability, or the advantages of socioeconomic privilege, or both. Consequently, people with these attributes and/or advantages move toward the high-impact region on the right-hand side of the model as they mature because they have what it takes to make a significant impact on the world. Whether that development leads toward the altruistic high ground in the back-right corner of the model, or the immoral low ground in the front-right corner depends on the individual's benevolent or malevolent inclinations, which can be shaped by his or her innate propensities, mentorship, education, the sociocultural and economic context, or any combination of these factors.

The right-side panel also magnetically repels those who lack high ability or who suffer from socioeconomic barriers that stunt their aspiration growth and talent development. These barriers usually derive from deprivation, stigmatization, and segregation (for analyses of socioeconomic barriers see Ambrose 2002, 2003, 2005b, 2005c; Fischer et al. 1996), Consequently, most nongifted or deprived people are confined to the low-impact region on the left side of the model and exert little influence in the world. A few deprived but outstanding individuals of high ability do make it into the high-impact, right-side region because their gifts, talents, creativity, or intelligence enable them to overcome the strong magnetic repulsion of their oppressive life circumstances.

Life positions represented by the numbers three, six, and nine on the right side of the model are sparsely populated because very small elites typically exert most control over their societies (Wolin 2008). Only a few are allowed to manipulate the levers of power and this region of the model is where most of the socioeconomic, political, and cultural power of a society exists. Moreover, those who reside in these locations typically arrive there through one of the following influences, or some amalgam of the two: (a) exceptional ability in the form of talent, creativity, intelligence, or some blend of these; and/or (b) the benefits of privilege such as wealth, support from lofty insider networking contacts and mentorships, and downright nepotism. In essence, a person in these regions can be anything from a paragon of high ability to someone of moderate ability but good fortune, to someone with unremarkable or even very weak intelligence and talent but bountiful resources and exceptional favoritism from powerful friends or relatives in the society.

Conversely, those populating the left side of the model at or near positions one, four, or seven are vast in number because the masses typically exert little to no influence over their societies, even in liberal democracies, which tend to be democratically nominal in today's corporate-dominated globalized environment (see Hacker and Pierson 2005; Wolin 2008). Moreover, those who reside in these locations typically arrived there through one of the following influences, or some amalgam of the two: (a) unremarkable or weak ability in the form of limited talent, creativity, intelligence, or some blend of these; and/or (b) the suppression of aspiration growth and talent development due to socioeconomic deprivation, stigmatization, and segregation.

Those populating the mid-range numbers two, five, and eight on the landscape also are numerous, much more so in nations that are somewhat egalitarian socioeconomically and much less so in highly stratified nations, which push the bulk of their populations into the powerless far-left side of the landscape. Most of those who operate in this mid-range arrive there by virtue of moderate abilities and/or moderate socioeconomic supports or barriers although some may have weak abilities augmented by favorable socioeconomic support or strong abilities hindered by socioeconomic barriers.

Interestingly, at least a few individuals can operate at more than one location on the landscape. Some exemplars of altruism are moral paradoxes making enormous, enduring ethical improvements to the world while also doing moral harm in the small scale. For example, Mohandas Gandhi catalyzed India's nonviolent escape from British colonial oppression but also treated some of those closest to him with indifference and cruelty (Gardner 1993). This locates him simultaneously at points three and seven on the model where he exerted the highest levels of positive, moral impact on millions while simultaneously doing mild harm to the world by treating a few miserably. While these latter actions are lamentable, we should avoid the temptation to dismiss Gandhi's influence on the grounds of hypocrisy. His human failings should not disqualify him as a moral exemplar because no human is infallible. Such disqualifications would rob us of most if not all positive exemplars and their useful messages. Table 4.1 shows some specific examples of moral life locations according to the numbers on the model.

Table 4.1 Examples of individual locations on the moral landscape (position on the model designated by number)

	Left side of the model	Center of the model	Right side of the model
Potential moral impact on the world	Low impact	Noticeable impact but not profound or widespread	Widespread, transformative high impact
Blend of ability & socioeconomic (SES) influence required for positioning at these locations	Insignificant or weak ability; or moderate ability + serious SES disadvantage; or high ability + severe SES disadvantage trap individuals on low-impact left side of landscape	Moderate ability + moderate SES advantage; or high ability + SES disadvantage; or low ability + very strong SES advantage enable location in moderate-impact left-to-right center of landscape	Low or moderate ability + enormous SES advantage; or high ability + significant SES advantage; or rare, outstanding ability overcoming SES disadvantage enable location on high-impact right side of landscape
Benevolent moral disposition and action	1. Impoverished parent who often provides guidance and compassion to children in a deprived neighborhood	2. Mother Hale, a poor African American widow, adopted, raised, and educated over 40 deprived children while helping scores of others including many who were born drug addicted or with HIV (see Lanker 1999)	3. Muhammad Yunus, Bangladeshi economist, Nobel Peace Prize winner, and "banker to the poor" lifts many of the world's poorest out of poverty by providing microcredit for widespread, small-scale entrepreneurship (see Yunus 2003, 2008)
Neutral moral disposition and action	4. Educator who goes through the motions to meet the demands of NCLB; does little to engage the moral imaginations of self or students; moral ambivalence subverts the opportunity to make a difference	5. Business executive whose innovative work transforms corporate procedures without generating either positive or harmful ethical implications; does significant work in the world but moral ambivalence limits moral impact	6. Gene Roddenberry, science-fiction author, writer and producer of Star Trek TV series and movie franchise among many other productions; did rare, highly influential work but made little moral impact (see Fern 1994)
Malevolent moral disposition and action	7. Street gang member who murders members of a rival gang due to conflict over drug-dealing turf; insatiable desire for material gain and self-aggrandizement motivates actions	8. Cult leader who exploits the labor of followers, commandeers their assets, or exhorts them to mass suicide; owner of third-world sweatshop exploiting desperate workers	9. Adolf Hitler undermined and overthrew the democratic government of the German Weimar Republic, catalyzed World War II, and engaged in massive genocide (see Brustein 1998)

Admittedly, placement of the specific examples in the locations in Table 4.1 is problematic. Individuals arguably could be placed in other locations. For example, Mother Hale is placed in location two because she did much more than most would or could do in similar circumstances. That places her well beyond location one. However, her influence didn't extend to the large-scale, regional or national level, which would have placed her in location three. Nevertheless, it is difficult to gauge the impact of an individual's influence over the long term. It could be that some of her protégés and their progeny have or will impact the world in profound ways due to her catalytic influence. In addition, her work may be even more impressive than the work of many better-known altruistic exemplars because it might have required more personal sacrifice, creativity, and diligence.

4.4.2 Additional Ethical Frameworks and Their Fit on the Moral-Ethical Impact Model

Most ethical constructs and other theories pertinent to morality can fit on the moral-ethical impact model. Examples included here are the Presbey-Arendt continuum and a distinction between ethical particularism and universalism.

4.4.2.1 The Presbey-Arendt Continuum

Power relationships in communities and nations fit on a continuum derived from the work of Arendt (1958/1998) and Presbey (1997). The following positions on the continuum are arrayed along the top arrow of Fig. 4.1: (g) free consent, (h) deceptive manipulation and propaganda, (i) coercion and threats of violence, and (j) actual physical constraint and violence. Position "g" is most conducive to group- and individual freedom, self-actualization, and widespread benevolent action while position "j" is least. An individual who helps a community or an entire nation achieve position "g" moves large masses of people toward the morally positive back sector of the model in Fig. 4.1. For example, Nelson Mandela, Desmond Tutu, and others pushed the nation of South Africa away from the malevolent valley in the front up the landscape somewhat toward the benevolent hill in the back. An individual who works to manipulate, deceive, enslave, or do violence to others moves toward the evil front of the model. A society that encourages free consent in its sociopolitical dynamics promotes transparent, egalitarian, democratic governance that works for the benefit of all citizens (Wolin 2008). Such a healthy sociopolitical context encourages creative, gifted people to move toward the lofty, altruistic back of the model. Conversely, a society that allows or enables talented, ambitious psychopaths to employ deceit, propaganda, coercion, and violence to commandeer the levers of power erodes whatever democracy it had established in the past. Such conditions wash many creative, gifted people down toward the malevolent valley in the front of the model.

4.4.2.2   Universalist Versus Particularist Morality

Some ethical philosophers (e.g., Gewirth 1998) distinguish between two important dimensions of morality. People who are guided by universalist morality may favor their own well-being and that of their family, ethnic group, or nation over that of outsiders. But they don't allow themselves to seriously impede the fulfillment of outsiders in pursuit of their own goals because they don't see their own wants superseding the needs of others. In contrast, a person guided by particularist morality adheres to the moral framework of a particular group and shows much less concern for the well-being of outsiders or humanity as a whole.

Particularist loyalty to one's own cultural, ethnic, religious, or national group has its merits because it provides strong frameworks for personal identity formation (Gutmann 2003). Nevertheless, excessive adherence to a particular group can create serious ethical problems. Particularists may be altruistic toward members of their own identity group but their kindness usually does not extend beyond to those different from them. They are likely to favor the frivolous wants of insiders over the desperate needs of outsiders. In an especially virulent example, fanatical patriotism and racist ethnic cleansing are desirable from within the particular ethical frameworks of some extremist right-wing groups but they definitely are immoral from the viewpoint of a universalist. Historically, other particularist ethical frameworks have been used to justify slavery, military conquest, and even genocide. For these reasons, Gewirth (1998) advocated universalism over particularism as a prerequisite for high moral development. The actions of individuals following particularist morality tend to show up anywhere just above the amoral zone in the middle of the moral-ethical impact model to the malevolent front while the actions of universalists tend to appear near the benevolent back of the model.

4.4.2.3   Irrational Action Within Globalized, Runaway, Neoliberal–Neoclassical Capitalism

As mentioned earlier, free-market, capitalism encourages individuals to view themselves as self-interested, atomistic, rational actors. In a globalized, free-market system guided primarily by neoclassical economic theory, regulatory rules diminish considerably (Appelbaum 2005; Babb 2001; Frank 2007; Kasser et al. 2007; Kuttner 1999; Madrick 2008; Nadeau 2003) largely leaving the ethics of socioeconomic action to individual choice. In such an environment, the only significant check on individual freedom is the legal framework of the society, which should prevent egregious misbehavior. However, as discussed previously, legality and morality do not always coincide. When the legal system is compromised by corruption it offers little protection from malevolent acts and may even *encourage* them. An extreme free-market system with a corrupted legal framework represents a perfect storm of ethical erosion that washes the collective behavior of millions downward from the amoral mid-regions of the model toward the dark malevolence of the valley at the front.

Examples of such erosion in the form of corrupt, immoral but legal actions perpetrated by cunning, gifted or talented individuals in neoliberal socioeconomic systems are ubiquitous. The few listed below are illustrative:

1. Repealing inheritance taxes by deceptively calling them "death taxes" (see Graetz and Shapiro 2005) is unethical because it shifts the tax burden from the highly affluent who can afford it to the deprived who cannot while seriously eroding equality of opportunity, thereby making a sham of the meritocracy we claim as the nurturing ground for the emergence of giftedness and talent.
2. Gifted lobbyists for the pharmaceutical industry collude with clever politicians in the establishment of laws that enable extortion of artificially exorbitant drug prices and other medical costs while nearly 50 million people cannot afford basic medical care in the United States (Goozner 2005).
3. The cigarette industry developed clever, deceptive marketing and lobbying practices to create a disinformation campaign aimed at sidestepping government regulation and undermining and suppressing scientific inquiry into the harmful effects of their products (Brandt 2007).
4. Gifted corporate leaders take advantage of international free-trade pacts they lobbied to establish. Free trade enables them to move capital around the globe freely to take advantage of the weakest labor laws and environmental regulations in impoverished nations (Appelbaum 2005; McMurtry 1999, 2002). In so doing, they maximize their own profits while eroding the well-being of American workers and ruthlessly exploiting third-world sweatshop workers.
5. Talented neoclassical economists and the policy makers who follow them implement economic systems that ignore the environmental costs of doing business while generating widespread environmental devastation (Nadeau 2003).

Many influential, gifted adults initiate these immoral practices with impunity because the American regulatory system currently suffers from corruption (Hacker and Pierson 2005; Wolin 2008).

These dynamics are signified by two of the arrows in Fig. 4.2. Utopian ideologies represent grand hopes for humanity, usually couched in ethical terms (Kumar 1987); however, they often go awry and lead to serious ethical erosion (Ambrose 2008). The utopian Third Reich's golden age of Aryan supremacy in Nazi Germany and Pol Pot's idiosyncratic, agrarian version of utopian communism in Cambodia were extreme examples. Morally hollow or misguided individuals who are gifted, talented, or creative leaders often catalyze and sustain such utopian movements. The downward sloping arrow of hegemonic utopian ideology in Fig. 4.2 represents the moral erosion utopianism often entails. The weaker, ghostly dashed arrow moving back up the hill toward relational-altruistic benevolence represents the self-deceptive high hopes of the ideologues at the core of the utopian conceptual framework.

The corrupt actions described earlier in this subsection provide evidence that neoliberal ideology, along with its close cousin, neoclassical economic theory, together represent another, very powerful utopian framework that is washing many bright, talented people down toward the malevolent front of the model (see Ambrose 2008,

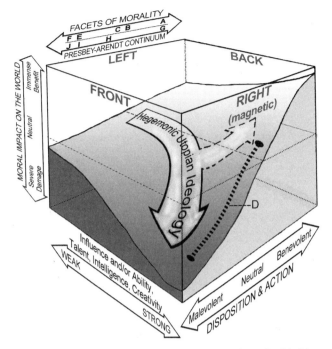

Fig. 4.2 Hegemonic, utopian ideology mapped onto the model of moral–ethical impact

and Green's Chapter 6 in this volume for additional analyses of these dynamics). When mapping neoliberal ideology and neoclassical economics onto the model, the downward sloping arrow of hegemonic utopian ideology represents the self-loving, self-aggrandizing, highly materialistic moral erosion of the current globalized socioeconomic system. The weaker, ghostly dashed arrow moving back up the hill toward relational-altruistic benevolence represents the somewhat less prevalent moral good that globalized capitalism actually does by encouraging economic vibrancy in some locales, as well as what it could do were it guided by stronger regulatory and ethical frameworks as recommended by various high-profile economists and political theorists (e.g., Chang 2002, 2007; Hacker and Pierson 2005; Madrick 2008; Wolin 2008) and by none other than the eighteenth-century philosopher-economist Adam Smith, the icon of free-market capitalism. According to Fleischacker (2004) and Muller (1995) Smith's strong moral messages have been ignored while his free-market advice has been magnified in recent decades. Smith actually recommended the use of regulation to countervail the excesses of marketplace greed. Gifted, neoliberal ideologues and those who follow their message see only the upward arrow and remain oblivious to the massive erosion represented by the downward arrow.

4.5 Implications for the Ethical Development of High Ability

Identity formation appears to be central to important forms of both altruism and malevolence (Gewirth 1998; Monroe 1996, 2004). To the extent that educators, parents, and policy makers influence the identity formation of bright young people, we must raise our awareness of the extreme positive and negative directions that formation can take. The tendency for dogmatic conceptual frameworks to ensnare human minds, even the brightest, can induce erosion toward the lower, malevolent regions of the moral-ethical impact model. Some highly gifted young people with leadership potential may be influenced to develop excessively grandiose, egocentric identities and apply their abilities to malevolent ends. Fortunately, the contributors to this volume provide additional ways to understand how and why people of high ability locate themselves at various positions on the landscape of the model. These insights are discussed briefly at the end of this chapter.

4.5.1 Clearing Dogmatic Fog

The preceding examples of ethical problems generated by the hegemony of neoliberal-neoclassical ideology highlight the issue of dogmatism and the extent to which it contributes to ethical erosion on the moral-ethical impact model. While some, perhaps many, of the powerful, talented ideologues and gifted corporate leaders who drive the neoliberal-neoclassical system might be morally bankrupt, highly egocentric, possibly even psychopathic, many others believe strongly in the ethical value of the system, emphasizing its freedom-enhancing capacities, for example. There is good reason to hypothesize that dogmatic attachment to conceptual systems makes large numbers of people, including gifted leaders, engage in malevolent acts while genuinely believing they are working for the greater good. Self-deception might be at play in such cases. Mele (2001) analyzed the dynamics of self-deception, showing that the phenomenon occurs when individuals hold excessive belief in things they want to be true, or unwarranted belief against something they want not to be true. The problem of self-deception can occur on a mass scale. Entire nations can self-deceive to the point of re-inventing their histories or engaging in self-destructive actions on the world stage (see Moeller 2001).

This hypothetical phenomenon of mass self-deception can be represented metaphorically as dogmatic fog drifting over the undulating landscape on the moral-ethical impact model. The fog of dogmatism hinders accurate perception of where one actually is on the landscape, deceiving some into believing they are on the moral high ground when, in actuality, they are sliding into the malevolent valley at the front of the model.

Of course, fog collects thickly on the malevolent low ground and thins out on the benevolent high ground because those most trapped in dogmatism are least likely to understand the harm they do. Conceptual systems capable of generating the fog can be ontological (assumptions about the nature of reality), epistemological (assumptions about the nature of knowledge), ideological, ethnocentric, cultural, religious, or any combination of these.

Ontological and epistemological dogmatism occur in scholarly fields (Ambrose 1996, 1998; Overton 1984; Pepper 1942) and might contribute to moral erosion indirectly; however, the ideological, ethnic, and religious forms of dogmatism are more germane to this analysis. While the neoliberal-neoclassical system provides an example of ideological dogmatism, ethnic dogmatism can come from the phenomenon of particularist morality (strongly favoring one's own identity group), which is mapped onto the model (see Fig. 4.1).

Religious dogmatism can generate another form of particularist morality that encourages moral erosion on the landscape of the model. The identity formation of most people worldwide, gifted young people included, heavily rests upon religious and spiritual influences from the surrounding culture. Moore (2000) and Stark (2003) illustrated the good and the harm monotheistic religions foment, with the harm extending up to and including genocide. Given both the promise and dangers of monotheistic religion, these influences on identity formation have powerful ethical implications. If otherwise gifted individuals stop short of deep, spiritual development, which tends to unite diverse peoples, while adhering to superficial, religious doctrine, which tends to alienate groups from one another, they will be more inclined to support or initiate hateful conflicts with those of other religious beliefs. They will consider outsiders somewhat less human and less worthy of compassion. Conversely, if they find ways to develop deep, inward, spiritual growth and move past the particularities of religious doctrine, they will become more compassionate, altruistic, and universalist in their moral approach to life. They will be more inclined to reach out and help others regardless of superficial differences.

Whatever form the dogmatic fog takes (ideological, economic, particularist ethnic or religious), young people of high ability will need help to peer through it. Fortunately, their expansive intellects and their propensities for panoramic global awareness (Gibson et al. 2008; Roeper 2008; Silverman 1993) make them capable of capitalizing on any guidance we can provide.

4.5.2   Watching for Excessive Self-Aggrandizement Within Warped Meritocracies

Consistent with the atomistic individualism encouraged by rational-choice theory, in describing the extremes of egocentrism Bohm (1994) pointed out that enormously gifted or talented megalomaniacs such as Alexander the Great have tended to become intensely self-focused and develop grandiose senses of their destiny in the world. In their minds, the grandiosity of their visions appears to justify whatever courses of action they take, no matter how harmful to others. In Alexander's case, he was so caught up in self-aggrandizement that he felt compelled to do no less than conquer and rule the world.

Alexander was an extreme case, but he illustrates a caution we must heed in our work with individuals of high ability. While we shouldn't burden the gifted with expectations that they must solve all the world's problems because they are gifted, we still should consider their future actions on the world because their high potential makes them more likely to impact the culture, socioeconomic system, and environment than their peers of lesser ability. Their potential ethical impact, whether positive or negative, magnifies the importance of attending to their moral development.

The ethical effects of megalomania can be magnified by socioeconomic and political contexts that are portrayed as far more meritocratic than they truly are. Self-aggrandizing megalomaniacs find justification for their vainglory when the societal context accepts or even lauds self-serving, possibly reprehensible actions as natural and any ensuing rewards as well-deserved outcomes from the exercise of meritorious creativity, talent, or intelligence. For example, today's globalized, corporate capitalism exalts self-love, materialism, and the exercise of domination over others while diminishing the value of community and concern for others (Kasser et al. 2007; McMurtry 1999, 2002), thereby warping the ethical fiber of its meritocracy. Moreover, forgetting ethics for a moment, even possession of material affluence and power might not emerge from outstanding talent, creativity, or intelligence but instead might accrue to individuals effortlessly on the basis of inheritance and birth privilege. In a system that protects such privileges and in which merit is underdefined (see Gates and Collins 2004; Sen 2000) morally vacuous individuals who lack ability can find themselves in "meritorious" positions of great power.

The dynamics of such a system raise issues about the nature of merit. First, a true meritocracy would not allow those with little ability into lofty positions of immense power. Second, it would not laud them as meritorious unless they actually accomplished great things. Third, it would establish clear criteria for what counts as merit and those criteria would not be dominated by materialistic self-interest. This last point is of most concern when considering moral development because it magnifies the importance of societal context. If educators and mentors of bright young people must swim upstream against strong ideological currents that undermine moral development they will need the help of wise policy makers to improve the prospects for moral development in the long term. In spite of strong, neoliberal ideological hegemony worldwide, some nations do a better job of others in providing equal opportunity for aspiration development (see Ambrose 2005c; Smeeding et al. 2002) and some are less caught up in materialistic value systems (see Inglehart 1997). Consequently, large-scale socioeconomic and political contexts conducive to stronger moral development exist and are worthy of attention by educators, and of emulation by policy makers.

4.5.3 Plotting the Chapters in This Book on the Model

Finally, the contributors to this volume reveal some additional dynamics of movement and location on the landscape of the moral-ethical impact model. Tom Green illustrates some ways in which economists of high ability trap themselves in somewhat myopic economic theory that washes them, and the millions they influence, downward toward the malevolent valley at the front of the model. Amit Goswami suggests ways that those in the world of business can avoid such ethical erosion and climb toward the high ground on the model by using creative thinking to synthesize commerce with ethics. Laurence Bove illustrates some ways in which conceptual framing and storytelling can help us resist the corrosive effects of power and domination in societies, which push large masses of people into the malevolent region. Richard Paul and Linda Elder argue for a stronger blending of critical thinking, creative thinking, and ethical reasoning to build the scaffolding needed for climbing toward the ethical high ground at the back. Deirdre Lovecky as well as Annemarie Roeper and Linda Silverman analyze many of the child-development dynamics that move individuals toward the powerful back-right corner. Deborah Ruf shows how family, school, and social backgrounds can distribute the gifted widely across the surface of the landscape. Robert Sternberg and Mary Jacobsen look for ways that gifted leaders can find the high ground themselves while encouraging others to do the same. Several authors emphasize the potential of instructional or mentoring frameworks for moving young people toward the high ground at the back of the model. Christy Folsom develops an instructional framework that synthesizes cognition with affect to give young people more strength for climbing the ethical high ground. Kay Gibson and Marjorie Landwehr-Brown generate a global learning framework that can attract the young and gifted to this high ground. Scott Seider, Katie Davis, and Howard Gardner argue that the value neutrality of human rationality requires us to support the good works of young people as they strive to reach the high ground. Barry Grant shows how some character education programs may be ineffective in their attempts to move bright young people toward the back of the model. Adam Martin and Kristen Monroe reveal some subtle identity dynamics that make some individuals navigate on the high ground of the model while the identity orientations of others keep them in neutral or malevolent territory. Meier Dan-Cohen also focuses on identity, discussing how societal values and legal frameworks can push us one way or another on the landscape. Maureen Neihart reveals some thought processes emerging from criminal logic, which pulls some bright people down toward the front, malevolent region. Michael Piechowski explores the strong emotions, energy, sensitivity, and spirituality that help some gifted individuals move toward the back-right corner of the model. Christopher Reynolds and Jane Piirto also explore the inner lives of the gifted, using depth psychology to reveal human interconnections with the potential for moving us upward toward the high ground en masse. Mark Johnson shows how we can slide unwittingly in one direction or another on the landscape because our cognition is shaped tacitly by metaphorical abstractions. David White discusses the problems caused by misunderstandings between those who adhere to differing cultural values and then uses philosophical arguments to resolve such problems. Following his advice may help many to avoid sliding down the slope toward malevolent cultural conflict. Chua Tee Teo and Yuanshan Cheng show how these cultural values vary considerably among several Asian nations. Of course, the movements and locations portrayed here oversimplify the nuances of our contributing authors' arguments; however, they do reveal the complexity of this conceptual terrain while suggesting new directions for future work on the ethics-high ability nexus.

4.6 Some Concluding Thoughts

There is far more ethical ground to cover than can be accomplished here. Studies of ethics and morality are extensive and reach into multiple academic disciplines. Conflicting views on ethics show up in most of these bodies of literature and require resolution or synthesis. Given the enhanced moral sensitivity of many gifted young people, and their likely magnified impact on the world when their abilities unfurl, we certainly need more light shed on ethics-high ability connections. In a world plagued with international conflicts, exploitative economic practices, and pending, world-transforming environmental disasters of our own making, understanding the ways in which gifted young people develop their identities and apply their talents has never been more important.

References

Ambrose, D. (1996). Unifying theories of creativity: Metaphorical thought and the unification process. *New Ideas in Psychology, 14*, 257–267.

Ambrose, D. (1998). Comprehensiveness of conceptual foundations for gifted education: A world-view analysis. *Journal for the Education of the Gifted, 21*, 452–470.

Ambrose, D. (2000). World-view entrapment: Moral-ethical implications for gifted education. *Journal for the Education of the Gifted, 23*, 159–186.

Ambrose, D. (2002). Socioeconomic stratification and its influences on talent development: Some interdisciplinary perspectives. *Gifted Child Quarterly, 46*, 170–180.

Ambrose, D. (2003). Barriers to aspiration development and self-fulfillment: Interdisciplinary insights for talent discovery. *Gifted Child Quarterly, 47*, 282–294.

Ambrose, D. (2005a). Aspiration growth, talent development, and self-fulfillment in a context of democratic erosion. *Roeper Review, 28*, 11–19.

Ambrose, D. (2005b). Contexts for aspiration development and self-fulfillment: International comparisons. *Gifted and Talented International, 20*, 60–69.

Ambrose, D. (2005c). Interdisciplinary expansion of conceptual foundations: Insights from beyond our field. *Roeper Review, 27*, 137–143.

Ambrose, D. (2008). Utopian visions: Promise and pitfalls in the global awareness of the gifted. *Roeper Review, 30*, 52–60.

Ambrose, D. (in press). *Expanding visions of creative intelligence: Interdisciplinary perspectives.* Cresskill, NJ: Hampton Press.

Appelbaum, R. P. (2005). Fighting sweatshops: Problems of enforcing global labor standards. In R. P. Appelbaum & W. I. Robinson (Eds.), *Critical globalization studies* (pp. 369–378). New York: Routledge.

Arendt, H. (1998). *The human condition* (2nd ed.). Chicago, IL: University of Chicago Press. (Original work published 1958)

Babb, S. (2001). *Managing Mexico: Economists from nationalism to neoliberalism.* Princeton, NJ: Princeton University Press.

Beckert, J. (2002). *Beyond the market: The social foundations of economic efficiency*. Princeton, NJ: Princeton University Press.

Bohm, D. (1994). *Thought as a system*. London: Routledge.

Brandt, A. (2007). *The cigarette century: The rise, fall, and deadly persistence of the product that defined America*. New York: BasicBooks.

Brustein, W. (1998). *The logic of evil: The social origins of the Nazi party, 1925–1933*. New Haven, CT: Yale University Press.

Chang, H. J. (2002). *Kicking away the ladder: Development strategy in historical perspective*. London: Anthem Press.

Chang, H. J. (2007). *Bad Samaritans: The myth of free trade and the secret history of capitalism*. New York: Random House.

Chirot, D., & McCauley, C. (2006). *Why not kill them all? The logic and prevention of mass political murder*. Princeton, NJ: Princeton University Press.

Csikszentmihalyi, M. (1993). *The evolving self: A psychology for the third millenium*. New York: HarperCollins.

Csikszentmihalyi, M., & Nakamura, J. (2007). Creativity and responsibility. In H. Gardner (Ed.), *Responsibility at work: How leading professionals act (or don't act) responsibly* (pp. 64–80). San Francisco, CA: Jossey-Bass.

Dabrowski, K. (1964). *Positive disintegration*. Boston, MA: Little Brown.

Dabrowski, K., & Piechowski, M. M. (1977). *Theory of levels of emotional development* (Vols. 1 & 2). Oceanside, NY: Dabor Science.

Damon, W. (2008). *The path to purpose: Helping our children find their calling in life*. New York: Simon & Schuster.

Damon, W., & Colby, A. (1996). *Education and moral commitment. Journal of Moral Education, 25*, 31–37.

Derryberry, P. W., Wilson, T., Snyder, H., Norman, T., & Barger, B. (2005). Moral judgment: Developmental differences between gifted youth and college students. *Journal of Secondary Gifted Education, 17*, 6–19.

de Waal, F. B. M. (2006). *Primates and philosophers: How morality evolved*. Princeton, NJ: Princeton University Press.

Fern, Y. (1994). *Gene Roddenberry*. Berkeley, CA: University of California Press.

Fischer, C. S., Hout, M., Jankowski, M. S., Lucas, S. R., Swidler, A., & Voss, K. (1996). *Inequality by design: Cracking the bell curve myth*. Princeton, NJ: Princeton University Press.

Flannery, T. (2006). *The weather makers: The history and future impact of climate change*. New York: Atlantic Monthly Press.

Fleischacker, S. (2004). *On Adam Smith's wealth of nations: A philosophical companion*. Princeton, NJ: Princeton University Press.

Folsom, C. (1998). From a distance: Joining the mind and moral character. *Roeper Review, 20*, 265–270.

Frank, R. H. (2007). *Falling behind: How rising inequality harms the middle class*. Berkeley, CA: University of California Press.

Gardner, H. (1991). The tensions between education and development. *Journal of Moral Education, 20*, 113–125.

Gardner, H. (1993). *Creating minds*. New York: HarperCollins.

Gardner, H. (Ed.). (2007). *Responsibility at work*. San Francisco, CA: Jossey-Bass.

Gardner, H., Csikszentmihalyi, M., & Damon, W. (2001). *Good work: When excellence and ethics meet*. New York: Basic Books.

Gates, W. H., & Collins, C. (2004). *Wealth and our commonwealth: Why America should tax accumulated fortunes*. Boston, MA: Beacon Press.

Gewirth, A. (1998). *Self-fulfillment*. Princeton, NJ: Princeton University Press.

Gibson, K. L., Rimmington, G. M., & Landwehr-Brown, M. (2008). Developing global awareness and responsible world citizenship with global learning. *Roeper Review, 30*, 11–23.

Goozner, M. (2005). *The $800 million pill: The truth behind the cost of new drugs*. Berkeley, CA: University of California Press.

Graetz, M. J., & Shapiro, I. (2005). *Death by a thousand cuts: The fight over taxing inherited wealth*. Princeton, NJ: Princeton University Press.

Grant, B. (1995). The place of achievement in the life of the spirit and the education of gifted students. *Roeper Review, 18*, 132–134.

Gruber, H. E. (1989). Creativity and human survival. In D. B. Wallace & H. E. Gruber (Eds.), *Creative people at work* (pp. 278–287). New York: Oxford University Press.

Gruber, H. E. (1993). Creativity in the moral domain: Ought implies can implies create. *Creativity Research Journal, 6*, 3–15.

Gutmann, A. (2003). *Identity in democracy*. Princeton, NJ: Princeton University Press.

Habermas, J. (1996). *Between facts and norms: Contributions to a discourse theory of law and democracy*. Cambridge, MA: MIT Press.

Hacker, J. S., & Pierson, P. (2005). *Off center: The Republican revolution and the erosion of American democracy*. New Haven, CT: Yale University Press.

Hague, W. J. (1998). *Is there moral giftedness? Gifted Education International, 12*, 170–174.

Hansen, J. E. (2005, December). *Is there still time to avoid 'dangerous anthropogenic interference' with global climate?* Paper presented at the American Geophysical Union, San Francisco, CA.

Hobbes, T. (1985). *Leviathan*. New York: Penguin Classics. (Original work published 1651)

Inglehart, R. (1997). *Modernization and postmodernization: Cultural, economic, and political change in 43 societies*. Princeton, NJ: Princeton University Press.

Intergovernmental Panel on Climate Change (2007) *Climate change 2007*: The physical science basis. Retrieved Feb. 2nd, 2007, from http://www.ipcc.ch/SPM2feb07.pdf

Kasser, T., Cohn, S., Kanner, A. D., & Ryan, R. M. (2007). Some costs of American corporate capitalism: A psychological exploration of value and goal conflicts. *Psychological Inquiry, 18*, 1–22.

Kumar, K. (1987). *Utopias and anti-utopias in modern times*. Oxford, UK: Blackwell.

Kuttner, R. (1999). *Everything for sale: The virtues and limits of markets*. Chicago, IL: University of Chicago Press.

Lanker, B. (1999). *I dream a world: Portraits of Black women who changed America*. New York: Stewart, Tabori & Chang.

Launis, V., Pietarinen, J., & Raikka, J. (Eds.). (1999). *Genes and morality*. Amsterdam/Atlanta, GA: Rodopi.

Lee, S.-Y., & Olszewski-Kubilius, P. (2006). The emotional intelligence, moral judgment, and leadership of academically gifted adolescents. *Journal for the Education of the Gifted, 30*, 29–67.

Lovecky, D. V. (1997). Identity development in gifted children: Moral sensitivity. *Roeper Review, 20*, 90–94.

Madrick, J. (2008). *The case for big government*. Princeton, NJ: Princeton University Press.

McMurtry, J. (1999). *The cancer stage of capitalism*. London: Pluto Press.

McMurtry, J. (2002). *Value wars: The global market versus the life economy*. London: Pluto Press.

Mele, A. R. (2001). *Self-deception unmasked*. Princeton, NJ: Princeton University Press.

Michaelson, M. (2001). A model of extraordinary social engagement, or "moral giftedness." *New Directions for Child and Adolescent Development, 93*, 19–32.

Moeller, R. G. (2001). *War stories: The search for a usable past in the Federal Republic of Germany*. Berkeley, CA: University of California Press.

Monroe, K. R. (1996). *The heart of altruism*. Princeton, NJ: Princeton University Press.

Monroe, K. R. (2004). *The hand of compassion: Portraits of moral choice during the Holocaust*. Princeton, NJ: Princeton University Press.

Moore, B., Jr. (2000). *Moral purity and persecution in history*. Princeton, NJ: Princeton University Press.

Muller, J. Z. (1995). *Adam Smith in his time and ours: Designing the decent society*. Princeton, NJ: Princteon University Press.

Nadeau, R. L. (2003). *The wealth of nature: How mainstream economics has failed the environment*. New York: Columbia University Press.

Overton, W. F. (1984). World views and their influence on psychological thoughts and research: Khun-Lakatos-Laudan. In H. W. Reese (Ed.), *Advances in child development and behavior* (Vol. 18, pp. 91–226). New York: Academic.

Pepper, S. C. (1942). *World hypotheses*. Berkeley, CA: University of California Press.

Piechowski, M. M. (2003). From William James to Maslow and Dabrowski: Excitability of character and self actualization. In D. Ambrose, L. M. Cohen & A. J. Tannenbaum (Eds.), *Creative intelligence: Toward theoretic integration* (pp. 283–322). Cresskill, NJ: Hampton Press.

Piirto, J. (2005). I live in my own bubble: The values of talented adolescents. *Journal of Secondary Gifted Education, 16*, 106–118.

Presbey, G. M. (1997). Hannah Arendt on power. In L. D. Kaplan & L. F. Bove (Eds.), *Philosophical perspectives on power and domination* (pp. 29–40). Amsterdam: Rodopi.

Roeper, A. (2008). Global awareness and gifted children: Its joy and history. *Roeper Review, 30*, 8–10.

Rosenau, J. N. (2003). *Distant proximities: Dynamics beyond globalization.* Princeton, NJ: Princeton University Press.

Runco, M. A., & Nemiro, J. (2003). Creativity in the moral domain: Integration and implications. *Creativity Research Journal, 15*, 91–105.

Sen, A. (2000). Merit and justice. In K. Arrow, S. Bowles & S. Durlauf (Eds.), *Meritocracy and economic inequality* (pp. 5–16). Princeton, NJ: Princeton University Press.

Silverman, L. (1993). The moral sensitivity of gifted children and the evolution of society. *Roeper Review, 17*, 110–116.

Singer, P. (2002). *One world: The ethics of globalization.* New Haven, CT: Yale University Press.

Smeeding, T., Rainwater, L., & Burtless, G. (2002). United States poverty in a cross-national context. In S. H. Danziger & R. H. Haveman (Eds.), *Understanding poverty* (pp. 162–189). Cambridge, MA: Harvard University Press.

Spreacker, A. (2001). Educating for moral development. *Gifted Education International, 15*, 188–193.

Sriraman, B., & Adrian, H. (2005). The use of fiction as a didactic tool to examine existential problems. *Journal of Secondary Gifted Education, 15*, 96–106.

Stark, R. (2003). *For the glory of God: How monotheism led to reformations, science, witch-hunts, and the end of slavery.* Princeton, NJ: Princeton University Press.

Sternberg, R. J. (2001). Why schools should teach for wisdom: The balance theory of wisdom in educational settings. *Educational Psychologist, 36*, 227–245.

Sternberg, R. J. (2005). WICS: A model of giftedness in leadership. *Roeper Review, 28*, 37–44.

Tannenbaum, A. J. (2000). Giftedness: The ultimate instrument for good and evil. In K. A. Heller, F. J. Mönks, R. J. Sternberg & R. Subotnik (Eds.), *International handbook of giftedness and talent* (2nd ed., pp. 447–465). Oxford, UK: Pergamon.

Tirri, K., & Nokelainen, P. (2007). Comparison of academically average and gifted students' self-rated ethical sensitivity. *Educational Research and Evaluation, 13*, 587–601.

Tolan, S. S. (1998). The lemming condition: Moral asynchrony and the isolated self. *Roeper Review, 20*, 211–214.

Trivers, R. (1971). The evolution of reciprocal altruism. *Quarterly Review of Biology, 46*, 35–57.

Wilson, E. O. (1978). *On human nature.* Cambridge, MA: Harvard University Press.

Wolin, S. S. (2008). *Democracy incorporated: Managed democracy and the specter of inverted totalitarianism.* Princeton, NJ: Princeton University Press.

Xiang, B. (2007). *Global "body shopping": An Indian labor system in the information technology industry.* Princeton, NJ: Princeton University Press.

Yunus, M. (2003). *Banker to the poor: Micro-lending and the battle against world poverty.* New York: Public Affairs.

Yunus, M. (2008). *Creating a world without poverty: Social business and the future of capitalism.* New York: Public Affairs.

Chapter 5
Identity, Moral Choice, and the Moral Imagination: Is There a Neuroscientific Foundation for Altruism?

Adam Martin and Kristen Renwick Monroe

Abstract We review recent work in moral psychology, the neurosciences, and religion to explore the biological and behavioral foundations of altruism. Building on previous work on the psychology of rescuers during genocide (Monroe 1996, 2004, 2008), we describe the altruistic disposition as a feeling "at one with all humanity", positing a perspective akin to Adam Smith's "impartial spectator" (1759/2004). Findings addressing the neuropsychology of religious experience, mindfulness-based psychotherapy and the psychology of terrorism can delineate the contours in the brain that might constitute a neuroscientific foundation for altruism. We close by discussing implications of our framework and suggest future hypotheses that could be tested as a result.

Keywords Altruism · Etiology of ethics · Identity · Impartial spectator · Mindfulness · Moral imagination · Neuroplasticity · Neuroscience · Religious experience · Self-other dichotomy · Self-transcendence

This volume creates a reference for the interdisciplinary field of creative studies, and related fields dealing with topics such as imagination, giftedness, talent, and intelligence. Such an enterprise naturally raises intriguing questions for scholars concerned with ethical philosophy, moral psychology, and political theory. In this chapter, we ask whether there may be a relationship between identity, moral psychology and what we call the moral imagination, defined as the ability to conceptualize certain options in response to ethical dilemmas.

Extensive work on moral choice during the Holocaust (Monroe 1996, 2004; S. Oliner and P. Oliner 1988; Reykowski 1992; Tec 1986) suggests identity acts as a cognitive menu, structuring the choice options found available to all actors, from

A. Martin (✉) and K.R. Monroe
UCI Interdisciplinary Center for the Scientific Study of Ethics and Morality, Social Science Plaza A, University of California, Irvine, CA 92697, USA
e-mail: abmartin@uci.edu, krmonroe@uci.edu

D. Ambrose, T. Cross (eds.), *Morality, Ethics, and Gifted Minds*,
DOI: 10.1007/978-0-387-89368-6_5,
ⓒ Springer Science+Business Media LLC 2009

supporters of genocide to bystanders and rescuers of Jews. One's sense of self in relation to others appears to limit moral choice by making some options available but not others, much as a menu in a restaurant presents the range of choices for diners or a computer menu limits the programs available. Just as it is hard to order sushi in an Italian restaurant, it is difficult to help victims of genocide without the prior ability to see that choice as an option available to the actor. This empirical finding highlights the importance of the moral imagination. Certain options simply may not be available because of the actors' idealized cognitive models about what it means to be a human being, what constitutes the good life, and what kinds of actions are appropriate for *people like me*.

This chapter begins with a brief discussion of how this anomalous phenomenon served to limit choices during the Holocaust. It then uses this empirical finding to construct an intellectual framework linking work in moral philosophy and moral psychology to work in neuroscience that may – eventually – suggest how the moral imagination links behavior to cognition. We hope this framework will help later scholars develop a plan for understanding what may be critical neurobiological changes that occur when people engage in certain ethical activities. In particular, we hope to be able to explain acts of moral courage or extreme altruism, in which people risk their lives for strangers because they feel a sense of self-transcendence through a sense of connection to all humanity.

We present our work in nine sections. In section 5.1 we begin by posing the problem, through reference to the empirical behavior that initially gave rise to our interest in understanding the moral identity. This empirical puzzle concerns what drove people to risk their lives to save strangers during World War II. In section 5.2, we discuss Adam Smith's concept of the impartial spectator, and its relation to absolute values. Recent advances in neuroscience, including the phenomenon of neuro-plasticity, hold out the possibility of biologically grounding Smith's theoretical ideas (section 5.3). Section 5.4 turns to recent work on the psychology of religious experience and its effects on psychological and moral development. This work may provide an entry point into understanding the way in which the normal ethical self is transcended so that, under certain conditions, the actor feels strongly connected to others through the bonds of a common humanity. Such ethical behavior – in the form of altruism – is the healthy, pro-social manifestation of *self-transcendence*. But a maladaptive form exists as well; this maladaptive form is described in sections 5.5 and 5.6 via recent literature on the psychology of terror and fanaticism, and how aspects thereof find parallels in models of non-altruistic "bystanders." Finally, sections 5.7 through 5.9 weave these different avenues of inquiry into general conclusions about the moral identity of altruism, including concluding remarks in the form of hypotheses for future research.

5.1   An Empirical Puzzle: Explaining Altruism Through Perceptions of Self in Relation to Others

We begin by assuming that the psyche is complex and varied. Explaining behavior or ethical action will require us to develop a dynamic theory, not a static portrait of the average personality. We focus on moral salience, defined as the psychological process in which the suffering of others is experienced as relevant for the actor (Monroe 2004). Empirically, we have tried to discern what factors move people beyond generalized sympathy for others to an urgent sense that it is imperative that they act to ameliorate the injustice or suffering endured by others. Much of our previous work (Monroe 1996, 2004) has been dedicated to elucidating the dynamics of this process under heroic conditions that constitute the ultimate test-case for extreme moral action, that of sheltering or rescuing Jews during the Holocaust. Such a situation presented an ideal moral dilemma in which we found individuals had quite distinct responses. These responses evinced radically different ways of conceiving oneself, the self in relation to other people, and the self in relation to the world in general. In reviewing the personal stories of such activist *rescuers*, a number of psychological themes kept recurring. One striking finding suggested that rescuers' decisions to aid Jews in evading or escaping the Nazis were frequently described as instinctual and spontaneous. Despite the life-and-death aspect of their acts, the rescuers of Jews seldom described their acts as the product of reflection or conscious choice. These decisions to act appear to derive more from the individual's sense of self in relation to others, which set the menu of choices, much as a restaurant menu limits the range of options for dinner.

Furthermore, rescuers' decisions were not just a function of the character or personality traits of the persons involved by themselves, as is described in the virtue ethics account of moral behavior; for virtue ethicists the emphasis is on a moral character from which moral acts evolve naturally. Instead, the rescuers we interviewed suggested that the critical factor behind their rescues was their perception of self in relation to others at the time of action.

We have described this process elsewhere in detail (Monroe 1996, 2004). But it is worth noting here that these findings appear to differ from traditional approaches to analyzing ethics, such as consequentialism, deontological ethics, or virtue ethics, which identify ethical decisions as being rooted in the weighing of costs and benefits (consequentialism), a categorical decision rule (deontological ethics), or inherent intentions or character traits (virtue ethics) respectively. Our empirical analysis of rescuers of Jews during the Holocaust led us to advance a different approach, one we describe as a perspectival model of altruism. It merits emphasis that the moral process discussed here is a relational one, one that all people have in actuality or potentiality.

The critical question then becomes: how do individuals acquire this perspective? What moves human beings along a kind of moral and psychological continuum from complete self-interestedness to complete identification with, sympathy for, and automatically acting on the behalf of others? In considering this, we now consider the ethical work of Adam Smith.

5.2   Adam Smith and the Impartial Spectator

If identity is a critical determinant of behavior we must ask how people arrive at a sense that a particular behavior is appropriate for people like them. This involves us in a consideration of universal moral values.

Critical to these tasks, we maintain, is the maturation and refinement of what Adam Smith (1759/2004) denoted as the "impartial spectator." *The Theory of Moral Sentiments* outlines how human communication depends on sympathy between agent and spectator, by which Smith meant the individual and other members of society. Smith employed the concept of an impartial spectator as a reference to help when deciding about the *propriety of action* or what Smith appeared to mean as whether or not the action is right. To do this, the actor has to imagine one's self in the situation of another, allowing for a kind of corrective factor by imagining how someone more impartial than the actor would react. Smith's work in this area used the term *sympathy* but in contemporary works, this term usually is interpreted to refer to empathy (a term not invented until long after Smith had died), and his theory of moral behavior is traditionally said to suggest that putting oneself in the place of another plays a critical part of the process driving moral or ethical action.

For our purposes, we consider Smith's *impartial spectator* as nomenclature for an actual process – one which well might have neurobiological underpinnings – that enables both pro-social behavior and greater ethical competence in the individual via adapting the mindset, perspective, and/or emotional state of others. We link this to Monroe's work describing the sense that rescuers described of feeling *at one with all humanity* and to psychological work linking morality with perspective-taking (Batson et al. 2003; de Waal 2008).

It might be inquired how these phenomena relate to religion. One of religion's principal sociological functions has been to sanctify and enforce pro-social behavior, if only within a particular faith's own reference groups, and via a link to universal moral values. Like many other writers of his time, even those who made reference to nature, not to a deity, Smith was interested in this ethical focus yet wished to make it more rational and universal, and thereby more humane. As Smith described it, "the spectator must, first of all, endeavor as much as he can to put himself in the situation of the other, and to bring home to himself every little circumstance of distress which can possibly occur to the sufferer" (Smith 1759/2004, p. 201).

Such a sympathetic faculty depends upon the ability of the individual to progressively approximate a "God's-eye view," whereupon the hopes, fears and desires of the individual are revealed as finite, partial, and transitory and should accordingly give way to that which is less finite, more impartial, and more enduring.

5.3   Free Will, Neuroplasticity, and Moral Psychology

The impartial spectator may be related to current advances in neuroscience in such a way that a coherent account of individual agency and an affirmation of the reality and freedom of the will may be posited. The work done by neuroscientists such as Antonio Damasio (1994) and Edelman and Tononi (2000) has begun to deal with questions of free will and moral agency in a manner anticipated by William James (1950). The dichotomy of thought and deed in this formulation is transcended in the phenomenon of attention, the control over which and the objects of which become the principal tasks of ethical prescription:

> In ... *The Principles of Psychology*, [William] James argued that the ability to fix one's attention on a stimulus or a thought and 'hold it fast before the mind' was the act that constituted 'the essential achievement of the will.' ... if one can make more or less effort, as one chooses, and so willfully 'prolong the stay in consciousness of innumerable ideas which else would fade away more quickly,' then free will remains a real scientific possibility. (Schwarz and Begley 2002, p. 17)

This process also may account for the phenomenon, noted by Aristotle, of the dissipation of moral energy, in which the needs of others become experienced as less important the more distant the person is from the actor.

While further empirical proof is obviously needed concerning these attention-based phenomena, there is some current evidence in the burgeoning research on neuroplasticity (Davidson, Kabat-Zinn, et al. 2003; Doidge 2007; Begley 2007) and attention (Posner and Rothbart 1998; Beauregard et al. 2001) that appears to corroborate the essentials of the James-Monroe account of ethical action. We would define this as a process in which the person, individual agency, the role of attention and the will, and the possibility of altruistic, selfless, pro-social behavior are critical.

This recently discovered phenomenon has shed new light upon the nature of consciousness, for the possibilities of individual agency, and upon the personal and social factors that enable or constrain ethical/altruistic behavior. We would argue that this seat of attention works in tandem with Smith's idea of the *impartial spectator*, but it only fully realizes this function with gradual habituation, learning, and practice. Attention is the task through which the *self* selects and ranks its priorities, and therefore its moral commitments.

We therefore can witness variation in both psychological growth and ethical competence in the degree, scope and duration of attention devoted to various topics. This scope narrows in some individuals such that the Other, whether as foreigners, enemies, or those simply socially distant find themselves on the periphery of this focus.

The degree of psychological maturity and the circle of ethical regard thus appreciably narrow in focus in direct proportion to the focus and rigidity of attention. In the opposite direction of psychological and ethical development, a more expansive definition of self and a more generous ethic of other-regarding behavior become possible as the focus of attention becomes more flexible, more inclusive, and more comprehensive:

> All progress in the social Self is the substitution of higher tribunals for lower; this ideal tribunal is the highest; and most men, either continually or occasionally, carry a reference to it in their breast. The humblest outcast on this earth can feel himself to be real and valid by means of this higher recognition. (James 1890/1950, p. 316)

Utilizing terminology akin to that of Adam Smith, James (1890/1950) observed that:

> it is probable that individuals differ a good deal in the degree in which they are haunted by this sense of an ideal spectator. It is a much more essential part of the consciousness of some men than of others. (p. 316)

5.4 Moving Toward the Neuroscience of Self-Transcendent Experiences

We now take insights from the previous works and weave them into a coherent theory of ethical behavior. We would argue that ethical conduct and psychological growth depend upon the progressive expansion of control and direction of the faculty of attention, and upon prudent choice of its focus and intensity.

Only within the last decade have neuroscientists and psychologists begun to understand and integrate the data concerning "self-transcendent" experiences into a coherent picture of what occurs in the mind and brain when such experiences take place. Any understanding of the *transcendent self* as the destination of Abraham Maslow's process of *self-actualization* (1968) or Mihalyi Csikszentmihalyi's (1990) dialectical description of the *flow*-imbued personality will need to draw upon such literature. However, in light of the affective salience and abnormality of *self-transcendence*, historically self-transcendence has been identified as a phenomenon with spiritual or supernatural overtones, and as such has been studied – ironically – under the rubric of *religious experience*. We wish to treat these as natural phenomena amenable to empirical scrutiny, and no religious interpretations will be advanced. They are the ways that "self-transcendence" has been identified and accomplished historically, and the neurobiological description of such phenomena can provide a key entry point into elucidating the ways that the "self" is both constructed and altered.

The "self-transcendent" modalities of conscious experience exist in a variety of forms, and it is the variety of such forms that can both help – or hinder – adaptive or pro-social behavior as a result. d'Aquili and Newberg (1998), Newberg and Waldman (2006) use SPECT (single photon emission computed tomography) studies that measure cerebral/cortical blood flow (as a proxy for cortical activity) to demonstrate that for contemplative Christian prayer and Buddhist mindfulness meditation, an increase in activity in the "attention" areas of the pre-frontal cortex is accompanied by reduced activity in the inferior parietal lobe of the right hemisphere, what Newberg and d'Aquili (1998) dubs the *orientation area*. This mediates an intense sense of present consciousness largely devoid of content save the object of contemplation, either a personal God or an ultimate reality, accompanied by a softening of the boundaries of the self and its spatio-temporal location. As Newberg described it, "if you could consciously decrease activity in your parietal lobes, you would probably feel a brief loss or suspension of self-awareness. You might also experience a loss of your sense of space and time" (Newberg and Waldman 2006, pp. 175–176). Newberg and d'Aquili found that both sets of subjects indeed underwent such experiences, indicating that such practices contribute to fundamentally altering the sense of self.

Mario Beauregard and Paquette (2006) have found contemporaneous evidence to bolster that of d'Aquili and Newberg, but they focused explicitly on the contemplative practices of a sample of Carmelite nuns (N = 15). In particular, they noted the affective activation of the caudate nucleus as well as the insula. Regarding the readings on the caudate nucleus, Beauregard and Paquette (2006) noted that "the caudate nucleus has been systematically activated in previous functional brain imaging studies implicating positive emotions such as happiness, romantic love, and maternal love" (p. 189). It merits emphasis that "self-transcendence" does not mean a disappearance of the "self-construct" as such, but an alteration of its boundaries and contents – as well as "ultimate concerns" (Tillich and Kimball 1964, p. 8) and priorities.

A sense of "self" is still retained, but its boundaries are for all practical purposes nonexistent – or, more to the point, the boundaries of the "self" encompass all that exists. Traditionally, as Durkheim (2001) have pointed out, such experiences were mediated through myth, ritual and ceremony, and the sense of connection with others was circumscribed as applying only to a certain social group. We should emphasize, however, that such an outcome is not predetermined; the scope of the unitive experience and the sense of connection it fosters could also "apply to all members of a religion, a nation-state, an ideology, all of humanity, and all of reality. Obviously, as one increases the scope of what is included in the unitary experience, the amount of overall aggressive behavior decreases" (d'Aquili and Newberg 1998, p. 188) We thus posit that at least some of the greater connection to all humanity felt by our "rescuers" can be explained via neurological processes such as these.

Additional insight into the neurobiology of "self-transcendence" is found in clinical applications of "mindfulness"-based anxiety and stress-related therapies. These phenomena are especially noteworthy since they illustrate the reality of directed neuroplasticity, the efficacy of the will, and the crucial role played by attention-as-moral agency, affirming both the reality and the importance of the "impartial spectator." The introduction of aspects of Buddhist psychology, known by the nomenclature "mindfulness," began among multiple independent clinical and research psychiatrists for example, Jeffrey Schwartz and Begley (2002), John Segal, Williams and Teasdale (2002), Jon Kabat-Zinn (2003), and Richard Davidson (2005). It has gradually acquired clinically formal applications as "mindfulness-based stress reduction," or MBSR. Schwartz was explicit in his debt to Buddhist concepts and practices in developing this treatment modality, viewing their most valuable contribution as:

> the ability it affords those practicing it to observe their sensations and thoughts with the calm clarity of an external witness: through mindful awareness, you can stand outside your own mind as if you are watching what is happening to another rather than experiencing it yourself.

Such a detached perspective has marked therapeutic benefits, since the practitioner can see "his thoughts, feelings, and expectations much as a scientist views experimental data—that is, as natural phenomena to be noted, investigated, reflected on, and learned from" (Schwartz and Begley 2002, p. 11). Besides straightforward clinical data, a wide variety of recent neurological studies demonstrate the physiological effects of such "mindfulness" treatments relating not only to brain structure and function, but in terms of dispositional affect and cognitive processing as well. Davidson (2005) reported on a study in which over the course of several weeks, left-sided anterior activity in the cortex was greater in practitioners of "mindfulness" meditation than controls. This activity has been demonstrably tied to greater positive affective style. Davidson and his colleagues interpret such findings as having crucial importance for affective style and interpersonal relations:

> It is our conjecture that such positive affective styles are also associated with higher levels of empathy and compassion, since these are characteristics that are described as being strongly present in meditation adepts who have spent a considerable time training these neural circuits. (Davidson 2005, p. 85)

The process of progressively refining attention in the prefrontal cortex thus contributes not only to a more detached, objective stance of judgment but also appears to prompt greater equanimity in one's orientation to the world (and others) as well.

5.5   Maladaptive and Positive Self-Transcendence

The maladaptive and psychosocially pathological forms of "self-transcendence" just discussed describe what takes place when the affective neurobiology of "self-transcendence" described in the previous section – whether by individual neurosis or ideological manipulation – becomes delimited to a given collectivity in the form of the "true believer," such as the religious fundamentalist and the political fanatic. The consequences of this perspective for interpersonal ethics are deleterious. There is no "person" per se that the true believer or terrorist is dealing with and this fact legitimizes all manner of inhumane treatment. Juergensmeyer (2003) hypothesizes that extremist violence is likely to occur:

> when the opponent rejects one's moral or spiritual position; when the enemy appears to hold the power to completely annihilate one's community, one's culture, and oneself; when the opponent's victory would be unthinkable; and when there seems no way to defeat the enemy in human terms. (p. 186)

The plausibility of such depictions diminishes as the irrational estimate of threat rises, both of which distort the image of the "Other" and encourage further alienation. Juergensmeyer calls this process "satanization," a dehumanization so stark that it empowers the self at the expense of an Other – not just in terms of violence or force, but symbols and spirit as well. The self and "Other" are clearly divided and identified in this scenario, and it is perceived that one cannot exist or flourish save at the expense of the other.

5.6 Empirical Resonance with This Approach: Monroe's Rescuers, Bystanders and Perpetrators

The above-described traits, and what they reveal about human agency, seem to closely track those moral distinctions we have observed in studies of bystanders, perpetrators, and rescuers of Jews during the Holocaust (Browning 1992; Glass 1997; Lerner 1992; Lifton 1986; Monroe 2008). Central to these empirical psychological and historical analyses are perceptions of self and "Other," perceived agency and autonomy of self, and the locus of attention upon self or others. Monroe (2008) described the "bystanders," as they describe themselves, as, reactive, helpless, and having a fatalistic mindset about what was happening. The Nazi individual during this time was an individual under siege, looking to their own embattled group first. This sense of a sharply demarcated self, with low possibilities of agency, and the psychology of aggrieved victimhood closely approximates the correlating symptoms described by Juergensmeyer as preceding another, similarly de-personalizing encounter – that of the fanatic or terrorist.

What if the indifference of the Holocaust bystander and the alienated hostility of the terrorist both spring from a common source – the delimitation of the psychological faculties associated with the "impartial spectator," occupying the attention of the individual with maladaptive and socially pathological priorities as objects? By contrast, what if the "rescuers" of Jews we profiled were people who consider themselves "connected to all human beings through bonds of a common humanity. Their idealized cognitive model of what it means to be a human being is far more expansive and inclusive than the model employed by bystanders or Nazis," as Monroe (in press) suggests? Most critically, their self-concepts, as defined by the focus of attention, seem to be inextricably tied to the security and autonomy of the self and its fulfillment of what Maslow deems the *hierarchy of human needs*, since the difference between "bystanders" and rescuers was the depth and breadth of their categories, encompassing a greater or lesser range of individuals and groups (Monroe 2006). If this explanation is valid, it corresponds not only to Juergensmeyer's work but also that of Maslow and Csikszentmihalyi, and moral agency and personal autonomy are closely tied to how independent the "self" is from social desires and fears, how able to resist pressures for group conformity and consensus through refusing to accept group restrictions on the focus of attention. This would suggest that for bystanders, more individuals and their sufferings are appropriate relevant objects of the "impartial spectator" than a group's cognitive schema would allow. These seem to reflect a basic orientation to the world (and the rest of humanity) into which different persons revert by default in situations of abrupt change or crisis. One turns its face to the world, the other turns away; one is open, and one is closed. It is this basic disposition, which is largely a function of the strength and focus of the attention of the "impartial spectator," that would explain the moral agency in Holocaust "rescuers," and that Juergensmeyer (2003) describes as social pathology at work in the minds of "true believers."

5.7   Moving Forward: Towards a Reformulation
of Ethical Theory

All these developments hold implications for a new theoretical framework for the political psychology of altruism. The moral imperative is not merely to avoid doing evil in the eyes of the "impartial spectator," but to combine such a disinterested, objective perspective with the individual's moral agency. The goal is thus to translate a temporary insight into a regular substrate of consciousness that participates in daily ethical relationships implicitly, almost as second nature.

Progressive consonance between the individual's attention and the ideal of the "impartial spectator" is analogous to the spiral path of psychological maturity and greater self-transcendence already outlined by Maslow and Csikszentmihalyi. The constructed "self" is a bio-psycho-social phenomenon, and each layer of the construct is linked to the others. It maintains its internal homeostasis (as well as its social and cultural homeostasis) by directing attention toward objects that seem to enhance the finite self or remove its finitude, and exhibits a strong bias away from engaging topics, objects, or individuals that would make that finitude more salient. The focus and strength of attention thus might be said to determine morality, and the focus and strength of attention may have evolved in certain ways to enhance human physical and social survival; the psychological dissonance that often occurs is that a concord between these two priorities does not always obtain. As neuroscientist Antonio Damasio noted (2003):

> the history of our civilization is, to some extent, the history of a persuasive effort to extend the best of 'moral sentiments' to wider and wider circles of humanity, beyond the restrictions of inner groups, eventually encompassing the whole of humanity. (p. 163)

Within this endeavor, progress in expanding this circle can rely not only upon genetic roots but also on epigenetic practice and praxis – being mindful of the Other, whether the family, the tribe, the nation, the species, or existence itself.

5.8   The Neurological Expression of This Approach

We are now in a position to speculate about how such a process finds its psychological and neurological expression. In line with Newberg and Waldman (2006), we can point to four components that inform human morals: the obvious evolutionary imperative toward survival, the growth of our cerebral cortex, pressures towards group solidarity, and a mental architecture to discern right from wrong. These factors all appear to contribute to the construction of a kind of moral continuum, between two idealized poles of self-regarding and other-regarding morality. Such a continuum is a function of the degree of connection felt between the self and others, with stark consequences: lack of connection creates more emotional distance, and so we are less likely to feel empathy toward those we do not know. When people feel distant from others, they can more easily trust others with less respect. Connection guides us to manifest our moral ideals (Newberg and Waldman 2006).

Increased growth along these dimensions should also result (or be correlated with) similar development in moral psychology. The attention paid to external and internal stimuli is intimately involved in different kinds of cognitive processing. Human beings apparently acquire their categories not from abstractions, but through exemplars – and these categories have an internal architecture of their own, with certain individuals or objects serving as the touchstone for a particular category, while others are of secondary or minor import (Newberg and Waldman 2006). This resembles the bundle of cognitive processes identified in the developmental theories of Maslow and Csikszentmihalyi and the moral theory of Adam Smith.

5.9   Crafting This Approach into Forms of Hypotheses to Test

Let us now try to put our approach into a form that can be tested empirically. Here, two reasonable extensions seem warranted. First, in persons with a fragile self-concept and low sense of self-agency, their increased needs for group affiliation and conformity may make them more susceptible to in-group/out-group dichotomizing, a similar way attention is directed and objects of consciousness are classified in Smith's model of the "impartial spectator" with varying degrees of "partiality." Their internally-structured categories thus are applied with reference to such "prototypical examples" that constrain and inhibit the flexibility of the focus of attention – not, by contrast, with reference to abstract rules or principles. Second, in individuals who are "self-transcendent" (as Maslow or Csikszentmihalyi might deem them, and/or who are "rescuers" in Monroe's paradigm), there may be a greater refinement and accurate/adaptive character to the focus of such attention, the valence it accordingly assigns to external persons or stimuli, and the consonance of such flexible behavior with broader, expansive categories or principles. Such individuals are more discriminating in their perceptions of self and "Other," have a greater sense of agency, more accurate assessments of what is and is not in their control, and therefore apply (and viscerally feel) a greater moral imperative to assist others, reflecting cognitive categories that more closely correspond to universalistic or humanistic values, since the categories of "Other" will not have been as negatively encoded neurologically in their emotional memory. Accurate self-awareness and appropriate functioning of attention is further posited to be both a learned skill, and an ethical and normative imperative.

We anticipate that the future applications of such work for political psychology and normative political theory will prove especially salient in discussions of the phenomenon of motivated reasoning or, more colloquially, what is known as *hot cognition*. In one revealing recent study, psychologist Drew Westen et al. (2006) and his colleagues devised a set of experiments during the American 2004 election cycle in which committed partisans (equal numbers of Republicans and Democrats) were presented with reasoning tasks about information threatening to their own candidate, versus the opposite party's candidate. Subjects consistently sought more accommodating rationalizations for the inconsistencies of their own candidate while being more critical of those of the opposing candidate. More sobering, the fMRI profiles of each set of partisans during the cognitive task displayed processing not associated with those brain centers known to be used in *cold* reasoning and conscious emotional management; instead, the hot cognition processes displayed seemed to reinforce beliefs, biases and prejudices already held, especially biases that were more critical of the Other. If this more emotionally-driven style of political cognition is as widespread in the population as Westen suggested in subsequent work (2007) (as much as 80% of the American electorate, for example), it bodes ominously for both political ethics and cognitivistic, deontological accounts of the same in empirical political theory, such as that of John Rawls (1971). Likewise, the notion of human decisions as driven by dispassionate, benefit/cost analysis has been further eroded by the discoveries of neuroeconomics (Zak 2004) and its insights into the biological bases of human cooperation and competition.

This suggests any accurate description of ethical decision-making in the near future will need to include biological, emotional, and relational dimensions. Scholarly models of ethical decision-making will need to allow for the critical inputs that tap into the basic personality of the decision-maker as well as the immediate influences on the actor at the moment of decision. These influences on the actor shape the actor's sense of self in relation to others. They are the aspect of identity that is self-reflective and highly flexible, not the static model of an actor's identity that currently dominates decision-making models and approaches. These requirements of an ethical decision-making personality are neurological and emotional, not merely rational, requirements, requirements that the framework we have presented above is designed to include.

We believe the framework we have erected and the literature surveyed thus far provides a number of possible avenues via which subjects' affective style, scope and scale of attention, and dimensions of ethical regard could be shaped by exercises in empathy, perspective-taking, and, especially, practices which temporarily altered or adjusted their usual model of the self. Clinical evidence suggests these modalities of treatment have been successful in treating emotional and neurological pathologies in matters of individual mental health; it would be a fruitful inquiry to see if they proved salubrious for moral, ethical, and political judgment as well. Encouraging scholars to think along these ethical lines would be a task not merely of encouraging the use of moral principles, but a move towards the kind of political psychotherapy Harold Lasswell (Ascher and Hirschfelder-Ascher 2005) originally envisioned, medicine not only for the mind, but for the heart and spirit as well.

In more concrete research terms, our current framework may have positive contributions to make to the current scholarly dialogue on the role of ethics in religion, and its impact on our society and politics. Recent literature in the field, both on the more scholarly end of the spectrum (Boyer 2001; Dennett 2006) and in the popular press (Harris 2004; Dawkins 2006; Hitchens 2007), have focused heavily on religion's alleged social pathologies, drawing their contemporary salience from the events of September 11th, 2001 and current events in the Middle East and elsewhere. In line with our previous attempts to deal with religiously charged issues in politics, such as scientific research on stem cells (Monroe 2008), we find this focus understandable, but somewhat misleading. Regardless of religion's truth or falsehood, religion constitutes a richly varied legacy for many members of society, and its impact on human ethics and morality is far more nuanced and complex than is frequently allowed by either its dogmatic supporters or detractors. Our line of thought provides an opportunity to assess the substance and consequences of religion at a level where it matters most, and offers answers to the question posed both in religious texts and by moral psychologists concerned with altruism: "But who is my neighbor?" (Batson et al. 1999, p. 445). Our own research suggests religion's impact should be judged not on the beliefs it proposes or the converts it makes, but the walls of identity it erects – and, as we have shown, it is the presence or absence of these walls that prove decisive for ethical conduct. Elucidating their presence or absence among the faithful of any politically salient religious group remains one of the most potent areas for future scholarly research.

5.10 Conclusion

In this chapter, we have attempted to demonstrate the ethical importance of the moral imagination. More particularly, we suggest how the moral imagination works through the perceptions of *self* in relation to others to set and limit the range of ethical options an actor finds available, both empirically and cognitively. We argue that the self is a cultural and biological construction that can be altered, and that states of "self"-transcendence hold key insights for how an individual's circle of reciprocal altruism can be expanded to include increasing numbers of human beings. Any discussion of altruism begins with the self, and where the self ends, self-transcendent altruism begins. It is worth quoting one of our "rescuer" interviewees, as he illustrates the links between the "self," bridging the self/other dichotomy, and the route to a more universalist ethics in a fitting way:

> I see the whole world as one living body, basically. But not our world only: the whole universe. And I'm like one of the cells. I'm as much a part of that as others. Without me, the universe doesn't exist anymore that my body exists without its cells. I think that we are as much together as the cells in our body are together. (Bert Bochove, Dutch Rescuer)

The existence of such individuals, and the moral worldview they propound, provides the clearest possible empirical verification of the possibility – and desirability – of providing a comprehensive description of one's constructed "self," and how one arrives at the ethical positions in daily life and in situations requiring moral courage. We believe this framework offers great potential for scholars interested in the importance of imagination – particularly the images we have of the Other – and we encourage others to build on our preliminary, theoretical work.

References

Ascher, W., & Hirschfelder-Ascher, B. (2005). *Revitalizing political psychology: The legacy of Harold D. Lasswell*. Mahwah, NJ: Lawrence Erlbaum.

Batson, C. D., Floyd, R. B., Meyer, J. M., & Winner, A. L. (1999). "And who is my neighbor?": Intrinsic religion as a source of universal compassion. *Journal for the Scientific Study of Religion, 38*, 445–457.

Batson, C. D., Lishner, D. A., Carpenter, A., Dulin, L., Harjusola-Webb, S., Stocks, E. L., et al. (2003). "As you would have them do unto you": Does imagining yourself in the other's place stimulate moral action? *Personality and Social Psychology Bulletin, 29*, 1190–1201.

Beauregard, M., & Paquette, V. (2006). Neural correlates of a mystical experience in Carmelite nuns. *Neuroscience Letters, 405*(3), 186–190.

Beauregard, M., Levesque, J., & Bourgouin, P. (2001). Neural correlates of conscious self-regulation of emotion. *Journal of Neuroscience*, 21, RC165.

Begley, S. (2007). *Train your mind, change your brain: How a new science reveals our extraordinary potential to transform ourselves*. New York: Ballantine Books.

Boyer, P. (2001). *Religion explained: the evolutionary origins of religious thought*. New York: Basic Books.

Browning, C. R. (1992). *The path to genocide: Essays on launching the final solution*. Cambridge, UK: Cambridge University Press.

Csikszentmihalyi, M. (1990). *Flow: the psychology of optimal experience*. New York: Harper-Perennial.

Damasio, A. (1994). *Descartes' error: Emotion, reason, and the human brain*. New York: G.P. Putnam.

Damasio, A. (2003). Looking for Spinoza: joy, sorrow, and the feeling brain. Orlando, FL: Harvest Books.

d'Aquili, E., & Newberg, A. (1998). The neurophysiological basis of religions, or why God won't go away. *Zygon: Journal of Religion and Science, 33*(2), 187–201.

Davidson, R. J., Kabat-Zinn, J., et al. (2003). Alterations in brain and immune function produced by mindfulness meditation. *Psychosomatic Medicine, 65*, 564–570.

Davidson, R. J. (2005). Neural substrates of affective style and value. In Y. Christen (Series ed.) & J.-P. Changeux, A. R. Damasio, W. Singer, & Y. Christen (Vol. eds.), *Research and perspectives in neurosciences: neurobiology of human values* (pp. 67–90). Germany: Springer.

Dawkins, R. (2006). *The God delusion*. Boston, MA: Houghton Mifflin.

Dennett, D. (2006). *Breaking the spell: religion as a natural phenomenon*. New York: Viking.

Doidge, N. (2007). *The brain that changes itself: Stories of personal triumph from the frontiers of brain science*. New York: Viking.

De Waal, F. (2008). Putting the altruism back into altruism: The evolution of empathy. *Annual Review of Psychology, 59*, 279–300.

Durkheim, E. (2001). *The elementary forms of religious life*. Oxford, UK: Oxford University Press.

Edelman, G., & Tononi, G. (2000). *A universe of consciousness: How matter becomes imagination*. New York: Basic Books.

Glass, J. M. (1997). *Life unworthy of life: Racial phobia and mass murder in Hitler's Germany*. New York: Basic Books.

Harris, S. (2004). *The end of faith: Religion, terror, and the future of reason*. New York: W.W. Norton.

Hitchens, C. (2007). *God is not great: How religion poisons everything*. New York: Twelve.

James, W. (1950). *The Principles of psychology*, Mineola, NY: Dover. (Original work published 1890)

Juergensmeyer, M. (2003). *Terror in the mind of God: The global rise of religious violence*. Berkeley, CA: University of California Press.

Kabat-Zinn, J. (2003). Mindfulness-based interventions in context: past, present, and future. *Clinical Psychology: Science and Practice, 10*(2), 144–156.

Lerner, R. M. (1992). *Final solutions: Biology, prejudice and genocide*. University Park, PA: Pennsylvania State University Press.

Lifton, R. J. (1986). *The Nazi doctors: Medical killing and the psychology of genocide*. New York: Basic Books.

Maslow, A. (1968). *Toward a psychology of being*. New York: Van Nostrand Reinhold.

Monroe, K. (1996). *The heart of altruism: Perceptions of a common humanity*. Princeton, NJ: Princeton University Press.

Monroe, K. (2004). *The hand of compassion: Portraits of moral choice during the Holocaust*. Princeton, NJ: Princeton University Press.

Monroe, K. (2008). *Cracking the code of genocide: The moral psychology of rescuers, bystanders and Nazis during the Holocaust. Political Psychology, 29*, 699–736.

Monroe, K., Miller, B., & Tobis, J. (eds.) (2008). *Fundamentals of the stem cell debate: The scientific, religious, ethical, and political issues*. Berkeley, CA: University of California Press.

Newberg, A., & d'Aquili, E. (1998). The neuropsychology of religious experience. In H. Koenig (ed.), *Handbook of religion and mental health* (pp. 76–95). San Diego, CA: Academic.

Newberg, A., & Waldman, M. R. (2006). *Why we believe what we believe: Uncovering our biological need for meaning, spirituality, and truth*. New York: Simon & Schuster.

Oliner, S., & Oliner, P. (1988). *The altruistic personality: Rescuers of Jews in Nazi Europe*. New York: Free Press.

Posner, M. I., & Rothbart, M. K. (1998). Attention, self-regulation, and consciousness. *Philosophical Transactions of the Royal Society of London, 353*, 1915–1927.

Rawls, J. (1971). *A theory of justice*. Cambridge, MA: Belknap Press of Harvard University Press.

Reykowski, J. (1992). Motivations of people who helped Jews survive the Nazi occupation. In Pearl M. Oliner et al. (eds.), *Embracing the other: Philosophical, psychological, and historical perspectives on altruism* (pp. 213–225). New York: New York University Press.

Schwartz, J., & Begley, S. (2002). *The mind and the brain: Neuroplasticity and the power of mental force*. New York: Regan Books.

Smith, A. (1759/2004). *The theory of moral sentiments*. New York: Barnes & Noble Classics.

Tec, N. (1986). *When light pierced the darkness: Christian rescue of Jews in Nazi-occupied Poland*. New York: Oxford University Press.

Tillich, P., & Kimball, R. (1964). *Theology of culture*. Oxford: Oxford University Press.

Westen, D. (2007). *The political brain: The role of emotion in deciding the fate of the nation*. New York: Public Affairs.

Westen, D., Kilts, C., Blagov, P., Harenski, K., & Hamann, S. (2006). The neural basis of motivated reasoning: An fMRI study of emotional constraints on political judgment during the U.S. Presidential election of 2004. *Journal of Cognitive Neuroscience, 18*, 1947–1958.

Zak, P. (2004). Neuroeconomics. *Philosophical Transactions of the Royal Society of London, 359*, 1737–1748.

Chapter 6
The Efficient Drowning of a Nation: Is Economics Education Warping Gifted Minds and Eroding Human Prospects?

Tom L. Green

> ...goods follow dollar votes and not the greatest need. A rich man's cat may drink the milk that a poor boy needs to remain healthy. Does this happen because the market is failing? Not at all, for the market mechanism is doing its job – putting goods in the hands of those who have the dollar votes.
>
> Samuelson and Nordhaus (2005, p. 38)

Abstract Humanity has put itself in great peril, as the impending demise of the nation of Kiribati due to global warming illustrates. This failure to act is in part due to the influence of mainstream economics. Economics is a challenging discipline that attracts many gifted individuals. Yet during their training, mainstream economists adopt, often unwittingly and despite believing their profession to be an exemplar of objectivity and dispassionate analysis, a deeply problematic ethical framework and worldview. This is shown by examining the analysis that mainstream economists have contributed to policy discussions on global warming, the profession's unfailing devotion to economic growth, and the evaluative criterion that underlies so much economic theorizing and analysis, namely economic efficiency. This chapter then explores how it is that the many gifted individuals who have become economists, often out of concern for the disadvantaged, could have been educated and socialized to adopt uncritically a morally problematic analytical framework and to provide analysis and policy advice with little reflection on its moral implications. Some changes to economics education might provide gifted future economists more sophisticated ethical bearings and improve the likelihood that their skills will contribute to finding more equitable and sustainable solutions to the pressing ecological and social problems confronting humanity.

Keywords Economic efficiency · Economics education · Economic growth · Ethics · Gifted adults · Global warming · Morality · Sustainability

T.L. Green
Interdisciplinary Studies Graduate Program, Green College University of British Columbia, 6201 Cecil Green Park Road, Vancouver, BC, Canada V6T 1Z1
e-mail: tgreen@ires.ubc.ca

D. Ambrose, T. Cross (eds.), *Morality, Ethics, and Gifted Minds,*
DOI: 10.1007/978-0-387-89368-6_6,

6.1 Economists as Overseers of Earth's Liquidation Sale

On World Environment Day, June 5, 2008, President Tong of the small South Pacific nation of Kiribati requested international assistance to permanently evacuate his nation of far flung atolls. Because international efforts to limit CO_2 emissions had been so weak, his nation was "beyond redemption." His people would have no choice but to abandon their already much diminished country, victims of sea level rise due to global warming.

A little over 10 years earlier, during my graduate course in environmental economics, my professor argued that it would be unethical for an economist, in his or her capacity as an economist, to favor policies that would achieve sustainability, if people's preferences as expressed in the marketplace revealed that they valued present consumption over protecting the environment. The economist's role, he argued, was to help society achieve efficiency. If people's purchases had demonstrated that they were unconcerned about sustainability, then the economist should help design policies that deplete the planet efficiently; to do otherwise would be undemocratic and paternalistic. Appalled, I raised myriad objections: the ability to express preferences in the market depends upon the existing allocation of wealth, so the poor are counted out; consumers do not have perfect information and may not know that their consumer behavior is undermining their grandchildren's future; advertisers manipulate consumer behavior; as citizens, individuals may vote for sustainability even if as consumers they ignore it. My arguments were moot because they did not fit within the economist's way of thinking. My professor's commitment to the efficient transformation of the Earth into a moonscape in support of consumerism, if that's what the count of dollar votes showed to be society's priority, was left unperturbed.

My professor was an ardent nature lover who openly admitted that his personal preference was that nature continue to flourish on Earth; his rapid rise through the academic ranks left no doubt that he was remarkably intelligent. Yet his intelligence had been so narrowly focused by his disciplinary training that the mostly unacknowledged ethical framework that underlay his economic perspective was leading him – like many of his peers – to advocate, under the banner of objectivity, that society take a morally problematic course of action (or inaction). In effect, his deeply engrained way of "thinking like an economist" was leading him to champion the consumer interests of those who have the most money and thereby get to vote in the market. As the Kiribati example so starkly illustrates, it is a framework that purports to balance catastrophic changes for those living at the margin of subsistence against the need for respectable return on investment for investors in coal-fired power plants and the ephemeral enjoyments and conveniences of that minority of humanity that can afford to fill up gas-guzzlers and jet away for a weekend in the sun. Corporate interests and the promotion of consumerism trump human rights; the present trumps the future; the lifestyles of those humans fortunate in the lottery of birth trump those incapable of escaping poverty, while at the same time, the interests of all other life forms are immaterial.

6.2   Thinking Like an Economist: Global Warming and Growth

In this commentary, I focus on a couple of core ethical issues that underlie economic analysis. To bring these issues to life, I draw on the analysis that mainstream economists have contributed to policy discussions on global warming and also on the profession's unfailing devotion to economic growth. These examples help illustrate how the economics profession has come to embed a deeply problematic ethical framework into its theorizing and its analysis, all the while believing itself to be an exemplar of objectivity and dispassionate analysis. I then ask how it is that the many gifted individuals who have become economists, often out of concern for the common good, could have been educated and socialized to adopt a morally problematic analytical framework.

6.2.1   Global Warming

Until the Stern report prepared at the behest of the British Government (Stern 2007) was published, mainstream economists typically produced analysis that implies that a rational approach to global warming should involve at most modest investments in mitigation (see for example Nordhaus 1982). This recommendation followed from using the profession's standard tool of cost–benefit analysis which assumes that it is desirable to maximize the summed utilities of per capita consumption. The costs of action, which largely occur in the present, are the costs of limiting greenhouse gas emissions and the foregone consumption such investments imply. The benefits of avoiding climate chaos occur in the distant future and hence add up to little because they are discounted (discounting can be thought of as the equivalent of taking into account the interest that will be earned on bank deposits, but in reverse; discounting is used to bring future flows of costs and benefits to the present, such that at a 5% discount rate, $105 to be received in a year would be worth the same as $100 today). When Stern came to the conclusion that the economically sound course of action was to take aggressive action to combat climate change, rather than being applauded for making the values that informed his framing of the problem explicit, and for recognizing that the scale of the issue he was analyzing pushed economic analysis to its limits, he was roundly criticized by his fellow economists for "radical revision of global-warming economics" (Nordhaus 2007, p. 687). In particular, he was chastised for selecting a very low discount rate that took greater account of the interests of future generations (see analysis of the reaction in Nelson 2008).

In part due to the influence of previous studies by mainstream economists, effective action on global warming has been deferred or watered down (Brown 1992; Spash 2002). As a result, the remaining time to take effective action before humanity finds itself in a state of great peril has been shortened, the costs of mitigation have increased, while the likelihood of failure and hence of human suffering have been much enhanced. The economic profession must shoulder responsibility for its part in encouraging inaction on climate change.

6.2.2 Economic Growth

Turning now to my second and related example, it is hard to be a card-carrying member of the economics profession without displaying almost religious support for uninterrupted economic growth. But continued growth implies ever increasing use of energy and raw materials and hence mounting pressures on the biosphere and accelerating deterioration of long term human prospects. If the global economy were to grow at 3% annually for another 100 years, world GDP would be almost 20-fold higher than present. In 2 centuries, world GDP would be over 350 times its present size. Consider this: the logic of growth explains how between 1982 and 2003, a mere 21 years, humanity used up as much oil as it did between the discovery of oil and 1981 (Hughes 2006). Recently, the United Nations millennium ecosystem assessment concluded that humanity is living beyond its ecological means and is degrading the very ecosystems on which its wellbeing depends (United Nations Environment Program 2005). Yet somehow, there is room for more growth.

When pressed, most neoclassical economists will concede that growth, if it entails a proportional increase in resource and energy use and waste emissions, must ultimately cease at some distant point in the future. Nevertheless, they have three standard arguments they use to defend growth for the foreseeable future, all of which are red herrings.

The first argument is that the market will recognize scarcity and prices will therefore adjust, such that scarce resources will be conserved and substituted with more abundant ones. The track record to date shows that while there are some instances where this mechanism may have applied to natural resources, at the aggregate level and for most "renewable" resources it is but wishful thinking (Rees 2002). Often, the mechanism goes in the reverse direction. Tuna gets scarce, the price goes up, so it pays more to chase down the last few fish (Ludwig et al. 1993).

The second argument is that we can substitute our growing stock of manufactured capital (e.g., machinery and computers) for diminishing stocks of natural capital (e.g., forests and fish stocks). However, manufactured capital and natural capital are more often complements than substitutes: more fishing boats will not substitute for collapsed fish stocks (Daly 1977/1992). Also, as stocks of natural capital are drawn down, the loss of ecosystem services formerly freely provided by nature implies that resource consumption must accelerate to avoid slippage in the standard of living. For instance, land, cement, steel and energy will be needed to build and operate a water purification plant to replace the service once freely provided by a now denuded forest.

The third argument is that technological progress will come to humanity's rescue, such that the ecological impact for a given amount of economic activity will decline over time. In this era when we have become used to computers doubling in memory and processing power every couple of years, this argument seems intuitively promising: we can seek to "dematerialize" the economy. But unlike computing which involves the manipulation of information that has no mass, most economic activity that supports human existence is inherently physical. We live in homes made of timber, cement and brick; dwellings built this year do not weigh half as much as those built last year. We should indeed seek to do more with less. However, while it is initially easy to find ways to improve the eco-efficiency of a given process or product, further improvements become more challenging. For instance, it is easy to reduce the fuel consumption of a car by switching six cylinder engines with high performance four cylinder engines. The improvements get more difficult and costly in switching from four cylinders to hybrids. The challenge and cost of squeezing that last bit of energy out of a gallon of gas increases exponentially as we approach limits imposed by the laws of thermodynamics, limits that despite the cornucopian beliefs of many economists no technology will ever be able to transcend. Therefore, the rate at which eco-efficiency improves over time will generally decline and hence will tend towards an asymptote, which it will not be able to improve upon. In contrast, growth compounds upon itself and is hence exponential. Thus, eco-efficiency is quickly overwhelmed by growth (Georgescu-Roegen 1971; Huesemann 2003). Commitment to continued economic growth is therefore a commitment to a path that is ultimately impossible but somewhere in the not too distant future implies dramatic collapse.

6.3   The Perplexing Inefficiency Implied by Economic Efficiency

For the critic, uncovering problems with the ethical framework of mainstream economics is a bit like stabbing a sponge: no matter where you aim, the sponge has no effective resistance to offer, but withdraw the knife and there is no visible wound that would show the attack took place. Members of the economics profession rarely take heed of criticisms that are based on philosophical or ethical arguments; a withering critique will be met with silence and economic theorizing and analysis will carry on as before. In part, this is because economics is a unified-insular discipline that tenaciously preserves its core assumptions and methods and denies that members of other communities of knowledge might have insights on economic matters (Ambrose 2006; Ambrose and Green 2009).

I believe the problem with the values adopted by economists can be usefully examined by focusing in on the concept of economic efficiency. Efficiency is the evaluative criterion that underlies much economic analysis, such as cost-benefit analysis studies that purport to inform humanity of the rational approach to climate change.

To begin this discussion it seems relevant to note that efficiency is a term that implies its own desirability, since it involves achieving a desired result without waste, of making productive use of resources; to be inefficient implies being wasteful, that there was a better way of achieving the desired end that was not followed. In our current era of deepening environmental concern, we are used to hearing of the promise and desirability of eco-efficiency or energy efficiency technologies and how they can help us reduce our burden on the planet. This desirability of efficiency, as a general concept, maps over to the term's usage in economics, without most people understanding exactly what an economist means or implies when he or she speaks of economic efficiency. I suspect that if there was greater public appreciation of what the economist's use of the term actually implied, there would be much less enthusiasm for its usage as an evaluative criterion to inform societal decisions.

What then is economic efficiency? A market is said to be economically efficient when no feasible reorganization of production or trade can make one person better off without making another person worse off. At first glance, this seems reasonable, even laudable: all improvements that are possible through market exchanges or through the production decisions of firms without making anyone worse off have been pursued. For example, I trade my excess apples for your excess potatoes; we both leave the marketplace owning a mix of apples and potatoes that gives us greater utility than we had when we entered. Adam Smith's invisible hand has carried out its magic. Not only that, but efficiency is given even greater lustre because it is linked to freedom – all market exchanges and changes in the production decisions of firms were carried out without coercion.

Now it should be noted that when introductory textbooks laud the market's ability to deliver efficient outcomes, they concede that this finding is premised on certain conditions being met. First, market participants are assumed to have perfect information, which is of course impossible. Second, the distribution of wealth is taken as given, which I will discuss further below. Third, there are no externalities. Externalities occur when the participants to a transaction cause an uncompensated impact on a third party: I sell you pesticides, you use them on your lawn and as a result your neighbor's child gets leukemia. As the economy grows and consumption increases, externalities tend to become more pervasive, as we see now with global warming. While it is important to understand what such assumptions imply to the social desirability of efficient outcomes and the likelihood of achieving them, they are not the focus of this critique and they are discussed extensively elsewhere (Lutz and Lux 1979; Bromley 1990; Daly 1977/1992; Hausman and McPherson 1996).

Although introductory economics textbooks typically (over)emphasize the distinction between positive (what is) and normative economics (what ought to be), they often fail to acknowledge that economic efficiency is a normative concept, erroneously insisting that it is a scientific, objective concept. For instance, in the internationally bestselling textbook by Mankiw, "Whereas efficiency is an objective goal that can be judged on strictly positive grounds, equity involves normative judgments that go beyond economics and enter into the realm of political philosophy" (Mankiw 2007, p. 148).

The achievement of efficiency is argued to be desirable because consumers will be provided with the largest possible combination of commodities while all resources will be fully utilized given available technology (Samuelson and Nordhaus 2005). As Mankiw puts it, with efficiency "...the pie is as big as possible" (Mankiw 2007, p. 148). Efficiency turns to being focused on maximizing consumption by those who are already drowning in material goods – hardly the loftiest of goals to guide humanity (Brown 1992). Yet note the value judgment involved in preferring more over less, in preferring a state where the economy is maxed out rather than one where production occurs at a more leisurely pace. That maximizing the economy's output might involve diminishing long-term human prospects or that some might prefer to live in a world where work is less frenetic is ignored. Indeed, in many instances economic efficiency ends up being a measure of "...the efficiency with which we destroy what is valuable" (Daly 1977/1992, p. 94).

I highlight the problematic relationship between efficiency and equity[1] before going one layer deeper. A little thought experiment quickly demonstrates that focusing on efficiency can lead society to accept some outcomes that are morally repugnant because of their implications for equity. Imagine a nation where the one rich person has all the wealth, while everyone else is destitute. Those who are destitute have nothing to offer to the rich person or to each other, and hence by the requirements of efficiency the only exchanges that might improve national wellbeing are disallowed, even if millions could be saved from starvation. This is because they would involve taxing the rich person's wealth and making that one person somewhat worse off.

Recognizing how severely limiting this version of efficiency is, in welfare economics a weaker version is typically used: the potential Pareto improvement criterion. An outcome is said to be efficient if the gainers could compensate the losers, whether or not they do (and in practice, it's exceedingly rare that they do). Again, deeply problematic: imagine a policy which makes our rich person twice as wealthy, even if it slightly deepens the destitution of the rest of society. So long as the increase in the wealth of the rich person exceeds the summed increase in everyone else's destitution, the wealthy person could, in theory, compensate the poor. The policy would therefore be deemed to be economically efficient by this more relaxed criterion. In the end, all that matters is that benefits exceed costs.

As the distinguished economist and philosopher Amartya Sen has observed, economists' choice of the term "efficiency" was itself "unfortunate" since at best this criterion describes "an extremely limited way of assessing social achievement" (Sen 1987, pp. 33–35). How have economists come to rely so heavily upon an incoherent analytical construct that lacks legitimacy (Bromley 1990)? Economic efficiency has its roots in utilitarianism – John Stuart Mill's "the greatest happiness for the greatest number" – a consequentialist ethical framework underlying most economic thought that is rarely acknowledged and whose deficiencies and full ethical ramifications are rarely understood by most economists (see for instance Smart and Williams 1973; Brown 1992; Hausman and McPherson 1996). Utilitarianism is in some senses a radical philosophy in that it can be used to argue for redistribution of wealth (since taking half the wealth from a very rich person might make that one person somewhat worse off, but it could do a whole lot of good were this wealth spent wisely on the poor, thus increasing society's net happiness). But as we shall see in a moment, while modern welfare economics has been erected upon utilitarian foundations, the radical implications of utilitarianism for redistribution have been sterilized by subtle amendments to the economists' rulebook.

While economists write about efficient outcomes leading to the most efficient use of resources (a mantra repeated in the textbooks), they are being imprecise and

---

[1] Economists are fond of pointing to a trade-off between equity and efficiency, but the matter is not so simple. For a technical treatment, see Greenwald and Stiglitz (1986) and Stiglitz (1991). I sidestep the trade-off issue here.

hiding a major gap in the argument. It is hard to imagine a more inefficient use of resources than that of our market-oriented, industrial societies. The rate of resource extraction, processing, consumption and ultimate disposal as waste emissions is staggering, and yet, the level of happiness and wellbeing achieved is disappointing, especially given the multitudes left destitute or living lives too close to the margins of survival. The side effect of all this resource use is that habitat is lost, renewable resource stocks crash, the atmosphere overheats while the planet is slowly poisoned by accumulating toxins (United Nations Environment Program 2005; Fischer et al. 2007). In short, our supposedly efficient use of resources leads to a joyless economy in rich countries (Scitovsky 1992) while foreclosing options for future generations and rendering their future more difficult.

A key but subtle problem is that an efficient outcome does not actually imply that resources are used efficiently, despite imprecise wording in economic writings to the contrary. This is because resources enter the efficiency equation only indirectly, in their role of helping consumers achieve utility in the context of market exchanges (Daly 1977/1992; van Staveren 2006). Because of the focus on exchange, resources that might be used outside of the market to support wellbeing, such as to support subsistence production, are rarely taken into account. Furthermore, the concept of utility needs to be unpacked.

Utility turns out to be a slippery concept – over time, as theoretical problems accumulated, economists decoupled utility from wellbeing. Instead, economists seek a veneer of scientific objectivity by focusing on the satisfaction of preferences. An individual's preferences are taken as given and economists learn what these preferences are by observing the consumer's marketplace decisions. The more preferences an individual is able to satisfy, the better off they are presumed to be. However, there are many reasons to doubt that the more an individual's preferences are satisfied, the higher their level of welfare will be (Hausman and McPherson 1996; van Staveren 2006). An individual's preferences might be to abuse substances, to street race, to maltreat animals and to read hate literature, but satisfying these preferences may do little for his or her wellbeing – or the wellbeing of the community.

To compound matters, in a misguided effort to embrace positivism and to enhance the scientific credentials of the discipline, economists banished interpersonal comparisons of utility. They cannot say whether a multi-millionaire or a pauper will benefit more from being handed a $10 bill, or whether I will benefit more from acquiring a Hummer than a subsistence farmer will benefit from owning a wind-powered irrigation pump. This despite economists' emphasis that one of the keys to "thinking like an economist" is recognizing that with increasing consumption of a good, there is decreasing marginal utility. I'll really enjoy one hotdog, moderately enjoy the second, and prefer an apple to a third. Hence, a wealthy person should get little benefit from an extra $10, while a poor person, having little money, should get great benefit. So to defend a position where comparisons between persons are disallowed, specious arguments get used. Maybe the millionaire's happiness is easily improved by one more trinket for his or her yacht and the poor person has a dour disposition that can't be lightened by a decent meal.

The redistributive argument contained within utilitarianism was thus sterilized, and economics became a profession that is biased to maintaining the status quo distribution of wealth. So even though, in cases where the distribution of wealth is highly unequal, the benefits to society at large from income redistribution are obvious, economists tend to see the issue as outside of their purview. Fortunately, the emerging field of happiness economics is helping to overturn the profession's longstanding refusal to engage in interpersonal utility comparisons since researchers are finding rigorous ways to measure how consumption or other economic factors affect wellbeing, thereby bringing issues of income distribution to the fore again (Frey and Stutzer 2002; Layard 2005).

Utility for some individuals who have purchasing power (recall that we need only concern ourselves with the plight of those who have the money to vote in the market) can be achieved in highly energy and resource intensive ways (van Staveren 2006). If I get utility out of buying a Hummer and cruising around town, the gas I use is no longer available to satisfy other human needs. If my buying a Hummer makes my neighbor feel inadequate unless he can demonstrate his worth by also driving a status symbol, so much the better for the economy, even though it implies that more resources will be used up to build and fuel the Jaguar. The steel embodied in my Hummer could have been made into two dozen wind-powered irrigation pumps for use in Africa. The African farmers might demand pumps at a political rally, arguing that without them, their communities will go hungry. However, since I was willing to pay more for the steel than the African farmers, my use of the steel must be more efficient than theirs, and therefore from the economist's standpoint the steel is going to its highest and best use. While the African farmers might desperately want irrigation pumps and derive great utility from them, they cannot back up their preferences with money and their needs are therefore irrelevant. In the cold terminology of economics, the farmers lack *effective* demand.

The cost–benefit analysis studies that economists contributed to the global warming debate have typically involved unquestioning acceptance of the existing distribution of income. This means that each person in effect gets one vote for each dollar of income or of consumption, so the life of someone in Kiribati is only worth a little more than 1/40th of that of someone in North America. Having Kiribati sink below the ocean is thus an efficient thing to do, since my preferences, as revealed in the marketplace, show driving my Hummer and flying off for a winter holiday gives me such utility – and I have the ability to back up my desires with cash – while the losses in income or consumption that the poor folk of Kiribati will experience from being flooded out of a homeland are modest indeed (Spash 2002, 2008).

In effect, the economist's framing of global warming has implied that protecting the environment is a luxury we may not be able to afford if we want to have a healthy economy, rather than acknowledging that the health of the biosphere is the basis for human life and the viability of the economy. Furthermore, because economics prioritizes enabling private consumption by individuals over meeting the need for public goods such as libraries, natural areas, and a healthy atmosphere, it gives insufficient attention to the importance of and potential for collective responses to challenges that affect society at large (Galbraith 1958/1998). Finally, most economic models used to date to assess the cost of mitigating climate change fail to capture that many climate-saving technologies actually pay for themselves (Lovins and Lovins 1991), while the costs of global warming have often been understated and offset by deducting supposed benefits of a warmer world such as better vacation opportunities (Spash 2002, 2008).

Can society really buy into the economic logic that concludes resources are efficiently used if steel goes to manufacture my CO_2-emitting Hummer rather than to build wind-powered irrigation pumps? Is it not obvious that an outcome that denied me the Hummer, saved Kiribati from submersion and enabled African farmers to grow more food would involve resources being used in a way that was more likely to support happiness in the world? It is time to drop economists' arbitrary definition of efficiency, which at best might be an intermediate goal, and to refocus economic analysis on the final goals of meeting human needs and supporting human welfare, indeed, of seeking the continued flourishing of the commonwealth of life (Brown 2007; Goodwin 2008).

6.4   How Do Economists Learn to Think Like Economists?

As the above analysis has shown, economists have embraced a problematic system of ethics, one that is at odds with the values commonly held by members of the general public, with the values promoted by the world's major religions or with the ethical insights of the great philosophers. It seems worth examining how economists have come to hold this system and why they defend it with a passion that belies their avowed self-identification as dispassionate scientists. How is it that so many gifted individuals, who are frequently motivated to choose the discipline of economics by a desire to ameliorate conditions for the poor (Nelson 2001), have been able to coldly write off future generations, people in locations vulnerable to climate change or people struggling with the consequences of ecological deterioration implied by growing levels of resource and energy consumption? How is it they are so good at mathematical models, but will not do some quick math to see the fallacy in believing the non-growing earth can sustain perpetual exponential growth of the economy? How is it that they have persistently dismissed critiques of limits to growth (see reactions documented in Georgescu-Roegen,1975, pp. 364–365), often with a hostile attitude that suggests they act as members of an academic tribe rather than as scientists in search of knowledge?

The answers to these questions would not matter if economics were but an intellectual pastime, but that is not the case. The pool of talented minds that makes up the higher echelons of the economics profession has obfuscated and frustrated policy responses to the most important issues of our time. More broadly, economic thought and analysis has pervasive influence on the design of human institutions and on societal decisions. An introductory version of the mainstream canon is taught to almost half of undergraduate students in North America, shaping societal attitudes towards economic policy. As institutions and decisions are shaped by economic theory, our social environment changes and thereby reshapes human behavior, such that with the passage of time, humans increasingly begin to resemble the selfish, rational and emotionally impoverished *homo economicus* that inhabits economic models and textbooks (Ferraro et al. 2005). Hence, the values and assumptions knowingly and unknowingly adopted by economists and incorporated into their theory, analysis and policy prescriptions is of critical importance to the opportunity set that humanity – and the commonwealth of life – will face in the future. By understanding how the talent that decides upon a career in economics gets misdirected and stymied, we can see the pathway to a solution.

Research suggests that studying economics, with its strong emphasis on rationality and self-interest, makes students greedier, less cooperative and more corrupt (Frank et al. 1993, 1996; Frank and Schulze 2000). Sociology has valuable insights to offer on the socialization and perpetuation of the economics profession (Fourcade-Gourinchas 2001; Fourcade 2006). Undergraduate courses in economics tend to select out students with social and environmental concerns since they are actively devalued by "the economist's way of thinking." Success in upper levels of economics requires high levels of mathematical aptitude and hence selects against gifted individuals whose talents or interests lie in other domains of knowledge. Advanced education in economics focuses on developing the student's skills at manipulating formal models that assume well-behaved, predictable systems rather than providing tools for understanding complex, unpredictable economic systems linked to complex natural systems (Ormerod 1998; Liu et al. 2007). This restricts students to looking at a small set of problems that fit within the parameters of the standard model rather than the problems that are most relevant to society. The focus on formal models means that ethical considerations are buried in the math and rarely brought to the student's attention.

Most doctoral programs in the United States have eliminated course requirements in the history of economic thought. Such courses would help students appreciate the roots of current ideas, to understand the preconceptions that underlie analysis and to see that theory once thought to be unassailable was later shown to be partial, deficient and coloured by the presumptions about scientific knowledge and the values of the era (Heilbroner 1990; Blaug 2001; Coleman 2005). Students pursing advanced degrees are discouraged by a demanding set of core courses from peering over the discipline's ramparts where they might learn from psychology, ecology, sociology, political science or philosophy. Were students to pursue such studies, fellow economists would not recognize this training as an improvement in academic credentials. A small number of top-ranked economics departments influence what is studied at second and third tier departments and provide the supply of newly minted Ph.D.s to replace retiring professors. It is difficult for an aspiring student to learn outside of the discipline's received canon. This is in part because there are so few economists trained in other traditions of economic thought such as feminist economics, institutional economics, or ecological economics. The small number of heterodox scholars that did earn Ph.D.s in recent decades often could not find academic appointments or had to accept appointments based in other departments (Lee 2004). Heterodox theory is considered to be off-base by the mainstream and hence not worth teaching.

The publish-or-perish university environment, in a context where the only journals that count towards securing tenure or other professional rewards require the use of formal models and filter out content that undermines the mainstream canon, restrict economists to playing in a sandbox where all problems must be amenable to translation into math and results must avoid disturbing the conventional wisdom. This focus on mathematical prowess and incremental contributions to existing theory leads to a discipline with little space for creativity, that neglects wisdom, eschews cross-disciplinary collaboration, and undervalues the use of empirical data. The end result is a profession that is "an extremely inefficient generator of substantively useful knowledge" (Reay 2007, p. 122). The knowledge that is generated in such circumscribed conditions provides poor guidance to the messy outside world where interactions between complex systems are ubiquitous and decisions have multi-faceted ethical dimensions. Worse still, economists do not realize the deficiencies of their training and the limitations of their ethical framework. Instead, they see themselves as stalwarts of objectivity and their economic analysis as providing guidance that, if only it was put into effect by society without the inevitable amendments that result from political compromise and meddling by non-economists, would increase opportunity and diminish waste.

Part of the problem with the economics profession is that it has yet to address its sexist heritage (Strober 1994; Ferber and Nelson 2003). One result, as Nelson (2008) convincingly argues, is that the economics profession has hypervalued detachment and has misunderstood the essence of objectivity. Somehow, economists have believed that evaluating the consequences of global warming, with consequences for those now alive and generations yet to come, "can be accomplished *without* recourse to ethical value judgements" (Nelson 2008, p. 442). Somehow, economists have come to believe that taking the existing distribution of income as given is an objective, value-free way to set up the analysis. Economics has become ethically impoverished (Sen 1987) in a way that would dismay Adam Smith, whose first book was on ethics (Smith 1790).

Nelson (2008) suggested that economists look to the medical profession for a better metaphor of objectivity: rather than idealizing detached and neutral observation, medical researchers are objective in terms of not prejudicing findings or slanting results. However, at the same time, one would hope that they are motivated to improve human health rather than being objective in the sense of being indifferent to it. Likewise, one would hope economists are in favor of the long-term persistence of Homo sapiens and the commonwealth of life with which we share this planet. Objectivity in this sense means being transparent about the moral positions and assumptions that underlie one's analysis and engaging a broader community of knowledge and experience in developing theory or to inform analysis.

6.5   Towards a More Efficient Use of Gifted Minds

In theory, the solution to improving the ethical content of economics, the ethical sophistication of economists and the relevance of economic theory is simple. Broaden
the economics curriculum, from the introductory level to the Ph.D. Teach the controversies in economic theory (Becker 2007), including schools of thought that are
critical of the neoclassical tradition. Encourage students to take an interdisciplinary
approach to their studies. Recognize that promoting emotional disengagement as a
virtue and downplaying consideration of right and wrong is a poor recipe for mental health, lessens one's potential for making substantial contributions to knowledge
that can better the human predicament and can lead to individuals who are skilled
at promoting policies that cause great human suffering with few moral qualms
(Haigh 2005, p. 39). Have students engage with real world issues, to value learning from beyond the campus gates, to engage with disadvantaged communities and
civil society. Drop the hypervaluation of formal modelling. Accept that economics
is inevitably entangled with ethics. The result? We might end up with what Goodwin (2008) has termed *contextual economics* based on the insight that:

> an economic system can only be understood when it is seen to operate within a so-
> cial/psychological context that includes ethics, norms and human motivations, culture,
> politics, institutions, and history and a physical context that includes the built environment
> as well as the natural world. (p. 43)

In practice, the solution to ensuring that the gifted individuals who become
economists have well-rounded training and are not ethically challenged is much
more difficult. The profession resists change and ignores its critics. It is able to do
so because it has the support of vested interests, since economics has long provided
a veneer of legitimacy to the status quo (Silva and Slaughter 1984; Heilbroner and
Milberg 1995; Reay 2007). Though there are some hopeful signs of change, the pace
is too slow given the urgent problems that confront humanity.

President Tong of Kiribati, who also happens to be a graduate of the London
School of Economics, argues that getting the economics right is "...not an issue
of economic growth, it's an issue of human survival."[2] Ultimately, as the plight of
the people of Kiribati illustrates, economic theory and policy is too important to
be left to mainstream economists, however well-meaning they might be. Ideally,
society will benefit from economists' considerable analytical skills (tempered with
new humility, infused with ethical sophistication and enriched by interdisciplinary
collaborations) directed at tackling the interlinked ecological, social and economic
crises of our era. We need their brainpower to help find a path forward, from an
economy addicted to growth and vulnerable to the slightest perturbation in consumer
spending to one that is confined to operating within the biosphere's limits. Markets,

---

[2] International Herald Tribune Online, "Leader of disappearing nation says climate change is an
issue of survival, not economics." At: http://www.iht.com/articles/ap/2008/06/05/asia/AS-GEN-
New-Zealand-World-Environment-Day.php. Accessed June 28, 2008.

institutions and economic policies must be shaped and guided so that they deliver human wellbeing in nations both north and south such that life can be sustained over the long term (Daly 2002; Lourdes 2003).

References

Ambrose, D. (2006). Large-scale contextual influences on creativity: Evolving academic disciplines and global value systems. *Creativity Research Journal, 18*: 75–85.

Ambrose, D., & Green, T. L. (2009). *The not-so-invisible hand of economics and its impact on high ability*, Manuscript submitted for publication.

Becker, W. E. (2007). Quit lying and address the controversies: There are no dogmata, laws, rules or standards in the science of economics. *American Economist, 51*(1): 3–14.

Blaug, M. (2001). No history of ideas, please, we're economists. *The Journal of Economic Perspectives, 15*(1): 145–164.

Bromley, D. W. (1990). The ideology of efficiency: Searching for a theory of policy analysis. *Journal of Environmental Economics and Management, 19*(1): 86–107.

Brown, P. G. (1992). Climate change and the planetary trust. *Energy Policy, 20*(3): 208–222.

Brown, P. G. (2007). *The commonwealth of life: Economics for a flourishing earth, Second Edition.* London: Black Rose Books.

Coleman, W. (2005). Taking out the pins: Economics as alive and living in the history of economic thought. *Economic Papers, 24*(2): 107–115.

Daly, H. E. (1992). *Steady state economics, Second Edition.* London: Earthscan (Original work published 1977).

Daly, H. E. (2002). Reconciling the economics of social equity and environmental sustainability. *Population and Environment, 24*: 47–53.

Ferber, M., & Nelson, J. (2003). *Feminist economics today: Beyond economic man.* Chicago, IL: University of Chicago Press.

Ferraro, F., Pfeffer, J., & Sutton, R. (2005). Economics language and assumptions: How theories can become self-fulfilling. *Academy of Management Review, 30*: 8–24.

Fischer, J., Manning, A., Steffen, W., Rose, D., Daniell, K., Felton, A., et al. (2007). Mind the sustainability gap. *Trends in Ecology & Evolution, 22*: 621–624.

Fourcade, M. (2006). The construction of a global profession: The transnationalization of economics. *American Journal of Sociology, 112*(1): 145–194.

Fourcade-Gourinchas, M. (2001). Politics, institutional structures, and the rise of economics: A comparative study. *Theory and Society, 30*: 397–447.

Frank, B., & Schulze, G. G. (2000). Does economics make citizens corrupt? *Journal of Economic Behavior & Organization, 43*: 101–113.

Frank, R. H., Gilovich T. D., & Regan, D. (1993). Does studying economics inhibit cooperation? *The Journal of Economic Perspectives, 7*(2): 159–171.

Frank, R. H., Gilovich, T. D., & Regan, D. (1996). Do economists make bad citizens? *The Journal of Economic Perspectives, 10*(1): 187–192.

Frey, B. S., & Stutzer, A. (2002). What can economists learn from happiness research? *Journal of Economic Literature, 40*: 402–435.

Galbraith, J. K. (1998). *The affluent society: 40th anniversary edition.* New York: Houghton Mifflin (Original work published 1958).

Georgescu-Roegen, N. (1971). *The entropy law and the economic process.* Cambridge, MA: Harvard University Press.

Georgescu-Roegen, N. (1975). Energy and economic myths. *Southern Economic Journal, 41*: 347–381.

Goodwin, N. (2008). From outer circle to center stage: The maturation of heterodox economics. In J. T. Harvey, & R. F. Jr. Garnett (Eds.), *Future directions for heterodox economics* (pp. 27–52). Ann Arbor, MI: University of Michigan Press.

Greenwald, B. C., & Stiglitz, J. E. (1986). Externalities in economies with imperfect information and incomplete markets. *The Quarterly Journal of Economics*, *101*: 229–264.

Haigh, M. (2005). Greening the university curriculum: Appraising an international movement. *Journal of Geography in Higher Education*, *29*: 31–48.

Hausman, D. M., & McPherson, M. S. (1996). *Economic analysis and moral philosophy*. Cambridge: Cambridge University Press.

Heilbroner, R. (1990). Analysis and vision in the history of modern economic thought. *Journal of Economic Literature*, *28*: 1097–1114.

Heilbroner, R., & Milberg, W. (1995). *The crisis of vision in modern economic thought*. Cambridge: Cambridge University Press.

Huesemann, M. H. (2003). The limits of technological solutions to sustainable development. *Clean Technologies and Environmental Policy*, *5*: 21–34.

Hughes, J. D. (2006). Energy supply/demand trends and forecasts: Implications for a sustainable energy future in Canada and the world. Presentation to Federation of Canadian Municipalities 2006 Sustainable Communities National Conference and Trade Show, Ottawa, February 2–4, 2006. Natural Resources Canada, Geological Survey of Canada, Calgary.

Layard, R. (2005). *Happiness: Lessons from a new science*. London: Penguin Books.

Lee, F. S. (2004). To be a heterodox economist: The contested landscape of American economics, 1960s and 1970s." *Journal of Economic Issues*, *38*: 747–763.

Liu, J., Dietz, T., & Stern, P. (2007). Complexity of coupled human and natural systems. *Science*, *317*: 1513–1516.

Lourdes, B. (2003). *Gender, development, and globalization: Economics as if all people mattered*. London: Routledge.

Lovins, A. B., & Lovins, L. H. (1991). Least-cost climatic stabilization. *Annual Review of Energy and the Environment*, *16*: 433–531.

Ludwig, D., Hilborn, R., & Waters, C. (1993). Uncertainty, resource exploitation, and conservation: Lessons from history. *Science*, *260*: 17–36.

Lutz, M. A., & Lux, K. (1979). *The challenge of humanistic economics*. Menlo Park, CA: Benjamin/ Cummings.

Mankiw, G. N. (2007). *Principles of economics*. Mason, OH: South-Western.

Nelson, J. A. (2008). Economists, value judgments, and climate change: A view from feminist economics. *Ecological Economics*, *65*: 441–447.

Nelson, R. (2001). *Economics as religion: From Samuelson to Chicago and beyond*. University Park, PA: Pennsylvania State University Press.

Nordhaus, W. D. (1982). How fast should we graze the global commons? *American Economic Review: Papers and Proceedings*, *72*(2): 242–246.

Nordhaus, W. D. (2007). A review of the stern review on the economics of global warming. *Journal of Economic Literature*, *45*: 686–702.

Ormerod, P. (1998). *Butterfly economics: A new general theory of social and economic behaviour*. London: Faber and Faber.

Reay, M. (2007). Academic knowledge and expert authority in American economics. *Sociological Perspectives*, *50*: 101–129.

Rees, W. (2002). An ecological economics perspective on sustainability and prospects for ending poverty. *Population and Environment*, *24*: 15–46.

Samuelson, P. A., & Nordhaus, W. D. (2005). *Economics*. New York: McGraw-Hill.

Scitovsky, T. (1992). *The joyless economy*. Oxford: Oxford University Press.

Sen, A. (1987). *On ethics and economics*. Oxford: Blackwell.

Silva, E. T., & Slaughter, S. A. (1984). *Serving power: The making of the academic social science expert*. Westport, CT: Greenwood.

Smart, J. J. C., & Williams, B. (1973). *Utilitarianism: For and against*. Cambridge: Cambridge University Press.

Smith, A. (1790). *The theory of moral sentiments*. London: A. Millar.

Spash, C. (2008). The economics of avoiding action on climate change. *Adbusters, 16*(1): 16–17

Spash, C. L. (2002). *Greenhouse economics: Value and ethics*. London: Routledge.

Stern, N. (2007). *The economics of climate change: The stern review*. Cambridge, UK: Cambridge University Press.

Stiglitz, J. (1991). The invisible hand and modern welfare economics (p. 41). Cambridge, MA: National Bureau of Economic Research.

Strober, M. H. (1994). Rethinking economics through a feminist lens. *The American Economic Review, 84*(2): 143–147.

United Nations Environment Program (2005). *Living beyond our means: Natural assets and human well-being. Statement of the millennium ecosystem assessment board*. Nairobi: UNEP.

van Staveren, I. (2006). *The ethics of efficiency*. Groningen: Human Development and Capability Association.

Chapter 7
The Continuous Nature of Moral Creativity

Mark A. Runco

Abstract Moral creativity is increasingly important in today's complex world because rapid technological advances with unpredictable consequences are magnifying the effects of creative thought and action as well as the importance of ethical guidance for what we do. This chapter explores the relationships between giftedness, creativity, and morality. It also outlines some empirical evidence for these interconnections. Continua are employed to illustrate how individuals can move toward higher levels of creativity and moral action. Creativity can lead toward both negative and positive directions on the moral continuum. Bright people can be creatively benevolent or creatively malevolent and the moral nature of their creations depends on the intertwining of their actions and values. There are some reasons for optimism that people can achieve positive moral development through creativity.

This chapter focuses on creativity in the moral domain. It explores relationships that exist between creativity (the focus of this chapter) and "ethical gifted minds" (the focus of the book) and outlines a number of practical implications for encouraging both morality and creativity. The starting point is a thought experiment:

Think for a moment about your students and/or your children (if any) and what ideals you have for their growth and development. Who do you want them to become? What characteristics are most important for them to develop and express? If you could somehow select or even guarantee specific characteristics for your students and children, what would they be?

Very likely you would like your students and children (real or hypothetical) to be happy and healthy. Suppose you are lucky enough to have happy and healthy children – what would be next? In all probability you would like them to be good people. You might operationalize this in terms of honesty, integrity, or honor, each of which can be subsumed under the umbrella of ethics and morality.

M.A. Runco
Torrance Creativity Center, University of Georgia, Aderhold Hall,
Athens, GA 30602
e-mail: Runco@uga.edu

D. Ambrose, T. Cross (eds.), *Morality, Ethics, and Gifted Minds*,
DOI: 10.1007/978-0-387-89368-6_7,

The idea that health and happiness are somehow primary and morality and ethics are just below implies a hierarchy, not unlike Maslow's (1970) *hierarchy of needs*. Significantly, the peak of that hierarchy (self-actualization) includes creative potential, which is the focus of this chapter.

The point of this simple thought experiment is merely that morality and ethics are of enormous and universal importance. And if creative talents are by chance inextricable from morals and ethics, they too are of the same importance. Indeed, even if extricable, creative talents might facilitate or support morality, in which case they are nearly as important. Admittedly creative talents are probably on most lists of ideals for students and children, especially because they are related directly to psychological and physical health (Richards and Runco 1998) and to adaptability and coping (Flach 1990; Runco 1994).

Keywords Differential reinforcement of other behaviors (DRO) · Hierarchy of needs · Passive resistance · Personal creativity · Self-actualization · Spontaneous integration of previously learned responses · Threshold theory · Volition

7.1 How Exactly Are Creativity and Morality Related to One Another?

The creativity of morals is becoming more and more important. This is in part because the world has gotten smaller, with easy travel and communication. Thus a rigid moral system can lead to conflict. Additionally, technology has boomed in the past 100 years and is growing at an ever-accelerating rate. Like most things, this has an upside but also a downside, a benefit but also a cost. Technology has given us atomic energy, but also the atomic bomb. It has given us the capability to engineer genes, but also the need to decide when that is an appropriate thing to do. A huge number of moral issues have arisen as a direct result of technological advance (McLaren 1993; Stein 1993), and if these issues are viewed as problems, it is easy to see how creativity has simultaneously become of utmost importance.

What of the question raised above about the relationship of creativity to "gifted minds?" This relationship has been described several times before (e.g., Albert 1990; Milgram 1990) but it should be summarized here, before moving on. There are different views, some suggesting that giftedness sometimes requires only convergent thinking and traditional intelligence. This view assumes that such convergent thinking and traditional intelligence are extricable from divergent thinking and the capacity for original ideation. Several empirical studies have suggested that they are indeed extricable, at least at certain levels of ability. This perspective is known as the threshold view or triangular theory (Guilford 1968; Kim 2005; Runco and Albert 1986). A very different theory posits that all gifted individuals are creative. This perspective is an attractive one, especially if *intelligence* is equated with the capacity to process information or merely memorize facts. In that light traditional intelligence, including that estimated with IQ tests, is unlikely to lead to productivity or achievement, and certainly will not lead to original insights or important breakthroughs. Actually, it is sufficient to acknowledge the different perspectives on the relationship of giftedness and creativity, articulate the assumption that creative talents are involved in most, and perhaps all, forms of giftedness, and turn to the possibility and definition of creativity in the moral domain.

How are creativity and morality related to one another? The answer is far from simple. That is because moral action is sometimes defined as "doing the right thing," but "right" assumes a value system, and that means that the action is consistent with existing values. Doing the right thing might therefore preclude creativity, given that creativity requires originality. It may be novelty, uniqueness, unusualness, or rarity, but in some way all creativity requires originality. One complication, then, is that too often moral action is tied to the status quo, while creative action is contrarian or at least highly unusual.

The situation is even more complicated because it is not tenable to entirely separate morality from creativity. Instead of viewing (a) morality as supporting the status quo, and therefore convergent and conventional, and (b) creativity as entirely different because it requires originality and divergence, my suggestion was to view each as representing intersecting continua (Runco 1993). We might then have one continuum representing possible moral actions, ranging from "low morality" (or immoral) to high morality, and a separate continuum representing creativity, with high creativity at one extreme and low creativity (lacking originality) at the other. This makes it easy to avoid the view that all morality is conventional and all creativity is unconventional. They are no longer opposites on one continuum but can instead sometimes be employed together in various complimentary ways.

This also makes it easier to understand gifted minds. Consider in this regard Henry David Thoreau, who spent a bit of time in jail and claimed that, in an unjust society, prison was the appropriate place for a moral individual. Along the same lines Gandhi remained a pacifist (and thus true to his morals) even when there was a need for rebellion (Wolpert 2002). His choices and behavior were highly creative – especially his innovation known as *passive resistance* – and yet they were unambiguously moral.

The two-continuum theory described above not only describes this kind of extraordinarily gifted mind. It also allows us to identify individuals or tendencies that fit in one of the other quadrants. (The two-continuum theory has them bisecting each other, so there are quadrants representing high and low levels of morality and creativity. It is similar to a 2 x 2 table though it is also important to retain the range of possibilities, which are allowed by a continuum rather than a simple dichotomous alternative). One such possibility is that there are creative persons who are immoral. That is probably accurate. There may be successful criminals, for example, who are successful precisely because they are creative. Eisenman (1999) found most incarcerated individuals to express only low levels of creative talent, but his was a limited sample, and if a criminal is incarcerated, it is unlikely that he can be viewed as successful, at least from the perspective of profit and loss. Law enforcement experts may disagree, but it is possible that the most talented and creative criminals tend to avoid incarceration, and therefore we know little if anything about them.

7.2 An Optimistic View

The two-continuum theory implies a kind of optimism. That is because a number of methods have been proposed and tested for the enhancement of creative talents; and if these are in fact effective, they might help us keep individuals out of two quadrants, namely the uncreative quadrants. Then again, that is not good enough. That would leave us with creative people, but only some of whom would be ethical! Clearly what is needed is to also encourage the transition from the various levels of immorality or low morality to clear-cut and consistent moral tendencies.

Before exploring that, something must be said about those techniques mentioned above for the encouragement of creative behavior. This is one point where we can again draw on Maslow's (1970) theory, for he described how people realize their potentials. This is not the same as acquiring something that is altogether new. Instead, it implies that there is the capacity for something, but it is not manifest until it is supported or encouraged. When it is manifest, it is not potential but actual performance (Runco 1995). Again there is a need to view morality and creativity as continua. Neither is just "entirely lacking" vs. "entirely fulfilled." The idea of continua reminds us that individuals are somewhere on a continuum, rather than completely lacking. That is why we can be optimistic. What is needed is to fulfill potentials, not construct something from nothing. The fulfillment of potentials is a matter of helping that individual move along the continuum towards higher levels of creativity or morality, or, hopefully, both creativity and morality.

Most humanistic efforts to fulfill potentials are fairly unobtrusive. Rogers (1970), for example, used *unconditional positive regard*, the idea being that each of us has the potential for self-actualization, and if allowed to be ourselves, we would mature in that direction and eventually become actualized. If we do not have such unconditional positive regard, we might conform to expectations and incentives and act in a fashion that is not consistent with our true selves, and as such would not be truly self-actualized. These ideas are particularly relevant because Roger's methods have been empirically tested, and individuals do seem to be more creative as a result (Harrington et al. 1987).

Two other methods for fulfilling potential should be mentioned. One is from Kohlberg (1987) and requires that individuals experience the challenge of dilemma. He felt that such challenges would exercise moral reasoning skills. My own recent suggestion for fulfilling potentials is somewhat more systematic but has yet to be empirically tested (Runco, in press). It is adapted from learning that has been empirical validated. At the heart of this method is the *spontaneous integration of previously learned responses* (Epstein 2003). This integration is practically ensured with differential reinforcement, but note that the reinforcement is given to discrete behaviors and not the terminal action. This is precisely why it might work to fulfill potentials. The discrete behaviors make up the potential, which is only potential because they are not initially integrated. After the learning experience, however, they are integrated and a potential is fulfilled. My outline of this procedure focused on creativity, with the capacity for original interpretations and discretion as the two discrete aspects of potential. Education can strengthen each such that they will be spontaneously integrated into actual creative action. Very likely moral reasoning can be included in this procedure as one of the discrete contributions.

Learning theory provides yet another reason for optimism. This is implied by the concept of *differential reinforcement of other behaviors* (DRO). This method was developed for self-injurious (e.g., autistic) individuals. Their attempts to injure themselves could be controlled via restraint, but when restrained they are not really learning anything and may in fact be given attention which serves to reinforce the self-abuse! The result is an increase in self-injurious efforts. DRO does not use restraint but instead provides clear and regular reinforcement for actions that are functionally incompatible with the self-abuse. If the preferred method of self-abuse were scratching, for example, DRO would target something requiring the hands and digits. If the hands are busy with the new behavior, they can't be used for scratching. The self-abuse is replaced by appropriate behaviors. This is relevant to the present discussion because it is quite possible that the spontaneous integration procedure discussed just above might be used to strengthen moral actions, and like DRO, these moral actions might keep the individual from acting in an immoral fashion.

7.3 Volition, Responsibility, and Creativity

Elsewhere I claimed that anyone encouraging or using creativity must be prepared to "take the good with the bad" (Runco 2008). This relates to the discussion of creativity and ethics but should be qualified. It is too general and in some ways it does not hold up. Certainly it does make sense that the dark sides of creativity must be accepted if they are unavoidable correlates or results. This is true of certain unfortunate tendencies of creative persons, as is apparent in studies of the mad genius and associations between creativity and psychopathologies (Becker 2000, 2001; Sass and Schuldburg 2000, 2001; Runco and Richards 1998) as well as some of the behavior problems of creative children (Kim, in press). These are frequently well beyond the control of the individual. But what of crime and other not uncommon correlates of creativity (Eisenman in press; Runco 1993)?

Unethical behavior can be avoided. Not to put too sharp a point on it, but it can be controlled. Values may be involved, but some part of ethical action is a decision. It is voluntary. Similarly, unethical action is also at least partly voluntary and a function of decisions. Thus the qualified position promised above is that "we must accept some bad with the good," the implication being that there are certain undesirable correlates and components of creativity that we must accept ("take with the good"), because they are involuntary, but others, involving morals and ethics, that we should not accept. They can be controlled and we should work to change them.

Given the thought experiment that opened this chapter, and the question about ideal students and children, this premise about control and volition might be applied to the classroom. As a matter of fact Gowan et al. (1979) referred to *creatively handicapped children*, the idea being that the creativity of this group causes problems in the classroom. Kim (in press) extended this line of thought and seemed to agree about "the good and the bad." She concluded that:

> It has been said that creativity is both a gift and a curse depending upon whether the creativity can be channeled into productive behaviors... [her research] exemplifies that since some students seem to handle their creativity well and excel while some students seem to let their creativity handle them and fail. It has long been thought that creativity can be a curse for some students in traditional school environments where it can lead to underachievement.

What is most important here is that creativity can lead in several different directions: moral action or immoral action, achievement or failure. The two continua described earlier in this chapter might be inadequate. It certainly makes sense to recognize different levels of achievement, with failure at the low end, but creative talents associated with some forms of achievement but also with some forms of failure. Further, achievement is sometimes a result of creative talent but sometimes a matter of luck or another kind of skill, such as impression management (Kasof 1995; Runco 1995).

7.4 Directionality and Causality

It is one thing to hypothesize this kind of relationship between morality and creativity. It is quite another to determine how the two are related in a causal fashion. After all, a correlation between the two may be indicative of (a) morality being the causal agent and creativity a kind of result; (b) creativity the causal agent and morality the result; (c) bidirectionality with morality and creativity each influencing the other; or (d) some hidden variable influencing both creativity and morality while they exert no causal influence on each other. Admittedly the two-continuum theory used throughout this chapter may imply causal independence, but only if the two continua are orthogonal. More importantly, the two-continuum theory is largely descriptive. It allows the morality and creativity to be separated, but this does not mean that they must always be separate. You can smoke cigarettes and not get cancer, or you might get cancer but not smoke, but sometimes smoking leads to cancer. The possibility that morality influences creative thinking was implied early in this chapter when moral action was described as entirely conventional and as such inhibiting creative thinking.

One possible hidden variable is conventionality. Conventions can inhibit creativity, but then again, most creative efforts use some conventions. It may influence creativity at all levels and often do so in a compelling way. It is, however, just one influence on the creative process. This can be explained using labels from Kohlberg's (1987) theory of moral reasoning. He described the highest level of moral reasoning as post conventional. This is characterized by ethical decision making that takes conventions into account (unlike preconventional moral reasoning) but allows autonomous judgment as well. It is thus informed but nonconforming.

Mature and intentional creativity is post-conventional. It takes conventions into account but the individual does not rely entirely on them. He or she may take liberties, adapt, or simply reject relevant conventions, or the creative idea may be a very simple but original extension of some convention. Creative thinking does not require a complete rejection of conventions. If it did we might conclude that morals were the causal agents in that they determine whether or not creativity was possible. This is clearly simplistic. If a person has an original idea but then decides not to act on it because it is contrary to his or her moral standards, both creative potential and those standards are influences. The latter win out because they are last in the process.

Another alternative is that creativity is the causal agent and determinant of moral decisions. This makes a great deal of sense if we recognize the role of volition, as suggested above. After all, suppose someone does the morally correct thing but does it only to fit in or please others? What if the morals have been so strongly ingrained that the individual is extremely uncomfortable considering any alternatives to them? He or she might be highly moral, but not really by choice. Can we give that individual credit for morality? It is really is just an act of conformity. Kohlberg (1987) described this kind of moral action as the least mature. The most mature was the post-conventional variety defined above. There the individual must be given full credit since the action is mindfully chosen. The individual considers the alternatives and chooses one; he or she is therefore responsible.

What if the individual takes this to the extreme and not only carefully considers the alternatives but in fact finds or constructs new alternatives? This would of course be incredibly useful whenever the problem at hand is a true dilemma. Dilemmas have two alternatives (hence the prefix). They are not like other kinds of problems. Other kinds of problems have a goal or objective and an obstacle. This kind of problem is solved by getting around the obstacle, or perhaps by removing it. But a dilemma involves a choice between two exclusive alternatives. There is usually some sort of loss; it is almost a no-win situation. That is because the alternatives are exclusive of one another. If the person takes option A, he or she has no chance of option B, and vice versa.

Yet this assumes that dilemmas are entirely dichotomous. That in and of itself should make us suspicious of them! How many things in life are so clear cut? Often there are numerous rather than just two alternatives, even if the range of options is not obvious. They might be found, however, by thinking in a creative fashion. In other words, an initially hidden option or solution might be found by thinking outside the box, or more accurately, outside the dichotomy. This conception of moral reasoning is consistent with many conceptions of creativity, including theories of divergent or lateral thinking, solution generation, and even paradigm shifts.

Many moral innovators seem to find new alternatives. That is what allows their innovations. Gandhi's *passive resistance* can again be cited; it is a wonderful example of a moral innovation. It allows passivism and rebellion rather than one or the other. It is outside the dichotomy. Not coincidentally, it strongly resembles the ethical perspective and *civil disobedience* of Henry David Thoreau. Both also can be tied to post-conventional creativity as well. They are conventional in their honoring passivism, yet creative in their originality and usefulness.

7.5 Empirical Evidence

There is more controlled empirical evidence suggesting a connection between creativity and moral reasoning. Mumford et al. (in press), for example, found creative problem solving to be empirically related to ethical decision making. Importantly, they explained the relationship between creative thinking and ethical decisions by including not just the generation of ideas as the basis of creative thinking but also the capacity to identify implications of actions. This is a useful point because individuals who know the implications of their actions are likely to see how they may influence other people and how they may fit or not fit with mores and cultural values.

Mumford et al. (in press) were aware that earlier theories of ethical thinking (e.g., Fromm 1973) supported a negative relationship between it and abstraction; and the latter is in some ways indicative of effective cognition. Then again, abstraction is used even early in life (e.g., when children abstract the rules of language and meaning of words without explicit tutelage), so Fromm's conclusion may not apply to mature cognition. This is a very important point given Kohlberg's (1987) theory that a universal ethic characterizes only the highest levels of cognitive maturity.

Kohlberg's (1987) theory of moral reasoning does suggest a caveat. He felt that cognitively mature individuals will tend towards a universal ethic, which means that they will all lean towards certain morals. It is as if their cognitive maturity shows them what is best or right. This is contrary to theories of moral relativity, but it certainly is possible that creative talents may indicate that the individual has the cognitive capacity to consider a full range of options and therefore will have a large amount of information at his or her disposal. That might in turn allow the person to make the best possible decision, which may for everyone involve prosocial action and similar universal values. No wonder Gruber (1993), in his breakthrough paper on creativity in the moral domain, concluded that "ought implies can implies create" (p. 3).

Still it is not surprising that Mumford et al. concluded that there may be a complex pattern of relationships between creative thinking and ethical decision making. In addition to Fromm's (1973) suggestions about abstraction and ethical behavior, some fairly recent empirical findings from Wyszack et al. (in press) indicate that creative talents can sometimes support deception. The basic idea is that creative thinking may provide an individual with ideas about how they might get away with certain selfish or otherwise immoral actions. It is almost as if a person says to him- or herself, "why conform to that morally appropriate action when there are these alternatives that better serve my own needs?" The potential for creative thinking will provide the person with the capacity to see all alternatives and options of all sorts, and some may be ethical, and some unethical. The point of the discussion above about volition, mindfulness, and control was that a judgment about morality must take more than the production of ideas into account. It must take intentions and other meta-cognitive aspects of the process into account.

7.6   Conclusions

Apparently both evil geniuses and benevolent luminaries can be creative. Indeed, it is quite possible that the primary difference between the two is in the values they hold. They may not differ at all in their cognitive capacities, intellectual talents, and creative potentials. Certainly it depends on how each of these things is defined, but the key point is that immoral and morally creative persons may be identical cognitively and dissimilar only in the values used and the subsequent decisions made.

Much of the creativity literature can be cited to further describe this possibility. That literature contains many descriptions of creative insights resulting from lateral or divergent thinking, or from some similar process that lead to unconventional ideas. Imagine a Venn diagram with conventional ideas in the smallest and innermost circle, slightly less conventional ideas in a moderately large circle which encompasses the conventional set of ideas, and a very large circle encompassing both of those and representing the set of "all possible ideas." Creative ideas would be found outside the innermost circles and would be well out towards the outer-most boundary.

One small point: Perhaps there is no boundary at all since this simple graphic is intended to capture "creativity" graphically and in relation to conventional tendencies. Creative ideas may be way "out there" and are sometimes outside existing paradigms. They may break all boundaries. Of course, the wildest possible idea is not guaranteed to be creative. Creative things are original, but also fitting. They solve a problem or fulfill some objective. It may be a personal objective, such as an artist finding the best way to capture an emotion, but still they have some fit or efficacy. Without that, original ideas are just original and not creative. Wild ideas may be original but are not necessarily creative. Thus we might even have one outer circle in the Venn diagram representing truly original and novel ideas, but ideas with some sort of connection with reality (thereby allowing for the fit or efficacy), and another circle in the diagram representing ideas that are wildly original and have not connection nor fit. These are probably viewed as bizarre or even psychotic.

Now imagine a division of that diagram containing creative ideas that are morally correct. They may fit the definition offered by Cropley et al. (2008) as benevolent. Then there is the section of the diagram that is exclusive of benevolent ideas and immoral. Ideas in this section may be malevolent. They may be creative and even effective, given some unsavory task or objective, but they fit that task and are original, and therefore are creative. They differ from ideas that are equally far removed from the center of our diagram, and equally creative, but they are creative in an immoral fashion.

Who could think in this fashion? Cropley et al. (2008) gave several examples in their description of malevolent creativity. The point here is that the creative process is independent of values. This is just another way of saying that they are the result of a creative process that can be used to construct benevolent creations, malevolent creations, or, theoretically, creations that imply no moral position.

Note the phrase, "independent of values." The creative process is probably not entirely free of values because values are necessary for the development of creative potentials and for the decisions that lead the individual to invest the resources that are necessary to produce creative ideas and insights. These are not moral or immoral values, however, but instead are those that allow the individual to recognize that creativity is a good thing that should be nurtured and practiced.

The most important aspect of creative morality may be the decision making, and the most important thing about decisions that they can go in various directions. They are not like reflexes nor even traits, both of that have predictable directions. An introvert will avoid social activity, for example, and a optimist will see the sunny side of life. But decisions are open-ended, so any time they are involved, the person may go one way, or another. It depends on the amount of effort expended, motives, values, situational factors, and so on. This is relevant because it is one thing to say that creative capacities are related to ethical decisions, but something completely different to say that creative talents guarantee ethical behavior.

The discussion in this chapter, and especially the concluding points, suggest a clear definition of creativity, and one that is itself useful in studies of creative morality. By definition creativity requires those two things: originality and usefulness. It does *not* require a moral basis. (That is another way of saying that the two things are best viewed as separate continua.) Yet most of the time it would be highly desirable if creative action was morally attractive. All of the moral issues facing humanity at this point in time could be addressed, and perhaps eventually solved.

Not surprisingly, this is again too simple. For one thing, it may be that conflicts and issues sometimes stimulate creative thinking, and morality. This is why Kohlberg (1987) looked to dilemmas; they challenge people and hopefully lead to increased moral reasoning. The same thing probably occurs on a societal level. Sometimes issues are ignored until they become critical. In that sense, progress is made not by removing all problems and issues but instead by addressing them as they arise. Some might even be embraced because they will demand attention and lead to progress. It may sound like I am concluding here by suggesting that moral issues are good things, but let's just say that I am concluding that we might restructure our thinking. Just as individuals can benefit by seeing value in problems and recognizing them as opportunities and useful challenges, so too can society accept diversity and disagreement as useful contributions to progress of all sorts, including in the domain of morality. All it takes for that restructuring is a bit of creative thinking.

References

Albert, R. S. (1990). Real world creativity and eminence: An enduring relationship. *Creativity Research Journal, 3*, 1–5.
Becker, G. (2000–2001). The association of creativity and psychopathology: Its cultural-historical origins. *Creativity Research Journal, 13*, 45–53.
Cropley, D., Kaufman, J., & Cropley, A. (2008). Malevolent creativity: A functional model of creativity in terrorism and crime. *Creativity Research Journal, 20*, 105–115.
Eisenman, R. (1999). Creative prisoners: Do they exist? *Creativity Research Journal, 12*, 205–210.

Eisenman, R. (2008). Creativity in prisoners: Conduct disorders and psychotics. *Creativity Research Journal* (in press).

Epstein R. (2003). Generativity theory as a theory of creativity. In M. A. Runco, & R. S. Albert (Eds.). *Theories of creativity* (pp. 257–293). Cresskill, NJ: Hampton.

Flach, F. (1990). Disorders of the pathways involved in the creative process. *Creativity Research Journal, 3*, 158–165.

Fromm, E. (1973). *The anatomy of human destructiveness.* New York: Holt, Rinehart, and Winston.

Gowan, J. C., Khatena, J., and Torrance, E. P. (1979). Educating the ablest–a book of readings on the education of gifted children. Itasca: Peacock.

Gruber, H. E. (1993). Creativity in the moral domain: Ought implies can implies create. *Creativity Research Journal, 6*, 3–16.

Guilford, J. P. (1968). *Creativity, intelligence and their educational implications.* San Diego, CA: EDITS/Knapp.

Harrington, D.M., Block, J. H., & Block, J. (1987). Testing aspects of Carl Rogers' theory of creative environments: Child-rearing antecedents of creative potential in young adolescents. *Journal of Personality and Social Psychology, 52*, 851–856.

Kasof, J. (1995). Explaining creativity: The attributional perspective. *Creativity Research Journal, 8*, 311–366.

Kim, K.-H. (2005). Can only intelligent people be creative? A meta-analysis. *Journal of Secondary Education, 16*, 57–66.

Kim, K.-H. (in press). Underachievement and Creativity: Are gifted underachievers highly creative? *Creativity Research Journal.*

Kohlberg, L. (1987). The development of moral judgment and moral action. In L. Kohlberg (Ed.). *Child psychology and childhood education: A cognitive developmental view* (pp. 259–328). New York: Longman.

Maslow, A. (1970). *The farther reaches of human development.* New York: Viking.

McLaren, R. B. (1993). The dark side of creativity. *Creativity Research Journal, 6*, 137–144.

Milgram, R. M. (1990). Creativity: An idea whose time has come and gone? In M. A. Runco, & R. S. Albert (Eds.). *Theories of creativity* (pp. 215–233). Newbury Park, CA: Sage.

Mumford, M. D. et al. (in press). Creativity and ethics: The relationship of creative and ethical problem solving. *Creativity Research Journal.*

Rogers, C. (1970). Toward a theory of creativity. In P. E. Vernon (Ed.). *Creativity* (pp. 137–151). New York: Penguin.

Runco, M. A., and Albert, R. S. (1986). The threshold hypothesis regarding creativity and intelligence: An empirical test with gifted and nongifted children. *Creative Child and Adult Quarterly, 11*, 212–218.

Runco, M. A. (1993). Creativity: Intentional and unconventional. *Creativity Research Journal, 6*, 17–28.

Runco, M. A. (Ed.) (1994). *Creativity and affect.* Norwood, NJ: Ablex.

Runco, M. A. (1995). Insight for creativity, expression for impact. *Creativity Research Journal, 8*, 377–390.

Runco, M. A., and Richards, R. (Eds.) (1998). *Eminent creativity, everyday creativity, and health* (pp. 99–106). Norwood, NJ: Ablex.

Runco, M. A. (in press). Simplifying theories of creativity and revisiting the criterion problem: A comment on Simonton's hierarchical model of domain-specific disposition, development, and achievement. *Perspectives on Psychological Science.*

Sass, L. A., & Schuldberg, D. (2000). Schizophrenia, modernism, and the 'creative imagination': On creativity and psychopathology. *Creativity Research Journal, 13*, 55–75.

Sass, L. A., & Schuldberg, D. (2000–2001). Introduction to the special issue: Creativity and the schizophrenic spectrum. *Creativity Research Journal, 13*, 1–4.

Stein, M. I. (1993). Moral issues facing intermediaries between creators and the public. *Creativity Research Journal, 6*, 200.

Wyszack, J., Runco, M. A., & Smith (in press). Deception and creativity. *Creativity Research Journal.*

Wolpert, S. (2002). *Gandhi's passion.* New York: Oxford University Press.

Chapter 8
Critical Thinking, Creativity, Ethical Reasoning: A Unity of Opposites

Richard Paul and Linda Elder

Abstract In this chapter, we argue for an intimate interrelationship between critical thinking, creative thinking and ethical reasoning. Indeed we argue for an underlying unity between them. We begin by establishing the interdependence of criticality and creativity in the life of the mind. That life is manifest in three basic forms: uncriticality, sophistic criticality, and Socratic criticality. Each of these forms of thought implies an ethically significant pattern, which we illuminate. This leads to the challenge of living an ethical life when humans so routinely confuse ethics with other modes of thinking. Thus, the most common "counterfeits" of ethics are analyzed at length. The chapter concludes with some important implications of the absence of any one of the triad in human thought, given their innate dependence on one another.

Ever since the nineteenth century, and increasingly thereafter, knowledge, reasoning, and insight have become more and more specialized and compartmentalized. The threads that unify them have become obscured. The threads that diversify them are now highlighted. Yet life itself is not compartmentalized. Reality does not offer itself up to us in sealed compartments. The various dimensions of who we are interact and interrelate. So it is with modes of thinking. The critical and creative dimensions of thought interpenetrate and interface with our capacity to reflect ethically. Each of the three is better understood in relation to the other two. Each deepens and develops one another.

If we would understand the creative mind, then we must study the manner in which it is dependent on criticality. If we would understand the critical mind, then we must study the way it is dependent on creativity. If we would understand the highest levels of criticality and creativity, we must study their dependence on

R. Paul (✉)
Foundation for Critical Thinking, P.O. BOX 220, Dillon Beach, CA 94929, USA
e-mail: paul@criticalthinking.org

L. Elder
Foundation for Critical Thinking, P.O. BOX 220, Dillon Beach, CA 94929
e-mail: cct@CriticalThinking.org

D. Ambrose, T. Cross (eds.), *Morality, Ethics, and Gifted Minds*,
DOI: 10.1007/978-0-387-89368-6_8,   117

ethical reflection. Intellectual work is a common denominator of all three: creativity, criticality, and ethical reflection. Intellectual constructs are their shared products (constructs such as novels, editorials, critiques). Intellectual traits are what take them to higher levels of functioning. Let us consider first how to overcome the dichotomy between thought that is fundamentally creative and thought that is fundamentally critical.

Keywords Creative thinking · Creativity · Critical thinking · Ethical reasoning · Ethics · Ethnocentricity · Intellectual dispositions · Intellectual traits · Morality · Sociocentricity · Socratic thinking · Sophistry

8.1   The Interdependence of Criticality and Creativity

The relationship between criticality and creativity is commonly misunderstood. One reason is cultural, resulting largely from the portrayal of creative and critical persons in the media. The creative person is often represented as a cousin to the nutty professor – highly imaginative, spontaneous, emotional, a source of off-beat ideas, but generally out of touch with everyday reality. The critical person, in turn, is wrongly represented as given to faultfinding, as skeptical, negative, captious, severe, and hypercritical; as focused on trivial faults, as either unduly exacting or perversely hard to please; lacking in spontaneity, imagination, and emotion.

These cultural stereotypes are not validated by precise use of the words '*critical*' and '*creative*.' For example, in *Webster's Dictionary of Synonyms*, the term 'critical' is given in the following definition:

> when applied to persons who judge and to their judgments, not only may, but in very precise use does, imply an effort to see a thing clearly and truly so that not only the good in it may be distinguished from the bad and the perfect from the imperfect, but also that it as a whole may be fairly judged and valued.

In *Webster's New World Dictionary*, the term "creative" is given three interrelated meanings: "(1) creating or able to create, (2) having or showing imagination and artistic or intellectual inventiveness (creative writing), and (3) stimulating the imagination and inventive powers."

Accordingly, *critical* and *creative* thought are both achievements of thought. *Creativity* masters a process of making or producing, *criticality* a process of assessing or judging. But there is more. The very definition of the word "creative" implies a critical component (e.g., "having or showing imagination [generativeness] and artistic or intellectual inventiveness [criticality]").

Thus, when engaged in high-quality thought, the mind must simultaneously produce and assess, both generate and judge the products it fabricates. In short, sound thinking requires both imagination and intellectual standards.

Throughout this chapter we elaborate the essential idea that intellectual discipline and rigor are at home with originality and productivity, and also that these supposed poles of thinking (critical and creative thought) are inseparable aspects of excellence of thought. Whether we are dealing with the most mundane intellectual acts of the mind or those of the most imaginative artist or thinker, the creative and the critical are interwoven. It is the nature of the mind to create thoughts, though the quality of that creation varies enormously from person to person, as well as from thought to thought. Achieving quality requires standards for assessing quality – hence, criticality.

To achieve any challenging end, we must have *criteria*: gauges, measures, models, principles, standards, or tests to use in judging whether we are approaching that end. What's more, we must apply these criteria in a way that is discerning, discriminating, exacting, and judicious. We must continually monitor and assess how our thinking is going, whether it is on the right track, whether it is sufficiently clear, accurate, precise, consistent, relevant, deep, or broad for our purposes.

We don't achieve excellence in thinking without an end in view. We design for a reason. We fashion and create knowing what we are trying to fashion and create. We originate and produce with a sense of why we are doing so. Thinking that is random, that roams aimlessly through half-formed images, that meanders without an organizing goal, is neither creative nor critical.

This is true because when the mind thinks aimlessly, its energy and drive are typically low, its tendency is generally inert, its results usually barren. What is aimless is also normally pointless and moves in familiar alliance with indolence and dormancy. But when thinking takes on a challenging task, the mind must come alive, ready itself for intellectual labor, engage the intellect in some form of work upon some intellectual object – until such time as it succeeds in originating, formulating, designing, engendering, creating, or producing what is necessary for the achievement of its goal. Intellectual work is essential to creating intellectual products, and that work, that production, presupposes *intellectual standards* judiciously applied. When this happens, creativity and criticality are interwoven into one seamless fabric.

Like the body, the mind has its own form of *fitness* or excellence. Like the body, that fitness is caused by and reflected in activities performed in accordance with standards (criticality). A fit mind can engage successfully in designing, fashioning, formulating, originating, or producing intellectual products worthy of its challenging ends. To achieve this fitness, the mind must learn to take charge of itself, energize itself, press forward when difficulties emerge, proceed slowly and methodically when meticulousness is necessary, immerse itself in a task, become attentive, reflective, and engrossed, circle back on a train of thought, recheck to ensure that it has been thorough, accurate, exact, and deep. Its *generative power* (creativity) and its *judiciousness* (criticality) can be separated only artificially. In the process of actual thought, they are one.

Such thought is systematic – when being systematic serves its end. It also can cast system aside and ransack its intuitions for a lead – when no clear maneuver, plan, strategy, or tactic comes to mind. And the generative, the productive, the creative mind has standards for what it generates and produces. It is not a mind lacking judiciousness, discernment, and judgment. It is not a mind incapable of acuteness and exactness. It is not a mind whose standards are vagueness, imprecision, inaccuracy, irrelevance, triviality, inconsistency, superficiality, and narrowness. The fit mind generates and produces precisely because it has high standards for itself, because it cares about how and what it creates.

Serious thinking originates in a commitment to grasp some truth, to get to the bottom of something, to make accurate sense of that about which it is thinking. This figuring out cannot simply be a matter of arbitrary creation or production. Specific restraints and requirements must be met, something outside the will to which the will must bend, some unyielding objectivity we must painstakingly take into account. This severe, inflexible, stern reality is exactly what forces intellectual criticality and productivity into one seamless whole. If there were no objective reality bearing down upon us, we would have literally nothing to figure out. If what we figure out can be anything we want it to be, anything we fantasize it as being, there would be no logic to the expression "figure out."

8.2 Three Forms of Criticality: Uncriticality, Sophistic Criticality, and Socratic Criticality

There are three forms of criticality manifested in human thought and action: un-criticality, sophistic criticality, and Socratic criticality (see the distinctions between uncritical persons, skilled manipulators and fair-minded critical persons in Paul and Elder 2006b). The first is intellectually undisciplined and unskilled (the uncritical thinker). The second is intellectually skilled but narrowly self-serving (the clever sophist regularly ignoring the rights and needs of others). The third is skilled and fair-minded (the skilled thinker regularly considering the rights and needs of others).

Historically speaking, the large mass of people is intellectually unskilled (and hence susceptible to domination by the clever and sophistic). The second largest group (those who are sophistic) regularly manipulate the uncritical. The third and smallest group (historically speaking) possesses traits of mind that the first and second lack, especially intellectual humility, intellectual integrity, and intellectual empathy. These traits, considered as an integrated intellectual/ethical complex, enable the Socratically critical person to recognize and do what the sophistically critical person, however cunning and clever, is unable to recognize or do. This should become apparent as we unfold each of the traits. Thus we begin with a brief explication of the term 'intellectual virtues or traits.' This is followed by short summaries of essential intellectual traits ("virtues of the intellect"). These traits, taken together in the human mind, represent the Socratic critical thinker.[1]

8.2.1 Intellectual Virtues or Traits

The traits of mind and character necessary for right action and thinking; the traits of mind and character essential for fair-minded rationality; the traits that distinguish the

---

[1] For deeper understanding of intellectual virtues, see Paul and Elder (2006a).

narrow-minded, self-serving critical thinker from the open-minded, truth-seeking critical thinker. These intellectual traits are interdependent. Each is best developed while developing the others. They cannot be imposed from without; they must be cultivated through encouragement and example. People can come to deeply understand and accept these principles by analyzing their experiences of them: learning from an unfamiliar perspective, discovering you don't know as much as you thought, and so on. They include, but are not limited to, intellectual sense of justice, intellectual perseverance, intellectual integrity, intellectual humility, intellectual empathy, intellectual courage, (intellectual) confidence in reason, and intellectual autonomy.

8.2.1.1 Intellectual Autonomy

Having rational control over one's beliefs, values, and inferences. The ideal of critical thinking is to learn to think for oneself, to gain command over one's thought processes, to see oneself as one is. Intellectual autonomy does not entail willfulness, stubbornness, or rebellion. It entails a commitment to analyzing and evaluating beliefs on the basis of reason and evidence, to question when it is rational to question, to believe when it is rational to believe, and to conform when it is rational to conform.

8.2.1.2 Intellectual Confidence in Reason

Confidence that in the long run one's own higher interests and those of humankind at large will best be served by giving the freest play to reason, by encouraging people to come to their own conclusions through a process of developing their own rational faculties; faith that (with proper encouragement and cultivation) people can learn to think for themselves, form rational viewpoints, draw reasonable conclusions, think coherently and logically, persuade each other by reason, and become reasonable, despite the deep-seated obstacles in the native character of the human mind and in society. Confidence in reason is developed through experiences in which one reasons one's way to insight, solves problems through reason, uses reason to persuade, is persuaded by reason. Confidence in reason is undermined when one is expected to perform tasks without understanding why, to repeat statements without having verified or justified them, to accept beliefs on the sole basis of authority or social pressure.

8.2.1.3 Intellectual Courage

The willingness to face and fairly assess ideas, beliefs, or viewpoints to which we have not given a serious hearing, regardless of our strong negative reactions to them. This courage arises from the recognition that ideas considered dangerous or absurd are sometimes rationally justified (in whole or in part), and that conclusions or beliefs espoused by those around us or inculcated in us are sometimes false or misleading. To determine for ourselves which is which, we must not passively and uncritically "accept" what we have "learned." Intellectual courage comes into play here, because inevitably we will come to see some truth in some ideas considered dangerous and absurd and some distortion or falsity in some ideas strongly held in our social group. It takes courage to be true to our own thinking in such circumstances. Examining cherished beliefs is difficult, and the penalties for non-conformity are often severe.

8.2.1.4 Intellectual Empathy

Understanding the need to imaginatively put oneself in the (intellectual) place of others to genuinely understand them. We must recognize our egocentric tendency to identify truth with our immediate perceptions or longstanding beliefs. Intellectual empathy correlates with the ability to accurately reconstruct the viewpoints and reasoning of others and to reason from premises, assumptions, and ideas other than our own. This trait also requires that we remember occasions when we were wrong, despite an intense conviction that we were right, and consider that we might be similarly deceived in a case at hand.

8.2.1.5 Intellectual Humility

Awareness of the limits of one's knowledge, including sensitivity to circumstances in which one's native egocentrism is likely to function self-deceptively; sensitivity to bias and prejudice in, and limitations of one's viewpoint. Intellectual humility is based on the recognition that no one should claim more than he or she actually knows. It does not imply spinelessness or submissiveness. It implies the lack of intellectual pretentiousness, boastfulness, or conceit, combined with insight into the strengths or weaknesses of the logical foundations of one's beliefs.

8.2.1.6 Intellectual Integrity

Recognition of the need to be true to one's own thinking, to be consistent in the intellectual standards one applies, to hold oneself to the same rigorous standards of evidence and proof to which one holds one's antagonists, to practice what one advocates for others, and to honestly admit discrepancies and inconsistencies in one's own thought and action. This trait develops best in a supportive atmosphere in which people feel secure and free enough to honestly acknowledge their inconsistencies, and can develop and share realistic ways of ameliorating them. It requires honest acknowledgment of the difficulties of achieving greater consistency.

8.2.1.7 Intellectual Perseverance

Willingness and consciousness of the need to pursue intellectual insights and truths despite difficulties, obstacles, and frustrations; firm adherence to rational principles despite irrational opposition of others; a sense of the need to struggle with confusion and unsettled questions over an extended period of time in order to achieve deeper understanding or insight. This trait is undermined when teachers and others continually provide the answers, do students' thinking for them or substitute easy tricks, algorithms, and short cuts that avoid careful, independent thought.

8.2.1.8 Fair-Mindedness

Having an intellectual sense of justice. Willingness and consciousness of the need to entertain all viewpoints sympathetically and to assess them with the same intellectual standards, without reference to one's own feelings or vested interests, or the feelings or vested interests of one's friends, community, or nation; implies adherence to intellectual standards without reference to one's own advantage or the advantage of one's group.

8.3 The Ethical Dimension of Human Thought: Ethical Reflection Intertwined with Creative and Critical Thought

For every human there are ethical considerations implied by the decisions they must make, the people with whom they interact, the context in which they live. In other words, there is an ethical dimension to our lives whether we recognize it or not, whether we take command of it or not.

Humans think ethically to the extent that they act so as to enhance the well-being of others, without harming or diminishing the well being of still others at the same time. We are capable of acting toward others in such a way as to increase or decrease the quality of their lives. We are capable of helping or harming. What is more, we are theoretically capable of understanding when we are doing the one and when the other.

The world we live in is a world of interdependence, of impacting the lives of many other persons and sentient creatures. As the world becomes increasingly more complex and humans become increasingly more interdependent, our ability to reason ethically becomes ever more important. And our ability to reason ethically directly depends on our skills in criticality and creativity. For example, ethical reasoning entails thinking critically about (i.e. taking command of) our native egocentric and sociocentric tendencies. It depends upon our ability to find creative means for dealing with these destructive predispositions. Similarly, to reason ethically depends on our ability to internalize, using skills of critical thought, fundamental ethical concepts and principles. And it depends on our ability to generate (using skills of creativity) reasonable solutions to ethical problems (as we critically apply ethical concepts and principles to such problems).

Though ethics is a rich and multifaceted domain of thought, we can begin to understand its foundations by considering the counterfeits of ethics, with which it is often confused, and from which it must be distinguished.

8.3.1   The Sociocentric Counterfeits of Ethical Reasoning

Skilled ethical thinkers routinely distinguish ethics from other domains of thinking such as those of social conventions (conventional thinking), religion (theological thinking), politics (ideological thinking) and the law (legal thinking). Too often, ethics is confused with these very different modes of thinking. It is not uncommon, for example, for highly variant and conflicting social values and taboos to be treated as if they were universal ethical principles.

Thus, religious ideologies, social "rules," and laws are often mistakenly taken to be inherently ethical in nature. If we were to accept this amalgamation of domains, then by implication every practice within any religious system would necessarily be ethical, every social rule ethically obligatory, and every law ethically justified.

If religion defined ethics, we could not then judge any religious practices – for example, torturing unbelievers or burning them alive – as unethical. In the same way, if ethical and conventional thinking were one and the same, every social practice within any culture would necessarily be ethically obligatory – including social conventions in Nazi Germany. We could not, then, condemn any social traditions, norms, and taboos from an ethical standpoint – however ethically bankrupt they were. What's more, if the law defined ethics, then by implication politicians and lawyers would be considered experts on ethics and every law they finagled to get on the books would take on the status of a moral truth.

It is essential, then, to differentiate ethics from other modes of thinking commonly confused with ethics. We must remain free to critique commonly accepted social conventions, religious practices, political ideas, and laws using ethical concepts not defined by them. No one lacking this ability can become proficient in ethical reasoning.

8.3.1.1   Ethics and Religion

Theological reasoning answers metaphysical questions such as: What is the origin of all things? Is there a God? Is there more than one God? If there is a God, what is his/her nature? Are there ordained divine laws expressed by God to guide our life and behavior? If so, what are these laws? How are they communicated to us? What must we do to live in keeping with the will of the divine?

8.3.1.2 Religious Beliefs Are Culturally Variant

Religious variability derives from the fact that theological beliefs are intrinsically subject to debate. There are an unlimited number of alternative ways for people to conceive and account for the nature of the "spiritual." The Encyclopedia Americana, for example, lists over 300 different religious belief systems. These traditional ways of believing adopted by social groups or cultures often take on the force of habit and custom. They are then handed down from one generation to another. To the individuals in any given group, their particular beliefs seem to them to be the *only* way, or the only *reasonable* way, to conceive of the "divine." They cannot see that their religious beliefs are just one set among many possible religious belief systems. Here are some examples of theological beliefs confused with ethical principles:

- Members of majority religious groups often enforce their beliefs on minorities.
- Members of religious groups often act as if their theological views are self-evidently true, scorning those who hold other views.
- Members of religious groups often fail to recognize that "sin" is a theological concept, not an ethical one. "Sin" is theologically defined.
- Divergent religions define sin in different ways but often expect their views to be enforced on all others as if a matter of universal ethics.

Religious beliefs, when dominant in a human group, tend to shape many, if not all, aspects of a person's life – with rules, requirements, taboos, and rituals. Most of these regulations are ethically neither right nor wrong, but simply represent social preferences and culturally subjective choices.

It is every person's human right to choose his or her own religious orientation, including, if one wishes, that of agnosticism or atheism. That is why there is a provision (Article 18) in the United Nations Declaration of Human Rights (Office of the High Commissioner for Human Rights 1948) concerning the right to change one's religious beliefs: "Everyone has the right to freedom of thought, conscience, and religion; this right includes freedom to change his religion or belief..."

Beliefs about divinity and spirituality are notoriously divergent and should therefore be non-compulsory. There is no definitive way to prove any one set of religious beliefs to the exclusion of all others. For that reason religious freedom is a human right. One can objectively prove that murder and assault are harmful to persons, but not that non-belief in God is.

That ethical judgment must trump religious belief is shown by the undeniable fact that many persons have been tortured and/or murdered by people motivated by religious zeal or conviction. Indeed religious persecution is commonplace in human history (Moore 2000). Humans need recourse to ethics in defending themselves against religious intolerance and persecution.

Consider this example: If a religious group were to believe that the firstborn male of every family must be sacrificed, every person in that group would think themselves ethically obligated to kill their firstborn male. Their religious beliefs would lead them to unethical behavior and lessen their capacity to appreciate the cruel nature of their acts.

Furthermore, a society must be deemed unethical if it accepts among its religious practices any form of slavery, torture, sexism, racism, persecution, murder, assault, fraud, deceit, or intimidation. Remember, atrocities have often been committed during religious warfare. Even to this day, religious persecution and religiously motivated atrocities are commonplace. No religious belief as such can justify violations of basic human rights.

In short, theological beliefs cannot override ethical principles. We must turn to ethical principles to protect ourselves from intolerant and oppressive religious practices.

8.3.1.3 Ethics and Social Conventions

All of us are, in the first instance, socially conditioned. Consequently, we do not begin with the ability to critique social norms and taboos. Unless we learn to critique the social mores and taboos imposed upon us from birth, we will inherently accept those traditions as "right."

Consider the history of the United States. For more than a hundred years most Americans considered slavery to be justified and desirable. It was part of social custom. Moreover, throughout history, many groups of people, including people of various nationalities and skin colors, as well as females, children, and individuals with disabilities, have been victims of discrimination as the result of social convention treated as ethical obligation. Yet, all social practices violating human rights are rejected, and have been rejected, by ethically sensitive, reasonable persons no matter what social conventions support those practices.

8.3.1.4 Socially or Culturally Variant Practices

Cultural diversity derives from the fact that there are an unlimited number of alternative ways for social groups to satisfy their needs and fulfill their desires. Those traditional ways of living within a social group or culture take on the force of habit and custom. They are handed down from one generation to another. To the individuals in a given group they seem to be the *only* way, or the only *reasonable* way, to do things. And these social customs sometimes have ethical implications. Social habits and customs answer questions like this:

- How should marriage take place? Who should be allowed to marry, under what conditions, and with what ritual or ceremony? Once married what role should the male play? What role should the female play? Are multiple marriage partners possible? Is divorce possible? Under what conditions?
- Who should care for the children? What should they teach the children as to proper and improper ways to act? When children do not act as they are expected to act, how should they be treated?
- When should children be accepted as adults? When should they be considered old enough to be married? Who should they be allowed to marry?

- When children develop sensual and sexual desires, how should they be allowed to act? With whom, if anyone, should they be allowed to engage in sexual exploration and discovery? What sexual acts are considered acceptable and wholesome? What sexual acts are considered perverted or sinful?
- How should men and women dress? To what degree should their bodies be exposed in public? How is nudity treated? How are those who violate these codes treated?
- How should food be obtained and how should it be prepared? Who is responsible for obtaining food? Who for preparing it? How should it be served? How eaten?
- How is the society "stratified" (into levels of power)? How is the society controlled? What belief system is used to justify the distribution of scarce goods and services and the way rituals and practices are carried out?
- If the society develops enemies or is threatened from without, how will it deal with those threats? How will it defend itself? How does the society engage in war, or does it?
- What sorts of games, sports, or amusements will be practiced in the society? Who is allowed to engage in them?
- What religions are taught or allowable within the society? Who is allowed to participate in the religious rituals or to interpret divine or spiritual teachings to the group?
- How are grievances settled in the society? Who decides who is right and who wrong? How are violators treated?

Schools traditionally function as apologists for conventional thought; those who teach often inadvertently foster confusion between convention and ethics because they themselves have internalized the conventions of society. Education, properly so called, should foster the intellectual skills that enable students to distinguish between cultural mores and ethical precepts, between social commandments and ethical truths. In each case, when social beliefs and taboos conflict with ethical principles, ethical principles should prevail. The following are examples of confusion between ethics and social conventions:

- Many societies have created taboos against showing various parts of the body and have severely punished those who violated them.
- Many societies have created taboos against giving women the same rights as men.
- Many societies have socially legitimized religious persecution.
- Many societies have socially stigmatized interracial marriages.

These practices seem (wrongly) to be ethically obligatory to those socialized into accepting them.

8.3.1.5 Ethics and Sexual Taboos

Social taboos are often matters of strong emotions. People are often disgusted when others violate a taboo. Their disgust signals to them that the behavior is unethical. They forget that what is socially repugnant to us may not violate any ethical principle but, instead, may merely differ from social convention. Social doctrines regarding human sexuality are often classic examples of conventions expressed as if they were ethical truths. Social groups often establish strong sanctions for unconventional behavior involving the human body. Some social groups inflict unjust punishments on women who do no more than appear in public without being completely veiled, an act considered in some cultures as indecent and sexually provocative. Sexual behaviors should be considered unethical only when they result in unequivocal harm or damage.

8.3.1.6 Ethics and Political Ideology

A political ideology provides an analysis of the present distribution of wealth and power and devises strategies in keeping with that analysis. It provides either a "justification" of the present structure of power or a "critique." It seeks either to protect and maintain the way things are or to change them. It seeks to change things in small ways or in big ways. It compares the present to the past and both to a future it projects.

Conservative ideologies "justify" the status quo or seek a return to a previous "ideal" time. Liberal ideologies critique the status quo and seek to justify "new" forms of political arrangements designed to rectify present problems. Reactionary ideologies plead for a "radical" return to the past; revolutionary ideologies plead for a "radical" overturning of the fundamental ("corrupt") structures. Conservative ideologies consider the highest values to be private property, family, God, and country. Liberal ideologies consider the highest values to be liberty, equality, and social justice (Lakoff 2002).

Ideological analyses have highly significant ethical implications. Put into action they often have profound effects on the well being of people. What is more, the ideologies officially espoused by politicians are often widely different from the personal ends they pursue. Virtually all political ideologies speak in the name of the "people." Yet most of them, in fact, are committed to powerful vested interest groups who fund their election campaigns. The same people often end up ruling, independent of the "official" ideology. Thus, in the post-soviet power structure, many of those who were formerly powerful in the communist party are now among the most prominent and acquisitive neo-capitalists (Meier 2003).

The bottom line is that politicians rarely act for ethical reasons. Struggling against each other for power and control, political movements and interests often sacrifice ethical ideals for practical advantage. They often rationalize unethical acts as unavoidable necessities (for example, "forced on them" by their opponents). And they systematically use propaganda to further vested interest agendas.

8.3.1.7 Ethics and the Law

Anyone interested in developing their ethical reasoning abilities should be able to differentiate ethics and the law. What is illegal may or may not be a matter of ethics.

What is ethically obligatory may be illegal. What is unethical may be legal. There is no essential connection between ethics and the law.

Laws often emerge out of social conventions and taboos. And, because we cannot assume that social conventions are ethical, we cannot assume that human laws are ethical. What is more, most laws are ultimately made by politicians, who routinely confuse social values with ethical principles. As we have said, their primary motivation is, except in special cases, power, vested interest, or expediency. For example, from 1900 through 1930, American politicians, in response to an electorate dominated by fundamentalist religious believers, passed laws that made it illegal for anyone, including doctors, to disseminate any information about birth control. The consequence was predictable: hundreds of thousands of poor and working class women suffered severe injuries or death from the effects of illegal drugs and unsanitary abortions. To "criminalize" behavior that goes against social conventions is one of the time-honored ways for politicians to get re-elected.[2] Here are some examples of confusing ethics and the law:

- Many sexual practices (such as homosexuality) have been unjustly punished with life imprisonment or death (under the laws of one society or another).
- Many societies have enforced unjust laws based on racist views.
- Many societies have enforced laws that discriminated against women.
- Many societies have enforced laws that discriminated against children.
- Many societies have made torture and/or slavery legal.
- Many societies have enforced laws arbitrarily punishing people for using some drugs but not others.

8.4 Acts That Are Unethical in-and-of-Themselves

For any action to be unethical, it must inherently deny another person or creature some inalienable right. The following classes of acts are unethical in-and-of themselves.[3] Any person or group that violates them is properly criticized from an ethical standpoint:

- Slavery: Owning people, whether individually or in groups.
- Genocide: Systematically killing with the attempt to eliminate a whole nation or ethnic group.
- Torture: Inflicting severe pain to force information, get revenge, or serve some other irrational end.
- Sexism: Treating people unequally (and harmfully) in virtue of their gender.
- Racism: Treating people unequally (and harmfully) in virtue of their race or ethnicity.

---

[2] The U.S. now has a higher percentage of its citizens in prison than any other country in the world (recently surpassing Russia) (Human Rights Watch, August 2008)

[3] See the website of Amnesty International for acts that are unethical in themselves: http://www.amnesty.org/

- Murder: The pre-meditated killing of people for revenge, pleasure, or to gain advantage for oneself.
- Assault: Attacking an innocent person with intent to cause grievous bodily harm.
- Rape: Forcing an unwilling person to have intercourse.
- Fraud: Intentional deception that causes someone to give up property or some right.
- Deceit: Representing something as true, which one knows to be false, in order to gain a selfish end harmful to another.
- Intimidation: Forcing people to act against their interests or deter from acting in their interest by threats or violence.
- Imprisoning persons without telling them the charges against them or providing them with a reasonable opportunity to defend themselves.
- Imprisoning persons, or otherwise punishing them, solely for their political or religious views.

8.5 Thinking Beyond the Opposites: Toward a Better and More Humane World

Critical, creative, and ethical thinking working together are intellectually more powerful than any one of these forms in isolation. This is especially obvious if one contemplates the opposites of any of the three combined with the other two. Thus, consider the implications of thought that derive from one of the following combinations.

8.5.1 Creative, Critical but Unethical

The combining of creativity and criticality with thinking that is unethical leads to a misuse of creativity and criticality. Indeed it is a dangerous combination, one that at present creates untold suffering where vested interest is combined with the ability to think critically and creatively about how to serve one's own or one's group's selfish desires without consideration for the rights and needs of relevant others. Consider, for example, highly intelligent and innovative thinkers devising ways of manipulating innocent people into behaving in ways which are not in their own interests.

8.5.2 Critical, Ethical, but Uncreative

The combining of critical and ethical with uncreative thinking suggests thinking that is in itself highly desirable being advocated in unimaginative or possibly boring, dull, or lackluster ways. Consider the many deep ideas, well thought out and ethically desirable, coming aground because they were expressed in un-inspired prose.

8.5.3 Ethical, Creative, but Uncritical

The combining of the ethical with the creative but uncritical suggests the many ways in which important ideas, highly desirable in themselves have been lost to us because they were, for example, unrealistically advocated.

Think of the ideal state of affairs: a world of ethically sensitive people who are not only intellectually imaginative and innovative, but also realistic and practical. Such ethical sensitivity, broadly encouraged and realized, would keep us focused on what is right and just (on that, for example, which protects the rights and fulfills the basic needs of all) while their ability to devise new and original ideas enable us not only to consider the raw possibilities before us, but to do so in such a way as to raise vital questions, gather relevant information, come to well-reasoned conclusions and solutions (testing them against relevant criteria and standards), think open-mindedly within alternative systems of thought, recognizing and assessing as need be their assumptions, implications, and practical consequences; and communicate effectively with others in figuring out solutions to complex problems.

It should be apparent that the three most important dimensions of human thought – the critical, the creative, and the ethical – are not only theoretically compatible – but that working in combination they are each raised to a higher level of functioning. Of course, it is eminently easier to explore theoretical possibilities and implications, and imagine what might or could be, than to create what should be, in the muck and mire of the real world. Nevertheless, if we fail to become clear about the unity that exists (at root) among the most powerful and desirable "opposites," we are likely to continue to set them up in opposition, conceive them in dilemmas we must choose between, rather than grasp them as possibilities we can, and hopefully someday will, think beyond, as we create a better and more humane world.

References

Human Rights Watch (2008). http://www.hrw.org/english/docs/2006/01/18/usdom12292.htm

Lakoff, G. (2002). *Moral politics: How liberals and conservatives think* (2nd ed.). Chicago, IL: University of Chicago Press.

Meier, A. (2003). *Black earth: A journey through Russia after the fall*. New York: W.W. Norton.

Moore, B., Jr. (2000). *Moral purity and persecution in history*. Princeton, NJ: Princeton University Press.

Office of the High Commissioner for Human Rights (1948). United declaration of human rights, http://www.unhchr.ch/udhr/

Paul, R. & Elder, L. (2006a). *Critical thinking: Tools for taking charge of your learning and your life*. Upper Saddle River, NJ: Pearson Prentice-Hall.

Paul, R., & Elder, L. (2006b). *The thinker's guide to fallacies: The art of mental trickery and manipulation*. Dillon Beach, CA: Foundation for Critical Thinking.

Chapter 9
Quantum Creativity in Business

Amit Goswami

Abstract This chapter shows how the quantum principles implicit in creativity, when properly applied, can help businesses not only with innovation but also with the evolutionary global changes that are coming our way. Deeper understanding of science derived from paradoxes revealed by quantum physics, show that consciousness is fundamental to the nature of reality. Implications for creativity and business derive from this understanding. I discuss how the creative process works for business innovations. I elucidate the preferred evolution of capitalism toward a new spiritual, ethical economic system and how businesses must adapt to it.

Keywords Brainstorming · Capitalism · Consciousness · Creativity · Creativity in business · Ethics · Flow · Quantum creativity · Quantum physics · Spiritual economics · Worldview

9.1 Business Within a New Science Framework

Recent developments in science (Goswami 2008) indicate that there is an evolutionary movement of consciousness going on right now. This evolutionary movement demands that our society as a whole must become more ethical, more inclined to put moral values at the center of societal activities. In this chapter I discuss creativity in business from this evolutionary ethical point of view.

The new science emerges from the implications of quantum physics, which present mechanistic scientists with difficult paradoxes not resolvable from within their familiar materialistic paradigms (Goswami 1995, 1996, 1999). Counter to Western-materialistic conceptions of reality, this deeper understanding of science

A. Goswami
Institute of Theoretical Science, 5203 University of Oregon, 453 Willamette Hall, Eugene, OR 97403-5203, USA
e-mail: agoswami@uoregon.edu

D. Ambrose, T. Cross (eds.), *Morality, Ethics, and Gifted Minds*,
DOI: 10.1007/978-0-387-89368-6_9,

reveals that consciousness is the ground of all being. The following tenets are rooted in the understanding that consciousness is fundamental and is not simply an epiphenomenon of material processes:

- The possibilities of consciousness are quantum in nature and are four-fold: material (which we sense); vital energy (which we feel, primarily through the chakras and secondarily through the brain); mental meaning (which we think)); and supramental discriminating contexts such as physical laws, contexts of meaning and feeling such as ethics and love and aesthetics (which we intuit). The material is called gross and the others make up the subtle domain of our experience.
- Conscious choice with real freedom takes place not in our ordinary ego-consciousness but in a unitive cosmic consciousness that we can call quantum consciousness. Traditionalists interpret this consciousness as God.
- When consciousness chooses from the quantum possibilities the actual event of its experience (with physical, vital, mental, and supramental components), the physical has the opportunity of making representations of the subtle. The physical (e.g., the human brain) is analogous to computer hardware; the subtle (e.g., the mind) is analogous to software.
- Our capacity for making physical representation of the subtle evolves. First, the capacity for making representations of the vital evolved through the evolution of life via more and more sophisticated organs to represent the living functions such as maintenance and reproduction. Next the capacity of making more and more sophisticated representations of the mental evolved. This is the stage of evolution we are in right now.
- Our ability to make direct physical representations of the supramental has not evolved yet, but we struggle to make these representations through the intermediary of the mind. Our spiritual life and our pursuit of happiness reflect this struggle.

Two recent trends in business are extremely noteworthy and are in consonance with the evolutionary movement of consciousness. The first is the widespread recognition by a substantial segment of business and industry of the importance of creativity and innovation. The second is the recognition that converting to eco-friendly "green" ideas, even ideas of resource sustainability, may not be detrimental to profit making.

Many businesses begin with creativity, somebody's innovative new idea for a product or a service. And as everybody knows, no innovation is forever as the central motif for running a business. Ideas build on ideas, innovations build on innovations. Completely new ideas arise to cause revolution – paradigm shifts in science and technology and our societies in general – and businesses have to reflect those changes. All of this requires creativity in business in an ongoing basis.

Organizations, and business are no exceptions, require structures and hierarchies, and reliance on past experiences to avoid chaos. This requires a lot of conditioned movements as well on the part of the personnel of a business.

Creativity and conditioning: businesses need both and it is a balancing act, like balancing yang and yin in Chinese medicine. Understanding the nature of creativity and conditioning is essential for doing the right balancing. But it is much more than that as I explain in a later subsection.

Why the importance of eco-friendliness and sustainability? Sadly, environmental pollution by business and industry has been taken for granted as a necessary evil for economic progress and job creation. And businesses have been quite satisfied with the assumption of infinite resources on which currently dominant economic paradigm is based (Daly 2007; Nadeau 2003). What prompted businesses to look for alternatives is the arrival of two undeniable emergencies: global warming (a direct effect of environmental pollution) and scarcity of oil leading to increased production cost for virtually all businesses.

9.2 Creativity and Worldview

How we look at creativity depends on our worldview. If we have an incomplete worldview that guides a business, a worldview that is incapable of explaining all the relevant aspects of creativity and creative innovations, the business will be compromised in carrying out its balancing act.

This is why businesses have to pay attention to the worldview changes that are at play right now, worldview changes that the late philosopher Willis Harman called *global mind change* (Harman 1988).

Currently, the worldview that guides businesses is a post-modern amalgam of scientific materialism, behavioral psychology, and existentialist philosophy. Scientific materialism denotes the idea that all things are material at base, all phenomena are due to movements of matter and matter alone. Behavioral psychology gives the idea that each of us is a product of psychosocial conditioning. This product I will label our ego, although the concept of the ego is not particularly popular with behavioral psychologists. Existential philosophy contributes the notion that existence precedes metaphysical ideas that therefore have to be mistrusted and denigrated – deconstruction is the fashionable word for this denigration.

Quantum physics is forcing us to abandon this worldview. In quantum physics, matter itself is less tangible and consists of possibility. A transcendent agent, a causal force that can act from *outside of all this* but affect things *inside of all this* is needed to convert the possibilities into actual events of manifest experience. Detailed considerations show that the causal agent for this transformation of possibility into actuality is consciousness that is the ground of all being. The causal force that consciousness uses to convert quantum possibilities into actuality is called *downward causation* consisting of choosing from consciousness's own possibilities – everything is consciousness, remember? (Goswami 1993).

The breakthrough in this way of looking at the world is that dualism – the dual existence of mind and matter that raises the unyielding question of how the two interact – is avoided. Similarly, if you want to designate this causal agent of *downward causation* as God, following tradition, you must not think of God separate from the world, which is dualistic thinking. Instead, the world is God. God is immanent in the world and also transcends it.

Once materialism – primacy of matter – is given up in favor of the primacy of consciousness, behaviorism and existential philosophy lose their credibility. If consciousness is the ground of being then obviously essence precedes manifest existence; in fact, essence is needed for manifesting existence.

And if the world consists of possibilities, psychosocial conditioning never can be said to exhaust our being; there are always new possibilities to manifest. There is always scope for creativity.

This worldview change will do business good all over the world. In recent times, the preponderance of the materialist worldview and the resulting deterioration of values in the USA has changed America from a can-do culture to a no-can-do culture in a hurry. This should be an object lesson for everyone.

9.3 Gross and Subtle Possibilities

Materialists have bamboozled us into believing that matter is the only thing although our experience says otherwise. Since our experiences comprise of two radically different varieties, one external and public (and therefore gross), the other internal and private (and therefore subtle), traditionally we always have distinguished between gross and subtle or matter and mind if you will.

In the last century, the psychologist Carl Jung classified our experiences in four categories: sensing, feeling, thinking, and intuiting (paraphrased from Campbell 1971). The gross we sense; the part of the subtle that we feel is called the vital body, the part that we think is the mental, and the part that we intuit is the supramental – the abode of archetypes such as truth, beauty, love, justice, and good. Correspondingly, consciousness carries with it four compartments of possibilities – physical, the manifestations of which we sense; the vital whose manifestations we feel; the mental whose manifestations we think; and supramental whose manifestations we intuit – from which it chooses its experiences. Notice once more that there is no dualism in this reckoning because consciousness nonlocally mediates the interaction between these compartments without the exchange of any signals.

The recognition that we consist of both gross and the subtle raises fascinating new questions for businesses which heretofore have concentrated only on the gross balance sheet. Likewise our economics has to be extended to deal with not only the gross but also with the subtle.

Businesses intuitively know about the importance of the subtle. For example, it is well known that a customer uses a product based not on an objective appraisal of the sensory uses of the product but also based on how he or she feels about it. Similarly, indiscriminate use of the objective game theory mathematics in economics does not always work because business decisions often are colored by people's feelings and intuitive hunches.

The fact is, subtle influences the gross; there is no way around it. Businesses do know about it implicitly. Look at the ads the automobile industry puts out for selling their products. If the considerations behind these ads were pure physical, the ads would talk about physical stuff only: mileage per gallon, durability, maintenance cost. Instead most ads talk about "sexy" stuff: how much speed you can get, how fast the car accelerates, how much pleasure you can get out of it; and sometimes more directly the ads point out the sex appeal of the car.

You must be familiar with the chakras; the new science explains them as the places where physical organs and their vital blueprints are simultaneously brought to manifestation. It is the movement of the vital at these chakra points that we experience as feeling. Movement at the three lower chakras is responsible for our instinctual negative emotions: fear, lust, and egotism. Many businesses, the auto industry is an example, try to sell their products by appealing to the lower chakras.

But the human condition is not limited to the low chakras; there also are the higher chakras starting with the heart where the movement of vital energy gives rise to noble or positive emotions – love, exultation, clarity, and satisfaction.

You can easily see that one can sell a product by appealing to the higher positive emotions also. For example, if a car advertisement says that the car covers 60 miles of distance for a gallon of gasoline, it does not sound sexy, but to an environmentally aware person, it is very satisfying.

It is usually said that in order to get ahead in a company hierarchy, employees must compete with one another. We are constantly reminded, it is a dog-eat-dog world as far as businesses are concerned – negative emotions again. But is that all? When the Japanese ways of running production lines (in which a single worker is responsible for a single finished product) became popular along with the slogan "quality is job one," businesses worldwide recognized the importance of job satisfaction that an employee derives from seeing his or her handiwork in a finished product. There is scope for higher emotion in businesses after all!

9.3.1 Creativity and the Subtle

To the materialist, creativity consists of making a new brain circuit for response to a new environmental stimulus and the reason that some people do it rather than others is their genetic endowment that makes them more survival oriented and competitive. This is a very myopic view. Worldview neutral creativity researchers define creativity as the *discovery of new meaning of value* (Amabile 1990). But the materialist is stuck: matter cannot even process meaning so how can they acknowledge meaning in connection with creativity?

In the consciousness based worldview, we acknowledge from the get go that creativity is an unusual experience of the mind; the brain circuits are made for the representation of the mind's new experiences. Mind is where we engage with meaning. Thus the creative experience consisting of a discovery or invention of new meaning involves the subtle mind. Actually discovery goes higher; it consists of a new look at a supramental archetype that requires a quantum leap – a discontinuous transition – from the mind. And invention consists of finding new meaning in already discovered archetypal contexts of meaning, which entails a quantum leap within the mind. Hence creativity always leads to better physical representations of the archetypes and this has value for us.

When you recognize this, clearly you must realize that creativity in business is more than exploring an innovative product to make more profit. The profit motive does not need to be given up, but it is secondary.

Look at the great innovations that begin new trends in business and industry. From electric bulbs to *postem* stickers, they all contributed to our capacity for meaning processing directly or indirectly – and therein is their value. The material profit is a by-product.

One of the evils of how we run things today is the rise of businesses that deal purely with money and no other business product (Bogle 2005). The above considerations clearly show that this is not a desirable trend. Money has no intrinsic value. Businesses that make money speculating on money have no scope for fundamental creativity and because there is no intrinsic value involved, there is no creativity, even situational innovation, period. What there is is cleverness and greed and catering to the worst of human instincts. So this is one lesson when considering creativity in business: keep yourself away from money-from-money business.

Money has no inherent meaning, but it does represent a promise of power. That people even consider entering a money-based business is a symptom of the overall social deterioration under the aegis of a materialist worldview. Making money on money is indeed a form of gambling. And just like legalized gambling, these businesses need to be controlled, for example, through taxation and regulation.

On the positive side of this lesson, the new science tells us that consciousness is evolving toward making meaning processing accessible to more and more people (Goswami 2008). When your business is tuned to add a meaningful product or service in your society and environment, it is in tune with the evolutionary movement of consciousness. When this happens then your intention (of a successful creative business) is backed up by the entire power of downward causation of nonlocal quantum consciousness, God if you will.

So remember that in terms of consciousness, there is only one purpose for your business whatever the content may be. It is to spread meaning processing to people. When this purposiveness is clearly expressed in your business dealings, they cannot fail.

9.4 Creativity in Business: How to Begin a Creative Business

I said before that businesses begin with a product. This statement is not quite right and needs to be modified. The correct statement is businesses take off when there is a creative product. Actually businesses begin with an conviction-carrying idea that there will be such creative products.

There is a great movie on the American game of baseball called *Field of Dreams* in which there is a great line: "Build it [the field] and they will come." This is true of businesses too. All you need is a faith in possibilities, quantum possibilities of the mind and your ability to harness them.

The co-founders of Apple Computers, Steve Jobs and Steve Wozniak, consulted with lawyers, venture capitalists, about all that it takes to set up a business without knowing exactly what they were setting up. Strangely, this openness of their minds was crucial to the profundity of the actuality they eventually established. In the same vein, Paul Cook, the founder of the Raychem Corporation said, "When we started, we didn't know what we're going to do. We didn't know what products we were going to make" (cited in Ray and Myers 1986, p. 140).

In this aspect creativity in business is no different from all other expressions of creativity, which all begin with questions, not with finished answers. For example, an important question is, Can I contribute to meaning this way, through establishing this business enterprise, meaning for me and for the people who use my product (or service)? Contrary to common sense, creative businesses begin with a seed of an idea – an intuition, a field of possibilities open to the new.

9.4.1 Being in Business

An golden oldie of Hollywood movies, a movie named *Executive Suite*, was based on a theme of a struggle between a conservative type (stay the course, no risk and no creativity) and a visionary (creative change or bust). The adventurer wins the executive suite and the business is able to continue in its dynamic creative way of changing the course as necessary.

Without risk-taking, many businesses die or are cannibalized by non-visionaries who have managed to amass even more power. But to have vision is not enough. To have the field is a good beginning, but one has to engage a process to manifest actualities, actual creative products from the field of possibilities, and only then people come.

To the naïve, business is busy-ness, being in business means being in busy action. Businesspeople are supposed to be always on the run, with do–do–do as their mode of operation. Businesspeople also have the image of needing to be in control all the time; they are not supposed to entertain the new, even in possibility, because of the fear of losing control. These are stereotypes of popular perception and are not universally true. Creative businesspeople are exceptions to all this stereotyping.

Look at it in another way. The bottom line of businesses is to make money, to make a profit. The fear of losing money gives you butterflies in your stomach, haven't you noticed? So the tendency is to analyze your past actions incessantly or to project the future so as not to repeat your mistakes. In other words, being in business seems synonymous with anxiety. Isn't the best way to cope with anxiety to do something? Not doing means inviting thoughts and thoughts beget anxiety. Right?

Not right. One of the great discoveries of the new era is that there is an antidote to the anxious mind – the relaxation response. To learn to relax is a better way to cope with anxiety. To learn to relax is to learn to be – being in your own company without judgment without incessantly creating the past or the future.

This sounds like living Zen and this is true:

Sitting quietly doing nothing.
The spring comes,
And the grass grows by itself.

Somehow the creative businessperson is an expert in living Zen – this being in the moment. Stanford professors Michael Ray and Rochelle Myers (1986) wrote a book, *Creativity in Business,* in which they quote a businessman, Robert Marcus of Alumax, famous in the 1980s for business success, to make the point:

We're an efficient company in terms of people per dollar. Although we're a two-billion-dollar company, we have only eight-four people in headquarters. Which isn't too many. We're doing the same thing, but we are not as big as Alcoa or Alcan. We're about a third of their size, but we have a tenth of the number of people in headquarters. It seems to work pretty well, so we're going to stick with it. ...
I will tell you some of the things we do. We don't have a lot of meetings. We don't write a lot of reports. We make quick decisions. You know, if it takes you a long time to make decisions, if you have a lot of meetings and write a lot of reports, you need a lot of people. We communicate very rapidly. We do it all by word of mouth. I don't write letters. I don't write reports. In fact, I don't know what I do. ... We play squash often. ...
I don't let time I allocate to some big parts of my life interfere with each other. I confine my business time, which is pretty much nine to five. ... I go out to play [squash] three times a week. And I don't feel really pressed by business. (pp. 144–145)

This (creative) businessman has learned to relax; he has developed a kind of equanimity about time. He has learned to complement the conventional do–do–do of the business mind by a be–be–be attitude. And this is the secret of his creativity in his craft.

So maybe being in business does not mean being busy all the time; instead it means how to be busy as needed and relax at other times, how to combine in tandem busy doing with relaxed being.

Another way of putting this was beautifully expressed by Rochelle Myers (in Ray and Myers 1986, p. 113) who suggested complementing living the adage "Don't just stand there, do something," with living the additional adage, "Don't just do something, stand there."

9.4.2 The Creative Process in Business: Do–Be–Do–Be–Do

So we come back to the creative process that creativity researchers have discovered for quite some time. It consists of four stages (adapted from Wallas 1926):

1. Preparation
2. Unconscious processing
3. Sudden insight
4. Manifestation

Preparation is doing: learning the ropes, learning what is already known, how others do this business. Preparation in business also is about finding venture capital, finding proper help to work out details and all that. Preparation also is about surrendering the judging anxious mind giving way to a curious don't-know open mind. Unconscious processing happens in relaxed being; we are not aware that we are processing our business questions, but processing is going on anyway in the state of unconscious, a state in which consciousness is not separate from its possibilities.

Why unconscious processing? Objects, thoughts even business thoughts, are possibilities of consciousness. When we are not collapsing them into actuality, possibilities spread as waves do. This is why technically we say, objects are waves of possibilities. If there is a proliferation of possibilities, there is more probability that they will encompass something new, something novel that contains the solution. Then insight can follow.

The process is not linear – a lot of preparation followed by a lot of unconscious processing. Instead, what is needed is an alternation of doing and being; like that Frank Sinatra line, do–be–do–be–do. Then insight.

To quote Robert Marcus again, "Always make sure you do the important things and do them well. And allow enough time for them" (cited in Ray and Myers 1986, p. 145). This is the trick, allowing enough time for a job allows do–be–do–be–do and enables creativity.

The insight is a quantum leap, a discontinuous transition in thought that comes with a surprise and a certainty. Once you have known that the creative process that includes being relaxed about your business actually produces certainties in your decisions, it becomes easier to trust relaxation, to trust the process that must include non-doing. So you can be relaxed about manifesting the insight.

9.4.3 The Joy of Flow

The big insights give businesses their big breakthrough products: big start up ideas like the internal combustion automobile or more recently, the search engine called google. For an established business, though, it is the little ideas, the little quantum leaps of everyday business activities that keep the business and the business people going smoothly, easy without effort. Again the do–be–do–be–do lifestyle of the businessperson is crucial.

When do–be–do–be–do is incorporated in the businessperson's modus operandi, a time comes when the gap between doing and being becomes so little that the shift is hardly noticeable. And if the being comes with a sense of surrender in which the doer refuses to resolve the usual conflicts of work problems with mere logical step-by-step thinking, when the business person truly hears the motto: the small business's three worst enemies...thinking too big...thinking too small...thinking too much, something special happens. The sense of the doer disappears and the doing happens by itself.

This easy without effort way of (creative) action is called the flow experience in creativity literature (Csikzentmihayi 1990). When one achieves this way of doing business, business itself becomes pleasure. Listen to Paul Cook:

> I am having the time of my life. I wouldn't change it for anything. I'm doing what I have always wanted to do, and it's every bit as exciting as I thought it was going to be when I wanted to do it. It is a thrilling experience, doing new things and leading the new technology to create new products for society. I couldn't want anything more. (cited in Ray and Myers 1986, p. 113)

9.4.4 Collective Creativity: Brainstorming

So far we have only spoken of individual creativity, which certainly is a cornerstone of businesses. However, businesses are special enterprises in the sense that in a business often an entire group works together toward a creative product. How does one apply do–be–do–be–do for collective creativity? One way is brainstorming, but not how it is conventionally practiced.

In conventional brainstorming, people sit around a table and they share their thinking about the problem at hand. The instruction is: no comment is dumb enough not to be shared. And everybody is instructed to listen without passing an instant judgment on a comment. The idea is that the power of divergent thinking believed to be an essential ingredient of individual creativity will prevail ever more strongly in brainstorming and lead the group to solution.

From the quantum creativity point of view, however, divergent thinking in actuality is only more ideas from the known. We never can reach the unknown that way. What is needed is divergence of meaning processing in our unconscious – new possibilities have to be entertained in our unconscious. In other words, what we need is not divergent thinking but divergent meaning processing in the unconscious.

This can be achieved in brainstorming easily by engaging the art of listening not only without expressed judgment but also with real internal silence. One should express of course and share; but all expressions, including those that create conflict must emerge from silence, not from the busy mind but from being itself. And the participants must not try to resolve conflicts, but allow conflicts to be processed in the unconscious. Conflicts are important because they enlarge the space of possibilities for unconscious processing.

9.5 Changing Current Big Business Practices: Spiritual Economics

Whereas in small businesses and start-ups creativity thrives, the story is quite different for big business corporations. For such enterprises, spreading meaning processing in the world is no longer the objective of business; the naked objective is to amass power. Today some multinational corporations have amassed more power than many nation states (Wolin 2008).

How did it get this way? To make a long story short, partly because of the oil crisis, partly because of the misuse of Keynesian economics, a situation called stagflation was created in the early 1980s due to which both decreasing business activity (consequently rising unemployment) and rapid inflation took place. Monitory economists found a solution called supply side economics that has been with us ever since.

Keynesian economics works on the demand side trying to increase employment via government spending, thereby creating demand that eventually increases business productivity and the economy gets moving again. With stagflation, this solution is dubious since it would certainly fuel inflation even further. Hence neoclassical supply side economics solves the problem by increasing money supply without creating demand. For example, supply siders cut taxes for the rich putting money in the pockets of rich people who will then invest and the investment will trickle down to ordinary people eventually. Of course, somebody has to bear the burden of tax cuts and of course the government does by running up high deficit financing by borrowing money.

Some economists claim that this supply-side economics has been able to solve the huge boom and bust cycles that used to plague free market capitalism. Now recessions are relatively soft and inflation is kept under control by government regulation of the money supply.

The downside is that like free-market capitalism, this system also is unstable. There is a limit to how far we can go with deficit financing without producing instability. So the instability of free-market capitalism (boom–bust cycle) is just replaced by a different kind of instability that is created by deficit financing, perhaps an even more disastrous instability. This has been emphasized by the economist Ravi Batra (1985). Also the limits of natural resources and the problem of increased environmental pollution for a consumer economy create further instability (Daly 2007; Nadeau 2003).

Furthermore, one direct consequence of supply side, free-market economics is that the rich get richer and the poor get poorer creating a huge gap and potential political instability (Wolin 2008). And finally, the middle class shrinks in size reducing meaning processing and creativity of the society as a whole – an altogether anti-evolutionary dynamic.

Multinationals and the growth of corporate power were a direct product of this change in economic policy. The rich did not invest in supplying venture capital and creating new small businesses that foster creativity. Instead, the rich saw an opportunity in amassing power through investing in already big corporations allowing them to become multinationals to reduce taxes and labor outlays even further. Multinationals can outsource to countries of developing economies with small labor costs and relaxed labor ethics and practices, never mind the job shrinkage in their home countries of well-developed economies. Much of the money of the rich also was used in speculative financial gambling.

Multinationals and big corporations are fundamentally not into meaning processing; they have replaced the search for meaning by instinctual greed and the resultant search for power. In multinationals, employment outsourcing guarantees that the middle-class labor of mature economies in developed nations is replaced by much more economically deprived workforces in economically developing countries. In this way jobs that were meaningful for one culture are rendered relatively meaningless for another culture. When meaning is not there, the question of creativity is moot. Labor that engages in outsourced production gets some material survival benefit, but that is practically all. They hardly get any enrichment of their lives in the subtle dimension.

Can gifted, creative people bring creativity back even in the operation of big corporations and multinationals? Can they solve the instability problem of boom–bust cycles without the supply-side deficit financing?

They can. A fundamental incompleteness of capitalism that was developed under the aegis of the philosophy of modernism in the eighteenth century, as a replacement for feudal and mercantile economics, is that it confined itself only to the material balance sheet of business enterprises and people who consume business products. But businesses are not only those that produce a material product; enterprises that produce subtle products – meaning, beauty, love, truth – they, too are easily can be seen as businesses. Examples are spiritual enterprises (like religions) and humanistic (like universities) and artistic enterprises (such as museums). In all these institutions, no doubt accounting is done differently, no doubt there is no material profit, but there also is no doubt that these differences are only superficial.

In truth, these "business" enterprises that are primarily dealers of the subtle, do often come with a material counterpart for their products whose value, however, cannot be based on material value alone. Similarly, business enterprises that deal with seemingly pure material products ultimately have subtle components as well, a point already made. Thus a more inclusive economics that treats the gross and the subtle on equal footing is needed. Such an economics is being developed (Goswami 2005) and the good news is that the problem of boom–bust cycles is solved without introducing the evils of supply-side economics.

The basic idea of such an economics is simply to include both the gross and the subtle in a business' balance sheet, be it predominantly material or predominantly subtle. The conventional wisdom is that subtle stuff cannot be measured, but this is not true any more (Goswami 2005). When we do extend the business balance sheet then a simple solution to the boom–bust cycle is to make up business and employment slack in the material sector through increased investment in the subtle that does not produce inflation because the subtle, being unlimited in resource (for example, there is no limit to love!), is not subject to the zero-sum game.

9.5.1 Creativity in Big Businesses Under Spiritual Economics

Now the big question, How can creativity be restored in big businesses that convert to spiritual economics? The answer is crucial.

Converting to spiritual economics implies that there is a shift in emphasis in how a business is run. A business is no longer an organization with one bottom line – material profit. Now it can be explicitly recognized that:

1. A positive showing in the production of subtle products also has value.
2. Labor can be paid not only in terms of gross material remuneration but also in terms of the subtle, for example by the gift of more leisure time, meditation breaks during work hours, and so forth.
3. With labor expenses thus under control, outsourcing can be considerably reduced and meaningful employment can be restored in economically advanced countries.
4. This restores meaning processing in people's life once again in economically advanced countries opening them to creativity.
5. Big corporations can take further advantage of its creative labor force by including the labor force in quality production, in research and in other creative activities as much as practicable.

When big businesses become producers of positive subtle energies through increased employee job-satisfaction, the whole society gets a creativity boost.

One can ask: Will this development not affect the developing countries adversely? Not necessarily. Don't forget that developing countries also need to convert to spiritual economics right away. Furthermore, developing countries need capital and market share for their exports. So long as attention is given to these aspects, developing economies are better off if freed from the relatively meaningless labor that outsourcing provides.

9.5.2 Creativity with Love: Eco-friendliness in Businesses

I have mentioned that many businesses are now aware that "green" business policies do not necessarily lead to "red" bottom lines of loss in profits. When gifted people in businesses adopt spiritual economics, green business policies follow automatically.

One great plus of spiritual economics over conventional free-market capitalism is that one no longer has to depend on consumerism to drive the economy. This means that the depletion of nonrenewable resources is much reduced. This also can reduce environmental pollution and mitigate global warming.

Spiritual economics allows our societies a less hurried lifestyle that is highly conducive to creativity. With eco-friendliness, the creativity is ever more enhanced because it is accompanied with love for the environment. With creativity and love providing an unprecedented quality of life, people's dependence on material pleasure as a substitute for happiness (in which way suffering in the subtle dimension of life is pushed under the rug so to speak) is lessened. In this way, a day may come when we will no longer need the high material standards of living. We may even hope that the reduced material standards will be provided by the renewable sources of energy (such as solar) at our disposal.

The possibilities are unlimited. In this map of our future, to achieve the creative end we envision, we also must use creativity as the means. Much creativity in the practice of businesses will be necessary to implement the paradigm shift in economics that is emerging.

References

Amabile, T. (1990). Within you, without you: The social psychology of creativity and beyond. In M. A. Runco & R. S. Albert (Eds.), *Theories of creativity* (pp. 116–134). Newbury Park, CA: Sage.

Batra, R. (1985). *The Great Depression* of 1990. New York: Simon & Schuster.

Campbell, J. (Ed.). (1971). *The portable Jung.* New York: Viking.

Csikzentmihayi, M. (1990). Flow: *The psychology of optimal experience.* New York: Harper Collins.

Daly, H. (2007). *Ecological economics and sustainable development: Selected essays of Herman Daly.* Cheltenham, UK: Edward Elgar.

Goswami, A. (1993). *The self-aware universe.* New York: Tarcher.

Goswami, A. (1995). Monistic idealism may provide better ontology for cognitive science: A reply to Dyer. *The Journal of Mind and Behavior,* 16, 135–150.

Goswami, A. (1996). Creativity and the quantum: A unified theory of creativity. *Creativity Research Journal,* 9(1), 47–61.

Goswami, A. (1999). Quantum theory of creativity. In M. A. Runco & S. R. Pritzker (Eds.), *Encyclopedia of creativity* (Vol. 2, pp. 491–500). New York: Academic.

Goswami, A. (2005). Toward a spiritual economics. *Transformation* (Vol. 19, issues 2, 3, and 4). Ojai, CA: World Business Academy.

Goswami, A. (2008). *Creative evolution.* Wheaton, IL: Theosophical Publishing House.

Harman, W. (1988). *Global mind change.* Indianapolis, IN: Knowledge Systems.

Nadeau, R. L. (2003). *The wealth of nature: How mainstream economics has failed the environment.* New York: Columbia University Press.

Ray, M., & Myers, R. (1986). Creativity in business. New York: Doubleday.

Wallas, G. (1926). *The art of thought.* New York: Harcourt, Brace & World.

Wolin, S. S. (2008). *Democracy incorporated: Managed democracy and the specter of inverted totalitarianism.* Princeton, NJ: Princeton University Press.

Chapter 10
What Cognitive Science Brings to Ethics

Mark Johnson

Abstract Empirical research on the nature of mind, thought, and language has profound implications for our understanding of morality. From a critical perspective, this research constrains the range of acceptable theories by showing that our abstract moral concepts are grounded in our bodily experience, are defined relative to prototypes, are structured by metaphor, and are tied to emotions. The new view of moral deliberation that emerges from this conception of embodied mind reveals important similarities between moral reasoning and what has traditionally been thought of as aesthetic judgment. Moral reasoning is an imaginative process of problem solving.

Keywords Cognitive science · Dewey, John · Emotion · Imagination · Metaphor · Moral concepts · Moral reasoning · Prototypes

The most exciting development in moral theory over the past 3 decades has been the application of recent empirical research on the nature of mind, thought, and language to deep questions about moral experience, deliberation, and justification. This interdisciplinary dialogue between science and ethics challenges the key assumption that the sciences are merely descriptive and explanatory and cannot have any normative weight in moral deliberation. Fortunately, the importance for moral theory of research on human emotions, conceptualization, reasoning, and judgment is coming to be appreciated in many circles.

The contributions from the cognitive sciences take two major forms, one negative and critical, the other more positive and constructive. The critical dimension argues that no theory of morality can be adequate if it is incompatible with our most reliable and tested scientific understanding of how the mind works. For example, if a moral system presupposes mistaken views about the role of emotions in human valuation, if it assumes empirically incorrect notions of moral categories or principles, or if it

M. Johnson
Knight Professor of Liberal Arts and Sciences, Department of Philosophy, 1295 University
of Oregon, Eugene, OR 97403-1295, USA
e-mail: markj@uoregon.edu

D. Ambrose, T. Cross (eds.), *Morality, Ethics, and Gifted Minds,*
DOI: 10.1007/978-0-387-89368-6_10,

is built on a view of reason that is empirically suspect, then we have good reasons for thinking that such a theory cannot be fully satisfactory (Flanagan 1991). On the more constructive side, the cognitive sciences can give insight into what human, and even more-than-human, well-being consists in and how it can be enhanced. It can also provide us with methods of inquiry appropriate for the resolution of morally-problematic situations. Let us consider very briefly both the critical and constructive sides of this project of naturalized ethics.

The most important contribution on the critical side has centered on the nature of concepts and reasoning. For example, any theory that defines morality as a system of rules or principles, binding on all humans and derivable from a universal human reason, must be profoundly inadequate, for several reasons.

First, consider the conception of moral concepts required by such a theory. If a moral rule is going to prescribe a definitive action for a given situation, then its key concepts must map directly onto certain aspects of our world. To cite just one example, if there is a moral rule forbidding the killing of a materially innocent person, then the concepts "killing", "materially", "innocent", and "person" must be applicable to experience in a highly determinate fashion. Moral Law theories of this sort have thus assumed that concepts can be defined by sets of necessary and sufficient conditions and can be applied in an all-or-nothing fashion – as in the idea that something is a person, or it is not, period.

However, extensive empirical work in psychology, linguistics, and philosophy has provided a very different view of the structure and function of human concepts. To begin with, very few of our concepts actually fit this classical view of category structure as defined by a discrete list of essential features. Instead, categories tend to exhibit prototypicality effects. There are central members, which typically instantiate some specific cognitive model, but then there are other less prototypical category members that do not share all of the defining features for the idealized cognitive models of the prototypes. Take the concept *person*. At a certain point in American history, the prototypical person was an adult, white, Christian, heterosexual male. African-Americans, women, children, Jews, and homosexuals were not granted the respect required toward anyone possessing moral personhood. Today, in many cultures, our category of moral personhood has been reconfigured around a new set of prototypical members that would include most of those individuals previously regarded as marginal, or even outside the category (as in the case of slaves in nineteenth century America). So, our moral concepts have complex internal structure and get applied relative to how a particular thing stands in relation to the prototypical members and to other less prototypical members. Moreover, prototypes are already established relative to our values, interests, and purposes, so they are contextually dependent.

Not only is there complex internal structure to our key moral categories, even more, there is often no monolithic set of defining features shared by all members of the category. This means that, even if there were universal moral principles, their application to cases would require non-formalizable judgments about where a certain individual falls within the internal structure of the category, and how that placement bears on our moral evaluations.

A second major problem with the classical theory of categories is its assumption that our moral concepts could be strictly literal and capable of a simple, direct application to a situation. There is now a substantial and growing body of empirical study of moral concepts, including cross-cultural comparisons, that reveals their metaphorical nature. Johnson (1993) shows how large parts of our Western moral traditions are understood via systematic conceptual metaphors. To cite just one example, there is a pervasive *MORAL ACCOUNTING* metaphor in which deeds are conceptualized metaphorically as valuable objects, well-being is understood metaphorically as wealth (accumulation of valuable states of being), moral transactions are regarded as economic exchanges, moral credit is accumulated by increasing the well-being of others, and moral assessment is a type of moral accounting (i.e., adding up one's moral credit and moral debits). Thus we say, "I couldn't possibly *repay* your kindness," "I *owe* you everything for what you've done for me," "She *earned* considerable *credit* through all her selfless acts," "His despicable actions *cost* him their respect," and "That scoundrel *owes a debt* to society for the crimes he committed." These are not just colloquial expressions of common morality. This and other key systematic metaphors have been the bases for philosophically sophisticated moral theories. To cite just one instance, classical utilitarianism is a systematic elaboration of Moral Accounting, in which that act is considered right or best which *maximizes* the greatest *quantity* of well-being. Jeremy Bentham (1789/1948) even took Moral Accounting so far as to propose a form of moral calculus for calculating which possible actions would generate the greatest moral value.

The non-classical, prototype-oriented, and metaphorical character of most of our ethical concepts makes cognitively implausible any ethical view founded on a literalist Moral Law theory of moral governance. This founding of moral systems on conceptual metaphors is not just a product of Western philosophical thinking. It appears to be cross-cultural, as, for example, in Edward Slingerland's (2003) analysis of the systematic metaphors underlying classic Chinese conceptions of morality.

Another important area of research concerns the role of emotions in moral thinking. Certain traditional views, perhaps most famously Kant's aprioristic moral framework, claimed that moral laws issue directly from an alleged pure practical reason, having nothing to do with emotions. According to Antonio Damasio's work showing the central role of emotion in various types of practical judgments, pure reason views of this sort fly in the face of the facts about human cognition. Damasio (1994) gives neuroscientific evidence of the necessity of a fully functioning emotional system for the performance of certain forms of practical reasoning in complex social and moral situations. Indeed, without emotions, any rational deliberations are ungrounded and even inappropriate, leaving reason wholly impotent. The whole idea of a Kantian "pure practical reason" is highly suspect, in light of what we are learning about how our rational processes appropriate sensory-motor parts of our brains (Gallese and Lakoff 2005).

The contribution of science to ethics is not limited only to these kinds of critical constraints on the range of possible moral theories. There is, in addition, a constructive side, and it requires a fairly radical rethinking of some of our most cherished notions about morality. The naturalistic perspective that emerges from cognitive science research locates moral deliberation in the context of an ongoing flow of organism/environment interactions or transactions. It was John Dewey who articulated this new experientialist view with his key insight that moral values are not brought to experience from beyond experience, in acts of a priori evaluation and judgment. On the contrary, Dewey (1922) argued, our principles, values, and possibilities for the resolution of morally problematic situations arise within those very situations themselves and make it possible for us to transform our current problematic state into a better one. There are no absolute, context-independent, eternal moral values or principles for such reflective transformation. Dewey's great idea was that ethical inquiry is a form of engaged problem solving, the adequacy of which has to be tested out in our ongoing experience. Ethical thinking is a form of imaginative dramatic rehearsal – a trying out of various possible directions our developing experience might take were we to make certain decisions, recognize certain values, and cultivate certain virtues. Moral reasoning of this sort is situated (historically, culturally, and personally), shaped by emotions, and reconstructive of our ongoing experience.

The radical part of Dewey's view is that moral reasoning is a type of embedded ethical problem solving that can only be critically evaluated by how well a certain course of action eventually leads to growth of meaning, to constructive cooperative action, and to the opening up of broader, more sensitive, and more comprehensive perspectives. On this view, ethical reasoning is not some allegedly formal procedure, and certainly not a form of mathematical computation. Neither is it a mere affirmation of personal preference. In its emphasis on qualitative judgment, Dewey's view is more like what we experience in artistic creativity and aesthetic judgment, than it is anything like rule following, mathematical calculation, or subjective fantasy. The goal of moral reasoning is to make experience richer, more varied, more harmonious, and more liberating. The application of cognitive science to aesthetic experience is thus more likely to help us understand what good moral thinking involves than is any articulation of moral rules or allegedly eternal conceptions of the good.

References

Bentham, J. (1948). *An introduction to the principles of morals and legislation.* New York: Hafner. (Original work published 1789).

Damasio, A. (1994). *Descartes' error: Emotion, reason, and the human brain.* New York: G.P. Putnam's Sons.

Dewey, J. (1922/1988). *Human nature and conduct.* In *The Middle Works of John Dewey, Vol. 14.* Jo Ann Boydston (ed.). Carbondale, IL: Southern Illinois University Press.

Flanagan, O. (1991). *Varieties of moral personality: Ethics and psychological realism.* Cambridge, MA: Harvard University Press.

Gallese, V., & Lakoff, G. (2005). The brain's concepts: The role of the sensory-motor system in conceptual knowledge. *Cognitive Neuropsychology, 22,* 455–479.

Johnson, M. (1993). *Moral imagination: Implications of cognitive science for ethics.* Chicago, IL: University of Chicago Press.

Slingerland, E. (2003). *Effortless action: Wu-Wei as conceptual metaphor and spiritual ideal in early China.* New York: Oxford University Press.

Chapter 11
Constructing Selves* Meir Dan-Cohen

Meir Dan-Cohen

Abstract A number of influential schools of thought converge on the view that human beings are self-creating: through our actions and practices, individual and collective, we define our identities and draw our boundaries. On this view, morality and law play a role in determining not only what we do but also who we are. Consequently, in devising behavior-guiding norms we must ask: what subjects will emerge from the practices and activities generated by a particular set of norms? And what considerations bear on the construction of selves through our normative engagements?

Keywords Autonomy · Dignity · Identity · Norms, personalized · Responsibility · Roles distant· Roles impersonal · Roles personal · Roles proximate · Roles role-distance · Self boundaries of · Self constructive view of · Self impersonal · Self-constitution · Social construction

The ambiguity of the title is intended. The title depicts the self as the product of construction while also referring to it as the one doing the construction. By this I mean to capture one of the most salient philosophical themes of the recent past. This theme is best seen against the backdrop of philosophy's age-long preoccupation with the nature of the human subject. Writers on this topic have over the years greatly disagreed about the most adequate description of the self and about its most important or essential characteristics. But this very disagreement testifies to a deeper agreement that some such description and characteristics exist and provide a necessary foundation or backdrop for morality, and by extension, for law and politics. The theme to which I have alluded consists in a large body of thought that questions this traditional approach. The view that "man has no essence" and must create his

M. Dan-Cohen
Milo Reese Robbins Professor of Law, 786 Simon Hall, University of California, Berkeley, Berkeley, CA 94720-7200, USA
e-mail: mdancohen@law.berkeley.edu

*This essay provides an overview of some themes pursued in greater detail in Dan-Cohen (2002).

D. Ambrose, T. Cross (eds.), *Morality, Ethics, and Gifted Minds*,
DOI: 10.1007/978-0-387-89368-6_11,
© Springer Science+Business Media LLC 2009

own, though originating at least as far back as the fifteenth century (see Pico della Mirandola 1956), was given new impetus and significance in the twentieth. The insight that the meanings we create, create us undergirds some of the most influential and otherwise diverse schools of thought, such as existentialism, postmodernism, and communitarianism. We can distinguish in this large body of thought two broad conceptions regarding the ways human beings define who they are, *self-constitution* and *social construction*. Though both share the view that as human beings we create ourselves, the former interprets the *we* distributively – each individual is the author of her own identity; whereas the latter interprets it jointly – social practices, discursive and otherwise, shape our selves. In either way, but most likely through some combination of both, the human subject is formed or constituted in the course of her life by actual engagements and experiences.

On this *constructive view*, the self is the largely unintended by-product of individual actions and collective practices, including those of law and morality, whose primary orientation is not the creation of a self but the accomplishment of some individual or collective goals. When we pursue our goals and promote our projects, individual or collective, we inescapably do another thing as well: we determine the composition of the self and draw its boundaries. The constructive view thus complicates and expands our normative agenda. Absent a stable, antecedently given human subject, subject and norms are now seen to be engaged in a dynamic and dialectic relationship in which neither side provides a starting point or a resting place relative to the other. The recognition that we are the products as well as the authors of our practices and norms confronts us with a double challenge: not just what to do, but also what to be. And so in devising our behavior-guiding norms we must glimpse their effects on who we are as well: what subjects will emerge from a system of activity generated by a particular set of norms?

In contemplating this second set of issues, a particular cluster of norms (by which I mean values, evaluative attitudes, practices, and the like) assumes center stage. I call them *personalized*, since they take individual human beings as their objects and so depend for their content and application on the composition of the self. Responsibility, autonomy, and dignity are prominent examples. To be responsible is, at least primarily, to be answerable for oneself; to be autonomous is to govern oneself; to have dignity is to be the locus of moral value and so to demand and attract respect toward oneself. So what precisely we're responsible for, how far our autonomy extends, and what merits respect, all crucially depend on what we take the self to be. Now since the personalized norms track the boundaries of the self, on the traditional view their scope can be determined by studying those boundaries. The constructive view denies this option. Since the personalized norms participate in constituting the self, the boundary they track is in part their own creation. To be sure, specific ascriptions of responsibility or affirmations of autonomy or expressions of respect are supported by a pre-existing vision of the subject: she did it, we say, or it's her own life, or her body. But when we probe such statements, philosophically or in cases in which they prove particularly contentious, it turns out that they rest at bottom on the sedimentation of myriads of similar statements in the past. If we wish to go beyond precedent or are forced to do so, what can we appeal to? What considerations can guide us if we confront the constructive enterprise head-on?

It is natural to approach this matter in the same way in which we treat the more familiar questions concerning how to act. Just as we choose what to do in light of what best suits our values and serves our interests, so supposedly we can also choose what to be in those terms. But a moment's reflection reveals the fallacy. When action is concerned, some values and interests are foundational since they are implicitly taken to provide the incontrovertible, rock bottom answer to the question of who we are. However the question what to be comes up precisely when we realize that the supposedly incontrovertible can be controverted and that the rock is made of sand. We cannot derive norms of construction from our values and interests, since the "our" is at this stage up for grabs.

An alternative, however, exists. Building codes in general consist in part in imperatives that express the very idea of construction, of creating any structure, rather than those that pertain to the construction of a particular one. A building code for the construction of selves is no different; it too includes some such purely *formal* criteria, the imperatives of having an identity at all, imperatives oriented toward what it is for a self to exist. Two sets of such imperatives can be briefly indicated. The first concerns the relationship among personalized norms. The thought that these norms all track the boundaries of the self does not by itself tell us where these boundaries ought to lie. It does nonetheless help draw them by introducing an important constraint. Seen as tracking the boundary of one and the same entity, personalized norms must be co-extensive, they must have the same scope. To see the significance of this point, consider our attitude toward responsibility. Responsibility often carries with it burdens and so we are tempted to evade it. One way to do so is by enacting a more minimal, narrowly circumscribed self. For example, when we learn that the law applies some of its most draconian measures to what we take to be the operations of will, we may respond by contracting the will's domain and instead describe various types of actions in a deterministic vocabulary designed to place them at the periphery of the self or even completely outside its boundaries. Awareness of the co-extensiveness of the personalized norms, however, alerts us to the risk inherent in this maneuver. Evacuating regions of the self in order to escape the burdens of responsibility has as corollary the contraction of the scope of our autonomy and dignity as well. The opposite is also true. People may incline to stake out claims to expansive autonomy and to wide-ranging grounds of respect. But here too, they must recognize the potentially undesirable constructive implications: since these claims involve expanding the self, they entail the assumption of greater responsibility as well.

In order to introduce the second set of structural imperatives, let me focus on a specific variant of the constructive view. This variant uses a dramaturgical imagery, according to which the self consists, at least in part, of the social roles that it enacts. To form a self, the roles must be integrated: they must form a dovetailing, interrelated, and interacting arrangement that we can imagine as possessing a certain 'density' or as forming a 'core'. But people can also occupy roles that are too tenuously connected to the elements forming that core to count as parts of the self. Such possibility, as well as the underlying spatial imagery, are implicit in the sociological notion of *role distance*, which denotes the possibility of enacting a social role without identifying with it and so without fully integrating it into the self (Goffman (1961a, b).[1] Though identification and detachment are not fixed properties of roles, a certain degree of uniformity in the style of enacting different roles exists: certain roles are more likely to be enacted at a distance than other roles. So we can roughly distinguish between *personal* or *proximate* roles and *impersonal* or *distant* ones.

Obviously, the choice between proximate and distant roles, or between a personal or impersonal style in enacting a role, has a crucial bearing on the topography of the self, with normative implications on such matters as responsibility, autonomy, and the like. How ought this choice be made? A cluster of structural imperatives that are implicit in ordinary speech and judgments provide at least part of the answer. We often experience ourselves and others as more or less *substantial*: we describe people as heavyweights or lightweights, as deep or shallow, as complex or simple, as having or lacking heft. The seat of these metaphoric qualities is the 'core' of the self. By forming the self's core, proximate roles give us substance and solidity. But these structural qualities come at a price of greater vulnerability to change. The fixity and rigidity of a dense core make it brittle: an alteration in or loss of a proximate role will send shock waves throughout the entire self, threatening to shatter its identity. Distant roles, by contrast, are in this sense sources of versatility and resilience. One weathers change better when one can assume or discard a distant role without significant repercussions in other parts of the self.

This tradeoff between the structural virtues of solidity and pliability suggests that the optimal topography of the self would contain a gradation of distances or some combination of proximate and distant roles, where the distances correlate with the degree of social stability or change. But attaining such a balance in a world marked by a high level of change poses a challenge and a dilemma. Identifying with roles that are transitory and insecure may become a trap to a self whose resilience will be weakened and whose vulnerability to identity-shattering experiences increased. But the more roles are kept at a protective distance, the less there is to protect; at the limit we face the specter of the impersonal self: insubstantial, desolate, and empty.

References

Dan-Cohen, M. (2002). *Harmful thoughts: Essays on law, self, and morality*. Princeton, NJ: Princeton University Press.

Goffman, E. (1961a). *Encounters: Two studies in the sociology of interaction*. Indianapolis, IN: Bobbs-Merrill.

Goffman, E. (1961b). *Asylums: Essays on the social situation of mental patients and other inmates*. New York: Anchor Books.

Pico della Mirandola, G. (1956). *Oration on the dignity of man*. (A. R. Caponigri, trans.). Washington, DC: Regency Gateway.

---

[1] Although I borrow the notion of role distance from Goffman, I employ it in ways that depart from his own use.

Chapter 12
Reflections on the Philosophy of Nonviolence and Peace Studies

Laurence F. Bove

Abstract This chapter outlines three challenges for persons who undertake serious inquiry into the philosophy of nonviolence and peace studies. It invites gifted individuals to consider the issues and opportunities in philosophical method, narrative ethics, and the transformative nature of memory.

Keywords Archaeology of peace · Interdisciplinary · Memory · Narrative ethics · Peace studies · Philosophy · Postmodern · Violence

In 1517, Erasmus of Rotterdam wrote his now famous *The Complaint of Peace* (Erasmus 2004). One of the first persons to call himself a citizen of the world, Erasmus, through the personification of peace, detailed how destructive violence, recrimination, and revenge were to the fabric of human life. Today, over 500 years later, we can just as well proclaim, "Peace Complains Still." One does not have to look far to see the effects of violence, revenge, and strife in the personal, social, and political relations around us.

As a possible antidote or corrective, the philosophical study of nonviolence has much to offer the individual and the common good because it fosters the application of theoretical and practical skills to make a positive difference in the world. In addition, as part of the emerging interdisciplinary field of peace studies, it provides an opportunity to engage in some of the greatest questions and challenges facing the human family. That is not to say that philosophers who direct their efforts to study nonviolence and peace naively think human violence and its attendant ignorance and willfulness will disappear. Likewise, a world without conflict would not be human, but rather a utopia. The tasks for philosophers attending to nonviolence are many, and I will present my reflections only on three areas, realizing there are many other important areas to articulate and that my reflections will be evocative rather than exhaustive. The three areas that offer much challenge and opportunity to those

L.F. Bove
Walsh University, 2020 East Maple Street NW, North Canton, OH 44720, USA
e-mail: lbove@walsh.edu

D. Ambrose, T. Cross (eds.), *Morality, Ethics, and Gifted Minds*,
DOI: 10.1007/978-0-387-89368-6_12,
© Springer Science+Business Media LLC 2009

drawn to nonviolence and peace studies are the study of methods, narrative ethics, and the role of memory in violence and revenge and its need for transformation.

Peace Studies, in its current state of development, is an interdisciplinary field that is growing and maturing. The philosophical tasks necessary to untangle the methodological issues are especially engaging. Embedded in current issues are methodological issues that arise out of the limitations of the Enlightenment and Postmodern assumptions and interpretive horizons. The challenge inspires an inquiry that demands new syntheses and the invention of new vocabulary and concepts to name the complex phenomena studied. The complexity of phenomena that constitute peace challenges the very assumptions of our methods.

As an interdisciplinary endeavor, peace inquiries delve into historical, cultural, theoretical, and practical phenomena that must be understood from many points of view simultaneously. Philosophers orchestrate the work, identify foundations, assess new vocabularies and articulate the coherency or lack of it as this trans-cultural, trans-disciplinary effort proposes and tests significant theses and findings. Adapting a phrase from Foucault, let's call this collective effort creating an "archeology of peace". The creation of an archeology of peace in turn calls for a collective effort that articulates efforts suitable to the task and is able to synthesize the achievements of the past as it presents new insights, understandings, and judgments essential to the task.

The ability to invite dialog and to let the nuances of the phenomena of violence, nonviolence, and peace emerge more exactly reflects the challenge facing us. The simultaneous unfolding of human and societal growth, the rise of asynchronous digital communications and the burden of a complex and conflicted series of histories lead to what may be called *postmodern vertigo*, the disorientation that results when seeking to understand a phenomenon in a global setting with all its diverse, simultaneous and contrapuntal development. Viewed from standard accounts of rationality, this seeming non-discursive mass of conflicting data and perceptions disorients and offers two inadequate extremes as remedy. One extreme is to resort to simple solutions that obscure complexity and interpret phenomena through one point of view. This often exacerbates and escalates conflict as each insulated point of view revels in itself justification and bias. On the other extreme, embracing complexity to the point of complete relativity and randomness offers the option of choosing one's truth and defending one's power.

Recovery from post modern vertigo must recognize and respond to the challenges while avoiding despair or the inability to function. As Camus reminded us, "Be Neither Victim nor Executioner" (Camus 1986). Persons can be drawn into the study of nonviolence and peace because they desire a world without conflict. But, when the realization occurs that conflict and power are ever-present, they must make a transition to accept conflict and power and yet seek to broaden the human family's ability to resolve personal, communal, and political conflict constructively. The practice of intentionality, analysis, synthesis, and intervention required in this emergent field of inquiry will bring together a community of praxis from many disciplines and areas of expertise to develop new horizons.

My final thoughts on methodology are that many of the insights, connections and methods have not yet been articulated adequately. The pioneers have urged us on and have been prescient. But, entering into, unpacking, understanding, and developing new ways to resolve ever more complicated and interrelated conflicts will require new connections, insights and behaviors that have as their net effect a maximizing of alternatives to violence. Consequently, the growing archeology of peace is a combination of theory and practice that is transformative to persons and groups – and a challenge to any status quo where violence and destructive power dominate.

In morality, one promising area that aids the peace effort is narrative ethics, the practice of ethical discourse through stories. The ability to create ethical discourse and analysis through stories has a long and distinguished heritage that traces back to biblical, Talmudic and, more recently, existential sources of Kierkegaard, Marcel, Levinas, and others. Narrative ethics contributes to the archeology of peace in a number of ways. The narrative genre provides a framework for clarifying and analyzing situations, explicating a topic, synthesizing the contributions of others, and articulating and defending a thesis in the philosophy of nonviolence.

The ethical dimensions of power and domination are an essential challenge for our global society. To have power that leads to human flourishing demands an understanding and a compassion that reaches to a level to which the Buddha pointed. Power over others that dominates has been accepted by many as normal. To unleash the powers of human flourishing and to overturn the oppression that is caused by systems that isolate and privilege calls for a focus of intelligence, understanding, judgment and care. Another ubiquitous phenomenon globally is *getting even*. Revenge in all its forms cries out for analysis and moral assessment. In both of these areas the narrative method fits extremely well because stories of domination and revenge are told so frequently that they take on a life of their own, part of a cultural landscape that is shared and accepted by friend and foe alike, without awareness of its moral dimension. Gifted individuals are needed to identify, interpret and assess these phenomena. In addition and more importantly, they need to reframe these behaviors so that others are provided with novel ways of behaving given the weight of history that each brings to the collective understanding. Another essential task is to connect new ideas to familiar stories. By its very nature a story connects ideas with symbols, with time, and with memory. The ability to connect relevant insights in novel ways assists the peace researcher in developing and articulating new horizons.

Einstein reportedly posited that we cannot solve difficult problems from the same level of thought we were at when we created them. In addition to domination, revenge, and reframing old stories, the narrative method can assist in addressing one of the thorniest problems in contemporary thought about the moral assessment of violence and nonviolence – moving from a discursive notion of rationality to a synchronistic notion of rationality, as intimated by Carl Jung in the early twentieth century (Jung 1973). The development of a global understanding requires this shift, and the narrative methods can contain the contrasts much like Plato's dialogues go through many aspects along the route of inquiry.

A global morality will grapple with developing these new tools, and the call to gifted minds that are compassionate are necessary for this work, which leads me to my last fundamental interest related to the archeology of peace, the nature and transformation of memory. As I scour stories from around the world two prime stories come to mind concerning the transforming power of memory, Saint Augustine's Confessions in Book Ten (Augustine 1998) and the sutras of Gautama Buddha (Nhat Hanh 1990).

Upon reflection, I have become very much concerned about the power and role of memory in the perpetuation of hurts, harm and violence. A cursory reading of Augustine and Gautama's stories shows that a transformation of memory is necessary to overcome the harms that one or the group endures. For Augustine, transformation of memory connects us to the godhead, but for Gautama it opens the path to enlightenment. Each of us is caught in the biases of our self and our society, and freedom from this takes place through transformative activities that result in nonviolence. This transformation goes from the personal to the communal. This does not auger the end of violence, but it does give calm acceptance to those who are nonviolent to strive and to understand more about what diminishes oppression. Saint Augustine would probably just say: "Blessed are the Peacemakers, for they are the Children of God" (Matthew 5:9).

References

Augustine, Saint, Bishop of Hippo and Chadwick, H. (1998). *Confessions*. Oxford: Oxford University Press.
Camus, A. (1986). *Neither victims nor executioners*. Philadelphia, PA: New Society Publishers.
Erasmus, D. (2004). *Complaint of peace*. New York: Cosimo Classics.
Jung, C. G. (1973). *Synchronicity; an acausal connecting principle*. Princeton, NJ: Princeton University Press.
New Testament. *Gospel According to Matthew*. (5:9).
Nhat Hanh, T. and Laity, A. (1990). *Transformation and healing: The sutra on the four establishments of mindfulness*. Berkeley, CA: Parallax Press.

Part IV
Emotion, Affect, and the Inner Journey

Chapter 13
Moral Sensitivity in Young Gifted Children

Deirdre V. Lovecky

Abstract This chapter explores the development of moral sensitivity from infancy through elementary years, using an empathy-based model. Moral sensitivity is the ability to act in a way that takes into account others' feelings and needs. Moral sensitivity requires awareness of another's suffering, and the desire to do something to alleviate that suffering. How gifted children might develop empathy within this model is explored. The effects of intensity and sensitivity are discussed within a framework of the asynchrony between what young gifted children feel and what they are able to do. Anecdotes, as well as preliminary research on empathy in gifted children, complement the descriptions of how gifted children struggle with issues related to moral sensitivity.

Keywords Asynchrony · Attachment · Attunement · Compassion · Empathy · Intensity · Moral sensitivity · Self-regulation · Temperament · Theory of mind · Veridical empathy · Video games · Young gifted children

When Jack was 3 years old, he did not want to bring food with peanuts to preschool because there was a boy allergic to peanuts who had to sit alone during snack time. Jack said he felt sad for him and wanted to sit with him so he would not have to be alone.

At age 5, Jack heard the story of the sinking of the Titanic. He was quite angry that there weren't enough lifeboats on board. What especially angered him was why the boat manufacturers and the safety inspectors had allowed that to happen.

At age 6, Jack and two of his friends had a summer lemonade stand. They earned about US$20 and decided to give the money to a local soup kitchen. Jack's mother helped the boys to shop for food and deliver it.

At age 8, Jack is a very sensitive boy. He is caring, shares treats, and offers to help others. On the other hand, he gets upset if he senses teasing or anger. He dislikes

D.V. Lovecky
11 Whiting St., Providence, RI 02906, USA
e-mail: grcne02940@aol.com

D. Ambrose, T. Cross (eds.), *Morality, Ethics, and Gifted Minds*,
DOI: 10.1007/978-0-387-89368-6_13,
© Springer Science+Business Media LLC 2009

conflict, seeing people get hurt or sick. His parents try to shield him from excesses of feeling, as he seems to "catch" feelings, and become overwhelmed by them.

Jack has shown empathy and compassion for others from an early age. Like descriptions of some other gifted children in the literature (Lovecky 1997, 2004; Silverman 1993a, b), he shows unusual compassion, caring and sensitivity for his age. Based on parental report and observations over several years of knowing Jack, his empathy, compassion and caring encompass many areas of his life.

This chapter explores some aspects of moral sensitivity in young gifted children, from infancy through elementary school. First, the chapter will define moral sensitivity. Then, how children develop moral sensitivity, and how it manifests in gifted children will be described. The asynchrony between gifted children's ability to empathize and ability to act will also be explored.

13.1   A Definition of Moral Sensitivity

Moral sensitivity is the ability to act in a way that takes into account others' feelings and needs. Moral sensitivity requires awareness of another's suffering, and the desire to do something to alleviate that suffering. Moral sensitivity starts at birth and develops through an individual's lifetime, gaining in complexity as an individual matures. Moral sensitivity, in its most complex form, requires both compassion and a sense of justice to decide how to alleviate the suffering of an individual or group.

Most of the research on gifted children has focused on moral reasoning. Tasks designed to measure advanced moral reasoning are based on either Piagetian moral tasks (Piaget 1965) or moral dilemmas (Kohlberg 1984; Rest 1979). Moral reasoning requires a high level of abstract reasoning, as well as the ability to "decenter" (Piaget and Inhelder 1969), that is, to move beyond egocentric concerns to appreciate another's perspective. In this model, moral identity is constructed over time as children learn to de-center.

There has been little research on whether gifted children differ from age peers on moral sensitivity using a model that emphasizes empathetic responding. Also, how gifted children might develop moral sensitivity has not been explored.

13.2   A Theory of Moral Sensitivity Based on Empathy and Compassion

13.2.1   Types of Empathetic Responses

Hoffman (2000) defined empathy as a vicarious affective response to another's distress. The feeling of distress precedes and directly precipitates a helping response. In his model, reasoning is not required to respond effectively, but the most mature stages of empathy do use reason as part of the process of deciding on a response.

Empathetic responses include both automatic reactions to distress (autonomic responding) and sympathetic responses based on an ability to assume another's perspective (Hoffman 2000).

13.2.1.1 Autonomic Responses

Autonomic responses start in infancy and continue throughout life. Because they are involuntary, they enable preverbal children and others in nonverbal situations to empathize with others in distress. *Mimicry*, which starts in the earliest days of life, consists of both imitation (of others' facial expressions and feelings) and feedback (from within the body as well as outside). An observer unconsciously imitates an expression and then experiences the feeling conveyed. Hoffman saw mimicry as a "hard-wired neurologically based empathy arousing mechanism whose two steps, imitation and feedback, are directed by commands from the central nervous system" (Hoffman 2000, p. 44). The discovery of the mirror neuron system in the human forebrain (Gallese 2003; Iacoboni et al. 1999), with its connections to the early emotion system of the right brain, suggests that such a substrate exists from birth. What this means is that the mechanism for learning and displaying empathy is likely "on-line" from the first hours after birth.

Hoffman (2000) also described *classical conditioning*, a process in which the feeling associated with an experience is repeated when part of that experience is repeated. For example, a smiling mother soothes her baby who then feels good. The baby is conditioned to feel calmer when seeing the mother smile. For Hoffman, *direct association* occurs when aspects of the situation remind observers of experiences in their lives that evoke feelings that fit the observed victim's situation. An example is a child who sees another child hurt herself. The sight and sound of the victim's distress remind the child of past experiences of pain, and this evokes empathy for the hurt child.

13.2.1.2 Sympathetic Responses

Sympathetic responses develop as children learn language. Hoffman (2000) described *mediated association* as feelings communicated through language, which allows distance between observer and victim. This provides mediating aspects in the expression of empathy: it allows the person a moment to decide what to do. For example, a verbal expression of sadness might elicit a different expression of empathy than might a sad face. In *role taking*, more complexity is added as the observer uses perspective taking to mediate the response (Hoffman 2000). The observer "walks in the other's shoes" and by assuming their perspective, offers an empathetic response that fits their need. As role taking develops, it allows empathetic responding to a victim's life situation, as well as to a present situation, and builds the basis for empathy with a whole distressed group. Justice results from the intersection of empathetic responses to the individual or group and a determination to do something to ease that individual's or group's plight (Hoffman 2000).

Seeking justice, therefore, starts not with reasoning that something is unfair or unequal, but in feeling empathetic distress for the person caught in the unfair situation. The feeling of empathetic distress in the face of injustice leads to the recognition of the injustice, which then arouses emphatic anger and the desire to do something about the situation. Hoffman (2000) suggested that most real-life dilemmas arouse empathy because they involve victims for whom one feels distressed. Empathy triggers moral principles and through these principles brings about moral judgment and reasoning.

People use all the stages of empathy throughout life. For example, imitating a smile can make a person feel happier even if they did not feel so before the action of imitating. This is still mimicry, even if an adult does it. It is not as if the previous stage disappears, but that other types of empathetic responding are developed as the child matures. Consequently, the process of adding dimensions to empathy allows for a more considered and appropriate moral response (Hoffman 2000).

13.3 Development of Empathy

Theorists who study development of empathy examined interactions between child and caregiver from the first days of life to discover the first signs of empathetic responding. Stern (1985/2000), building on earlier work of Ainsworth (1969), described how infants develop a sense of self through early relationships. At the same time, Hoffman (2000) studied early empathy in young children.

13.3.1 Moral Development in Infancy

13.3.1.1 Mirroring, Attunement and Attachment

From birth to about 2 months of age, infants develop a "sense of emergent self" (Stern 1985/2000). Infants begin to make sense of the incoming world and their own feelings and reactions to it. This is not a conscious process, but a time of first experiencing and starting to become aware of sensations. Between the caregiver and the infant, from the infant's point of view, is no space. In this domain of emergent relatedness, self and other are still really one.

By the age of 2 months, babies start to have a sense of themselves as physically separate beings, with their own feelings. Self is an entity of physical sensations, actions, and emotions with continuity over time. This Core Self, developing from about 2–6 months of age, first recognizes a sense of being separate from the other, and then a relationship with the other (Stern 1985/2000). The baby with a Core Self does not yet know as a cognitive fact that the mother is a separate being; instead, this is something the baby senses. In this domain of core-relatedness, the child experiences self and other as different beings with different feelings, actions, and presence.

Sensitivity to others' distress starts soon after birth. Newborn infants react by crying at the sound of another infant crying (but not to their own recorded crying) (Simner 1971; Sagi and Hoffman 1976). This is the first stage of empathetic development, mimicry, and Hoffman (2000) refers to this stage as "the newborn reactive cry."

During this time, caregivers provide a sense of security for the baby not only by attending to physical needs, but also by playfully mirroring the baby's actions. This mirroring allows the baby to feel understood, the beginnings of empathy. Soon after that, infants start to engage in imitative behavior, first, of their caregiver's emotional facial expressions. Ainsworth (1969) and Stern (1985/2000) saw the development of imitation as following from the mother's first efforts to attune to her baby. Over time, the baby and mother develop a reciprocal relationship of imitation and feedback. Mothers use this system to teach babies how to soothe and calm by slowly varying the tempo of their imitation of the baby. As the baby follows the mother's lead, he/she calms and soothes. At other times parents slightly change the tempo and intensity of the imitation to help the baby arouse. This helps the infant learn emotional and behavioral self-regulation.

Between the 7th and 9th month, the infant becomes a subjective self (Stern 1985/2000). At this stage of development, the child discovers that self and other are not all that is out there. There are other minds too, with their feelings, presences, actions and continuity. Mental states and feelings can now be read and attuned to. Thus, in the earliest months the baby was imitating; now, the baby is relating.

As the baby becomes a subjective self, the process of attunement changes (Stern 1985/2000). Instead of just imitating the baby, parents start to alter communications with the baby based on how they read the baby's feelings. At the same time, the baby starts to read the parent's feelings. This process of attunement means that caregivers and babies engage in mutual interactions to which each contributes, and each feels the response of the other. This helps the baby learn about expressing feelings, entering into relationships and learning more about self-regulation. Caregivers no longer imitate the action, but instead, imitate the feeling intensity and tempo expressed. The baby experiences "feeling felt" (Siegel 1999).

As the baby experiences empathy, he/she also starts to develop a capacity to react with empathy. By 9 or 10 months of age, Hoffman (2000) described children who responded to the distress of others by seeking comfort for themselves. He called this stage of empathy development, *egocentric empathetic distress*. Because children at this age "catch" feelings so readily, they are unsure when they experience distress where it is coming from. Thus, distress of their own, and distress "caught" from another are treated as the same thing.

By age 8 or 9 months of age, children not only respond with empathy to the distress of others when they are bystanders to the other's suffering, but also respond when they have caused the other's pain, for example by hitting. This does not mean they recognize their role in causing the pain, rather they respond empathetically to the distress they observe (Hoffman 2000).

As young children learn how to predict and depend on the parents' response, they develop an inner sense of security and attachment to the parents. Children who are securely attached can depend on the parents to be there for them. They develop into independent, capable and resilient people with internal security about their role in establishing relationships throughout life (Siegel 1999).

13.3.1.2 Temperament

Some children may have such intense reactions to the environment, or are so sensitive to stimulation that they can be difficult to soothe. Others may need so much stimulation that it is difficult for a parent to provide it in the quantities needed. When parent and child are matched in temperament, or when the parent can take into account the child's temperament well enough, attunement can help ameliorate temperament problems. Thus, children who are easily overaroused can learn to tolerate more stimulation if the parents slowly teach them to adapt to small increases. These children then become securely attached. However, if parents and child are very different in temperament, if the child is unable to accurately perceive the mother's expressions, as are children with autism (Blakemore and Frith 2003; Harris 2003), or if the parent is unable to adjust for the child's temperament needs, misattunement is much more likely to result in insecure attachment (Ainsworth 1964; Thomas et al. 1968).

13.3.1.3 Attunement, Sensitivity and Gifted Children

While gifted children are often described as more intense (feeling emotions deeply) and more sensitive (reactive to low levels of sensation or emotion) than average children (Lovecky 2004; Piechowski 2006; Roeper 1982; Silverman 1993a), gifted children show better behavioral self-regulation than average children (Calero et al. 2007). Some gifted children, however, are exceptionally intense and sensitive to many types of stimulation. The more intense the feelings experienced, the more likely it is that children will have difficulty with developing self-other boundaries, because they will be more quickly overwhelmed by feelings. The more sensitive to feeling highly aroused by many types of stimulation, the more likely it is that the child will have trouble regulating emotions and behavior. Thus, not only are these gifted children likely to feel aroused by more things, but also they are more likely to have intense emotional experiences in situations in which others might not feel much at all. Overall, they are less likely to be emotionally resilient.

The parents of these exceptionally intense and sensitive gifted children need to be "super attuners" in order to help their gifted babies learn to feel calm, secure and attached. These children need, from the earliest days of life, more from the parents than most gifted children need. Anecdotal reports from the parents of more than 35 gifted children with IQ over 170 suggested that, for the children who appeared securely attached, early attunement was intensified on the part of the parent around activities chosen by the child (often activities that more average children were as yet unable to do, such as talking, reading, using numbers). One parent described the process as "learning to listen" to what her child was really asking for when she made what seemed to be overwhelming demands for attention (Lovecky 1997). Nevertheless, young gifted children with intense emotions and high degrees of sensitivity are at risk for insecure attachment, difficulty in self-regulation and other emotional problems.

13.3.2 Moral Development in Toddler Years

13.3.2.1 Development of Empathy from 15 Months to 3 Years

As the child begins the second year of life, new organizing principles develop. Not only does the baby need the parent's engagement in play, but also in expanding emotional and social repertoires. Babies observe the facial expression of the parent when directed to a particular object. This *social referencing* means the baby looks at the parent to see how the parent feels about the object, and then assumes that same facial expression (Gopnik et al. 2000; Stern (1985/2000).

At around 15–18 months the child develops a sense of verbal self (Stern 1985/2000). Now the world is open to him/her because things can be labeled, discussed, categorized and known. Children and parents use talking to relate to each other. Feelings are not only responded to in nonverbal ways, but are directly acknowledged and labeled for the child. As the child becomes more verbal, he or she begins to recognize basic feelings in self and others. Parents and children still imitate and attune, but the imitation is extended beyond parents to other adults, and it is delayed in time. The child has internalized an image of the parent and is now able to recapture the sense of that parent, even when the parent is not present (Stern). Thus, the child can begin to self-sooth and regulate based on recall of previous experiences.

As children become more verbal, they become cognitively aware of themselves as separate beings with their own feelings. This self-recognition begins about the same time as when a child can recognize the self in a mirror at 18–24 months (Lewis and Brooks-Gunn 1979; cited in Hoffman 2000). Along with this recognition of self as a separate person comes further empathetic development. As children are able to separate themselves from others, they start to recognize that distressed feelings can belong to another. Hoffman calls this stage: *quasi-egocentric empathetic distress*. Children start to recognize that other people have feelings and thoughts, though they still do not recognize that what is thought or felt might be different from what they would think or feel – they have no theory of mind yet (Perner et al. 1987). Because of this, if another is distressed or hurt, they will try to offer comfort by getting what would comfort them, such as their own mother or comfort object (Hoffman 2000). This beginning empathy is a direct response to the experienced feeling of the other.

13.3.2.2   Gifted Children and Moral Sensitivity in Toddler Years

Several anecdotes in the literature suggest advanced empathetic concern for others. Sara Jane (Silverman 1993b), at age 2, watched a television report about an earthquake in Russia that left thousands homeless. A very sensitive and empathetic child, she asked her parents to send the money in her piggy bank, which they did. The following Christmas, at age 3, she requested her presents be given to needy children, stating that she had all she needed and that some children would not get gifts. Performing these actions allowed Sara Jane to decrease distressed feelings within herself.

Hoffman (1994) described 15-month-old Michael, struggling with another child over a toy. When the other boy started to cry, Michael let the boy have the toy, but he still cried. Michael went and got his own teddy bear to comfort the boy, but this didn't work. Then, Michael paused for a moment, went into the next room and brought back the boy's teddy bear. The boy stopped crying. According to Hoffman (2000), the usual age for such a transaction would be preschool years.

Gifted toddlers who perform acts of compassion based on empathy are rare because most gifted toddlers would be unable to extrapolate from a situation in which they witness suffering in an unknown person to a solution. It is outside their life experience, and so they could not imagine a response. Few gifted children could act as Sara Jane did, thinking of offering money to help others. More gifted children may be like Michael, performing acts of kindness for people in their own lives, using objects and actions already familiar to them, like giving a toy or a hug to offer comfort.

13.3.2.3   Moral Asynchrony in Toddler Years

Asynchrony is the perceived difference between the empathetic feelings aroused by witnessing suffering and the ability to do something to ease the suffering. When asynchrony occurs, the child feels distressed.

For example, Sara Jane was very upset by the news report of the Russian earthquake. However, because she was so young, the act of giving her money could relieve her distress. The suffering she saw was dealt with by her act. Because even a gifted toddler like Sara Jane does not have a sense of the big picture, he/she could not imagine continued suffering. Gifted children of this age act in the moment, and once they feel they have done something, their distress decreases.

Asynchrony occurs when gifted toddlers become overwhelmed by feelings they experience when witnessing someone upset. They quickly seek comfort for themselves, then, from this safer position, ask questions about what they are witnessing. These children ask questions that sound to an outsider as if they have no empathy at all, when actually, the reverse is true. Intense and sensitive gifted children are especially prone to overarousal of empathetic feelings, and they need not only reassurance in the moment, but also assistance in making a positive response, for example, what to say or do to help someone feel better.

13.3.3   Moral Development in Preschool Years

13.3.3.1   Development of Empathy from 3 to 5 Years

In preschool years, empathy continues to develop as children learn that emotions can be different for different people, for example, that different people can feel differently about the same situation. This occurs as they develop the ability to "read" others' minds. Essentially, they have developed a *theory of mind*, which allows them to understand, on a simple level, that others have thoughts and feelings of their own, not identical to the child's. Language ability, especially the development of pragmatic and conversational ability, predicts ability to solve theory of mind tasks. Children who are advanced in language ability are advanced in their theory of mind performance, unless they have an autistic spectrum disorder (Milligan et al. 2007). Thus, those gifted children with early language development are likely to be advanced in solving theory of mind tasks. This means they are also likely to have an earlier understanding of basic perspective taking.

Developing a theory of mind, or understanding another's perspective, is not an all or none process. It develops slowly over time with most 2- to 3-year-olds not able to understand that another might have different thoughts. By age 5, the majority of children are able to make this assumption (Wellman et al. 2001).

Empathy development in preschool age children follows a similar path. It includes both feeling for another in distress and beginning to imagine how to alleviate that distress in a way that would specifically help that person. As children develop a theory of mind, they start to show *veridical empathy* (Hoffman 2000). For example, to offer comfort, a child would find the other child's blanket or mother rather than his/her own. This ability to offer comfort that fits reflects the child's underlying development of an autonomous self, a self aware that others' feelings, desires and needs are not the same as one's own. Hoffman sees veridical empathy as a more mature empathy because it is the scaffolding of empathy used throughout life.

Veridical empathy does not fully develop until elementary years. Most children show quasi-egocentric empathy through preschool, responding to another's suffering without a real awareness yet that the other can have a different perspective. Thus, the comfort given tends to be what the child finds comforting or has observed to be comforting to the other child (Hoffman 2000).

Preschoolers not only feel empathy, but also begin to develop prosocial behaviors such as helping, turn taking, and sharing. Hoffman (2000) reported that when 4-year-olds were asked the reason why they shared, the most common one given was empathy-based: it made the other child happy; when they didn't share the other child was sad. The most common nonempathetic reason given was to avoid a fight.

Research has shown that by age 4 and 5, naturally occurring prosocial behaviors such as sharing (but at a cost to the child) were correlated with sympathy/empathy (Eisenberg et al. 1988, 1999). Furthermore, early spontaneous sharing was related to prosocial and compassionate behaviors that had a cost to self at later ages and into adulthood. Thus, the beginning of justice, based on compassion for others, is built by early lessons in sharing and helping.

13.3.3.2 Gifted Children and Development of Moral Sensitivity in Preschool Years

Parents of gifted children at the Gifted Resource Center of New England described empathetic and compassionate acts by their young children. For example, Jack's level of empathy was advanced for his age. His feeling sad for the boy with the peanut allergy, and his action of not bringing peanut foods to school, suggests Jack, at age 3, had some ability to take the other boy's perspective (veridical empathy) by thinking how he'd feel if he had to sit alone.

Erin, age 4, participated in a study on empathy at the Gifted Resource Center of New England. Erin spontaneously shared all the pretend cookies in the test scenario, stating that the other children would feel sad if she kept them all. Her score on an empathy scale (Bryant 1982) was at the level of a first-grade child. Her mother's report about Erin's behavior suggested much spontaneous sharing with friends and more than usual kindness and helpfulness with her 18-month-old brother.

Piechowski (2006) described Steven, in a preschool class for gifted children, as a sensitive boy, aware of peers' needs and feelings. He would call the attention of the entire preschool class to a classmate in need of physical or emotional comfort.

At the Roeper School in Michigan, Roeper (1995) described gifted preschoolers who would comfort other children upset over the separation from parents. The consoling children described an awareness of knowing how the distressed children felt based on remembering how they had felt previously. Hoffman (2000), in contrast, reported similar behavior in empathetic 6- to 7-year-old children.

What do these anecdotes tell us about empathy in gifted children? Certainly, the children depicted here felt for others. Most were able to take some kind of action to relieve the suffering they observed. Some, like Steven and Erin, relieved the situation by performing a prosocial behavior – sharing or helping. A few, like Jack and the children at the Roeper School, acted because they knew how something might feel to the other person, based on how it might make them feel. These very young gifted children were able to see what was needed and to respond to the need with something that was helpful, a demonstration of veridical empathy.

13.3.3.3 Moral Asynchrony in Preschool Years

Asynchrony can arise when intense and sensitive gifted children, overwhelmed by the distress they feel coming from another, become overaroused. Then, unable to modulate their distress, they become unable to respond to another. These children become distressed not only by the distress they observe, but by their own distress. This empathetic overarousal (Hoffman 2000) can occur any time strong feelings are "caught" from another. Silverman (1993a) described M, age 3, who, while loving and compassionate, could not stand to hear a baby crying and put his hands over his ears. His feelings also were easily hurt.

Preschool age gifted children who are highly empathetic can also experience asynchrony when they are in situations where there is nothing immediate they can do to help. When Emily was 5, she visited one of her new friends from kindergarten, just after Christmas. Emily noted how few presents her friend had received. Emily was very careful not to reveal how much she had received from Santa, only naming one or two gifts when asked. Emily was profoundly sad when her mother explained that her friend was poor, and nothing could be done to help. Emily was so disturbed that she would not invite the friend to her own house, and in fact, after this, only saw this friend at school. Emily dealt with her distress by sharing treats and toys with this friend. Emily planned that when she was an adult she would do something to help children who were poor.

Initially Emily was overwhelmed by her feelings of sadness. She was an empathetic child, understanding that she would hurt her friend's feelings if she named all she had gotten as gifts. The asynchrony occurred when she had no way to deal with the poverty she witnessed and the disparity with her own circumstances. All she could do was keep the friendship at school where she could share her treats and toys.

13.3.4 Moral Development in Elementary Years

13.3.4.1 Development of Empathy from 6 to 11 Years

In the early elementary years, a cognitive shift from more concrete to more abstract thinking allows children to consider more than one aspect of a situation at a time, and to consider context (Piaget and Inhelder 1969). This cognitive shift allows the introduction of true perspective taking. This shift is a gradual process so that younger children still have trouble considering more than their own perspective, but by later elementary years, children are able to consider several perspectives. At that point they are really able to put themselves in someone else's shoes.

By early elementary years, children start to be able to understand that how someone else feels might be the same as how they would feel in a similar situation. Hoffman (2000) suggested that prior to age 6 or 7, children can respond empathetically, but may not realize that their distressed feeling was caused by the other's situation. By age 6 or 7, children are able to understand that their own feelings of sadness or upset are the result of what they witnessed happening to another. Thus, veridical empathy allows the child to start truly empathizing with the other. By age 8 or 9, Hoffman suggested that children start to understand that the same event can cause opposed feelings (e.g., sad and happy). Some children of this age are also able to start understanding from another's point of view – a role-taking perspective. Thus, empathy starts to include an ability to think of how a different other might feel in a situation.

By later elementary years many children are able to start to use role taking in understanding another's distress. Thus, they can look beyond the immediate situation and understand something of a person's life situation that may (or may not) contribute to the current situation. They can see beyond the surface and begin to understand that the face that is shown may not reflect the feelings underneath (Hoffman 2000).

In later elementary years, children are increasingly able to take into account the circumstances or context of the situation. By age 8, children develop awareness that recent experience plays a role in someone's future response. They consider another's previous experience in inferring feelings in a similar situation. For example, a child will understand that someone who had a bad experience in a situation might be reluctant to repeat the situation. They would start to understand and take into account mitigating and extenuating circumstances (Hoffman 2000).

Older elementary age children are able to predict another child's feelings given their life circumstances, provided they have information directly about those circumstances. For example, they would understand that a friend would be sad because his baby sister died, even if he doesn't look sad at that moment. Younger children are still caught in the saliency of the moment – the other child looks happy, therefore, he is happy. The older child would understand that he might feel momentarily happy but would still be sad too (Hoffman 2000).

Empathetic feelings of injustice start to be raised by specific knowledge of the suffering of others. While younger children can be angry about something they perceive as unfair, feelings about injustice occur when the child is old enough to understand that someone did not deserve their plight. This feeling of unfairness translates into a feeling of injustice and a desire to right the wrong done to the other. However, it is the ability to take another's experience into account, understand his or her perspective and his or her life condition in the framework of a principle of justice that makes for empathetic feelings of injustice, not just a feeling of unfairness (Hoffman 2000).

Temperament issues are related to empathy for elementary-age children. Emotional intensity interacts with self-regulation of feelings and behavior in predicting children's level of empathy. Children low in self-regulation were low in empathy and sympathy no matter what the level of intensity. Children who were moderate or high in emotional regulation showed increasing empathy/sympathy with increasing levels of intensity. Thus, emotional intensity can predict empathy/sympathy, if children are at least moderately able to self-regulate (Eisenberg et al, 1994). With gifted children, therefore, the key is how sensitive they are (related to self-regulation), not how intense (depth of feeling).

13.3.4.2 Gifted Children and Development of Moral Sensitivity in Elementary Years

There are many anecdotes about the empathy, compassion and caring of older gifted children. Jack, described at the start of this chapter, showed many empathetic behaviors in early elementary school. Feeling for the victims of the Titanic and getting angry at the ship manufacturers and government for allowing too few lifeboats suggests an empathetic anger unusual for age 5 or 6. Selling lemonade, then giving the money to the poor is also unusual for a child of his age.

Sara Jane continued to show empathetic behavior in elementary school. At age 6, she contacted a local soup kitchen and organized a Christmas drive for needy children (Silverman 1993b). For Emily's 10th birthday, she requested that her family take her to a fundraiser at a local orphanage. There they donated all the money that would have been spent on her presents. The following Christmas, she asked her parents to return with a big box of toys.

Some recent news stories suggested that children who want to help others by organizing specific fundraisers are somewhat older. For example, one recent news story described how 8-year-old Zachary Haines and his 6-year-old sister, Abby, watched a news report about homelessness. They decided to raise money, for a local homeless shelter where families with children lived. With their parents help, they raised almost $10,000 and presented the money to the Rhode Island Family Shelter (Jefferson 2007). Many other such stories suggest that wanting to help others is not just limited to gifted children. All the children, including those who are gifted, had their parents' help in organizing and executing their compassionate efforts. Thus, it is not whether the child had help in alleviating the suffering witnessed, but the age of awareness of the suffering, and that one can actually do something to help that may be somewhat earlier for gifted children who are empathetic (age 5 or 6).

13.3.4.3   Moral Asynchrony in Elementary Years

Concerns about moral issues can produce the distress of asynchrony for gifted children in elementary school in several ways. As with younger gifted children, asynchrony can arise when extremely sensitive gifted children feel overwhelmed by the amount of suffering they witness. When the child's ability to self-regulate is compromised, the child is unable to act empathetically.

Another type of asynchrony occurs with some gifted boys as they immerse themselves in the peer culture and adopt attitudes of indifference. Over time, their concerns for others at a distance begin to disappear as they adopt the idea that violence is a solution for many problems (Lovecky 1994). Because some current research suggests that boys may become desensitized to other's pain by playing violent video games (Funk et al. 2003, 2004), these gifted boys may actually experience a decrease in empathy for others as they play these games. The asynchrony between their own previous empathetic caring and their later desensitized selves becomes apparent to parents. The boys, however, think their desensitized, less empathetic self is more acceptable.

Some older elementary exceptionally empathetic gifted children have the ability to understand suffering in a wider context than age peers. Consequently, they are asynchronous with age peers in what they consider to be important. The world of school can seem superficial when they are concerned about larger issues. Emerging teen interests in age peers can seem alienating to these gifted children. They are at risk for depression if they have no peers with whom they can be their true selves.

13.4   Research on Empathy in Gifted Children

A search of the literature found a paucity of research articles about empathy and gifted children. Chan (2007) studied leadership competencies in gifted Chinese youth. These children perceived that they had greater strengths in social skills and utilization of emotions than in regulation of emotions or empathy. There were no gender or age effects for empathy, though there were for social skills (gender) and utilization of emotions (age). A high level of empathy may not be related to leadership ability.

At the Gifted Resource Center of New England, preliminary work on empathy was completed with a small sample of gifted children. Using the Bryant Empathy scale (Bryant 1982), eight gifted children, ages 4–13, were compared to their mothers, tested on the adult equivalent test (Mehrabian and Epstein 1972). Results showed that scores of the younger group of children (ages 4–8) were significantly lower than scores of the older group (10–13), an age trend found in the literature (Bryant 1982; Eisenberg et al. 1996; Lennon and Eisenberg 1987, cited in Eisenberg et al. 2006). Scores for most of the gifted children were above average. Five of the eight were more than 1 SD above average for their ages, using Bryant's (1982) norms. Thus, though preliminary, this research suggests that gifted children can show higher levels of empathy than average children, and that empathy levels increase in gifted children as they mature.

13.5   Conclusion

Not all gifted children show advanced moral sensitivity. Some are not very empathetic at all; others may be more average in their expressions of empathy. Nevertheless, it may be that a higher percentage of gifted children than average children show unusual empathy. It may be that some gifted children pass through, not only the stages of cognitive processing and moral reasoning sooner than age peers, but also, the stages of empathy. They may assume a more advanced mode of caring for others at an earlier age than peers. Much more research is needed.

If the sensitivity and empathy of at least some gifted children do develop on an earlier trajectory than that of average children, it points to the special needs of gifted children as a group for support and understanding of their advanced caring about others and reasoning about moral issues. It suggests that their education needs not only to be accelerated academically, but also that they need teacher support and a peer environment where they can develop skills to deal better with their advanced moral sensitivity.

References

Ainsworth, M. D. S. (1964). Patterns of attachment behavior shown by the infant in interaction with his mother. *Merrill Palmer Quarterly, 10*, 51–58.

Ainsworth, M. D. S. (1969). Object relations, dependency and attachment: A theoretical review of the infant-mother relationship. *Child Development, 40*, 969–1026.

Blakemore, S. J. & Frith, U. (2003). How does the brain deal with the social world? *NeuroReport, 14*, 1–10.

Bryant, B. K. (1982). An index of empathy for children and adolescents. *Child Development, 53*, 413–425.

Calero, M. D., Garcia-Martin, M. B., Jimenez, M. I., Kazen, M., & Araque, A. (2007). Self-regulation advantage for high-IQ children: Findings from a research study. *Learning and Individual Differences, 17*, 328–343.

Chan, D. W. (2007). Leadership competencies among Chinese gifted students in Hong Kong: The connection with emotional intelligence and successful intelligence. *Roeper Review, 29*, 183–189.

Eisenberg, N., McCreath, H., & Ahn, R. (1988). Vicarious emotional responsiveness and prosocial behavior: Their interrelations in young children. *Personality and Social Psychology Bulletin, 14*, 298–311.

Eisenberg, N., Fabes, R. A., Murphy, B., Karbon, M., Maszk, P., Smith, M., O'Boyle, C., & Suh, K. (1994). The relations of emotionality and regulation to dispositional and situational empathy-related responding. *Journal of Personality and Social Psychology, 66*, 776–797.

Eisenberg, N., Fabes, R. A., Murphy, B., Karbon, M. Smith, M., & Maszk, P. (1996). The relations of children's dispositional empathy-related responding to their emotionality, regulation, and social functioning. *Developmental Psychology, 32*, 195–209.

Eisenberg, N., Guthrie, I. K., Murphy, B. C., Shepard, S. A., Cumberland, A., & Carlo, G. (1999). Consistency and development of prosocial dispositions: A longitudinal study. *Child Development, 70*, 1360–1372.

Eisenberg, N., Spinrad, T. L., & Sadovsky, A. (2006). Empathy-related responding in children. In M. Killen & J. G. Smetana (Eds.), *Handbook of moral development* (pp. 517–549). Mahwah, NJ: Lawrence Erlbaum.

Funk, J. B., Buchman, D. D., Jenks, J., & Bechtoldt, H. (2003). Playing violent video games, desensitization, and moral evaluation in children. *Journal of Applied Developmental Psychology, 24*, 413–436.

Funk, J. B., Baldacci, H. B., Pasold, T., & Baumgardner, J. (2004). Violence exposure in real life, video games, television, movies and the Internet: Is there desensitization? *Journal of Adolescence, 27*, 23–39.

Gallese, V. (2003). The roots of empathy: The shared manifold hypothesis and the neural basis of intersubjectivity. *Psychpathology, 36* (4), 171–180.

Gopnik, A., Capps, L., & Meltzoff, A. N. (2000). Early theories of mind: What the theory can tell us about autism. In S. Baron-Cohen, H. Tager-Flusberg, & D. J. Cohen (Eds.), *Understanding other minds (2nd Ed.)* (pp. 50–72). New York: Oxford University Press.

Harris, J. C. (2003). Social neuroscience, empathy, brain integration, and neurodevelopmental disorders. *Physiology and Behavior, 79*, 525–531.

Hoffman, M. L. (1994). Empathy, role taking, guilt, and development of altruistic motives. In B. Puka (Ed.), *Reaching out: Caring, altruism and prosocial behavior* (pp. 196–218). New York: Garland.

Hoffman, M. L. (2000). *Empathy and moral development: Implications for caring and justice.* New York: Cambridge University Press.

Iacoboni, M., Woods, R. P., Brass, M., Bekkering, H., Mazziotta, J. C., & Rizzolatti, G. (1999). Cortical mechanisms of human imitation. *Science, 286* (5449), 2526–2528.

Jefferson, B. M. (2007, March 15). Their hearts are with the homeless. *The Providence Journal.* Available: http://www.projo.com/ri/northkingstown/content/SCNKSHELTER15_03-15-07.

Kohlberg, L. (1984). *The psychology of moral development*. New York: Harper & Row.

Lovecky, D. V. (1994). The moral gifted child in a violent world. *Understanding Our Gifted, 6,* 1, 3.

Lovecky, D. V. (1997). Identity development in gifted children: Moral sensitivity. *Roeper Review, 20,* 90–94.

Lovecky, D. V. (2004). *Different minds: Gifted children with AD/HD, Asperger Syndrome and other learning deficits*. New York: Jessica Kingsley.

Mehrabian, A. & Epstein, N. A. (1972). A measure of emotional empathy. *Journal of Personality, 40,* 237–247.

Milligan, K., Astington, J. W., & Dack, L. A. (2007). Language and theory of mind: Meta-analysis of the relation between language ability and false-belief understanding. *Child Development, 78,* 622–646.

Perner, J., Leekam, S. R., & Wimmer, H. (1987). Three-year-olds' difficulty with false belief: The case for a conceptual deficit. *British Journal of Developmental Psychology, 5,* 125–137.

Piaget, J. (1965). *The moral development of the child* (M. Gabain, Trans.). New York: Free Press. (Original work published 1932)

Piaget, J. & Inhelder, B. (1969). *The psychology of the child.* (H. Weaver, Trans.). New York: BasicBooks. (Original work published 1966)

Piechowski, M. M. (2006). *Mellow out, they say. If only I could: Intensities and sensitivities of the young and bright*. Madison, WI: Yunasa Books.

Rest, J. (1979). *Development in judging moral issues*. Minneapolis, MN: University of Minnesota Press.

Roeper, A. (1982). How the gifted cope with their emotions. *Roeper Review, 5* (2), 21–24.

Roeper, A. (1995). Finding the clue to children's thought processes. In R. C. Medeiros, L. K. Silverman, & P. Espeland (Eds.), *Annemarie Roeper: Selected speeches and writings* (pp. 22–38). Minneapolis, MN: Free Spirit.

Sagi, A. & Hoffman, M. L. (1976). Empathic distress in the newborn. *Developmental Psychology, 12,* 175–176.

Siegel, D. J. (1999). *The developing mind: How relationships and the brain interact to shape who we are*. New York: Guilford.

Silverman, L. K. (1993a). The gifted individual. In L. K. Silverman (Ed.), *Counseling the gifted and talented* (pp. 3–28). Denver: Love.

Silverman, L. K. (1993b). Social development, leadership, and gender issues. In L. K. Silverman (Ed.), *Counseling the gifted and talented* (pp. 291–327). Denver: Love.

Simner, M. L. (1971). Newborn's response to the cry of another infant. *Developmental Psychology, 5,* 136–150.

Stern, D. N. (1985/2000). *The interpersonal world of the infant* (First paperback edition). New York: Basic Books.

Thomas, A., Chess, S., & Birch, S. G. (1968). *Temperament and behavior disorders in children*. New York: New York University Press.

Wellman, H. M., Cross, D., & Watson, J. (2001). Meta-analysis of theory-of-mind development: The truth about false belief. *Child Development, 72,* 655–684.

Chapter 14
The Inner World of the Young and Bright

Michael M. Piechowski

Abstract William James (1902) made the connection between intensity of character (ardor) and moral action more than a 100 years ago. In the 1960s and 1970s,
when cognitive psychology supplanted behaviorism, moral development was seen
as development of moral judgment through reasoning. However, reasoning does not
guarantee that behavior will follow the dictates of reason. Behavior follows what
one believes and feels to be right rather than what one thinks is correct. Emotional
rather than cognitive development is the key to congruence between moral motivation and behavior. Dabrowski constructed his theory of emotional development
from the study of lives of gifted and creative people. The theory provides insight
into emotional life of the gifted and into what motivates moral action.

Keywords Character development · Emotional development · Emotional giftedness · Emotional intensity · Emotional life themes · Emotional sensitivity ·
Emotional tension · Empathy · Entelechy · Extraversion · Giftedness · Imagination ·
Introversion · Intuition · Mirror neurons · Multilevel disintegration · Overexcitability: psychomotor, sensual, imagination, intellectual, emotional · Positive
maladjustment · Psychological types · Psychosynthesis · Self-actualizing

14.1 Giftedness as Energy

Gifted children tend to be more active than regular children displaying higher energy level, whether physical, intellectual, or emotional. Prodigies are examples of an
extraordinary concentration of mental energy. The energy of the electric current in
the nerve tissue becomes interest, passion, sustained effort, perseverance, creative

M.M. Piechowski
119 Ski Ct., Madison, WI 53713, USA
e-mail: spirgif@earthlink.net

D. Ambrose, T. Cross (eds.), *Morality, Ethics, and Gifted Minds*,
DOI: 10.1007/978-0-387-89368-6_14,
© Springer Science+Business Media LLC 2009

flow, ecstasy, caring, compassion, or spiritual experience. A greater than average intensity, sometimes very great and extreme, makes for experiencing life at a high pitch. Countless sensations of extended range of hue and nuance, thoughts racing and tumbling over each other, often on many tracks at once, memories, desires, and a rich tapestry of feelings produce a multidimensional apprehension of the world, one's life and its possibilities.

The excess of energy Dabrowski called *psychomotor overexcitability* because it has to be discharged using one's muscles whether, for instance, to release the bottled up steam after sitting still or throwing oneself into action. For example, a gifted 16-year old girl said: "I get filled with energy when I need that energy. And, of course, I release it by doing the thing that got me excited in the first place" (Piechowski 2006, p. 40). Psychomotor overexcitability differentiates between gifted and nongifted students (Ackerman 1997; Bouchard 2004; Tieso 2007). Overexcitability stands for the capacity of being stimulated to a high degree and sustaining it for extended period of time.

Sensory experience for gifted children, and adults especially, tends to be of a much richer quality because so much more detail, texture, contrast, and distinction is coming into awareness. What is pleasant is liked with a passion, what is unpleasant is disliked intensely. Dabrowski called it *sensual overexcitability*. For example, in the words of a 16-year old: "I seem to notice more smells than a lot of other people. I love dark, musty smells and earthy smells, herbs and things like that. I love the smell of clean air in spring and tree blossoms and things and the smell of clean bodies, esp. hair" (Piechowski 2006, p. 48). When sensual overexcitability joins with emotional overexcitability, the experience becomes much richer and more meaningful. For example, a 17-year old girl said, "I like yellow for it seems warm and full of joy" (Piechowski 2006, p. 46). In an intimate relationship sensual and emotional elements go together.

14.2 Intellectual Energy

Intellectual overexcitability is the characteristic by which gifted children are most often identified. In a happy turn of phrase, Frank (2006) said that intelligence is about the ability to solve problems, but overexcitability is about the passion for solving them. When the emotional and mental energies meet, the mind supplies the energy of sustained concentration while emotional energy drives interest (passion). Interest is one of the basic emotions (Izard 1971).

Intellectual energy has certain consequences: relentless questioning, critical thinking, and evaluation. For instance, gifted adolescents responded to the question, *What gets your mind going?* by mentioning the irresistible attraction of brain teasers, logical puzzles, theories and controversies. More significantly, some have mentioned "challenging anything accepted by society," their way of resisting conformity: "One good thing [is that] I try to think about my beliefs – political and religious – so that I won't believe things just because my parents do"

(Piechowski 2006, p. 64). This may lead to a crisis in families with rather strict and orthodox religious faith or political adherence. Gifted adolescents are likely to question the foundations of their faith, and may find it wanting. To a highly gifted young person doubts about beliefs present themselves almost inevitably, consequently they may precipitate a crisis of worldview, in other words, a moral crisis.

The price of questioning can be twofold. One, in environments that do not value questioning one quickly meets with resistance and even rejection. Two, self-questioning may create self-doubt and the fear of going crazy: "I probably spend too much time thinking about my own thinking, analyzing myself and analyzing the analysis. I sometimes psych myself into thinking I am going crazy" (Piechowski 2006, p. 63). It may be interesting to note that the great Sir Francis Galton tried thinking paranoidally and was startled how quickly he became paranoid.

14.3   Imagination

Gifted children tend to have excitable *imagination* that is especially rich, abundant, and surprising in creative individuals (Piechowski 1999). With imagination a whole universe of unlimited possibilities opens up to us. Imaginal experience can be real and remembered as such, "as if it really happened."

The subject of invisible friends (imaginary playmates) has not received much attention in gifted literature other than noting that gifted children tend to have many more such companions than other children (Terman 1925; Hollingworth 1942/1977) and that creative adolescents often keep them from childhood (Davis 2003; Piirto 2004). That children distinguish pretend play from everyday reality is well established (Singer 1975; Singer and Singer 1990). However, the role of invisible friends in social development, in gaining sense of competence and overcoming fears, though studied in regular children, has not received much attention in regard to gifted children. Imaginary companions usually are not secret but they do belong to the child's own world. Attempts on the part of adults to interact with them swiftly lead to their disappearance by natural or unnatural means (Taylor 1999). Imaginary playmates are real to the child and one may wonder whether the experience is accompanied by sensations of sound, warmth, or touch that are felt. The answer is that it is.

Cohen and MacKeith (1991) examined 64 accounts of imaginary worlds. The degree of elaboration – creation of histories, languages, multiple characters (in one case as many as 282), and the early age when they are begun (six or seven or even younger) – indicates that the young weavers of these worlds were highly gifted. The experience of being in an imaginary world can be "as real as real." For example: "I also had a magic boat in my youth for a while. It had an outboard motor but I found that too noisy. I've never been clever with engines and there were always problems about petrol, so I discarded the idea" (Cohen and MacKeith 1991, p. 57).

Imaginary is usually taken to mean *not real*. But imaginary playmates and imaginary worlds are lived with the full range of sensory experience and vivid memory. The brain appears to make little distinction between something that is vividly imagined from something that is experienced from an outside sensory input (Damasio 2003). Therefore, to allow for the "as real as real" quality of experience, a more fitting term is *imaginal* (Singer 1975; Watkins 1990).

14.4   Emotional Energy and Funneling of Emotional Tension

Emotional overexcitability, manifested in a wide range of emotions and feelings, addresses the passionate nature of gifted and creative people – their emotional intensity. But it is emotional sensitivity that moves to compassion, caring, and responsibility. The significance of deep and perceptive feeling lies in *empathy as a way of knowing*, another little explored ability of the gifted.

Gifted children are often misunderstood exactly because they can be so greatly stimulated and because they perceive and process things differently. Their excitement is viewed as excessive, their high energy as hyperactivity, their persistence as nagging, their questioning as undermining authority, their imagination as not paying attention, their persistence as being disruptive, their strong emotions and sensitivity as immaturity, their creativity and self-directedness as oppositional disorder. They are the wild tall poppies that many forces conspire to cut down to size (Gross 1998).

The concept of overexcitability suggests that the overall picture of an individual's personal energy is worth investigating. Certain situations impede the natural flow of this energy. For a naturally active person inactivity leads to a buildup of energy, which presses to be discharged. For a naturally active mind a boring day at school, or at a meeting, has to be worked off by engagement in an intensely absorbing mental task, otherwise sleep won't come (Tolan 1994). Emotional tension also builds up energy which then seeks release in nervous habits, sensual easement of tension (e.g. drinking, eating, shopping, sex), or excessive worrying. Nervous habits and workaholism are a psychomotor way of funneling of emotional tension, the sensual way lies in oral compulsions, among others (Piechowski 2006).

14.5   Emergent Themes

The varieties of expressions of each overexcitability have been collected from open-ended questionnaires (Piechowski 2006). While quantitative studies are good for group comparisons and catching general trends in the data, it is the content of responses that reveals the quality of experience and features of emotional life (Piirto 2004).[1] The expressions and manifestations of overexcitability have been

---

[1] Three different studies provided 158 OEQs (open-ended) with a total of about 5,000 responses from 79 boys and 79 girls, ages 9–19; the majority were teens (? ?; Piechowski and Colangelo 1984; Piechowski and Miller 1995). The first study used an OEQ with 46 questions, subsequently replaced by a 21-item open-ended OEQ.

listed in a number of sources (Cline and Schwartz 1999; Piechowski 1991, 2003, 2006; Piirto 2002, 2004; Silverman 1993).

The themes that emerged from review of the responses give a fairly good picture of the many dimensions of inner life of gifted children and adolescents (Piechowski 2006). A sampling of themes is presented in Table 14.1. Yoo and Moon (2006) developed a 47-item inventory of problems identified by parents of gifted children requiring counseling. Quite a few of the items in their inventory

Table 14.1 Themes in research on the inner lives of the gifted

Piechowski (2006)	Yoo and Moon (2006)
Intensity and sensitivity	Hypersensitivity
High personal energy – physical and mental	
Funneling of emotional tension: psychomotor: nervous habits sensual: eating, drinking, etc. intellectual: a mind that can't slow down imaginal: doomsday scenarios emotional: excessive worrying (expecting the worst)	
Sensual delights: appreciation increases with age	
Intellectual energy interest as a basic emotion the role of empathy in intellectual probing passion for finding and solving problems relentless questioning and its consequences: resistance in others, self-doubt in oneself testing assumptions and beliefs: adolescent crisis of worldview spatial thinking	Low self-esteem
Imaginal experience is imagination valued or source of annoyance? imagistic thinking, e.g., metaphors precise visualization: spatial and vivid absorption: experiencing with full sensory engagement communication with nature invisible friends (aka imaginary companions) imaginary worlds how real is a self-created reality?	
Emotional experience emotional intensity as "too much" predominance of positive affect friendships transcend stereotypes affectional bonds with family, animals, and places the self in adolescence: elusive, fragmented, multiple, or confident sense of responsibility: the burden of "the gift" being different perfectionism entelechy empathy and a calling to action empathy as a way of knowing triggers of conflict resistance to compulsion anger, insecurity, and self-consciousness coping with depression coping with fears coping with death	Pressure to meet expectations sense of being different perfectionism conflict with teachers, fighting with peers noncompliance anger/frustration depression isolation, loneliness anxiety, fearfulness recent loss/grief suicidal ideations
Typology of emotional growth rational–altruistic ("judging" or J) emotional–introspective ("perceptive" or P)	
Emotional giftedness the high end of emotional intelligence	
Spiritual giftedness facility for transpersonal experience	
Multilevel development unilevel vs. multilevel developmental process	

identify similar themes, for instance, hypersensitivity, anxiety and fearfulness, low self-esteem (self-doubt), pressure to meet expectations (burden of "the gift"), perfectionism, conflict with teachers or classmates, noncompliance (resistance to compulsion), depression, loss and grief (coping with death), and so on.

14.6 Intensity and Sensitivity

Emotional overexcitability is about what stimulates the person's feelings and emotions. It is further differentiated into emotional intensity and sensitivity. Emotional *sensitivity* corresponds in many ways to emotional intelligence, the ability to perceive and respond to nuances of emotion and feeling in others, in oneself, and in group interactions. It may be so acute that it becomes hypersensitivity. Emotional *intensity* (passion) is about the amount of energy being expressed. With some people the intensity of their expression is so great that it may be felt as a pressure wave. Intensity of concentration, and their passion for a subject or talent, distinguish gifted children; as one of them said: "A passion is something that rules your life. You want to know everything that there is to know and you want to be the best at it. An interest is something that is cool, and you would like to know more, but if you don't that's okay too" (Schultz and Delisle 2006a, p. 90).

Emotional life of the gifted encompasses so much that only a few selected themes can be discussed (Table 14.1). In the responses to the OEQ positive feelings predominate. The dominant affect tends to be love, compassion, caring, optimism, appreciation of beauty, and the like. Bonds of deep affection involve parents and siblings, pets and favorite places, whether it is grandma's house, an orchard, a spot by the river, or backstage of the school theater.

The role of contact with nature in our emotional well-being has received very little attention. With the worsening environmental condition of the planet and growing urbanization, the opportunity for children to spend time in nature and explore it has all but vanished (Louv 2005).

Younger children have much empathy for the natural world. They empathize with a wilting plant, a tree whose limb is cut off, a crushed spider, and rise in indignation against maltreatment of living things. We belittle it by calling it animism because we don't see the moral imagination of the child who identifies with what is living and seems sentient. This feeling is extended to stuffed animals or any objects of which the child is especially fond. When we grow up we still do it, too, when we identify with our car or piece of jewelry (Piechowski 2006).

Gifted adolescents describe friendships in terms of intuitive connection and mutual understanding on a deep level. Friendships transcend gender stereotypes and are as easily formed between boys and girls as between boys only or girls only. Introverted and nonathletic gifted youngsters have a particularly difficult time finding friends – they are a minority (nonathletic) within a minority (gifted), which may be further compounded by any degree of "geekiness" (Anderegg 2007; Tannenbaum 1962).

Being intense is an ineradicable part of the gifted self. To most people being intense means "too much," creating an obvious challenge to find friends of similar level of intensity and passion. When asked how they see their own self (identity), some said that their self is unknown, elusive, or hidden; some described themselves in opposites. For example, a 16-year gifted girl said: "For every adjective I can think of there is one that contradicts it entirely: artistic but can't write neatly (so you've seen), lovable, yet a bitch; shy but loud, mature but silly, calm but 'spastic,' together yet ready for a nervous breakdown" (Piechowski 2006, p. 174). Others saw themselves as competent yet highly self-aware and weighed down by the burden of "the gift." For example, a 17-year old boy said this about himself (Piechowski 2006, p. 178):

> I am an existence perched in a precarious balance above the abyss of failure, sorrow, despair, and everything else associated with people of misfortune. I am held up by a few slender supports, among them self-confidence and a few raw talents and abilities. Forces weighing down on these supports…are the responsibility accompanying ability and the expectations of others…. The supports have bent but not broken, dipping into the chasm, but always rebounding with renewed strength.

Struggles with self-doubt, low self-concept, and lack of self-acceptance are common. In adolescence the self keeps changing – awareness of having many selves, or even being split into a thousand fragments, is not unusual. It's part of emotional growing and developing one's identity, which may be intensified in the process of multilevel development.

Because they are aware of the larger picture and their frame of reference may be the whole universe, gifted adolescents may feel as a little "insignificant human speck in the vast universe trying to make something of itself but will probably not succeed" (words of a 15-year old, Piechowski 2006, p. 172). But they can also feel predestined for their mission in life, an inner imperative called *entelechy* (Lovecky 1990). In such cases the qualities of will and self-determination become prominent and will clash with compulsory demands and authoritarian commands.

For gifted young people it is not always easy to admit being talented. The expectations of others for gifted children "to fulfill their potential" (as if one could know what that is) create pressure that is an unwelcome burden, because already one of the outstanding dominant traits of most gifted young people is a feeling of responsibility. Expectations and pressures from others rob them of their own initiative only to make the responsibility weigh all the more heavily on their shoulders. They are well aware of it. The question, who owns "the gift," is rarely considered (Clark 2005).

14.7   Sense of Fairness and Empathy: A Natural Response

The value of working for the common good is something gifted children understand readily. One teacher of the gifted said this about the difference in teaching gifted and regular students:

> One thing I have not realized until I returned to the regular classroom was that gifted students' heightened ability to perceive connections meant that I extensively used their empathy for others to teach broad concepts at a depth I find difficult to even start to address with my current classes. The empathy made the abstract very personal. Most of my current students cannot get beyond their own narrow world, and for some, not even beyond their skins. (Frank 2006, p. 166)

Gifted children's quick empathic response to the needs of others, their misfortunes and tragedies has been well documented (Lewis 1992; Lovecky 1992; Piechowski 2003; Roeper 2004, 2008; Silverman 1994; Waldman 2001) yet, obviously, it is not true of all gifted children. The statement quoted above shows the gifted students' capacity for empathy as a way of knowing. Sense of fairness and empathy are strong feelings that compel a person to act – to offer help when help is needed, to oppose injustice, to redress wrongs suffered by innocent persons. It's the essence of moral action.

The capacity for empathy as part of gifted children's intellectual makeup is something that deserves more attention. We have come late upon the knowledge that rational thought is ineffectual without feeling. In a study of individuals who showed a curious defect – an ability to solve moral problems through reasoning but inability to respond to emotionally charged pictures of human suffering – a lesion was found that severed the connection between the reasoning and feeling functions of the brain (Damasio 1994). A patient with this type of lesion remains unimpaired on tests of intelligence, moral reasoning, and the like. The impairment is revealed in the lack of emotional response to human tragedy and the inability to arrive at a decision when given the choice to exercise preference for, say, Wednesday versus Friday for the next appointment. In Damasio's view, this exposed the error in Descartes' saying "I think therefore I am" instead of "I feel therefore I am," and, one might add, "Because I feel, I can evaluate my reasoning." Evaluation as a process of appraisal involves feeling to decide that something is more desirable or less desirable than the alternative (Bowlby 1969). Centuries of placing reasoning above feeling now seems a pretty foolish enterprise since one cannot work properly without the other.

Tannenbaum (1998) pointed out that we tend to look at giftedness only in positive light and that we leave out gifted people who do harm, whether on a small or large scale. For a gifted person without emotional overexcitability there is no imperative to feel compassion or to be moved to altruistic action. To be effectual, morals and ethics need the engine of the heart. One-sided, harsh emotions like ambition, striving for power, ruthless competition, a drive to win at all cost (without regard for cost to others) can be found in gifted people lacking compassion and caring. There is no lack of examples: a secretary's of defense fascination with precision bombs, a Nobel Prize winner making inappropriate remarks about female brains, financial whizzes and manipulators bringing ruin on thousands of people, amoral presidential advisers, writers and film makers depicting violence and evil for their thrill value, and the list goes on.

14.8 What Causes Conflict for the Gifted

Being gifted inevitably leads to conflict. Gifted adolescents described their conflict with those who brag, are insensitive and irresponsible. Clearly, these behaviors offend their empathy, caring and sense of fairness. A frequently mentioned conflict arises with teachers who do not accept students' views, their knowledge, and their questions, in short, teachers who do not show respect for their students (Piechowski 2006; Schultz and Delisle 2006a, b).

Being forced to act against one's will raises *resistance to compulsion*, a much overlooked but very basic phenomenon (Seligman 1975; Piechowski 2006). Gifted students, and the creative ones especially, react very strongly and viscerally when they are denied choice and respect. Procrastination, refusal to work, as well as learning difficulties are born from this kind of resistance. Also being forced to adhere to a belief one has not chosen. The students then assert, by any means possible, their self, individual identity, right to be heard, respected, and given choice (Roeper 1998). In such situations resisting to be dominated could be viewed as taking a moral stance to preserves one's integrity.

They have fears. Holding to a high standard for themselves they fear making a fool of themselves. Those who are introverted and emotionally sensitive tend to lack self-confidence and suffer agonies when having to speak in front of an audience. They fear not doing well, of not being the best (many are those who feel they have to be the best), they fear failing in their responsibilities, not fulfilling their goals. As one boy said, the list of possible failures is pretty frightening (Piechowski 2006).

They also think of death, a subject that has received too little attention in gifted literature and in school. As one boy said, "can't ask questions related to life, only the textbook" (Schultz and Delisle 2006a, p. 53). Grant (2002, p. 13) observed, "the important topics in educating gifted children are self, meaning, sex, relationship, community, life, purpose, ethics, spirituality – the Most Important Things in Life," subjects that are for the most part avoided. Thinking of death makes some gifted children delve into the meaning of their role in life. Encountering violent death of others – by accident and murder – forces such questions with even greater urgency. Not all are afraid of death. Some expressed curiosity about the process of dying and wished to be able, when the time comes, to be conscious of their own dying and making the transition into the great unknown. Others, however, feared the finality of death and especially of their parents and loved ones more than their own. As for explanation of what happens after death they are divided between those who accept standard explanations offered by religion and those who don't (Piechowski 2006).

Gifted adolescents prefer to cope with their problems on their own. In a study of bullying, Peterson and Ray (2006) found that rather than report it and ask for help, gifted students chose to handle it themselves. Sometimes it meant to just grit their teeth, endure, and not complain. This may explain why despite their overexcitabilities, the suicide rate of gifted young people is not higher than their nongifted counterparts (Cross 1996; Cross et al. 2006).

14.9 Emotional Giftedness

Emotionally gifted children have deep empathy and respond to the needs and hurts of others (Roeper 1982). Such children cannot rest until they have set things right for others. This is especially noteworthy when the other is a stranger or someone disliked, e.g., when a child makes a special effort to be friendly to the class bully as did one 10-year old girl. Intimidating others, she explained, was his way of covering his own insecurity. Another girl, upset over her teacher's unfair treatment of a classmate, took her own paper, tore it into pieces and threw it into the wastebasket to show her moral outrage at the teacher's prejudice. There are also mediators and peacemakers. Terry, a gifted 9-year old was a natural leader but he often held back when he worked in groups to allow others to shine. One day he defended an "at risk" student, a boy who received a black eye in a wrestling tournament. The other boys teased him about the incident and embarrassed him. Terry told them, "you all know it was an accident so drop the subject." His tone was so sincere and authoritative that the boys ceased their teasing.

To be emotionally gifted is to dare to act on one's awareness. If there are hungry people one feeds them and makes sure they won't go hungry from now on. If one sees someone in distress one offers relief. Unfairness and injustice call for defending people's rights. Strongly felt caring becomes the motivation for altruistic behavior.

Strongly felt empathy moves quickly to action. Heather Tobis Booth, co-director of Citizen Action in Chicago recalled how, when she first encountered injustice, she reacted instantly (Witty 1991):

> I was in first grade at P.S. 200. I arrived in the schoolyard one morning and saw a little black boy named Benjamin surrounded by some other kids. They were picking up stones and starting to throw them, because they believed he had stolen this girl's lunch money. I ran up to him and stood beside him. And they stopped. I remember thinking something like "you don't treat people like this."

Compassion may move a youngster to personal sacrifice. A highly gifted high school student decided that after graduation he was not going to the university but to work with the homeless.

There are many preteens and early teens who take up social action on behalf of others, actions that become large scale operations extending over many states, or even many nations. For example, raising thousands of dollars for deaf and blind children, victims of abuse, sending over 100,000 books to African children, providing suitcases for children going into foster homes, providing kid packs for children victims of domestic violence whose parents are in jail, are only a few of the ingenious, effective organizational efforts that are motivated by compassion in these very young people (Lewis 1991; Piechowski 2003; Silverman 1994; Waldman 2001).

Emotional giftedness represents the high end of emotional intelligence. Mayer et al. (2001) devised ways of measuring components of emotional intelligence. In one of their tests they asked teenagers how they handled emotionally difficult situations: "Think about the last time you were out with some friends and they wanted to do something you were uncomfortable with." Mayer et al. hypothesized that emotionally gifted adolescents will resist going along with unsavory intentions of their friends. The results confirmed the hypothesis. Consequently the concept of emotional giftedness was validated. The biological basis of emotional giftedness becomes open to research with the discovery of mirror neurons. These neurons are engaged in empathy and understanding the moods and intentions of others. They are more strongly activated in people who score higher on an empathy scale (Gazzola et al. 2006).

Emotional giftedness at advanced level of development is represented by Eleanor Roosevelt, Etty Hillesum, Peace Pilgrim, Paul Robeson, A. J. Muste, Bishop Tutu, all profoundly spiritual persons, and can be also found in case studies of self-actualizing people (Brennan and Piechowski 1991; Mróz 2002; Payne 1987; Piechowski 1990). In their research on moral commitment, Ann Colby and William Damon studied 23 moral exemplars who dedicated their lives to the poor, world peace, civil rights, ethics in business and in medicine, sanctuary movement, and the like (Colby and Damon 1992). They found that those who were moved to action by compassion had an easier time keeping a peaceful heart than those who were fighting social injustice. In other words, being inspired by altruistic love appears to diminish conflict and friction. Fighting for social justice makes conflict and friction unavoidable.

The first piece of research exploring the application of Dabrowski's theory to the personality of a teacher of the gifted is Frank's (2006) study of an inspirational teacher. The criteria of multilevelness applied by Frank revealed an authentic individual, thoughtfully and deliberately engaged in a teaching grounded in the moral foundation of his advanced level of development. The effectiveness of this teacher lay in his Socratic method as an empathic and moral education that can be called teaching for life in the truest sense.

14.10   Positive Maladjustment

Mayer et al. (2001) realized that the young people in their study who took a stand in opposition to peer pressure displayed what Dabrowski named *positive maladjustment*. Positive maladjustment is a term for opposition to unethical behavior and moral compromise, self-interest and prejudice. It means standing by one's ideals and having the fortitude to stand alone (Dabrowski 1970). When empathy and sense of justice inspire action to help and protect others then emotional giftedness and positive maladjustment overlap (Piechowski 1997a). Resisting peer pressure for drugs, sex, and subversive acts are examples of positive maladjustment in which empathy and caring play a lesser role.

Standing by one's beliefs and ideals is not uncommon for gifted teens. Here are two examples (Piechowski 2006). A 16-year old gifted student was asked the question *How well do you like being all by yourself?* She replied:

Depends – all on the circumstances. I can take standing alone – if I have to. I spent 7 years of my life (almost 7) as a social outcast because I refused to conform to some demands of my society or couldn't conform to others – I'm not at all likely to be afraid of ostracism now.

To be true to oneself may indeed require a person to stand alone at times. The following is a reply to *What situations bring you in conflict with others?* A 16-year old girl said:

My opinions are quite different from other students my age. This many times brings conflict between someone in my class and myself. For example, many kids in my class don't think drinking is dangerous and I do. I don't believe in it and I believe it is a waste of time. This sometimes causes a hassle. Another thing my classmates disagree with me on is styles. Many students buy clothes because they are "in style." I don't. If I like them I get them, if I hate them I leave them at the store "in style" or not! (Piechowski, 2006, p. 209)

14.11 Fostering Emotional Growth as Character Development

Examining emotional life leads to the question of how to give it proper attention and help cultivate it. One way is to lead psychosynthesis exercises, or any other guided imagery designed with similar focus. Psychosynthesis techniques are designed for personal and spiritual growth (Ferrucci 1982). Among the principal elements of personal growth are: training one's will as an executive faculty (i.e., operating by choosing a course of action rather than forcing oneself), training for concentration, learning about different parts of one's personality, finding one's inner authority and guidance from within, working toward a synthesis of conflicting parts of oneself, practicing a sense of purpose (Piechowski 2006, Chapter 20).

I have been leading psychosynthesis exercises for a number of years, first with undergraduate students, then with gifted children aged 10–17 (Piechowski 2006, Chapter 20). Gifted children, with very few exceptions, have great capacity for detailed visualization and absorption in the imaginal experience. These techniques have also been adapted for elementary age children (Fugitt 2001; Murdock 1988). Another way of attending to emotional life is through group process devoted to emotionally charged issues. In a safe space, where no judgment or criticism is allowed to interfere with the process, teens discuss feelings, family, relationships, and the future (Peterson 1995).

14.12 Emotional Growth and Psychological Types

Jung's (1971) concept of psychological type identifies four continuous personality dimensions from extroversion to introversion (E–I), from sensation to intuition (S–N), and from thinking to feeling (T–F). One would expect these dimensions to correspond to the overexcitabilities, for instance thinking to intellectual or feeling to emotional. However, there is very little correlation between overexcitabilities and these dimensions (low correlation for sensual and imaginational with F, and no correlation for psychomotor, intellectual, and emotional). The reason is this: the Jungian dimensions are different constructs from overexcitabilities. They refer to *habitual* ways of dealing with the data of experience, the overexcitabilities refer to the *heightened* capacities for both apprehending and generating the data of experience (Lysy and Piechowski 1983). A further distinction into judging (J) and perceiving (P) was introduced by Myers and Myers-Briggs (Myers and Myers 1995). There is a significant correlation (.37) between imaginational overexcitability and type P (Lysy and Piechowski).

The gifted are evenly divided between extroverts and introverts (Hawkins 1998; Cross et al. 2006). The higher the level of giftedness, the frequency of both the intuitive (N) and the perceiving (P) type rises dramatically (Meckstroth 2006). The highly gifted Rhodes scholars are more than ten to one intuitive, and type P is close to twice as frequent as type J. In the general population of high school students it is just the opposite: the intuitive type is about five times less frequent than the sensation type (Myers and Myers 1995). This is one significant source for the gifted feeling "different," consequently not fitting in school – their predominant type is opposite of that of mainstream students and teachers (Cross et al. 2006). The prevalence of the intuitive type is consistent with higher frequency of multilevel developmental potential among the gifted.

Myers and Myers (1995) described the "judging" type as oriented toward action by personal executive power of will and choice, while the "perceiving" type as oriented toward embracing experience: "The judging types believe that life should be willed and decided, while the perceptive types regard life as something to be experienced and understood" (p. 69). From analysis of responses rated as emotional overexcitability two types of emotional growth have been identified in gifted adolescents: rational–altruistic and introspective (Piechowski 1989). They correspond exactly to the judging/perceiving distinction. Thus one validates the other as the two typologies were derived independently.

The rational–altruistic type so far has not been analyzed into internal components. The introspective type has eight intrapersonal components. Although on the surface people of the J type, being organized and planful, fit society's yardstick for defining a "good citizen" they are nevertheless capable of deep inner life (Lysy and Piechowski 1983; Piechowski 2006). Schools clearly prefer J type students because they tend toward achievement and tend not to buck the system unless their logical thinking and strong sense of fairness see a violation of basic principles and rights.

14.13 Multilevel Development

Theories that address moral development tend toward a "progression from rigidity, self-absorption, and dependence on authority to more sophistication, flexibility and independence as mature persons" but differ as to "what causes movement from one stage to the next" (Tannenbaum 1998, p. 99). For Dabrowski true moral development begins with the experience of inner conflict between lower and higher levels in oneself. The lower levels contain all that one finds in oneself unbecoming, even disgusting and reprehensible. The higher levels contain all that one finds desirable and ideal. It is a "multilevel" conflict. This concept of "multilevelness" can be applied to almost any behavior and human phenomenon. Its great value lies in making possible to sort out experience and behavior according to level. For instance love on a low level will be possessive, dominating, and controlling, while love on a high level will be nonpossessive and with the highest regard for the object of love (Dabrowski 1977). The theory found confirmation in cross-cultural validation of overexcitability profiles and in several empirical tests (Falk et al. 1997, 2008; Piechowski 1975, 2008).[2] Dabrowski linked the potential for multilevel development with the strength of emotional, intellectual, and imaginational overexcitabilities.

For the understanding of emotional growth of gifted children, the distinction between a unilevel and a multilevel developmental process is the most relevant (Piechowski 2008). In *unilevel process* values are relative rather than universal, inner conflicts are recycled rather than resolved, relationships with others do not have a steady footing. Trying every new trend, following fads, being guided primarily by others' opinions is an individual without a psychological center. The shifting nature of the person's identity depends on the circumstances. Such is often the self of an adolescent. When the process intensifies it becomes *unilevel disintegration*.

A change comes when the person begins to tire of this state of affairs with its meaningless emotional treading water and growing malaise. The search for a way out starts with the realization of the possibility of a more meaningful focus in life. A sense of higher and lower in oneself opens new horizons. Sensing the possibility of something higher in oneself engenders the feeling of inferiority, not to others but toward oneself. It is an inferiority before one's unrealized, more evolved and ideal self. Soon this feeling of inferiority toward oneself is followed by an array of inner currents and rifts with descriptive names like disquietude with oneself, dissatisfaction with oneself, positive maladjustment, and so on. What they all have in common is the vertical axis of self-evaluation, that judges the distance from the higher in oneself, which attracts, and grows a stronger reaction against the lower in oneself, which repels. Dabrowski firmly believed that moral exemplars share human values that are universal. His theory details out the process of development through inner transformation (Dabrowski 1967).

When we can spot in a young person an inner dialogue, self-judgment, distress over a moral conflict, we have in front of us a *multilevel* process. The intro-

---

[2] Additional empirical support comes by way of a positive correlation (.44) between the Jungian intuitive type (N) and developmental level, and that all five overexcitabilities correlated with developmental level: psychomotor .26, sensual .31, intellectual .57, imaginational .38, emotional .59 (Lysy and Piechowski 1983). Furthermore, on detailed scrutiny, Dabrowski's construct of Level IV corresponds exactly to Maslow's description of self-actualizing people (Piechowski 2008). When two independent sets of observations and constructs converge, we can be confident that a real phenomenon has been identified.

spective emotional growth mentioned earlier, has eight components, which help recognize the specifics of the multilevel emotional development in adolescents. They are: (1) awareness of growing and changing, (2) awareness of feelings, interest in others and empathy toward them, (3) occasional feelings of unreality, (4) inner dialogue, (5) self-examination, (6) self-judgment, (7) searching, problem-finding, asking existential questions, and (8) awareness of one's real self (Piechowski 1989; 2006). The values in such a process can be both individual and universal; the feelings toward oneself can be rife with inner conflict or they can be showing an emergent self-direction; feelings towards others will be sincerely democratic and displaying awareness of interdependence. In cases of intense inner conflict, suffering, inner seeking, and depression, the process becomes *multilevel disintegration*. This process may become very deep and may be misunderstood. How to read the signs and how to assist through counseling has been described elsewhere (Jackson et al. 2009; Jackson and Moyle 2009).

Let me close with an example of a boy awakening to the realization that competition in which there are winners and losers clashes with the virtue of caring, a distinctly moral concern. Here are replies, two years apart, from a boy confronted with asking himself, *Who am I?* When he was 15 he wrote: "I feel that I am a person who is on the earth that is destined to use his abilities and talents to his fullest. This is simply what I think I really am." He gave it much thought over the next two years. At 17 he recognized a moral conflict between getting ahead and being considerate of others (Piechowski 2006, p. 210):

> The answer to this question has changed over the past few years. A few years ago I was a person who wanted things for himself. Now I am trying to change that person to a person who wants to contribute to others and the world not just himself. Obtaining this type of person in this world is not that easy. The one thing that is a roadblock is competition. Not necessarily losing to other people, but beating them. How can I compete to get into medical school when a doctor is supposed to build people's confidence and restore their sense of security? The process is self-defeating.

It is not hard to see that this kind of thinking guided the lives of Gandhi, Eleanor Roosevelt, Paul Robeson, Peace Pilgrim, Bishop Tutu, and many others who follow their inner voice.

References

Ackerman, C. (1997). Identifying gifted adolescents using personality characteristics: Dabrowski's overexcitabilities. *Roeper Review, 19*, 229–236.

Anderegg, D. (2007). *Who they are and why we need more of them*. New York: Jeremy P. Tarcher/Penguin.

Bouchard, L. L. (2004). An instrument for the measure of Dabrowskian overexcitabilities to identify gifted elementary students. *Gifted Child Quarterly, 48*, 339–350.

Bowlby, J. (1969). Attachment and loss (Vol. 1). *Attachment*. New York: Basic Books.

Brennan, T. P., & Piechowski, M. M. (1991). A developmental framework for self-actualization: Evidence from case studies. *Journal of Humanistic Psychology, 31*, 43–64.

Clark, C. (2005). Personal communication, 12 February 2005.

Cline, S., & Schwartz, D. (1999). *Diverse populations of gifted children.* Upper Saddle River, NJ: Merrill/Prentice-Hall.

Cohen, D., & MacKeith, S. A. (1991). *The development of imagination: The private worlds of childhood.* London: Routledge.

Colby, A., & Damon, W. (1992). *Some do care: Contemporary lives of moral commitment.* New York: Free Press.

Cross, T. L. (1996). Examining claims about gifted children and suicide. *Gifted Child Today, 19,* 46–48.

Cross, T. L., Cassady, J. C., & Miller, K. A. (2006). Suicide ideation and personality characteristics among gifted adolescents. *Gifted Child Quarterly, 50,* 295–306.

Dabrowski, K. (1967). *Personality-shaping through positive disintegration.* Boston, MA: Little, Brown.

Dabrowski, K. (1970). *Mental growth through positive disintegration.* London: Gryf.

Dabrowski, K. (1977). *Theory of levels of emotional development* (Vol. 1). Oceanside, NY: Dabor.

Damasio, A. (1994). *Descartes' error: Emotion, reason, and the human brain.* New York: Putnam.

Damasio, A. (2003). *Looking for Spinoza: Joy, sorrow, and the feeling brain.* Orlando, FL: Harcourt.

Davis, G. A. (2003). Identifying creative students, teaching for creative growth. In N. Colangelo & G. A. Davis (Eds.). *Handbook of gifted education,* 3rd ed. (pp. 311–324). Boston, MA: Allyn & Bacon.

Falk, R. F., Manzanero, J. B., & Miller, N. B. (1997). Developmental potential in Venezuelan and American artists: A cross-cultural validity study. *Creativity Research Journal, 10,* 201–206.

Falk, R. F., Yakmaci-Guzel, B., Balderas, R. A., Chang, A., Sanz, P. S., & Chavez-Eakle, R. A. (2008). Measuring overexcitabilities: Replication across five countries. In S. Mendaglio (Ed.). *Dabrowski's theory of positive disintegration* (pp. 183–199). Scottsdale, AZ: Gifted Potential Press.

Ferrucci, P. (1982). *What we may be: Techniques for psychological and spiritual growth.* New York: Jeremy P. Tarcher/Putnam.

Frank, J. (2006). *Portrait of an inspirational teacher of the gifted.* Unpublished doctoral dissertation, University of Calgary, Calgary, Alberta.

Fugitt, E. D. (2001). *He hit me back first!* Development of the will in children for making choices. Torrance, CA: Jalmar Press.

Gazzola, V., Aziz-Zadeh, L., & Keysers, C. (2006). Empathy and the somatotopic auditory mirror system in humans. *Current Biology, 16,* 1824–1829.

Grant, B. (2002). Looking through the Glasses: J. D. Salinger's wise children and gifted education. *Gifted Child Quarterly, 46,* 6–14.

Gross, M. (1998). The "me" behind the mask: Intellectually gifted students and the search for identity. *Roeper Review, 20,* 167–173.

Hawkins, J. (1998) Giftedness and psychological type. Journal for Secondary Gifted Education, 9, 57–67.

Hollingworth, L. S. (1942/1977). *Children above 180 IQ.* New York: Octagon Books.

Izard, C. E. (1971). *The face of emotion.* New York: Apple-Century-Croft.

Jackson, P. S. and Moyle, V. F. (2009). Integrating the intense experience: Counseling and clinical applications, 105–125.

Jackson, P. S., Moyle, V. F., & Piechowski, M. M. (2009). Emotional life and psychotherapy in light of Dabrowski's theory, 439–467.

James, W. (1902). *The varieties of religious experience.* New York: Modern Library.

Jung, C. G. (1971). *Psychological types. Collected works* (Vol. 6). London: Routledge & Kegan Paul.

Lewis, B. (1992). *Kids with courage.* Minneapolis, MN: Free Spirit.

Louv, R. (2005). *Last child in the woods: Saving our children from nature-deficit disorder.* Chapel Hill, NC: Algonquin Books.

Lovecky, D. V. (1990). Warts and rainbows: Issues in the psychotherapy of the gifted. *Advanced Development, 2,* 65–83.

Lovecky, D. V. (1992). Exploring social and emotional aspects of giftedness in children. *Roeper Review, 15*, 18–25.

Lysy, K. Z., & Piechowski, M. M. (1983). Personal growth: An empirical study using Jungian and Dabrowskian measures. *Genetic Psychology Monographs, 108*, 267–320.

Mayer, J. D., Perkins, D. M., Caruso, D. R., & Salovey, P. (2001). Emotional intelligence and giftedness. *Roeper Review, 23*, 131–137.

Meckstroth, E. A. (2006). Personal communication, 3 August, 2006.

Myers, I. B., & Myers, P. B. (1995). *Gifts differing: Understanding personality type*. Palo Alto, CA: Davies-Black.

Mróz, A. (2002). *Rozwój osoby wedlug teorii dezyntegracji pozytywnej Kazimierza Dabrowskiego* (Individual development according to Dabrowski's theory of positive disintegration). Unpublished doctoral dissertation, Catholic University of Lublin, Lublin, Poland.

Murdock, M. (1988). *Spinning inward: Using guided imagery with children for learning, creativity & relaxation*. Boston, MA: Shambhala.

Payne, C. (1987). *A psychobiographical study of the emotional development of a controversial protest leader*. Unpublished doctoral dissertation, Northwestern University, Evanston, IL.

Peterson, J. S. (1995). *Talk with teens about feelings, family, relationships, and the future*. Minneapolis, MN: Free Spirit.

Peterson, J. S., & Ray, K. E. (2006). Bullying among the gifted: The subjective experience. *Gifted Child Quarterly, 50*, 252–269.

Piechowski, M. M. (1975). A theoretical and empirical approach to the study of development. *Genetic Psychology Monographs, 92*, 231–297.

Piechowski, M. M. (1989). Developmental potential and the growth of the self. In J. VanTassel-Baska & P. Olszewski-Kubilius (Eds.). *Patterns of influence on gifted learners: The home, the school, and the self* (pp. 87–101). New York: Teachers College Press.

Piechowski, M. M. (1990). Inner growth and transformation in the life of Eleanor Roosevelt. *Advanced Development, 2*, 35–53.

Piechowski, M. M. (1991). Emotional development and emotional giftedness. In N. Colangelo & G. Davis (Eds.). *Handbook of gifted education* (pp. 285–306). Boston, MA: Allyn & Bacon.

Piechowski, M. M. (1992). Giftedness for all seasons: Inner peace in time of war. In N. Colangelo, S. G. Assouline, & D. L. Ambroson (Eds.). *Talent development. Proceedings of the 1991 Henry B. and Jocelyn Wallace National Research Symposium on Talent Development*. Unionville, NY: Trillium Press.

Piechowski, M. M. (1997a). Emotional giftedness: The measure of intrapersonal intelligence. In N. Colangelo & G. A. Davis (Eds.). *The handbook of gifted education*, 2nd ed. Boston, MA: Allyn & Bacon.

Piechowski, M. M. (1997b). Emotional giftedness: An expanded view. *Apex, A New Zealand Journal of Gifted Education, 10*, 37–47.

Piechowski, M. M. (1999). Overexcitabilities. In M. Runco & S. Pritzker (Eds.). *Encyclopedia of creativity*. New York: Academic.

Piechowski, M. M. (2003). From William James to Maslow and Dabrowski: Excitability of character and self-actualization. In D. Ambrose, L. Cohen, & A. J. Tannenbaum (Eds.), *Creative intelligence: Toward a theoretic integration* (pp. 283–322). Cresskill, NJ: Hampton Press.

Piechowski, M. M. (2006). *"Mellow out," they say. If I only could: Intensities and sensitivities of the young and bright*. Madison, WI: Yunasa Books.

Piechowski, M. M. (2008). Discovering Dabrowski's theory. In S. Mendaglio (Ed.). *Dabrowski's theory of positive disintegration* (pp. 41–77). Scottsdale, AZ: Gifted Potential Press.

Piechowski, M. M., & Colangelo, N. (1984). Developmental potential of the gifted. *Gifted Child Quarterly, 28*, 80–88.

Piechowski, M. M., & Miller, N. B. (1995). Assessing developmental potential in gifted children: A comparison of methods. *Roeper Review, 17*, 176–180.

Piirto, J. (2002). *"My teeming brain": Understanding creative writers*. Cresskill, NJ: Hampton Press.

Piirto, J. (2004). *Understanding creativity*. Scottsdale, AZ: Great Potential Press.

Roeper, A. (1982). How gifted cope with their emotions. *Roeper Review, 5*, 21–24.

Roeper, A. (1998). The "I" of the beholder: An essay on the self, its existence, and its power. *Roeper Review, 20*, 144–149.

Roeper, A. (2004). *My life experiences with gifted children*. Denver: DeLeon.

Roeper, A. (2008). Global awareness and gifted children. *Roeper Review, 30*, 8–10.

Schultz, R. A., & Delisle, J. R. (2006a) *Smart talk: What kids say about growing up gifted*. Minneapolis, MN: Free Spirit.

Schultz, R. A., & Delisle, J. R. (2006b). *More than a test score: Teens talk about being gifted, talented, or otherwise extra-ordinary*. Minneapolis, MN: Free Spirit.

Seligman, M. E. P. (1975). *Helplessness*. San Francisco: W.H. Freeman.

Silverman, L. K. (Ed.). (1993). *Counseling the gifted and talented*. Denver: Love.

Silverman, L. K. (1994). The moral sensitivity of gifted children and the evolution of society. *Roeper Review, 17*, 110–116.

Singer, J. L. (1975). *The inner world of daydreaming*. New York: Harper & Row.

Singer D. G., & Singer, J. L. (1990). *The house of make-believe*. Cambridge, MA: Harvard University Press.

Tannenbaum, A. J. (1962). *Adolescents' attitudes toward academic brilliance*. New York: Bureau of Publications, Columbia University.

Tannenbaum, A. J. (1998). Giftedness: The ultimate instrument for good and evil. In N. Colangelo & S. G. Assouline (Eds.). *Talent development IV. Proceedings of the 1998 Henry B. and Jocelyn Wallace National Research Symposium on Talent Development* (pp. 89–120). Scottsdale, AZ: Great Potential Press.

Taylor, M. (1999). *Imaginary companions and the children who create them*. New York: Oxford University Press.

Terman, L. M. (1925). *Mental and physical traits of a thousand gifted children* (Vol. 1). Stanford, CA: Stanford University Press.

Tieso, C. L. (2007). Patterns of overexcitabilities in identified gifted students and their parents: A hierarchical model. *Gifted Child Quarterly, 51*, 11–22.

Tolan, S. S. (1994). Psychomotor overexcitability in the gifted: An expanded perspective. *Advanced Development, 6*, 77–86.

Waldman, J. (2001). *Teens with the courage to give*. Berkeley, CA: Conari Press.

Watkins, M. (1990). *Invisible guests: The development of imaginal dialogues*. Boston, MA: Sigo Press.

Witty, M. C. (1991). *Life history studies of committed lives*. Ph.D. dissertation. Northwestern University, Evanston, IL.

Yoo, J. E., & Moon, S. M. (2006). Counseling needs of gifted students: An analysis of intake forms at a university-based counseling center. *Gifted Child Quarterly, 50*, 52–61.

Chapter 15
Depth Psychology and Integrity

F. Christopher Reynolds and Jane Piirto

Abstract Investigators of depth psychology turn studies of the psyche toward the unconscious, believing that the ego consciousness typically receives excessive emphasis. When depth psychology is applied to high ability and creativity, often-hidden aspects of human ability come to the fore. These include notions of the collective unconscious, the transcendence of the psyche, the presence of archetypes, unbidden, positive inspiration, and the darker side of human nature. Consequently, the gifts of bright, creative people can be both blessing and poison, and can have strong influences on moral–ethical issues. Educational implications include more attention to inspiration in the arts and the search for inner truth.

Keywords Adolescent psychology · Creativity · Depth psychology · Integrity · Jung, Carl · Hillman, James · Popular culture · Summer programs · Talent in domains · Teaching French

Depth psychology, by making the unconscious or soul its first principle, traces its lineage to the roots of Western culture. The Socratic dictum, *Knowledge is virtue*, invites us into the individual's often tragic struggle to know the good and to do it. In our literature, concern for what is ethical has been at the heart of education for 2,500 years. Hillman (1975, 1983) traced the tradition of soul through Jung, Freud, Schelling, Vico, Ficino, Plotinus, Plato and Heraclitis. In all, whether it be Plato's (1952) condemnation of the Sophists for the mass merchandising of an imitation of virtue, Plotinus' (1991) call for a higher inspiration than socially dictated civic virtues, or Jung's (1959) appeals to avoid collective possession by entering into the darkness of our own psyches, the recurring theme is of the apparent surface of

F.C. Reynolds (✉)
Berea Public Schools, Berea, OH 44017, USA
e-mail: spiriman@aim.com

J. Piirto
Schar College of Education, Ashland University, OH 44805, Ashland
e-mail: janepiirto@mac.com

D. Ambrose, T. Cross (eds.), *Morality, Ethics, and Gifted Minds*,
DOI: 10.1007/978-0-387-89368-6_15,
© Springer Science+Business Media LLC 2009

ego-consciousness and the depths of the unconscious below that surface. The source of this virtue has always found its home in the depths.

It follows that if the depths are the unconscious, any penetrating discussion of ethics will require us to always see through our ego-consciousness into what lies hidden, forgotten, unacknowledged, just below the surface in even our best-intended judgments and actions. Our certainty is always full of holes and hidden motives, founded upon fictions (Hillman 1983) that present themselves as facts. This is troubling. However, the tradition of depth encourages us to enter into the trouble which that understanding produces, because it is precisely within that stance that authentic virtue and higher inspiration might inform us.

Students, parents, and the public expect educators to embody integrity. The idea of integrity originates from the Latin (*integer*) and the Tamil (*tag* – a game in which one is touched). Beebe (1992) explicated the term and its meanings in a depth psychological way with reference to the therapeutic relationship. This chapter will attempt to transfer these concepts to the educational setting, with an emphasis on the education of the talented. While numerous works have been written from this point of view, about ethics in the psychotherapeutic setting, (Edinger 1992; Guggenbuhl-Craig 1995; Marlan 2005; Monick 1987; Neumann 1969; Zoja 2007), few have been written using a depth psychological approach to ethics in education.

Young, would-be teachers are cautioned about ethics in their pedagogical courses. They receive warnings, admonitions, and advice about what to do and not to do in various settings and situations that may arise. Professors of education, themselves former teachers, recall situations where their own integrity was developed through the crucibles of practice, of working within schools, and with students, colleagues, parents, and others. But integrity also develops out of conflict, when one or the other, the educator and the student, have themselves felt violated. This violation can be caused, one by the other, by the institution of school itself, by the community in which the school is located, by the parents of the student or the family and friends of the teacher. Though this conflict can have negative results, often, when those involved have worked through the experience, they come out of it bonded more closely and more intensely.

Learning, as Plato has said in the *Phaedrus* (1952), is an encounter between the teacher and the taught that is erotic (not necessarily sexual, but fraught with love and regard; love being the exposure of one's vulnerability to the other's, and regard being the gaze of recognition, of feeling "seen" by the other). The encounter is mutual. The teacher becomes the taught and the taught becomes the teacher when this happens in the relationship. The class may be large or small, but each, the teacher and the taught, feels a thunderbolt, a prickling, a physical sensation that this moment of *educare* is made tangible in the physical response of the body to the encounter. This happens to all teachers and to all students when true learning takes place.

A depth psychological approach to the question of integrity focuses on what lies beneath the surface (in the depths) of common or uncommon encounters and situations found within the educational enterprise. This chapter is organized to discuss (a) notions of the personal and collective unconscious; (b) the transcendence of the psyche; and (c) the presence of archetypes, including their unbidden positive inspiration as well as their relation to the darker side of human nature. We offer recommendations as well as examples that focus on images within schools and in the popular culture, with an emphasis on the bright and talented students.

15.1 The Notion of the Personal and the Collective Unconscious

Though accessed and utilized by the Mesmerists in the 1700s (Reynolds & Piirto 2005), knowledge of the unconscious and its effects on waking life did not return into Western awareness until the 1900 publication of Freud's *Die Traumdeutung*, translated as *The Interpretation of Dreams* in English. It is important to recognize that along with his description of the unconscious, Freud understood its dreaming mode as the primary method of resolving moral conflicts between the various complexes and societal norms. In his assumption, he reasserted with the tradition mentioned above that, when faced with questions of conscience, the ego complex was only the surface character in a larger drama of psychological wholeness. Ethical understanding resulted from finding a way of cooperation between the conscious and unconscious. Likewise, any moral striving that left the unconscious split off from the conscious was neurotic, and therefore, problematic.

In 1912, with the publication of *Symbols of Transformation*, Jung (1959) made an even stronger case for including the unconscious depths in any moral discussion. For him, Freud's personal unconscious of the patient's complexes did not go deep enough. Beneath what we now call the *personal unconscious* was the *collective unconscious*, also referred to as the *objective psyche*.

Clearly, if the ego's role was as a surface player for Freud, with Jung and the psychological plunge into collective unconscious, the ego complex became a tiny archipelago (Hollis 1996) rising out of a vast ocean. Its existence was much more precarious and prone to being overwhelmed by larger forces. That is precisely how depth psychologists explained the evils of the twentieth century's two world wars, and its murderous mass movements. For them, the modern person, unaware of the unconscious, both personal and collective, was pathologically prone to seek meaning in the anonymous possessive emotional forces of mass movements (Fromm 1941).

15.2 Transferring Depth Psychological Principles to the Classroom

Neumann (1969) sounded three main themes that continue to frame depth psychology's work and goals. Our first recommendation for transferring concepts of integrity from the analytic hour to the classroom is that those educators who honestly wish to wrestle with matters of deepest importance and teach the exceptional with integrity need to incorporate those themes into their own teaching.

Neumann's (1969) themes were, first, that at that time in history, all institutions and collective entities had lost their capacity to assist the modern individual, because the individuality being called forth by the times was at odds with collective thinking and wearing the collective mask. He described how schools, churches, governments – all collective bodies – were enemies to individuality. Second, because the self-destructive forces within the human psyche had reached world-annihilating proportions, there was a moral obligation to acknowledge the power of and enter into a relationship with the unconscious, especially in order to confront and admit the evil that finds shelter in our own attitudes, assumptions, and self-esteem. To do this, Neumann urged us to move away from the "old ethic" (p. 4) whereby we would seek perfection by splitting ourselves into "good" and "bad" and then proceed to identify with only the "good" and deny the "bad" part of ourselves. He encouraged a "new ethic" where we chose wholeness instead of perfection, "to sacrifice the principle of perfection on the altar of wholeness" (p. 6). In depth psychology, this wholeness seeks to make conscious and integrate all elements of the psyche, not only the good, but also those elements which are unwelcome, rejected, even evil – that which Jung called *shadow*. Neumann wrote, "Acceptance of the shadow is the essential basis for the actual achievement of an ethical attitude towards the 'Thou' which is outside me" (p. 8). He urged that "The individual must work through his own basic moral problem before he is in a position to play a responsible part in the collective" (p. 9).

His third theme was that, at a time when the power of the collective had reached such influence, the general attitude toward those who were exceptional was to label them "criminals" (p. 39). He wrote, "The revolutionary (whatever his type) always takes his stand on the side of the inner voice and against the conscience of his time" (p. 39).

His book was an urgent call to the reader to have the courage to break free from the collective, to enter into the unknown of the unconscious, and to be respectful toward those that the collective labeled as wrong, crazy, criminal, inferior, evil, or alien, for they may be the very ones who are ushering in the renewal of the culture.

It is a daunting task to break free of the collective, to enter into one's own unconscious, and more humbly, to reverently approach the outcast, but that does not hinder us from bringing those ideas into the classroom setting and inviting our students to do so. The first author, as a French teacher, uses French literature and art to teach to Neumann's three themes. One of Existentialism's founding ideas, "L'existence précède l'essence" (Sartre 1943) described quite well the first task of breaking away from the collective. For Sartre, an individual's life was nothing more than existence until the moment of truth came, when in a self-creating act she moved against the sickening influence of the group. Such information is like food for the exceptional, because it empowers their urge for freedom and honors their profound feelings of loneliness. Further, Sartre coined the term, *Le regard*, to describe the shaming, judgmental "gaze" that those of the collective use to keep would-be individuals under control. Albert Camus's (1942) novel, *L'Étranger*, offers the opportunity to address Neumann's (1969) "old ethic" because it allows for the values society calls "good" to be questioned with the brutal honesty that made the main character, Meursault, so dangerous.

Entering into the unconscious and honoring the imagination can be done using Surrealist art and St. Exupéry's *Little Prince* (1944) to allow the students' dreams to become part of their educational process. Sardello (1995) encouraged us to employ the ideas of depth psychology with more confidence, and liberate dreams from the analyst's office. The first author has done that in the classroom for the past 25 years. He has observed many students work independently with their own dreams for guidance, inspiration and healing. As a teacher, he honors their dreams with the same respect that the depth tradition encourages. Through dreaming, especially if given importance by teachers through childhood and adolescence, the students can follow Freud's royal road to the unconscious and there become aware of both the light and dark of their psychological selves. Some learn how to live with wholeness and not perfection.

Finally, André Breton's (1952) original goal for surrealism was a "deepening of the foundations of the real" (p. 4) by creating a union of the conscious and the unconscious. That is the same goal as that of depth psychology and of this essay. Including the notion of the personal and collective unconscious into our educational psychology is the foundation that makes true integrity possible.

15.3 The Transcendence of the Psyche

It was Jung's publication of *Symbols of Transformation* in 1912 that shattered and ended his collaboration with Freud. This established the collective unconscious as an integral player in psychological healing and wholeness. Jung amplified the psychological experiences of a certain Miss Miller to demonstrate their mythic, archetypal contents, which extended far beyond her personal life experiences. He noted in the epilogue that had he worked with her, he would have handled the case in such a way as to honor the symbols that were breaking into her consciousness. He wrote, "For patients in this situation it is a positive life-saver when the doctor takes such products seriously and gives the patient access to the meanings they suggest" (p. 442).

It took incredible courage for Jung to publish *Symbols of Transformation*. It represented a restoration of fully-developed archetypal, what we now label holistic, understanding of humanity that is the signature of the lineage of soul traced by Hillman (1975, 1983). He dared to re-assert that to understand humanity, nature, and the cosmos in a whole way, they must be understood as material, psychological, and spiritual. What Jung had discovered in himself and his patients was that complete psychological health included lived experiences of inner divinity that he called the self. Note the intermingling of the physical, psychological, and spiritual when Jung (1959) wrote that for the individual, the *self* was "his wholeness, which is both God and animal – not merely the empirical man, but the totality of his being, which is rooted in his animal nature and reaches out beyond the merely human towards the divine. His wholeness implies a tremendous tension of opposites paradoxically at one with themselves" (p. 303).

Likewise, full inclusion of a depth psychological approach to ethics in education requires the teacher to be able to tolerate and suffer within herself and within her students that same tremendous tension of opposites between the animal nature and the divine that Jung elucidated. Beyond issues of professional integrity in the classroom, as teachers, when approaching the most pressing ethical issues of our times, such as terrorism, global warming, mass extinction, genocide, genetic engineering, and so on, depth psychology offers a possibility of a saving grace called *the transcendent function* (Jung 1959).

Depth psychologists have found that the psyche, if given time and permission to suffer the extreme tension of the opposites inherent to an ethical dilemma, can create out of itself a solution that allows those opposites to be transcended. This transcendence occurs not by overcoming the bifurcation, but by expanding to a greater wholeness that allows the formerly warring pair to co-mingle in a third possibility, a symbol or image of transformation. The transformational merging of the opposites into a new, more expansive psychological capacity is the source for authentic integrity and the virtue that is knowledge and not imitation. In this tradition, virtue is native to the individual soul's goodness, but it cannot be taught. It must come forth by being led out. Which is where the teacher comes in.

15.4   The Presence of Archetypes

The collective unconscious is made up of archetypes. Jung (1959) described them as the numinous, universal, and inherited patterns, which, taken together, constitute the structure of the unconscious which "possess a certain autonomy and specific energy which enables them to attract, out of the conscious mind, those contents best suited to themselves" (p. 232). Hillman (1975) saw archetypes as "the deepest patterns of psychic functioning, the roots of the soul governing the perspectives we have of ourselves and the world" (p. xiii). For depth psychology, the solar hero, sword, swan, swarm, lunar heroine, beauty, love, justice, temperance, sacrifice, rebirth, the basic recurring stories, characters, divine and demonic powers that appear in all cultures in all times, came into existence because they are archetypes. As such, they are still present now, ever influencing, shaping and weaving into our lives. In the analytic relationship, Jung found that "there is a dangerous isolation which everyone feels when confronted by an incomprehensible and irrational aspect of his personality" (p. 442). The curative effect of archetypal knowledge was that, for the individual in the experience, what at first seemed incomprehensible and irrational opened into profound meaning when brought into conscious relationship with its archetype. The images, stories and wisdom belonging to a particular archetype, the collective, impersonal, mythic, and thus eternal basis of the experience, gave a context, a larger pattern within which the isolating aspect of the personality, if integrated, became a healing force that helped the individual come home to his or her own humanity.

We have found that the same curative effect occurs in the educational setting. If what is incomprehensible and irrational can be placed by the teacher upon the wider context of an image, story, myth, or biography, the student feels seen and understood. She gratefully feels she is part of the flow of life as opposed to alien and isolated. A full exploration of archetypes is beyond the scope of this chapter; however, there are two archetypes that we have found most useful when approaching issues of integrity in a whole way. They are the shadow and the daimon.

15.4.1 The Shadow

The shadow is the opposite or complement of the ego and contains qualities the ego does not claim, but which are still part of the personality. In fact, at the beginning of deepening awareness, it is the unconscious itself. Because shadow is often associated with inferiority and shame, it's not a place individuals volunteer to go, even though they are aware of it and constantly drag such feelings around with them. The fairy tale, *Iron Henry*, also known as *The Frog Prince* (Grimm & Grimm 1944), is a wonderful story to share with students. It gives youth permission to feel bad about themselves and urges them to respect the depressions that drag them down. In fact, The Frog Prince offers a process of how to embrace and learn from shadow instead of trying to get over it. In the original, this did not happen with a kiss, but in a fit of rage where the princess threw her hated inferior partner in life against the wall. In his lecture series, *Myths of the Family*, Hillman (1997) offered nine themes in adolescence that are typical in analysis but that families and schools generally deny. They are nine different kinds of frogs, if you will. He encouraged teachers and families to grant teens permission to enter and to assist them into shadow. To initiate them into the deepening of their wholeness allows them a more joyful morality based on the love of life as opposed to the fear of it. Depth psychology contends that going into the dark is a necessary rite of passage in order to move forward and embrace adulthood. Hillman's themes were,

- Fascination with death
- Overwhelming sense of shadow, inferiority, unworthiness and evil
- First profound falling in love and opening to the mysteries of the erotic
- Unexplainable illness
- Desire for ordeals
- Experiences and thoughts about God and religion that may never come again
- Great need for beauty
- Extreme loyalty to friends
- Accidents that take the student out of the normal routine

In our Summer Honors Institute for talented teenagers, for which we have received grants for 19 years, we begin the weeklong experience with wreaths of ivy about our heads (to simulate laurel), and a telling of Plato's "Allegory of the Cave" by one of the philosophy or classics professors who teach in the Institute. In the cave, the people stare at shadows on the wall, but when they go outside the cave, they see the sunlight, and when they go back into the cave, they realize that the shadows have been illusions, and enlightenment comes from being in the open sun. The Platonic ideal of the world of immutable forms, existing only in the mind, is an apt metaphor for what we seek to provide these students with their bright minds. We do not dwell on the shadows, except to say they are false representations of the ideal form in the mind. The depth psychological perspective and the psychologists who teach in the institute (Michael Piechowski and Diane Montgomery) further enlighten the students by teaching them about the necessity for the integration of the shadow into the whole. Madeline L'Engle (1997) wrote about the necessity for the creator to integrate both shadow and light. "It took me a long time to realize the importance of the shadow in keeping things in creative balance," (p. 6) she said. She further noted that the sun stands for the intellect and the shadow stands for intuition: "In the Western world we have become overdependent on the intellect, burdening ourselves with the need for scientific proof, and suffering great imbalance when we forget that fact and truth are not the same thing" (p. 8). That is why we have spoken up for the depth psychological way of knowing, the "poetic way of knowing" with our gifted and talented (Reynolds & Piirto 2005, 2007).

In the film, *The History Boys* (Hytner 2006), a group of intellectually gifted working class boys are groomed for the entrance examinations for elite universities in the UK. They will have a chance to jump social classes if they get high scores on the examination, and social justice will be achieved. The whole idea that gifted children can rise beyond their station by virtue of their intelligence is one of the essentialist beliefs that are foundational to the field of the education of the gifted and talented. Their teachers embody the shadow side of the virtuous teacher archetype; one is a fondler of young boys; one is a fraud who himself never passed the exam; one is the old-maid schoolteacher whose life is supposed to be fulfilled in teaching but is not. The students themselves show their shadow sides: one is a compulsive liar and cheat, another a thief, still another a seducer. That these teachers and students can attain a virtuous denouement despite the ascendancy of shadow is the moral of this mythic story.

The school is called to integrate, rather than shame and split off the shadow. To well-behaved kids, who, when they are out of class, live out violent fantasies in virtual games like Halo and Grand Theft Auto, who put on their iPods and live in a musical world of sex and violence, depth psychology would say, let's honor the perspective and life force that comes through; let's acknowledge split-off, hard-to-admit emotions; let's find ways for the individual to live in relation to the shadows imaged by the video games and sexual songs.

The power of shame is known well enough. Miley Cyrus was thought to lack integrity when she was encouraged to bare a shoulder by artist photographer Annie Liebowitz in *Vanity Fair*, and because of her virginal reputation, she was made to feel shame, while young girls stride the halls of schools and the corridors of malls showing their derrieres and their nipples in imitations of Victoria Secret models, while young boys hide their bodies in baggy pants that fall to the rear end crack, and their slim legs are lost in folds of denim. They wear t-shirts that are several sizes too big, and even their sports clothes have evolved to hide their bodies, while young female athletes display themselves in briefs and bikinis, lunging on the sand volleyball courts, on tracks and on tennis lawns, showing their breasts, muscular arms, and toned rippling skin.

Shame is embodied in the dress of boys, and shamelessness in the dress of girls, a stark turnabout from what schools have sought to enforce in the form of dress codes. Girls have always been admonished to wear skirts of a certain length, tops of a certain cut, while boys were admonished to wear suits, ties, or certain types of shoes. In the early years of this millennium, schools required belts so that pants would not fall down to reveal underwear that was in itself minimal, as in thong, another term that invites the primitive interpretation. For the bright youth, pressure exists, just as it does for all youth. To not conform in dress and in attitude provokes taunting, bullying, and the resultant shame. The shadow side of shame is guilt, the senex or negative father, who imposes a distrust and inhibition against doing what the student is good at – thinking brilliantly or creating outstanding work in a domain of talent. As Beebe (1992) said, shame is confounded by guilt, and both belong to the shadow side of the lightness of giftedness. Depth psychologists urge people to "embrace shame" (Beebe 1992, p. 61). This enables the person to integrate the shadow and its light. Whereas the Freudian and Eriksonian view of shame is to help people feel better about it, the depth psychological view is to integrate it, so that the person is not "ashamed of shame" (p. 62).

Schools have always denied the shadow and have used shame as a tactic to force conformity on students, and perhaps the most susceptible to this tactic are those who strive to be "good," as the bright and talented often do, seeking to learn from and to please the authorities for reasons that are diverse, but which have to do with succeeding in the institution, moving on to the next step in education, getting high grades, meeting expectations, and the like. To integrate the shadow with the positive results obtained from such conformity to the demands of the authorities requires depth psychological work. The second author spilled melted chocolate on her dress while in a home economics class as a senior in high school, and her teacher required her to sit in the class in her slip (an undergarment) while she demonstrated to the class how to remove chocolate stains from wool. I had forgotten that I won the Betty Crocker Homemaker of the Year award, but the shame of sitting among the other girls (thankfully in those days there were no boys in home economics classes), took many years to be turned into an amusing story for her own students about how teachers use shame with good students. Shame operates to contain.

The image of the traditional school, which is often presented in dreams as a contained room with a writing board in front, desks lined up in rows, and windows on one side but not on the other is a place where bright and talented students often do well. They sit near the windows, embracing the light of *educare*. They get good grades, their teachers are pleased, they do well on assessments, and are encouraged to pursue further years within this contained space, or perhaps, to become leaders and teachers within this institution. They seldom move to the dark side, where the doors lead to long hallways within which are other restless souls, trooping in and out of similar rooms, up and down stairs, or into vast parking lots. The students study and do what they are supposed to. Few rebel, and those who do are usually in the arts, especially in rock music, where learning to read musical notes and to follow band leaders' directions are not valued. The society, though, admires the talented rebels, imbuing them with a mystical quality, where they are admired and even worshipped, as they "play" and play.

That Tupac Shakur was a small boy in an urban school for gifted children (where the second author was his school principal), whose IQ was tested at three standard deviations above the mean is seldom mentioned; that his parents were underground in the Black Panthers, and that his rebellious lyrics came from a consciousness that was nurtured in good schools, is one of the ironies that embodies the dream of the classroom with light on one side and darkness on the other. He moved into the collective unconscious from his verbal talent for pointed lyrics, and his subsequent murder by rival musicians has become the stuff of myth for the society. Collective consciousness sets up what people are supposed to be doing; where there is disruption is where the collective unconscious is breaking forth. Shakur's life as a gifted child and as a societal rebel are illustrative of the collective consciousness moving into the collective unconscious.

Solutions are in the attempt to integrate; traditional tales told of manhood and womanhood. The movie *Juno* is an example (Reitman 2007); the character Juno deals with shadow in a savvy and healing way, despite her insipid boyfriend. In our times, the masculine is not in a serpent, as in the myth and fairy tale; he is inactive and bland. The whole image of the bright boy in popular culture is of the evil hacker who wants to take down the government through cunning and because it will illustrate how bright he is; he'll get recognition from his peers, the pod of other bright hackers. Another example is the quest of Harold and Kumar (Leiner 2004), good gifted boys, to have a plateful of fatty sliders at the White Castle. They themselves are sliders, and they wander the back highways of New Jersey where you can only turn right. Another example is the world-wide obsession with talent searching, where panels of expert judges admit the worthy to the domain, discussing esoteric dance postures or calling their music "pitchy." They are the Sophists of the day, mass merchandising in the imitation of soul, not recognizing the revelation of what true soul is. In the incarnation of You Tube, "broadcast yourself," the populace searches for true soul and when they find it, it goes viral, as people use technology for amplification of their inner needs, in a dream-like forwarding of images to each other by email. We're looking at something that's never been. The popular video that embodies joy, "Where in the Hell is Matt" (You Tube 2008), has spread throughout the world as people hop up and down in a frenzied, smiling, tribal dance that resembles rituals thought to be extinct. At this writing the 2008 version had over 9 million viewings.

15.5 The Daimon

A whole understanding of exceptionality is greatly assisted when incorporating the archetype of the daimon or genius. In the depth tradition, the daimon is the semi-divine guarantor of our life's purpose. It is that element of our psychology that both nudges us forward at crucial moments when we are in the right place, and afflicts us with symptoms when we are missing the mark. Of the daimon, Hillman (1996) wrote, "The talent is only a piece of the image … only when the talent serves the fuller image and is carried by its character do we recognize exceptionality" (p. 45). In describing the Pyramid of Talent Development, Piirto (2004) used the image of the thorn as a metaphor for the motivation to develop one's inborn talent. She likened the thorn to the daimon, tracing its history through Plato, Jung and Hillman.

However, the presence of the daimon can also presage evil, darkness, and crime, for it is reckless, heedless, passionate, and eternally and pathologically adolescent. With that in mind, it is useful to remember that the term "gift" also meant "poison" in old German. The first author has worked with many brilliant students who were often suspended, arrested, or who spent time in the psychiatric ward. Hillman (1996) is helpful in how a teacher can best proceed. He encouraged seeing and honoring the daimon, that which was great within the soul, but also grounding it and giving it the means to "cool." The teacher helps to cool the daimon through depth of knowledge and the capacity to withstand the tensions of paradox that inevitably arise when working in this style. For example, the absolute revolutionary zeal of a student was cooled by his learning about quantum physics, socialism, and the socialist parties in Europe. With another student, the urge to punch lockers when angry was cooled through his learning to bake bread and to use his anger to prepare the dough. With yet another, her tendency to depression was cooled by learning of the descent into darkness found in the book, *Women Who Run with the Wolves* (Pinkola-Estes 1992). Approaching the ethics of each student individually is not moral relativism, but it is respecting each student's inner truth. That is the most important thing we do as teachers.

References

Beebe, J. (1992). *Integrity in depth*. College Station, TX: Texas A & M University Press.
Breton, A. (1952). *Conversations: The autobiography of surrealism*. (Mark Polizzoti, trans.) New York: Paragon House.
Camus, A. (1942). *L'Etranger [The Stranger]*. Paris: Gallimard.
Edinger, E. (1992). *Ego and archetype*. Boston, MA: Shambala.
Fromm, E. (1941). *Escape from freedom*. New York: Rinehart.
Freud, S. (1900). *The interpretation of dreams*. Leipzig/Vienna: Franz Deuticke.
Grimm, J., & Grimm, W. (1944). (M. Hunt, trans.) *The complete Grimm's fairy tales*. New York: Pantheon Books.
Hillman, J. (1975). *Re-visioning psychology*. New York: Harper Colophon Books.
Hillman, J. (1983). *Healing fiction*. Woodstock, CT: Spring.
Hillman, J. (1996). *The soul's code*. New York: Random House.
Hillman, J. (1997). *Myths of the family* (Cassette recording). Woodstock, CT: Sound Horizons.
Hytner, N. (2006). *The history boys*. Motion Picture. UK: Free Range Films.
L'Engle, M. (1997). Light's companion *Parabola, 22*(2), 6–9.
Guggenbuhl-Craig, A. (1995). *Power in the helping professions*. Dallas: Spring.
Hollis, J. (1996). *Swamplands of the soul: New life in dismal places*. Toronto: Open Court.

Jung, C. G. (1959). Symbols of transformation. *Collected Works*. Vol. 5. Princeton, NJ: Bollingen Foundation.

Jung, C. G. (1969). On the nature of the psyche. *Collected Works*. Vol. 8. Princeton, NJ: Bollingen Foundation.

Leiner, D. (Director.) (2004). *Harold and Kumar go to White Castle*. Motion Picture. United States: New Line Cinema.

Marlan, S. (2005). *The black sun: Alchemy and the art of darkness*. College Station, TX: Texas A & M University Press.

Monick, E. (1987). *Phallos: Sacred image of the masculine*. Toronto: Open Court.

Neumann, E. (1969). *Depth psychology and a new ethic*. Boston, MA: Shambala.

Piirto, J. (2004). *Understanding creativity*. Scottsdale, AZ: Great Potential Press.

Pinkola-Estes, C. (1992). *Women who run with the wolves*. New York: Ballantine.

Plato (1952). The Phaedrus. In *Great books of the western world*, Vol. 7. Chicago, IL: Encyclopaedia Britannica.

Plotinus (1991). (S. McKenna, trans.) *The enneads*. New York: Penguin Classics

Reitman, J. (2007). *Juno*. Motion Picture. United States. Fox Searchlight Pictures.

Reynolds, F. C., & Piirto, J. (2005). Depth psychology and giftedness: bringing soul to the field of talent development. *Roeper Review*, 27, 164–171.

Reynolds, F. C., & Piirto, J. (2007). Honoring and suffering the thorn: Marking, naming and eldering. *Roeper Review*, 29, 48–53.

Sardello, R. (1995). *Love and the soul: Creating a future for earth*. New York: HarperCollins.

Sartre, J. P. (1943). *L'Etre et le neant. [Being and essence]* Paris: Gallimard.

St. Exupéry, A. (1944). *Le petit prince. [The Little Prince]* Paris: Gallimard.

Zoja, L. (2007). *Ethics and analysis*. College Station, TX: Texas A & M University Press.

Part V
Recognizing and Guiding Ethical High Ability

Chapter 16
Morality, Ethics and Good Work: Young People's Respectful and Ethical Minds*

Scott Seider, Katie Davis, and Howard Gardner

Abstract We contend that the formation of the contemporary mind should emphasize the development of respect and ethics. Individuals with respectful minds welcome differences between themselves and other individuals and groups and seek to work effectively with all parties. Individuals who possess ethical minds acknowledge their membership within numerous local, national, and international communities; they consider the effects of their actions upon these communities. The multiple intelligences of human beings – particularly logical–mathematical intelligence and the personal intelligences – are the core capacities upon which policymakers and practitioners must call when seeking to foster young people's respectful and ethical minds. Here, we offer a number of experiences that can enhance relevant facets of young people's logical–mathematical and personal intelligences and help them to employ their intelligences in prosocial ways.

Keywords Booster shots · Crystallizing experiences · Ethical mind · Good work project · Good work toolkit · Horizontal supports · Internal supports · Logical–mathematical intelligences · Multiple intelligences theory · Personal intelligences · Respectful mind · Vertical supports · Wake up calls

S. Seider (✉)
Boston University School of Education, 2 Silber Way, Boston, MA 02215, USA
e-mail: seider@bu.edu

K. Davis
Harvard Graduate School of Education, 204 Larsen Hall, 14 Appian Way, Cambridge, MA 02138
e-mail: ked491@mail.harvard.edu

H. Gardner
Harvard Graduate School of Education, 201 Larsen Hall, 14 Appian Way, Cambridge, MA 02138
e-mail: hgasst@pz.harvard.edu

*The research reported in this chapter was supported by the Carnegie Corporation, the MacArthur Foundation, and the Rockefeller Brothers Fund.

D. Ambrose, T. Cross (eds.), *Morality, Ethics, and Gifted Minds*,
DOI: 10.1007/978-0-387-89368-6_16,
© Springer Science+Business Media LLC 2009

It is difficult to turn on the news or open a newspaper in twenty-first century America without learning of yet another high-profile ethical lapse. The millennium began with the demise of Enron, Arthur Andersen and WorldCom in some of the largest cases of corporate fraud in our nation's history. Since that inauspicious beginning, dozens of our nation's top athletes have been caught using illegal drugs to gain a competitive advantage in sports such as baseball, cycling, and track; leading academics and intellectuals have published books with passages plagiarized from other sources; and congressmen, senators, and cabinet members have been implicated in a bribery scandal involving illegal lobbying and campaign contributions. In *The Cheating Culture*, David Callahan (2004) described these and more mundane examples of unethical behavior as having become routine over the past 2 decades. Likewise, interviews with hundreds of young professionals by our colleagues at the Good Work Project have revealed that, as they enter the real world, many young adults believe the competition to get ahead *necessitates* such ethical compromises (Fischman et al. 2004). Scholars have found a similar mindset to be prevalent amongst high achieving high school students as well (Howard 2007; Pope 2003).

This state of affairs leads to numerous questions and concerns from a variety of stakeholders. For scholars, such widespread ethical lapses raise questions about the nature of morality and ethics as well as questions about where our beliefs about these concepts originate. For policy-makers and practitioners, this "cheating culture" raises more pragmatic questions about the types of ethical frameworks that are desirable for the communities in which we live and what can be done to achieve and sustain such frameworks. In this chapter, we consider the questions of both sets of stakeholders. We begin by offering a scholarly perspective on the nature of morality and ethics and then utilize this perspective as a foundation for considering which ethical frameworks to privilege and how to go about instilling them in young people.

16.1 Conceptualizing Morality

One question posed by scholars concerns the nature of morality and ethics. A substantial line of scholarship conceives of morality as linked to a particular individual's intelligence. One of the founding fathers of intelligence testing, Lewis Terman, argued that children with high IQ's were not only more intelligent than their peers but possessed stronger moral characters as well (Terman 1925). Hollingworth (1942) added that individuals with IQ's over 180 demonstrated greater concern for ethical issues than their less gifted peers. Likewise, Lovecky (1992), Roeper (2003), and Silverman (1994) all have reported that intellectually gifted individuals describe deeper concerns for the needs and feelings of others than their less gifted peers. In seeking to explain these perceived links between intelligence and morality, Clark and Hankins (1985) reported that gifted individuals are more likely to read newspapers than less gifted individuals, and thus are more attuned to local and world events with ethical implications. Mendaglio (1995) added that gifted individuals demonstrate a superior ability to take the perspectives of others.

While the scholarship described above seeks to establish a link between intellectual giftedness and morality, another body of scholarship on morality in the "real world" calls this link into question. S. Oliner and P. Oliner (1988) compared the characteristics of German citizens who served as rescuers during the Holocaust to those who served as bystanders, and Colby and Damon (1992) examined the qualities and traits possessed by 23 adult moral exemplars. Both sets of scholars found that the moral exemplars in their respective studies did not demonstrate particularly strong moral reasoning skills. As Colby and Damon observed, "Pondering moral problems is not the same as dedicating one's life to their solution... The will to take a stand may derive from a source entirely different from the ability to arrive at sophisticated intellectual judgment" (p. 6). In short, both the Oliners and Colby and Damon concluded that sophisticated moral reasoning skills do not necessarily correlate with prosocial behavior. Supporting this perspective is neuroscience research that has found some individuals who suffer brain damage in particular regions of their frontal lobes to lose their sense of right or wrong, despite maintaining normal results on IQ tests (Anderson et al. 1999). Such a finding underscores the claims made by the Oliners and Colby and Damon that morality is not simply a sub-set of intelligence.

16.2   Origins of Morality

A second question taken up by scholars concerns the origins of morality. The individual perhaps most responsible for turning the lens of developmental psychology to issues of morality was Lawrence Kohlberg (1981, 1984). Following in the tradition of Piaget, Kohlberg (1981) developed a stage theory of moral development that asserted individuals could deepen their moral reasoning skills (and thereby their moral actions) through both experience and education. Kohlberg (1984) assessed the moral reasoning ability of individuals by gauging their reaction to a series of vignettes that described moral dilemmas. Believing that morality was a trait that could be nurtured and deepened, Kohlberg and his protégés also utilized these vignettes as an educational tool for promoting moral development.

While Kohlberg remains the founding father of contemporary morality research, a number of scholars in recent years have questioned whether individuals can meaningfully deepen their moral reasoning abilities in the manner suggested by Kohlberg. Greene (2001) has asserted that, "There is a growing consensus that moral judgments are based largely on intuition – 'gut feelings' about what is right or wrong in particular cases" (p. 847). As evidence of this claim, he pointed to fMRI studies in which people exposed to personal moral dilemmas demonstrated greater neural activity in regions of the brain that regulate emotion and social cognition. Haidt (2001) concurred that the moral reasoning process described by Kohlberg and Piaget has been overemphasized. Rather, Haidt argued that, "People have quick and automatic moral intuitions, and when called on to justify those intuitions they generate post hoc justifications out of a priori moral theories" (p. 823). Likewise,

Hauser (2006) reported that most individuals who offered strong opinions on moral and immoral actions in regards to dilemmas involving harm to others were unable to provide justifications of these moral judgments. In short, these scholars conceive of morality as a far more intuitive trait than did Kohlberg. In fact, Hauser and Haidt have gone so far as to argue that individuals are born with a "universal moral grammar" that frames their conceptions of morality as they progress through childhood, adolescence, and adulthood.

16.3 Morality and MI Theory

Our own perspective on these debates is impacted heavily by our beliefs about intelligence and human capabilities. The theory of multiple intelligences (developed by one of this chapter's authors) defines intelligence as a set of computational capacities that individuals use to solve problems and create products relevant to the society in which they live (Gardner 1983, 1999, 2006a, b; Gardner et al. 1996a). These capacities – linguistic, logical–mathematical, spatial, musical, bodily-kinesthetic, naturalistic, interpersonal and intrapersonal – form the basis of all complex cognitive capacities including moral judgments. MI theory further conceives of intelligence as a combination of presumably heritable potentials and of skills that can be acquired and enhanced by appropriate experiences. In other words, while one individual may be born with a particularly strong potential for musical intelligence, other individuals can strengthen their musical intelligence through study and practice.

As proponents of MI theory, we conceive of an individual's moral judgments as deriving – like all computational capacities – from a combination of heritable traits and learned behaviors. However, it is important to note that MI theory conceives of the existing eight intelligences as *amoral* – that is, neither intrinsically moral nor immoral. Martin Luther King Jr. serves as an example of an individual with tremendous linguistic intelligence, but so too does Adolf Hitler. King chose to *utilize* his linguistic intelligence for a highly moral purpose while Hitler did the opposite. In other words, there is nothing inherently moral (or immoral) about any of the intelligences. Each can be put to benevolent *and* malevolent ends.

In sum, then, MI theory is an account of how the mind is organized that asserts *all* cognitive activity calls upon one or more of the eight intelligences. Thus, we consider the multiple intelligences to be the core capacities upon which policymakers and practitioners must call when seeking to foster young people's commitment to ethical thought and action. However, we believe the question of "which" thoughts and actions should be privileged in this endeavor falls outside the purview of a scientific theory and into the realm of values.

The realm of values, of course, is precisely the arena of the policymaker – the individuals who offer a vision of how things should be in a particular community; create buy-in for this vision among colleagues and constituents; and gather the resources necessary to make this vision a reality. In the remainder of this chapter, then, we assume the hat of a policymaker in order to offer our perspective on *which* values a particular community should privilege and *how* to increase the number of citizens who buy into and live by these values. The foundation upon which our perspective on these policy questions rests is the scholarly conception of morality and the intelligences we have laid out here; namely, that any cognitive activity – including those involving issues of morality – must call upon one or more of the multiple intelligences.

16.4 Privileging Respect and Ethics

In *Five Minds for the Future*, writing as a policymaker, Gardner (2007) argued that the most important prosocial uses to which the contemporary mind should be directed are the development of respect and ethics. Respect and ethics call on both of the personal intelligences (particularly interpersonal intelligence); in addition, ethics calls on logical–mathematical intelligence.

Interpersonal intelligence involves the ability to consider the thoughts, feelings, beliefs, and perspectives of other people. Such an ability is crucial to treating other individuals with respect and developing a genuine appreciation for diversity. Logical–mathematical intelligence allows individuals to make calculations and consider abstract problems. This intelligence is crucial for developing the abstracting ability to consider one's ethical responsibilities vis-à-vis a role. To say a bit more about this process, children tend to conceive of themselves primarily as individuals, and perhaps, additionally, as filling the roles of son or daughter, sibling, grandchild, and friend. These youngsters do not yet possess the capacity to conceive of other (more abstract) roles that they also fill such as citizen of a particular town, state, country and planet, or roles they will one day fill such as worker, colleague, or professional. The capacity to recognize these more abstract roles and to understand the responsibilities that accompany them typically do not develop until adolescence and draw heavily upon one's logical–mathematical and interpersonal intelligences. In the sections that follow, we consider the processes by which young people may develop respect and ethics as well as the ways in which parents, educators, and policymakers can foster the development of young people's respectful and ethical minds.

16.4.1 The Respectful Mind

Individuals with respectful minds welcome differences between themselves and other individuals and groups while simultaneously seeking out common ground with such individuals and groups. The development of the respectful mind calls primarily upon an individual's interpersonal intelligence and includes learning to reject caricatures and stereotypes of individuals from other groups as well as giving such groups the benefit of the doubt when it comes to reflecting upon their actions, intentions, customs, and practices. In short, when we speak of fostering a young person's respectful mind, we aspire to more than engendering in this young person a tolerance for difference but, rather, a genuine valuing of difference.

Cultivation of an individual's respectful mind, then, is quite different from ignoring or overlooking differences in ethnicity, religion, race, gender, nationality, sexual preference, and the like. In fact, recent scholarship has demonstrated that ignoring such differences is nearly impossible. Human beings across a variety of backgrounds and cultures demonstrate a nearly instinctive tendency to recognize and value individuals that they perceive to be similar to them, and to be wary of those they perceive as different or "other" (Aboud 1988; Augoustinos and Rosewarne 2001; Davey 1983; Dunham 2007). Peter Singer (1981) has noted that evolutionary forces lead human beings to overvalue "self, kin and clan" but believes that we can utilize our reasoning skills to combat this evolutionary tendency and expand our circle of care to include a much wider population of groups and individuals.

Exemplars of the respectful mind are the German citizens studied by S. Oliner and P. Oliner (1988) who took on extraordinary risks to protect Jews from the Gestapo in Nazi Germany. Not surprisingly, the approximately 50,000 German citizens willing to assume this dangerous role represented less than one tenth of 1% of the German population. In their study of these individuals, the Oliners found that Germans who served as rescuers were three times less likely than bystanders to offer stereotypes about Jews and two times less likely to offer stereotypic comments about any group. The rescuers in the Oliners' study were also twice as likely as bystanders to note similarities between themselves and Jews. Finally, almost 40% of the Germans who served as rescuers described their obligation to alleviate the suffering of a stranger as equal to their responsibility to alleviate the suffering of a friend. In short, the German citizens who protected Jews from the Nazis during World War II recognized differences between themselves and Jews, but also acknowledged their commonalities as well. In this way, these rescuers are exemplars of the respectful mind in action. As the Oliners concluded, what distinguished the rescuers from the nonrescuers was their "feeling of responsibility for the welfare of others, including those outside their immediate familial or communal circles" (p. 249). These individuals are courageous examples of Singer's (1981) assertion that individuals possess the capability of expanding their circle of care beyond "self, kin and clan."

16.4.2 The Ethical Mind

Individuals who demonstrate use of their ethical minds recognize their role as members of a local, national and international community and consider the effects of their work and actions upon these different communities. Such a mindset calls upon an individual's logical–mathematical and interpersonal intelligences; it requires an ability to reflect upon the needs of other individuals, organizations, and the public as well as the resolve to play a role in improving the lot of those whose needs are significant. While the development of the respectful mind involves supporting young people in considering their relationship and responsibilities to other persons, the development of the ethical mind involves encouraging young people to reflect upon their responsibilities to their emerging roles of citizen and worker.

Cultivation of the ethical mind results in individuals who can articulate the values and principles with which they approach their roles as citizen and worker. Beyond simply an ability to articulate these principles, however, individuals with highly developed ethical minds keep these principles in mind as they go about their work and lives. When they find themselves tempted to take actions or pursue ends that are in conflict with these principles, they take steps to realign their actions. Importantly (which is not to say, easily), individuals who demonstrate use of their ethical minds do not allow self-interest to overrule their principles. For example, if an individual believes nepotism to be an unethical means of advancement, then he or she will turn down an opportunity for promotion proffered by one's new father-in-law or the offer by a longtime mentor to grease the skids for admission into a favored graduate program. As these examples make clear, actually living out the principles one believes to be ethical (or "walking the talk") is not easy.

An exemplar of an individual demonstrating use of his ethical mind is tennis great Arthur Ashe. In each of the many roles that he assumed over the course of his lifetime, Ashe strove to act in keeping with his principles and to the benefit of others. As an athlete and African American, when Ashe discovered that there was no definitive work on the history of African American athletes, he set out to write the work himself. The fruit of his labor, *A Hard Road to Glory*, was published in 1988. As a citizen of the world, Ashe took it upon himself to campaign against apartheid in South Africa. He founded an organization, Artists and Athletes against Apartheid, to raise awareness of apartheid worldwide and to lobby for sanctions against the South African government.

Finally, when Ashe found himself in the role of one of the world's most famous victims of AIDS, he recognized his obligation to serve as a spokesman for efforts to combat the disease. In the last years of his life, he founded the Arthur Ashe Foundation for the Defeat of AIDS with the goal of raising money for research into treating, curing and preventing AIDS. In his memoir, Ashe and Rampersad (1993) admitted that, "I do not like being the personification of a problem, much less a problem involving a killer disease, but I know I must seize these opportunities to spread the word." In the many different roles that Ashe assumed over the course of his lifetime, he strove to meet the responsibilities that each role demanded and to consider the needs and well-being of others less famous and less fortunate than himself. He is an exemplar of an individual with an aptitude for many different types of intelligence who sought to use these intelligences in ethical ways and in the service of ethical pursuits.

16.5 Fostering Respectful and Ethical Action

When considering *how* to foster respect and ethics, here, again, the scholar can offer insights to the policymaker. Specifically, the GoodWork Project offers a number of insights into this important endeavor (www.goodworkproject.org).

The GoodWork Project is a multi-site collaboration led by psychologists Howard Gardner, William Damon and Mihaly Csikszentmihalyi; these researchers seek to illuminate the supports and obstacles to producing work that is excellent in quality, carried out in an ethical manner, and engaging to its practitioners. The project's hundreds of interview with teenagers and young professionals have revealed that, as they enter the real world, young adults often feel enormous pressure to perform what we call "compromised work." Specifically, we have found that young workers know what it means to perform good work and aspire to be good workers some day; however, many of these young people believe the competition to get ahead necessitates ethical compromises (Barendsen and Gardner, in press; Fischman et al. 2004). Our interviewees included winners of the Intel/Westinghouse high school science competition who had lied about their data collection methods in order to make their experiments more compelling; Ph.D. candidates at top-tier universities who had cut methodological corners in their haste to publish ahead of competitors; and young actors of color whose eagerness for paid work had led them to take roles that they felt propagated stereotypes about their ethnicity or culture.

We offer these examples to make the point that otherwise intelligent, ambitious young people come to numerous moral and ethical crossroads as they proceed towards adulthood. Fortunately, our interviews with young workers (as well as more seasoned workers) revealed a number of factors that can encourage respectful and ethical behavior. These factors include vertical, horizontal, and internal supports; booster shots; and wake-up calls.

16.5.1 Vertical Supports

Vertical supports are the individuals ahead of our young workers on the career (or life) ladder who serve as mentors, coaches and paragons (Fischman et al. 2004). In childhood and adolescence, these mentors are typically parents, teachers and coaches. However, as individuals reach late adolescence and early adulthood, their deepening autonomy brings them into contact with a greater diversity of adults who can assume these roles – at work, in religious organizations, through professional associations, recreational activities and so forth. In their roles as workers and citizens, these older figures provide models of respectful and ethical behavior (Pianta 1992). Many of the young workers in our study described their own moral identities as a blend of the practices and perspectives they had acquired from the various mentors in their lives. We refer to this practice as *frag-mentoring* – the piecing together of a coherent value system from several different sources (Barendsen and Gardner, in press).

Young workers can also learn much from paragons with whom they share few face-to-face encounters. A deeply principled CEO can teach much to his or her young employees through the company's established practices for interacting with clients and competitors; treatment of employees; reigning in of compensation for top executives; corporate philanthropy; and intolerance for unethical practices or shady dealings. Likewise, historical figures such as Abraham Lincoln or international figures such as Nelson Mandela can serve as paragons of ethical behavior for young workers who take the time to read and learn about their lives and values. Though Eleanor Roosevelt and Franklin Roosevelt had flaws, one can still learn from and be inspired by their examples. Recent scholarship suggests that contemporary young Americans have more difficulty than previous generations citing public figures whom they admire (Gibbons and Gomes 2002). Such difficulty is not particularly surprising in an era when the foibles and failings of public figures are quickly and widely disseminated; however, it is concerning that a side effect of this heightened media glare may be the loss for contemporary young Americans of a powerful source of mentors and paragons.

Finally, a number of the veteran workers in our study noted that they had also learned powerful lessons about how *not* to behave from older individuals whom they perceived to be acting disrespectfully or unethically. We refer to these negative role models as anti-mentors or tormentors. In the best of circumstances, young workers seek to emulate the examples offered by positive coaches and paragons in their lives while actively avoiding replication of the disrespectful and unethical behaviors they recognize in anti-mentors.

16.5.2 Horizontal Supports

Hersh (2007) has observed that, in the contemporary United States, young people have decreased their reliance on older mentors and increased their reliance upon peers for guidance about how to live their lives. Damon (2008) agreed that, "Most adolescents and young adults…value their friendships highly and respond to them in ways that cannot be replicated by [older] adults" (p. 102). The prevalence of the Internet has allowed such guidance to be sought, not only from friends living down the street, but also from strangers living thousands of miles away.

Our own interviews with young workers revealed that the colleagues with whom they work closely exerted a substantial influence upon their beliefs about respectful and ethical behavior. Perhaps not surprisingly, if one arrives day after day at a work environment in which disrespectful treatment of clients or lower level employees is the norm, it is difficult for even the best-intentioned young workers to maintain their perspective on respectful actions.

Of course, it is often the case – particularly in larger organizations – that young workers seek out colleagues with whom they share similar perspectives. Workers interested in cutting corners or skimming off the top will seek out likeminded colleagues. Likewise, young workers who prioritize the respectful and ethical dimensions of their work are more likely to associate with other highly principled workers (Damon 2008). In this way, an individual's peer group can serve to reinforce respectful or disrespectful (as well as ethical or unethical) behavior (Moran and Gardner 2006).

16.5.3 Booster Shots

Individuals of all ages require periodic opportunities to "recharge" their commitment to respectful and ethical action. These booster shots can come in the form of an opportunity to discuss the beliefs, values, and principles underlying a commitment to respect and ethics; however, inoculations against a downward moral slide can also be catalyzed in an organization through reading a particular book, screening a film or participating in a workshop that allows for reflection about each individual's responsibilities to his or her role (Fischman et al. 2004).

One example of a booster shot comes out of the GoodWork Project itself. Following our study of the supports and obstacles to doing good work in journalism, several members of the GoodWork team led by Dr. William Damon developed a short "traveling curriculum"; this curriculum offered journalists and editors in newsrooms across the country the opportunity to reflect upon the ethical dimensions of their work. It opened up for discussion and reflection the actual dilemmas raised by journalists interviewed during the GoodWork in Journalism study. In a field that is facing tremendous pressure via the Internet and bloggers to sacrifice high-quality reporting and investigative undertakings for up-to-the-minute postings, many of the participants welcomed this reminder about their ethical responsibility to conduct accurate, fact-based reporting.

A second example of a booster shot invigorated an entire activist community. Though it may be difficult to recall, at the outset of the twenty-first century there was little public consensus in the United States about whether the actions of human beings contributed to global warming. This public uncertainty proved challenging for environmental groups that were campaigning for heightened environmental regulations as well as for increased personal responsibility for the environment.

In 2006, the campaign against global warming received a robust booster shot in the form of politician-turned-activist Al Gore's documentary "An Inconvenient Truth." This film about anthropogenic global warming became one of the highest grossing documentaries in American history. In 2007 Gore received two unique accolades. He was awarded the Nobel Peace Prize for his role in heightening awareness of man-made climate change and acting as "the single individual who has done most to create greater worldwide understanding of the measures that need to be adopted" (Gibbs and Lyall 2007, p. 1). And then, as well, he was awarded an Oscar for Best Documentary Feature. Through the creation and wide dissemination of this powerful documentary, Gore offered a substantial booster shot to an entire community of environmental activists. For the first time, it became politically incorrect to ridicule the idea that global warming reflected human practices.

16.5.4 Wake-Up Calls

Wake-up calls come in the form of shocks about some previously unconsidered (or little considered) aspect of the world. Damon (2008) and colleagues at the Stanford University Center of Adolescence have described the sequence of steps by which adolescents and young adults arrive at a sense of purpose as involving two distinct wake-up calls or moments of revelation. The first of these wake-up calls occurs when an individual identifies an aspect of the world in need of repair or improvement, and the second occurs when the individual realizes that he or she has the potential to play a role in addressing this concern.

As an example, the GoodWork Project considered the developmental trajectories of the Schweitzer Fellows, a group of young medical workers who are dedicated to providing healthcare to underserved populations in the United States and the developing world. In describing their motivation for addressing these humanitarian needs, a number of the Schweitzer fellows described "transformational" or "crystallizing" experiences that had inspired their decision to focus upon a particular population or social problem (Fischman et al. 2001). Examples of such experiences included witnessing abject poverty on a trip to Haiti and visiting an orphanage in Eastern Europe that had too few resources to care for its charges. In each of these cases, the young worker came away from a particular experience feeling an ethical obligation to ease the suffering of a particular population (see also Seider 2006, 2007 for a description of frame-changing experiences among young service-workers). These wake-up calls served to strengthen the Schweitzer Fellows' commitment to carrying out their work in a manner that made the world more just.

16.5.5 Internal Supports

The preceding descriptions of vertical and horizontal supports, booster shots and wake-up calls all share the commonality of offering an individual support or inspiration from interpersonal (i.e., external) sources. However, an individual's commitment to approaching her professional or civic roles in an ethical manner can be buttressed (or weakened) by intrapersonal means as well. Individuals who demonstrate a keen aptitude for recognizing their own beliefs, values, motivations, strengths and weaknesses can often take steps to provide themselves with a personalized booster shot. Specifically, individuals with strong intrapersonal intelligence can recognize the periods when their ethical resolve is weakening and take steps to reverse this process. Such steps may include seeking out a particular book, film, class, or conversation that the individual knows will serve as an invigorating reminder of his or her ethical obligations. For example, one of the young workers in our study – an African American college student at a prestigious university – cited *The Autobiography of Malcolm X* as a text that he had turned to repeatedly over the past several years when he felt he needed a reminder about the ends towards which he ultimately wished to utilize his education. Surrounded by classmates whom he believed to be primarily interested in the financial gains that their diplomas could yield, he recognized his own need to seek out guidance from a paragon of activism and African-American empowerment. Even more powerful than reading about a topic may be seeking out a project, apprenticeship or other opportunity for hands-on learning with colleagues and mentors who demonstrate a deep concern for the ethical obligations of their respective roles and fields.

16.6   The Toolkit

The GoodWork Toolkit is our attempt to put theory into practice and offer a booster shot of our own. The toolkit includes a number of the real-life ethical dilemmas which emerged from our interviews with young workers as well as activities and discussion guides that draw upon these dilemmas. We believe that the combination of dilemmas, activities and discussion prompts will prove useful to educators in engaging their students in deep reflection about the merits and challenges of pursuing work in a manner that aligns with their beliefs and values.

The Toolkit is currently being piloted in several secondary schools and universities in the United States and abroad, and we have now led mini-courses on pursuing meaningful work and a meaningful life at a number of our nation's most prestigious universities. It is too early to draw definitive conclusions about the impact of the Toolkit upon the young workers who have engaged with its content. Encouraging respect and ethics is not easy, and in fact recent scholarship by one of this paper's authors highlights the possibility of curricula intended to deepen the ethical orientation of young adults actually having the opposite effect upon its participants (Seider 2008ba, b, c). As a result, we have no doubt that the Toolkit will undergo many revisions and adaptations as we learn more about its effect upon students and young professionals. However, refining the Good Work Toolkit's ability to serve as an effective booster shot strikes us as an endeavor worthy of attention and continued refinement. We anticipate that experiences based on the toolkit should enhance relevant facets of logical–mathematical and personal intelligences, and should in addition help students to employ their intelligences in prosocial ways.

In his memoir penned in the final year of his life, Arthur Ashe and Rampersad (1993) wrote that, "As never before, our moral, intellectual and material wealth will depend on the strength, skills and productivity of our youth." We believe that the effectiveness with which scholars, policymakers, parents, and practitioners can work together to develop our children's respectful and ethical minds will dictate their approach to the important roles of worker and citizen, which they will soon inherit.

References

Aboud, F. (1988). *Children and prejudice*. New York: Basil Blackwell.

Augoustinos, M., & Rosewarne, D. L. (2001). Stereotype knowledge and prejudice in children. *British Journal of Developmental Psychology, 19*(Pt 1), 143–156.

Anderson, S., Bechara, A., Damasio, H., Tranel, D., & Damasio, A. (1999). Impairment of social and moral behavior related to early damage in prefrontal cortex. *Nature Neuroscience, 2*, 1032–1037.

Ashe, A., & Rampersad, A. (1993). *Days of grace: A memoir*. New York: G.K. Hall.

Barendsen, L., & Gardner, H. (2009). Good for what? Young workers in a global age. In A. Linley, S. Harrington, & N. Page (Eds.), *Oxford handbook of positive psychology and work*. Oxford, UK: Oxford University Press.

Callahan, D. (2004). *The cheating culture: Why more Americans are doing wrong to get ahead.* New York: Harcourt.

Clark, W., & Hankins, N. (1985). Giftedness and conflict. *Roeper Review, 8,* 50–53.

Colby, A., & Damon, W. (1992). *Some do care: Contemporary lives of moral commitment.* New York: Free Press/Macmillan.

Damon, W. (2008). *The path to purpose: Helping our children find their calling in life.* New York: Free Press.

Davey, A. (1983). *Learning to be prejudiced: Growing up in multi-ethnic Britain.* London: Edward Arnold.

Dunham, Y. (2007). *Assessing the automaticity of intergroup bias.* Unpublished doctoral dissertation. Harvard Graduate School of Education.

Fischman, W., Schutte, D., Solomon, B., & Lam, G. (2001). The development of an enduring commitment to service work. In M. Michaelson & J. Nakamura (Eds.), *Supportive frameworks for youth engagement* (pp. 33–45). New York: Jossey-Bass.

Fischman, W., Solomon, D., Greenspan, D., & Gardner, H. (2004). *Making good: How young people cope with moral dilemmas at work.* Cambridge, MA: Harvard University Press.

Gardner, H. (1983). *Frames of mind: The theory of multiple intelligences.* New York: Basic.

Gardner, H. (1999). *Intelligence reframed: Multiple intelligences for the 21st century.* New York: Basic.

Gardner, H. (2006a). *Multiple intelligences: New Horizons.* New York: Basic.

Gardner, H. (2006b). Response to my critics. In J. Schaler (Ed.), *Gardner under fire* (pp. 277–344). Chicago, IL: Open Court.

Gardner, H. (2007). *Five minds for the future.* Boston, MA: Harvard Business School Press.

Gardner, H., Kornhaber, M., & Warren, K. (1996a). *Intelligence: Multiple perspectives.* Fort Worth, TX: Harcourt Brace.

Gardner, H., Kornhaber, M., and Wake, W. (1996b). *Intelligence: Multiple perspectives.* Fort Worth, TX: Harcourt Brace.

Gibbons, P., & Gomes, P. (2002). *A call to heroism: Renewing America's vision of greatness.* Boston, MA: Atlantic Monthly Press.

Gibbs, W., & Lyall, S. (2007, October 13). Gore shares peace prize for climate change work. *The New York Times,* p. A1.

Greene, J. (2001). From neural "is" to moral "ought": What are the moral implications of neuroscientific moral psychology? *Nature Reviews Neuroscience, 4,* 847–850.

Haidt, J. (2001). The emotional dog and its rational tail: A social intuitionist approach to moral judgment. *Psychological Review, 108,* 814–834.

Hauser, M. (2006). *Moral minds: How nature designed our universal sense of right and wrong.* New York: Ecco.

Hersh, R. (2007). Terms of engagement. *AACU Peer Review, 9,* 30–31.

Hollingworth, L. (1942). *Children above 180 IQ: Origin and development.* New York: World Book.

Howard, A. (2007). *Learning privilege: Lessons of power and identity in affluent schooling.* New York: Routledge.

Kohlberg, L. (1981). *The philosophy of moral development.* Cambridge, MA: Harper & Row.

Kohlberg, L. (1984). *The psychology of moral development: The nature and validity of moral stages.* New York: HarperCollins.

Lovecky, D. (1992). Exploring social and emotional aspects of giftedness. *Roeper Review, 15,* 18–25.

Mendaglio, S. (1995). Sensitivity among gifted persons: A multi-faceted perspective. *Roeper Review, 17,* 169–172.

Moran, S., & Gardner, H. (2006). Extraordinary achievements: A developmental systems analysis. In W. Damon, R. Lerner, D. Kuhn, R. Siegler, N. Eisenberg, A. Renniger, & I. Sigel (Eds.), *Handbook of child psychology, 6th Ed.* New York: Wiley.

Oliner, S., & Oliner, P. (1988). *The altruistic personality: Rescuers of Jews in Nazi Europe.* New York: Free Press.

Pianta, R. (1992). *Beyond the parent.* San Francisco, CA: Jossey-Bass.

Pope, D. (2003). *Doing school: How we are creating a generation of stressed-out, materialistic and miseducated students*. New Haven, CT: Yale University Press.

Roeper, A. (2003). The young gifted girl: A contemporary view. *Roeper Review, 25*, 151–153.

Seider, S. (2006). Frame-changing experiences: A key to the development of a commitment to service-work and social action in young adults. *Journal for Civic Commitment*. Fall.

Seider, S. (2007). Catalyzing a commitment to community service in emerging adults. *Journal of Adolescent Research, 22*, 612–639.

Seider, S. (2008a). "Bad things could happen": How fear impedes the development of social responsibility in privileged adolescents. *Journal of Adolescent Research, 23(6)*, 647–666.

Seider, S. (2008b). Resisting obligation: How privileged adolescents conceive of their responsibilities to others. *Journal of Research in Character Education, 6(1)*, 3–19.

Seider, S. (2009). Overwhelmed and immobilized: Raising the consciousness of privileged young adults about world hunger and poverty. *International Studies Perspectives, 10(1)*, 60–76.

Silverman, L. (1994). The moral sensitivity of gifted children and the evolution of society. *Roeper Review, 17*, 110–116.

Singer, P. (1981). *The expanding circle: Ethics and sociobiology*. New York: Farrar, Strauss & Giroux.

Terman, L. (1925). *Genetic studies of genius: Mental and physical traits of a thousand gifted children, Vol. 1*. Palo Alto, CA: Stanford University Press.

Chapter 17
Gifted Minds and Cultural Differences: Facts vs. Values

David A. White

Abstract The guiding theme of this chapter follows David Hume's split between facts ("is") and values ("ought"). A program of analytical investigation is described, its purpose to allow gifted minds to see how values differ between and among cultures, especially "mainstream" American values in relation to selected non-American values. The argument is that if this program is followed, students will develop receptive dispositions – encompassing recognition, understanding, and appreciation – toward ethical values differing from their own. If acted upon, these dispositions enhance the tendency to accommodate, rather than be threatened by, culturally diverse values.

Keywords Cultural values · Culture · Curiosity · David Hume · Emotion · Fact · Freedom · Individual · Justice · Pedagogical · Perception · The good · Understanding

The following is an essay in the original sense of the word, that is, an attempt or a trial. The subject is large, the approach is reasoned but decidedly speculative, the educational program outlined for gifted minds is bold. The reader may or may not agree with some or all of what is asserted and argued, but thoughtful reservations or even a straightforward refutation of what follows will require the reader to reflect on important issues and, perhaps in the process, to produce something better. If so, then the essay will have achieved its end.

That gifted students argue among themselves is hardly an insight into their behavior, as is the observation that they argue about the same things everyone argues about. For example, what does it mean to be fair? This is clearly a crucial value since it seems obvious that everyone – including even the gifted – ought to be treated fairly. Now if fairness means justice, then a dispute among gifted students about fairness could be resolved, at least theoretically, by producing a definition of justice acceptable to all concerned and rigorously applied to particular circumstances. End of argument. But now consider honesty. Defining honesty as, say, always telling the

D.A. White
Philosophy Department, DePaul University, Suite 150, LPC, 2352 North Clifton, Chicago, IL 60614, USA
e-mail: dwhite6886@aol.com

D. Ambrose, T. Cross (eds.), *Morality, Ethics, and Gifted Minds*,
DOI: 10.1007/978-0-387-89368-6_17,
© Springer Science+Business Media LLC 2009

truth seems much more straightforward than defining justice as "being fair," since what exactly fairness means as a definition will be subject to considerable disagreement. But other questions arise pertaining to the value of honesty – for example, should we *always* be honest? It seems intuitively obvious that we should always be fair to others, but are there circumstances, complex and convoluted, when dishonesty would produce more good than mindlessly mouthing the truth?

Justice and honesty as values often permeate classroom settings, and their precise nature can and frequently does engender disputes. But shift the arena of concern from the classroom to the United States as a whole. The same two values are just as commonly confronted and also just as commonly disputed, except that on a national scale these values affect much more than classroom protocol, field trips, grading, etc. Is the Iraq war just or unjust? Is gay marriage just or unjust? Were the nation's leaders honest in representing the situation that led to war? It is belaboring the obvious to note that what is acted on because it is perceived as just and what is said, or not said, in the name of honesty may have repercussions that are, without exaggeration, life and death matters.

There are, of course, many differences about values within the U.S., and these differences are reflected in electoral contexts via the phenomenon of "values voters." The resulting tensions concerning disagreements about values and implications derivable from values fuel much national social commentary, controversy, and political debate. But now extend the context of values even further, from their disputed nature within a country to the question of values between countries, especially countries characterized by drastically different cultural environments. Given these differences, disputes about divergences of values between countries and their resident cultures should be expected as the rule rather than the exception. But differences in cultural values where the cultures in question are widely disparate will doubtless generate even more heated arenas for dispute, and at this level the disputes quickly reach an intensity where violence between the disagreeing cultures looms as an unavoidable means for resolving the conflict.

What happens in a small but real way when gifted students dispute among themselves concerning the nature of values becomes globally magnified and correlatively significant when the arena of contention contains cultures defined by clashing values. Resolving as many of these disputes as possible would seem clearly to be for the best for all concerned, especially when the differences in question involve entire cultures rather than merely entire classrooms. What role then can gifted students play if, hypothetically, they were to be thrust into the middle of such a cosmopolitan and complex arena? Reflective consideration of a famous position maintained by an important modern philosopher produces an answer to this question.

17.1 Facts vs. Values

A celebrated argument by the Scottish philosopher David Hume (1711–1776) has cast a long shadow on the subsequent history of philosophy and, in a finely filigreed yet serpentine process, has also contoured an important area of popular thinking – that is, that values are essentially private matters defined solely by individual preference. Hume's argument concerns whether one can justifiably reason from something which *is* the case – a fact – to the conclusion that this same something *ought* to be the case – a value. In short, does "is" imply "ought"? Hume reasoned to the conclusion that the answer is no. Consider then a series of examples to illustrate the apparently unbridgeable gap between "is" and "ought."

1. "I am patient with others" therefore "Everyone ought to be patient with others." I am patient since I hold patience to be a value. This attitude toward patience is a fact about me. But if I then conclude that therefore everyone ought to be patient, this inference is unwarranted since, following Hume, a fact (I am patient) does not imply a corresponding value (Everyone ought to be patient). Indeed, the fact that I have been patient with others does not even imply that I myself ought to be patient with others, since I can always change my mind as to whether what has been my practice in this regard will continue to be my practice. After all, life is short and if I need something done right away in order to suit my interests, then why not pester, browbeat, and harass whoever is available to provide this good? From this perhaps brutally pragmatic perspective, patience is indeed a virtue – but only for losers and the meek of heart. When I want or I need something, I want or need it right now! So much then for the value of patience.

2. "Marriage is a union between a man and a woman" is an example of a fact about the interpersonal relationships of many cultures. However, as a factual claim it also implies, or more accurately (with Hume alertly peeking over our shoulder) points to, an attitude about marriage that constitutes a value. This added dimension becomes evident if the sentence says: "Marriage is *and should be* a union between a man and a woman." But the addition of these three little words causes considerable uproar in terms of clashing values. Traditionalists about marriage, perhaps strengthened in their conviction due to religious considerations, will insist that marriage defined and limited to a man and a woman represents both a cultural fact as well as a cultural value. In contrast, those who see marriage as more a legal union characterized primarily by affection and shared interests between the parties (rather than the procreation of children – although not precluding the raising of, say, adopted children) will reject this value because it artificially limits their choices and desires for individual fulfillment. The value they appeal to is based on marriage seen as a union satisfying only certain conditions, indeed a union both legally and psychologically achievable regardless of the gender of the parties involved. But, the response might be, are not "family values" in some way essentially compromised if the adults in the family are the same gender?

3. A final example, this one deployed as a syllogism:

   "Hurricanes can damage property and kill human beings."
   "Some people have assisted hurricane victims."
   "Therefore, everyone ought to assist hurricane victims in some way."

The first two propositions as premises are clearly facts; the conclusion, ostensibly derived from the conjunction of the two premises via syllogistic mechanics, is clearly a value. For Hume, such a conclusion does not follow from these premises. It would indeed be noble if humanity were to band together, every single one of us, to assist all those around the globe who have suffered in one way or another because of a hurricane or any dire consequence resulting from nature's destructive capriciousness. But to impose this nobility as a moral necessity, derivable from these two – or, indeed, any – facts is to make a substantial error in reasoning. Facts are one thing; values are completely different. It follows then that values cannot be derived from facts.

17.1.1 Values: The Individual and the Good

The first example above concentrates on the self, the second is limited to a relation between two and only two individuals (ruling out polygamy for the sake of simplicity), the third example generalizes from the actions of a group of people to all people. But in all three cases, the value appealed to is universalized in the sense that those who maintain each value see it as a value *for everyone*. Thus everyone should be honest, everyone should view marriage as between a man and a woman, everyone should be compassionate and forthright in assisting anyone mired in hardship because of a natural disaster. However, again for all three cases, the apparently desirable value cannot be justifiably produced from these or any underlying facts.

It does not appear as if rational argument will resolve this difference. And, if so, this lack of resolution indirectly supports Hume's position. What, if anything, can then be done about this seemingly unbridgeable chasm between facts and values?

The following is an account, reasoned but speculative, offering one possible explanation for the logical chasm Hume saw between facts and values. Consider honesty. It is a fact that some people are honest most of the time, and it may be a fact that a few people are always honest. For these individuals, honesty is a very important value. However, in the world we live in, many people, perhaps most, have told the occasional "white lie" and the reason why is significant. We will return to that reason presently. And it is also obvious that some people have lied through their teeth, with their reasons for this seemingly unpraiseworthy course of action again significant.

But given the predominance of honesty in most human affairs, why can't one argue that since some people are honest most of the time [fact], therefore all people ought to be honest [value]? Let us examine why people lie, that is, why they violate or simply ignore the value of honesty. Depending on the depth of analysis introduced, many reasons are possible to account for the fact of lying but present purposes do not require an exhaustive review of these reasons. Here are common examples. If a gifted student lies about his or her participation in, say, an action forbidden by the teacher, the rationale for that lie is the conviction that the consequences facing the student when telling the truth and admitting participation are, or are believed to be, somehow worse than the consequences of telling the lie (where, it can be assumed, the student is convinced that the lie will not be discovered).

In other words, the lie is motivated by a certain vision of, to state the point very broadly, what is good for that individual. The student does not want to endure any form of punishment – therefore, to avoid punishment, the lie is told; after all, life without punishment is clearly better than life with punishment. The same motivational analysis can hold for a white lie. If a student asks another student for an aesthetic assessment of clothing or a change in physical appearance, student A will tell student B, the questioner, that "it looks fine" when student A might in truth feel that the phenomenon under scrutiny is a disaster. Why will A tell B this fib (i.e., a lightweight lie)? The reason is that A believes that B will feel better by hearing approval than by an honest but disapproving comment – in short, that it is good for B to feel pleased with B's exterior change. For both types of lie then, the underlying rationale is based on a certain understanding of the good, and that the end – enhancing someone's good, justifies the means – telling a lie (or fib) in order to accomplish this end.

People, gifted students and everyone else, disagree about the nature of what is truly good. I suggest this fact of disagreement is one factor that establishes barriers between and among human beings such that something seen as a value by one person might not be seen as a value by another person. Imagine a world where everyone agreed on what is good and, in addition to this fundamental agreement, everyone agreed on what means should and should not be used in order to achieve this good. This is a utopia, of course. But in such a world, it is also easy to imagine that *everyone* would be honest because everyone could realize that to be dishonest could in some way harm or crimp another's access to his or her share of the good. Thus, if it is reasonable to generalize from the single example of honesty, in this earthly paradise no conflict would arise between facts and values. And the explanation for the lack of conflict is that there would be complete harmony among its inhabitants, both collectively and individually, between what was thought to be for the best and what was desired as means in order to achieve what was best. This hypothetical world might enjoy a wide variety of clear and distinct differences – whether in geographical configuration, forms of government, types of entertainment, styles of clothing, and so on, but with respect to the good and means to achieve that good, everyone would be in perfect harmony with everyone else.

Return now to the real world: the one marked by disagreement, unrest, conflict, violence, war, and genocide (this list is not exhaustive of human frailties). In this world, the uniformity and harmony just sketched do not exist. But also in this world, another factor contributes to the situation regarding conflict between facts and values now under scrutiny. The individual enjoys a degree of autonomy – or at least this autonomy is, in the present world, accorded to individuals of certain countries and in certain cultures. If a gifted student believes that her future good depends on being dishonest, then there is a disconnect for that individual between what she envisions as the good and the value of honesty. For her, embracing honesty as a value in all circumstances makes no sense if such an embrace would lead her into a state of affairs where, as a result of acting according to the value of honesty, her perceived good was in some way impaired or diminished. So for this individual, what is a value for many will not be a value she endorses and adopts as part of her individual value system. From this perspective, values are wholly private affairs.

In the popular mind, a reality such as honesty is construed as a value, the moral force of a value is felt internally, and precisely this feeling, as emblematic of the distinctive signature of a value, spurs us to action in the name of these values. But individuals differ as to what they think is the good and what means they think are appropriate for realizing that good. Therefore, so the thinking goes, since people are different, their feelings are different; as a result, values may not be shared since different people may not feel the same way about the same value. Two people may indeed share the same value, but that this value is so shared is a fact about these two people and does not, as a fact, strengthen the conclusion that everyone *ought* to share the value these two people share.

The key word is *individual*. Human beings are individuals. As individuals, they differ as to what is the good and what means are appropriate for realizing that good. But since at least some of us accord a fundamental level of respect to human beings *as individuals*, we do not think it justified to legislate what we now refer to as "values" for everyone. Why? Because if an individual does not think and feel a certain way about fundamental realities (e.g., the good) then there is no justification for compelling that individual to rethink, or, as it were, "refeel," what to that individual is clear and obvious. If someone's desire for the good in life is defined by the acquisition of fame, or wealth, or power, then the "value" of honesty might interfere in some cases with the realization of that goal. Hence, the lack of concern, for that individual, in accepting honesty as a value which *ought to be* incumbent on all of his or her spoken discourse.

If this analysis is heading in the right direction, it is the value placed on the individual as such that serves as the underlying pivot for the conflict David Hume recognized between what is and what ought to be. "Ought" is a word with various meanings, but in this context an "ought" refers to a morally desirable outcome: something we do because we believe it is good to do so. But what is a desirable outcome for me, as my good, might not at all be a desirable outcome for you. Hence we disagree on "values," since we disagree on what sorts of things we should be doing with our lives with respect to attaining the good and also how we should go about attempting to achieve these good ends. What I think is good might not be identical to what you think is good, but since you and I are both individual human beings, why should either of our visions of the good be considered mandatory and desirable for the other person?

17.1.2 Value and Culture

Hume's distinction between fact and value is also relevant at the level of cultures, but appreciating its relevance requires a bit of background reflection. The concept of a culture is, in general, a polyglot affair, excluding very little in its operational definition. Thus, contributing factors to the concept of a culture include history, religion, philosophical heritage, political dimensions, popular moral beliefs, art, modes of entertainment, even geographical boundaries. However, enumerating accurately and exhaustively the constituent elements of a culture is not as important, at least in the present context, as properly understanding what might be called the metaphysical character of a culture.

A culture is an *organic whole of parts*. A culture has a mode of existence – or, to be less professorial – a life of its own, just as the individual human beings who exemplify or partake of that culture have lives of their own. Each element in a culture thus bears a living relation to every other element. Depending on the elements, this relation may be intimate and intense or removed and distant. But the essential point to keep in mind is that considering and isolating a given feature of a culture with the intention of approximating a full understanding and appreciation of that feature entails identifying and, if possible, experiencing as many of the "live" relations connecting that feature with other elements of the culture. To isolate a given element of a culture, thereby fixating on that element to the exclusion of its relations to other elements, is to denature that element and to falsify its reality as one part of a vibrant, complex whole.

Hume's denial that values can be inferred from facts was localized within a given culture, with the relevant parties either individuals or groups of individuals disputing about what should or should not be the case based on what has or has not been the case. But now the context is much broader, at least in terms of the number of people involved – and disputes arise not just between individual human beings all resident within one culture but rather between entire cultures with, it may be assumed, each culture containing large populations of individuals. And yet the relevant contrast established by Hume's position remains, in principle, the same.

Call two cultures A and B, and keep in mind our assumption that a culture as such is a kind of social unity, akin to the organic unity of a living being. A relevant analogy may now be drawn based on Hume's position: just as one person cannot infer that what is of value to him or her ought to be a value for someone else, so one culture that accepts a given value cannot expect another culture to embrace that value. The logical tension between facts and values, between "is" and "ought," remains in force at the macro level of cultures just as it does at the micro level of individual people. The question now becomes whether, from the more global perspective of cultural differences, some values are more threatening, disruptive and potentially destructive than others.

17.2 A Hierarchy of Values

One way of deploying values so that their significance becomes more evident for our purposes is to arrange them hierarchically into types with a view toward inter-cultural relevance, that is, the status values have insofar as they may span different cultures. Here is one such hierarchy.

17.2.1 Peripheral Values

A peripheral value is functional, as the name suggests, on the periphery of human interaction. Politeness, for example, is a value that many, but not all, cultures attempt to instill in children when they are still very young. Thus to visit a culture that does not value politeness requires typically that one must fend for oneself and not expect much in the way of graciously proffered assistance from those native to that culture. But the resulting inconveniences are, as a rule, minor in their effect and produce little more than hurt feelings or some lost time. Civilization as it manifests itself throughout the world and in a variety of ways within diverse cultures will survive, for example, the advent and proliferation of cell phones, but the current outcry about the increasingly impolite usage of this device testifies to the inherent appreciation of politeness as a value worth encouraging, perhaps to the point of trumpeting the need for legislation in order to preserve that value against this kind of irritating (for many!) technological encroachment. In general, peripheral values affect quality of life but not to the point where the qualitative dimension so affected touches anything truly significant or fundamental. If everyone were rude to everyone else all the time, life would be difficult and strained, but not insufferable and still well worth the effort to endure such sustained slights while we go about our business of pursuing human happiness.

17.2.2 Derivative Values

Very few cultures would not put a high value on loyalty. But only a moment's reflection is required to appreciate that loyalty is a derivative value. Thus, should lower level officers in Hitler's Gestapo have been loyal to their leaders? The point is that the justification of loyalty as a value depends necessarily on what or whom one is loyal *to*. Since it is entirely possible for a government, or an illegal organization such as the mafia, to be unjust at its core, then it may be argued that loyalty to such a social entity cannot be defended. In a word, loyalty is a derivative value depending on the nature of the object of the loyalty in question, although generally stated it is good to be loyal, just as it is good to be polite. But whereas being polite is benign, a social lubricant derived from acknowledging a basic respect earned by all human beings simply through being human, being loyal can, depending on the object of loyalty, produce serious problems in a culture where the value of loyalty is revered without any qualification whatsoever.

17.2.3 Core Values

The most obvious value at this, the highest level of normative concerns – hence the use of *core* as part of its rubric – is surely freedom. Or at least freedom enjoys this privileged status in some of the world's cultures. But to appeal to freedom in this context lacks explanatory force unless certain fundamental distinctions are drawn. Thus untrammeled freedom, the freedom to do literally anything and everything, is readily recognized as an invitation to chaos. If, to introduce a crude example, I am free to pummel people who get on my nerves, then anyone is free to pummel anyone (including me!) for the slightest provocation. Other examples of unrestrained freedom, much more obviously harmful to the individuals involved, will quickly come to mind.

In order to block the imminent chaos that would result from freedom without limits, distinguish between freedom *from* and freedom *to*. The former may be illustrated by freedom from apparently arbitrary forms of governmental restriction; the latter by freedom to seek self-realization, whether in external considerations, such as style of clothing, or more fundamental concerns, such as education. Freedom *to* has readily recognizable limits, such as those involving potential or actual harm to other individuals; thus, to repeat the previous example, I do not have freedom to pummel others just because they irritate me; or if I do so pummel, I can expect punishment if caught doing so by authorities. Much could and should be said to develop these two senses of freedom, but the relevant perspective here, as illustrative of a core value, is freedom *to* and an example will illustrate why this value is indeed taken as fundamental.

Freedom *to* addresses the heart of an individual's quest for self-realization. Thus there is a fundamental value in believing that human beings should be free to seek as much education as is deemed fit for their well-being. It follows then that discrimination in education by reason of gender or race should not exist. Without this value in place and thoroughly inculcated throughout the fabric of a given culture, those excluded from education will have their lives affected in failing to be in a position to realize their full potential as human beings. Education within a cultural setting is, of course, rigorously regulated by a variety of laws, both in terms of content and the processes involved in disseminating that content. But if a culture is defined, in part, by freedom *to*, then the right of access to education is freely given to any and all who wish to pursue that particular avenue of self-realization. From this perspective, freedom *to* is, in a way, a preeminent value, since its animating presence in a culture will allow an individual to choose, for example, to be loyal or to be polite (or, of course, to be both). Thus the core value of freedom may be seen to ground the possibility of derivative and peripheral values, as sketched in the above hierarchy. Core values therefore reflect a fundamental conception of what it means to be human, with, as suggested, freedom occupying a privileged status at this level of our values hierarchy.

17.3   The Clash of Values: A Schema for Strategic Accommodation

Cultures differ, in part, because they embody different values. These values can and often do clash, producing both minor and potentially cataclysmic conflicts. The first step in dealing with this kind of volatile situation is to identify a value and then determine whether this value is shared between cultures. If it is not shared, then, as noted above, Hume's position emerges. Culture A maintains a certain value; culture B does not accept this fact about culture A's value-structure; as a result, the value in question, which is a fact for culture A, does not enjoy the corresponding normative status in culture B. Otherwise stated, the fact that a certain value is held in one culture does not imply that another culture must also accept that value as a fact. Such differences breed conflict, only now not conflict between individuals at odds with each other on value issues but between disputing cultures as densely populated social wholes.

Consider, for example, a cultural approach to the core value of freedom limited by a religious conviction that sternly limits individual choices, say in clothing, diet, and entertainment. It is important to realize that the surface differences just listed are precisely that: differences directly experienced because they are immediately perceivable on the surface of life. However, the root cause for these differences lies in a much more fundamental difference – a distinctly defined understanding of the value of freedom. In a culture characterized by a broadly-based value of freedom, what one wears, eats, and does for entertainment is up to individual choice; other cultures restrict these choices because they restrict the value of freedom, which allows a much wider selection of available options.

We may now offer a statement of principle derived from the values hierarchy just enumerated: A conflict in values will tend toward a non-rational resolution as the conflict in question ascends the hierarchy of values. Thus two cultures with opposing views on the value of politeness will hardly decide to settle their differences in this regard on the field of battle. In fact, the two cultures are much more likely to agree to disagree, as the saying goes, as to the ultimate propriety of politeness. Such a difference is not worth pursuing to the point of embracing violence, other than the denatured violence inherent in snippy comments about the supposed interpersonal insensitivity of culture X or Y. Nor is it likely that disagreements about the nature of loyalty, a derivative value, will similarly lead to armed conflict. The practice of loyalty may in some circumstances exacerbate violent conflicts once these conflicts have been initiated, but it will never by itself be the instigating cause of conflict. However, when a core value – such as freedom – is under dispute, then human beings become fully engaged since the presence of and limitations on this value affect the complete fabric of their lives. At this level, virulent opposition between or among cultures concerning a given value must be approached with extreme care.

The question then becomes whether this seemingly unbridgeable logical gap between a cultural "is" and a commensurately cultural "ought" can somehow be narrowed. The following analysis argues that such narrowing can occur in a qualified sense. It should be emphasized that this account is not intended to "refute" Hume on the gap between facts and values, between "is" and "ought." It is intended only to bring the two spheres of concern in apposition to one another so that the emergent differences can be dealt with in a certain way.

This type of resolution is based on two conditions:

(A) *The values of a given culture should be situated within a sufficiently large con-*
text in order to appreciate the value per se as well as the effects this value may
have within the culture as a whole.

Although a given value may have originated within a specific area of a culture (e.g., its religious foundation), the more fundamental the value, the greater
its influence radiates throughout all areas of that culture. Recall that for present
purposes a culture is not a set of discrete elements, any one of which can be
withdrawn or replaced without effect on some, perhaps all, of the other elements; rather, a culture is an organic whole so that any one of its determinate
parts may, and in some cases will, affect any and all of its other determinate
parts. Therefore, to understand why a culture embraces a given value, it is
incumbent on the resident of another culture, one not sharing that value, to
reproduce, or at least to attempt to approximate, the full cultural experience of
someone born into and sharing all the values of the given culture.

To approach understanding a difference in values, it is necessary to connect
the alien value with fundamental features of the culture within which that value
is esteemed. The more inclusive the cultural context surrounding this value,
the more likely that the gap between fact (that the value in question is held by
another culture) and value (that its status as a value is not shared by one's own
culture) can be narrowed. The following principle now becomes operational:
the greater the degree that the full context surrounding the acceptance of a value
in a given culture is understood, the more likely those in different cultures who
do not accept this value will accommodate it peacefully or in a non-combative
way. At this juncture, the second condition takes effect:

(B) *The degree of acceptance of a given value for anyone residing outside the*
culture embracing that value depends on the extent to which the factual cir-
cumstances underlying the introduction and adoption of a value enter one's
complete experiential framework.

This experiential framework may be subdivided as follows: Definition, Perception,
Understanding. Each element of the framework is now discussed.

17.3.1 The Relevance of Definition

Consider freedom as an exemplary instance of a core value not shared to the same
extent by all cultures. As mentioned, the dual perspectives on freedom introduced
above represent a characterization of freedom rather than a technical definition of
freedom as a concept. Values at the core level are inherently slippery and difficult
to situate into neatly constrained conceptual packages. Thus the account relevant
for present purposes is not definition in the sense often advanced by professional
philosophers, as a set of necessary and sufficient conditions, but rather as a useful
marking off of conceptual territory so that the concept under analysis can be more

clearly recognized when it has become the object of scrutiny. This is an approach to definition with a built-in proviso anticipating the reality of disputes even after the definition has been produced and publicized, given the fundamental depth and complexity of the core values for which definitions are sought. But the argument is that it is incumbent on anyone seeking to appreciate cultural differences in the area of values to employ all available avenues of critical thinking in order to win at least an approximation of the value in question. Without such an account in place, however rough around the conceptual edges it may be, additional inquiry into the nature and effects of a value within a given culture will lack any sense of direction.

17.3.2   Perception and Value Recognition

Definition in this modified sense, although crucial, is only one factor of the requisite experiential framework. It is not sufficient to envision values from a purely intellectual perspective, as if it were possible to aim the mind directly toward a given value and, laser-like, ignore the penumbra of circumstances surrounding it. To understand the place of a value in a culture, it is essential to situate – or, more fundamentally, to "see" – that value by being aware of what envelops it within the culture as a whole. An emphasis on perception as integral to the process of understanding and appreciating must therefore be introduced. The full context of circumstances surrounding a value, everything seen, heard, felt, touched, must be brought into the forefront so that the gamut of human experience comes alive in determining the nature of that value as well as its import to the human beings who exist according to its directives. It may be helpful then to think of perception not simply as an arid arena in abstract epistemology with a multitude of arcane conceptual difficulties but rather, more simply and immediately, as an encompassing and enlivening receptacle that houses values. As a result, to describe a value is also to account for and attempt to articulate the ensemble of perceptual avenues that radiate from and to that value. From this perspective, values *per se* and the experience of values cannot be divorced from one another, since the latter provides the former with its power and relevance to the totality of human concerns.

17.3.3   Understanding, Emotion, and Values

Once definition and perception have been explicitly introduced, it is possible to analyze the connection between understanding and the receptivity to and accommodation of values in one culture that are foreign to the values held by individuals in another culture.

The principle is that understanding engenders acceptance and toleration. In this context, understanding does not mean the rarified, purely conceptual following of a demonstration as exemplified in mathematics or physics, but rather recognizing that if one were placed in a different cultural framework, one would feel through the medium of the emotions the moral weight of the value native to that culture. Emotion is here used broadly, covering the general attitude one may experience when in the presence of a value exhibited at the level of immediate perception (e.g., seeing someone dressed very differently from what is the norm in one's resident culture). The resulting sense of appreciation would not bridge the gap between one's own cultural values and the value that had been scrutinized to the extent of embracing that value – in this respect, Hume's separation of values from facts still stands. But this emotional or felt response, in conjunction with the purely theoretical statement of the definition of the value, would confer on the student of diverse cultural values a richer, more nuanced comprehension of why that value has the status which it enjoys in that culture.

From a more abstract perspective, this kind of appreciation is possible on condition that understanding and feeling intersect at certain key points. However, this is an intersection enabled, as it were, by movement on the part of the understanding that receives its direction from the purely cognitive grasp of a value in terms of its definition. As a result, a concerted effort must be made by the individual seeking to grasp the import of a foreign value (for someone living in accordance with that value) to experience materials and settings in a cognitive way so that the springs of moral feeling will be activated and directed toward a feeling of receptivity.

17.4   Gifted Minds: Values, Context, and Understanding

The complex intersection of different strands of cognition required to understand and appreciate divergent cultural values points to a certain kind of intelligence, competently represented by gifted minds, as especially receptive to actualizing this dimension of understanding. The following characteristics are, we will assume, resident in the structure of the gifted mind. It should be emphasized that these characteristics are not introduced as criteria for assessing students as gifted. Rather, it is assumed that the gifted population has already been identified and that a class of students so comprised could, with interest and insight, apply their abilities as embodied in these characteristics to divergences in cultural values. Once this level of understanding has been applied, it is possible to narrow the gap between facts and values, even and especially when this gap separates diverse cultures.

17.4.1   Curiosity

Gifted minds possess an inherent desire to pursue what is out there, especially in regions of the world that may be distant from their immediate environment (Howe 1999; Janos and Robinson 1985). This is a level of curiosity that will inspire the gifted mind to engage with a broad spectrum of phenomena. This spectrum will incorporate the contemporary prevalence of a multi-media approach to the problem. Thus facts presented in a variety of formats – films, drama, music and art forms, literature, popular culture – will be studied in order to determine the definitions of values and to discriminate differences between values found in distinct cultures. For example, what other cultures construe as freedom – or its lack – will vivify the desire to witness first-hand how this value is manifested in that culture's forms of life. In this regard, the number of pictorial evocations of divergent cultural practices available on the internet is large and growing exponentially. Care must be taken to access appropriate materials, of course, but the immediacy of this material is noteworthy and relevant.

17.4.2   Analytical Ability

The industriousness of the gifted mind will be challenged by this variety of content, ranging as it will over many disparate forms of human activity (Sternberg 1997). From a purely philosophical perspective, the initial phase of the problem will be formulating a definition of a given value. This definition must be fair to the array of material providing the "stuff" of the definition and yet it must still be codified and expressed in terms approximating logical canons of definition. Producing this kind of account will require both a high degree of integrative ability given the broad-based experiences embodied in the cultural manifestations listed above as well as the analytical skill to "break down" a mass of disparate data so that the value in question – freedom is our hypothetical case in point – can be approached with due attention for stating as precisely as possible just what that value is insofar as it emerges in another culture. The goal will be the formulation of a definition of the target value as a central focus for studying and appreciating the differences and divergences animating the nature and structure of this value when it is placed in apposition with a parallel value in our culture.

17.4.3   Sense of Justice

The gifted mind has an inherent sense for recognizing parameters necessary to determine what is fair (Janos and Robinson 1985; Gardner 1997). This sense will be tested and sharpened by appreciating, in the midst of the differences determined by due integration and analysis of relevant source materials, the values of other cultures. This dimension of justice will engender an affinity for recognizing the purpose of a given value, and for its *rightness* relative to the culture within which it is currently dominant. The resulting respect for this value will derive from a sense of justice exhibited not at the more immediate level of one person treating another person fairly, but at the more general and therefore less obvious level of one culture respecting the values of another culture. In the case of non-discriminatory education, for example, a culture endorsing this policy as a value insofar as it is a consequence of a certain apprehension of freedom could still respect another culture that does not sanction such liberal access to education, even if the culture with the more extensive sense of freedom might wish that an equivalent sense of freedom could be instilled in the other culture.

In the process of thinking about the values of other cultures, the gifted can appreciate the difference between those values and commensurate values in their home culture. And, in general, the more that gifted minds are exposed to different values, the greater will be their understanding of these values and the greater likelihood that they can suggest ways of accommodating the differences between values as these differences characterize distinct cultures. If as a minimal but necessary condition justice is characterized as a kind of fairness between and among certain parties – cultures in the context at hand – then gifted minds will be in a position to determine, or at least to suggest, ways to be fair to differences engendered by the values of other cultures.

The analysis offered above concerning the foundations for Hume's sharp split between facts and values appealed to fundamental differences emerging at the level of determining the good, either for oneself or for the culture in which one resides. As a result, one phase in discussing whether or not, or the extent to which, a given value is just will be to situate the analysis in as broad a normative context as possible – that is, by posing questions to students in terms of the nature of the good. Should the good include all or only some members of a culture? Should there be a good encompassing all cultures as interactive members, a pertinent perspective given the many senses in which the world as a whole is continually shrinking? What elements should comprise the good – Pleasure? Wealth? Fame? Longevity? Love and friendship? Eternal salvation? Some intricate combination of all these ends? It is unlikely that discussion pursuing this topic will produce a consensus of final and unexceptional answers, but both teacher and class as a whole will achieve a revitalized awareness of the importance of thinking about values from this extremely general perspective. The more that a consensus concerning the nature of the good can be established, the less likely that subsidiary disputes will arise concerning values more restrictive in scope and effect than "the good as such."

17.4.4 The Pedagogical Challenge

Even if the above program is accepted as theoretically cogent, anyone associated with the practical business of educating gifted minds – or, indeed, educating anyone – cannot help but consider the immense demands made on teachers in order to actualize this program in a real classroom with real students. Here are the principal pedagogical components:

> Mastering the content of another, perhaps in some ways alien culture, and focusing on as many aspects of that culture as possible relative to the value under analysis

Analyzing this content in order to produce a clear, coherent account of that value

Searching throughout as many media sources as possible to locate materials drawn from the target culture, which will best situate the value within the students' field of receptivity

Developing a presentation of this material to produce for gifted minds the most informed and sympathetic comprehensive effect

Integrating the material with more traditionally defined and presented curriculum.

To succeed in such extensive preparation, development, and presentation is asking a great deal of teachers. But if teachers of gifted minds look to the world as their classroom, insofar as the students in front of them will play out their lives within this world, the personal rewards as well as the seriousness of the challenge will inspire these teachers at least to investigate this approach to values as a viable option in the instruction they provide for their students.

17.5 Values: Appreciation, Accommodation, and Beyond....

To understand a value that conflicts with one's own value, that is, to think as well as to feel a certain degree of clarity concerning why that value is held to be such by people in different cultures, will tend to temper negative response to that value. Thus to recognize the connections between that value and the rest of the person's basic humanity is to place oneself in the same general framework as that individual. This apposite context will increase the student's appreciation for why the value is embraced as a value, even if it does not convince anyone living in a different culture to introduce that value as one of his or her own. Since this level of understanding is a subtle merger of a purely analytical grasp of definition joined with a concerted feel for context and the ramifications of values radiating throughout that context, it has been argued that gifted minds are especially receptive to implementing this kind of broad-based understanding.

The point is not utopian – that is, let the gifted rule the world and all will be peace and harmony. However, if the above analysis is generally sound and gifted minds take the lead in implementing this approach to understanding values, there may be a ripple effect as the gifted take their places in society. When the gifted establish positions throughout their respective environments – the arts, education, science, business, politics – this attitude of receptivity toward and understanding of divergent cultural values instilled in their world-view cannot help but foster a greater awareness of – and, it may be assumed, sensitivity toward – differences in values with at least some of the people with whom gifted minds interact. This will be a prime instance of leading by a form of compassionate example toward an informed acceptance of these values rather than merely rejecting them through some compelling force, whether subtle in the form of propaganda or more bluntly secured through sheer unvarnished political will. To the extent that this receptivity reaches through the ranks, it may be hoped that the country will become a more humane environment for the general acceptance of difference, and for an attitude of restraint whenever differences in values reach the point where confrontation appears inevitable.

If it can indeed be determined through the diversified sense of understanding characterized above how a value becomes established in a different culture, it will increase the possibility that a cultural clash concerning values can be resolved, or at least eased, since the elements elevating that characteristic to the level of a value will be in view. As a result, arenas of discussion will open up based on cultural commonalities such that representatives of the conflicting cultures can, with properly sympathetic motivation, reasonably analyze these elements in hopes of developing fertile compromises that preserve both the common ground they share as well as the irreducible differences in values that separate them.

With this receptivity for accommodation in place, the divergences in value estimation between cultures can at least be lessened in intensity so that if a conflict in cultural values should become intractable, there will nonetheless be a level of respect for this difference such that neither culture will have a serious or premeditated interest in attacking the other simply by virtue of this difference. Each side in such a dispute will surely be impressed by the degree and extent of knowledge of their culture manifested by the other side, assuming of course that both sides have prepared in the same or similar ways. It is worth emphasizing in this regard that the complex and subtle understanding invoked here will, if successfully engendered, apply not only to the United States in its interaction with other cultures, but to any native culture relative to other cultures that diverge from the boundaries of that native culture with respect to conflicting values. However, even if cultures are entrenched with their own values, the efforts of a culture on one side of the dispute to initiate an irenic resolution of the disagreement can at least lead to a peaceful approach to discussion based on as complete an awareness of the disputed value as possible.

These are clearly noble aspirations, but their implementation lies in a perhaps distant future, and after serious and sustained commitment to the procedures outlined above. The practice of determining as precisely and rigorously as possible how we see the values of other cultures will help us appreciate how other cultures discern and respond to our values, and such breadth of vicarious experience is invaluable. This recognition becomes especially crucial if the conflict between opposed values is deemed fundamentally incapable of resolution, whether by political leaders, the general populace or both. For if it is then deemed advisable to consider initiating a change in another culture's values, the above analysis implies that there will be as many factors relevant to the success of such a change as there are elements within the culture affected by that value. The complexities involved in such an attempted change will be daunting, but recognition of the full spectrum of these complexities is the only way to prepare for the many kinds of activities and realities that will be affected by such a change.

The modes of response one culture should pursue if its core values are threatened by another culture's aggressiveness is a matter to be decided by the political leaders of the culture under pressure. In a democracy, of course, these decisions must, or at least should, be undertaken with the consent of the citizenry at large. Although some may deem it unfortunate if not tragic, even in a democracy, the practice of war, and violence generally, will doubtless remain live options as means to preserve the values animating the democracy. But the philosophical and pedagogical perspective sketched above, if put into practice and found coherent and penetrating, suggests that although the inevitability of confrontation concerning core values is perhaps undeniable given the world's complexity, the inevitability of war as an apparent solution to such confrontation may not appear quite as palatable to so many in the upper reaches of power and influence.

As technological advances along with other factors continue to shrink the world, gifted minds are uniquely qualified to contribute to exploring and, in the long run, adopting more rational and congenial ways to understand divergent values as these values define other cultures, and to confront the hard fact that these fundamental differences in value are the root cause of so many of the world's conflicts. As things stand now, these differences are indelibly etched into the broad panoply of human consciousness; how gifted minds and people in general respond to these differences is an element in our collective educational environment with the potential to be aimed toward the pursuit of a sustainable global harmony which, one would like to hope and believe, exemplifies what is best for all concerned.

Note: The author would like to thank Juliana V. Vazquez for her careful and incisive editing of this chapter.

References

Gardner, H. (1997). *Extraordinary minds*. New York: Basic Books.

Howe, J.A. (1999). *The psychology of high abilities*. New York: New York University Press.

Janos, P. & Robinson, N. (1985). Psychosocial development in intellectually gifted children. In F.D. Horowitz & M. O'Brien (Eds), *The gifted and talented developmental perspectives* (pp. 37–74). Washington, DC: American Psychological Association.

Sternberg, R. (1997). A triarchic view of giftedness: theory and practice. In N. Colangelo & G. Davis (Eds), *Handbook of gifted education*. 2nd. Ed. (pp. 43–53). Boston, MA: Allyn and Bacon.

Chapter 18
Eastern Perspectives: Moral and Volitional Education of Gifted Students

Chua Tee Teo and Yuanshan Cheng

Abstract While provision for the education of gifted students in East Asia is ongoing, specific efforts in moral education are not known to the external world. Viewed from an Eastern perspective, this chapter briefly discusses moral education in talent development in Singapore, China, Indonesia, South Korea and Thailand. It then reports an empirical study that compares the differences in moral attributes and leadership qualities of gifted primary school students in Singapore with similar qualities of non-gifted students in Singapore and in China using the Moral and Leadership Subscale of the Self-Knowledge Checklist (SKC). Statistical analyses show no significant difference on moral attributes between the Singapore sample of gifted students and their non-gifted peers. Compared to a sample of non-gifted primary students in China, both Singapore samples of gifted and non-gifted students had significantly lower moral attribute scores. In addition, the Singapore gifted sample showed a significantly higher level of leadership attributes than the two non-gifted samples in Singapore and in China. Implications of the study are discussed in the context of modern Eastern culture and values. Recommendations for the teaching of gifted students in moral education are proposed in a framework of *Knowledge, Volition & Action*.

Keywords China · Eastern values · Gifted · Leadership · Moral attributes · Non-gifted · Self-knowledge · Singapore · Volition

Human powers, gifts and talents, are various in their kind and extensive in their range. The ills that face humanity today are not due to a lack of intellectual prowess but derive from a lack of education in moral choice. The outcomes in the phenomenal world come about as a manifestation of what people decide to do with their intelligence, putting their thoughts into deeds. While education to develop academic

---

C.T. Teo (✉) and Y. Cheng
Psychological Studies Academic Group, Blk 2 Level 3 Room 78 (General Office), National Institute of Education, 1 Nanyang Walk, Singapore 637616
e-mail: chuatee.teo@nie.edu.sg; yuanshan.cheng@nie.edu.sg

D. Ambrose, T. Cross (eds.), *Morality, Ethics, and Gifted Minds*,
DOI: 10.1007/978-0-387-89368-6_18,
© Springer Science+Business Media LLC 2009

talents and non-academic gifts are important, the education of the heart and soul in spirituality and morality is as important, if not more so. The harm done by a less intelligent person is not as detrimental as the evil committed by a highly intelligent person. J. K. Rowling, in her speech to graduates at Harvard University's 357th Commencement on June 5, 2008, said that what we achieve inwardly will change outer reality ("We do not," 2008). Gifted or talented or otherwise, we are the captains of our own ships. It is the core of our human being, our inner self, that decides what to do with our natural endowments and acquired capacities.

No matter how intelligent or gifted a person is, the first obstacle to the manifestation of talents into outward performance is the person himself or herself. First, the person has to overcome his or her own laziness, lethargy, and lassitude. This is a battle to beat oneself of one's bad habits, the conscious choice and willful exertion to be engaged in a fruitful endeavor as in learning, thinking, discovering, designing, writing, painting, producing or any other useful work. This is the first moral deed a gifted individual could render in service of the self. It is thus evident that the making of a moral choice affects talent development.

This chapter outlines eastern perspectives in talent development with regard to moral education in several Asian countries including Singapore, China, Indonesia, South Korea and Thailand. It discerns the differences between eastern and western moral educational stances, and then expound on the understanding of volitional, moral and spiritual development in general. Implications and suggestions for the moral and spiritual development of gifted and creative students also are given.

18.1 Moral Education for Gifted Students in Asian Countries

Gifted education in the People's Republic of China (P.R.C.) has been ongoing for the last 30 years in experimental schools. It started at the University of Science and Technology of China in Anhui Province with special classes for very young talented children around 12–14 years of age. This brought more attention to gifted education. However, today the Chinese Ministry of Education does not fully support schools in separating students into special classes according to talents, thus only a few schools for the gifted are located in Beijing and other large cities while not every province hosts a school for gifted education.

Gifted education is commonly known as education for supernormal children in China. Usually, gifted children spend a shorter time covering the content knowledge meant for average children. The curriculum for gifted students and research related to giftedness, brain functioning, talent development and effects of special educational and intervention programs are under the purview of organizations like the Institute of Psychology, a sub-organization of the Chinese Academy of Sciences. Lessons in moral development usually are conducted twice a week, according to a brief interview with Professor Shi Jiannong at the Institute. These lessons are designed to develop the gifted children in personal, familial and social morality and ethics. Moral reasoning and explanations are incorporated with stories and discussions pertaining to real life practices in morality.

Indonesia has an acceleration class program for their gifted students (Kamdi 2004). These are special classes in mainstream schools at primary, secondary and senior high school levels. Acceleration in learning is practiced for gifted students in English language, mathematics and science. Moral education is not taught separately but infused into the subject matter especially in subjects without acceleration such as civics, history and religion. For subjects in which no acceleration is provided, the gifted students study with non-gifted students together in mixed-ability classes.

In South Korea, gifted students attend special classes or pull-out programs affiliated with various universities in science and technology. Such programs are centrally orchestrated by the Institute for Gifted Students (IGS) of the Korea Advanced Institute of Science and Technology (KAIST). The gifted students undertake studies in physics, mathematics, biology, chemistry, technology, and art as well as interdisciplinary science. To date, there is no explicit moral education provision for gifted students in Korea.

In Thailand, gifted and talented students are usually taught in special schools with small class sizes of about 15 students. The curriculum consists of acceleration and enrichment programs. Other advanced-placement programs, talent-development projects in science and technology and various support activities are provided by institutions and relevant agencies (Thailand Education System 2008, pp. 98–99). Moral education is not known to be included in the efforts to provide learning for the gifted and talented. Formal monitoring of gifted education programs in Thailand is conducted by the National Centre for the Gifted and Talented, a government agency. The Prime Minister's Office also has set up an Institute for Gifted and Innovative Learning (IGIL) to promote gifted education.

In Singapore, gifted education is under the purview of the Ministry of Education's Gifted Education Branch and takes the form of self-contained classes in good mainstream schools. The Gifted Education Branch undertakes the selection of students into the program, designs the curriculum, trains teachers, and coordinates science research programs and other enrichment activities for primary and secondary students. Since its inception 25 years ago, the Gifted Education Program (GEP) always has a "civics and moral education" (CME) component, which all mainstream students also experience in a weekly lesson. The GEP however devises its own affective education curriculum and has formalized it in a GEP AE Model theoretical framework (Ministry of Education 2004). It aims to teach moral values given in the CME curriculum, citizenship and leadership education, a curriculum of conscience and service to community, and finally career awareness. It utilizes a three-pronged approach of deliberate instruction of desired values, dispositions and life-skills; infusion of values into the academic curriculum and then the conscious application of these values into real life as in allowing the gifted students to conduct service-learning projects as well as their involvement in co-curricular activities, camps, Individualised Study Options (ISO), other special programs and community projects, with the overall aim of character development.

Creatively gifted people appear to have greater courage to be different and to be odd or weird, and thus to have a greater tendency to do what they like, in some cases going beyond moral boundaries and legal constraints. Many famous creative people, such as Bertrand Russell, Oscar Wilde, Mahatma Gandhi, Emma Goldman, and Galileo Galilei, have spent time in jail (Runco 2007, pp. 140–143). This makes the teaching of moral education to the gifted and creative urgent and pertinent. Yet many Asian countries, while struggling to establish basic educational programming for gifted students, have simply overlooked this important aspect of moral education in the curriculum. How many eminent adults, such as politicians, commit unlawful acts? How many successful terrorist bomb attacks, are being masterminded by brilliant minds? The evil that those of lesser minds could commit is not as severe as the harm an intelligent person could do. By moral education, we mean the business of "getting reinforced by some benefit to another" (Schulman 2002, p. 499), and learning to refrain from harming others through conscious education in school and at home. Gifted and creative young students need to be taught in a manner such that that they become truly concerned about the well being of others.

18.2 Moral Attributes of Gifted and Non-gifted Students in Singapore and China

A comparative study of the moral attributes of gifted and non-gifted students in Singapore and China in the primary schools was conducted recently using the Moral and Leadership subscale of the Self-Knowledge Checklist (SKC) developed by the first author. This SKC subscale consists of 18 items on a 9-point Likert scale. It is a self-report of the extent or degree to which a person feels that he or she is truthful, selfless, sincere, responsible, humble, caring, has integrity, leadership and other moral qualities. The following is a sample of questions from the Moral and Leadership SKC subscale:

- I am truthful.
- I have integrity.
- I am trustworthy.
- I am selfless.
- I do not bully others.
- I care for all.
- I know I have no prejudice.
- I am a responsible person.
- I am able to take charge of a project.
- I generally direct the activity in which I am involved.
- I live to do good and to bring happiness to others.
- I wish to serve humanity when I grow up.

Factor analyses revealed two factors on the SKC subscale, with the first factor (factor 1) pertaining to moral attributes or virtues and the second (factor 2) relating to leadership qualities. The first factor of moral attributes or virtues is comprised of 14 items and reports a Cronbach's Alpha of .94. The second factor consists of four

Table 18.1 Table of means for moral and leadership SKC subscale for primary gifted and non-gifted students in Singapore and non-gifted students in China

	N	Mean	Standard deviation
Virtues or moral attributes (factor 1)			
Singapore gifted	347	6.56	1.14
Singapore non-gifted	169	6.45	1.40
Chinese non-gifted	971	7.09	1.93
Leadership attributes (factor 2)			
Singapore gifted	347	6.30	1.57
Singapore non-gifted	169	5.81	1.95
Chinese non-gifted	971	5.47	2.37

items and reports a Cronbach's Alpha of .85. Both factors of virtues and leadership attributes are meant to measure the moral character of the gifted students in the primary GEP when first designed.

A MANOVA was used to find out if a combination of the two measures of moral character varies as a function of culture as represented by gifted and non-gifted students in Singapore and non-gifted students in China. Simply, it tests whether mean differences between the Chinese and the Singaporean groups on a combination of the two factors on the Moral and leadership SKC subscale are likely to have occurred by chance. The MANOVA also provides statistical matching groups as random assignment to groups was not possible.

The MANOVA was performed with the two factors of moral character as dependent variables and with the three groups of students in the two countries as independent variable. The results show a significant main effect (Wilks' Lambda = .096; $F_{(2,1483)} = 7016.736$; $p < .001$). Table 18.1 gives the respective means and standard deviations.

For the moral or virtues subscale, ANOVA shows a significant difference across the three groups ($F_{(2,1484)} = 18.81$, $p < .001$, effect size = .03). Tukey post hoc tests show significant differences between Chinese non-gifted students and Singapore non-gifted students ($p < .001$) and between Chinese non-gifted students and Singapore gifted students ($p < .001$). However, no significant difference is found between Singapore gifted and non-gifted students.

Similarly, significant differences were reported across all three groups on the leadership subscale ($F_{(2,1484)} = 19.05$, $p < .001$, effect size = .02). Results of Tukey post hoc tests show significant differences between Singapore gifted students and Singapore non-gifted students ($p < .001$) and between Singapore gifted students and Chinese non-gifted students. However, no significant difference is reported between Chinese non-gifted students and Singapore non-gifted students.

It appears from the results of the study that Singaporean gifted students were significantly higher in the mean scores on the leadership aspect of character than Singaporean non-gifted students and Chinese non-gifted students. With regard to virtues or moral qualities, the Chinese non-gifted students have reported a significantly higher mean score than their Singaporean counterparts, both gifted and otherwise. Singaporean gifted and non-gifted students reported no significant difference in virtues and moral attributes although the gifted sample has reported a higher mean score.

In another study by Teo and Cheng (2008) comparing the moral attributes of secondary non-gifted students in China and Singapore, similar results were found. Using the same Moral and leadership SKC subscale, secondary Singapore students were found to have significantly higher leadership scores and lower mean moral or virtues score (Teo and Cheng 2008).

The above analyses show that under normal classroom conditions, that is, without special educational intervention on moral character, be it in deliberate virtues or leadership development, Chinese students in mainstream education appear to exhibit greater moral and virtuous attributes than Singaporean gifted students. Singaporean gifted students on the other hand, show significantly higher leadership scores. Such differences may be understood if we examine the value systems of the two countries.

18.2.1 Chinese Values

China with its rich cultural heritage of 5,000 years has been evolving and acquiring new values after the impact of communism on Chinese ancestral values and Confucian ethics. The modern Chinese values cannot be taken as pure reflection of Confucianism and/or communism. The second author believes that Chinese society today is characterized by five basic values, which include equity, country before self, self improvement and self-perfection, familial piety of respect and brotherhood/camaraderie, and social harmony.

The Chinese have a strong sense of egalitarianism, which is a remnant of communism. Social equality is always a governmental priority. A public toilet cleaner for example, will not hesitate to initiate a handshake and extend a helping hand towards a white foreigner in the belief that there is no caste system or hierarchy in society. A Chinese person is neither inferior nor egoistically superior toward his or her fellow beings. Leadership is not top-down; it is perceived as service. This is evident in the significantly lower mean leadership scores of the Chinese students in comparison with their Singaporean peers as leadership items measure the ability of a single person to lead. For example, Chinese students tend to score lower on the item:

• I generally direct the activity in which I am involved.

The patriotism of the Chinese people, putting the country before self, was witnessed by the world when Beijing hosted the games of the XXIX Olympiad in 2008. Sacrifices made in time and money to host the event successfully were shaped by the values of each person involved in the games. Westerners might think that ethics were violated when another person sang in the place of the young girl floating across the stadium. However, to the young performer and her family, and the rest of the country, if someone else could do the job better to bring glory to the country, then it was acceptable as long as the singer was acknowledged. Sacrificing the self for others symbolizes a rather high state of moral behavior. Perhaps this is the reason why the Chinese cohort of students was found to be significantly higher in their mean moral attributes score than the Singapore samples.

With respect to the value of self-improvement and self-perfection, as mentioned by the chairperson of the Chinese organizing committee at the opening ceremony of the 2008 Olympics, the Chinese believe that one has to develop and perfect himself/herself in various aspects of knowledge, morality, and skills before one could contribute to the family, the society, and the country. In addition, a person with a good moral character is one who has strong familial values of respect for elders, care for the young, and love for and brotherhood with peers. The Chinese emphasize camaraderie. They will not hesitate to sacrifice themselves for their "brothers." In this light, the Chinese tend to be more selfless than others. Chinese students are likely to score higher on the items:

- I am selfless.
- I care for all.

More recently, the Chinese government has been emphasizing social harmony. It is known that the Chinese are encouraged to live in unity and harmony with their fellow beings, with nature and with the entire universe. Chinese students may score higher for the items:

- I know I have no prejudice.
- I do not bully others.
- I live to do good and to bring happiness to others.

Note that China after opening its doors also accepted an influx of western culture and values. The Chinese values previously discussed are limited to those observed in the study and they are pertinent to primary school Chinese students.

18.2.2 Singaporean Values

Though Singapore is seated in East Asia, it is a hybrid of eastern and western cultures. Compared to China, Singapore certainly was exposed earlier to western values. The government of Singapore has always striven to maintain familial and citizenship values in the schools and in society. Schools work hard to foster national identity, to allow all students to understand the challenges facing Singapore, to feel for the country and to be able to contribute to society when they grow up. The Ministry of Education aims to nurture young Singaporeans to be morally upright, rooted to Singapore, peaceful and gracious members of a multi-racial society and to have good work attitudes locally and globally (Ministry of Education 2008). Character building for young Singaporean students is a composite of moral and civics education, national and citizenship education, and social-emotional learning. Gifted students in Singapore are nurtured in the same ethical tenets as students in the mainstream (Ministry of Education 2004). This is perhaps the reason why the mean moral attribute scores for gifted and non-gifted students in the study were not significantly different.

Being a smaller country with limited resources, Singaporeans are pragmatic and realistic people and meritocracy is prized. The Gifted Education Program at its inception was meant to nurture intellectual and leadership resources for the nation. It is no surprise to find that the sample of gifted Singaporean students had significantly higher mean scores on the leadership subscale than the sample of non-gifted students as well as the sample of non-gifted students from China.

18.3 Discussion

The results of the study would have been more meaningful if the Moral and Leadership SKC subscale had been administered to primary Chinese gifted students and gifted students in western countries. Nevertheless, mean scores of the three samples indicate that the respondents were clearly above the median of the 9-point Likert scale on moral attributes. This suggests that the gifted and non-gifted primary students in Singapore and China had moral attributes well above the median as depicted by the Moral and Leadership SKC subscale. More eastern samples of gifted students need to be tested before a generalization may be made.

If gifted students in Singapore do not have higher mean moral attribute scores than the non-gifted students in China, then educators need to consider incorporating eastern perspectives and philosophy into the curriculum for moral education of the gifted students. Young people in the east may be more obedient but as they become smarter, they begin to query why they should be good and why they should abide by what the adults suggest when the adults may not be as intelligent or moral as they are. Traditional eastern societies seem to promote a sense of self-respect or dignity and respect for others, familial values of filial piety, loving the nation before self, diligence, positive work attitude and a sense of pride in work, and many other virtues such as being trustworthy, kind, respectful, caring, courteous and living in harmony and unity with people.

Confucius (479 B.C./2005), the great teacher in ancient China, defined a good man as a person with five qualities – reverence, lenience, confidence, diligence and benevolence Confucian ethics may be considered a form of virtues ethics. Reverence means that one should respect others as oneself; lenience means that one should understand and tolerate others; confidence means that one should believe in others and be trustworthy; diligence means that one should be devoted to work with heart and soul; and benevolence means that one should do good to others. Confucian followers approved of the wise and the good and as a result wise good people are highly honored in Chinese societies. When highly intelligent students have moral qualities, we expect that their contributions to society will be tremendous.

18.4   Effective Methods to Teach Gifted Students Morality: The Knowledge, Volition, and Action Framework

As gifted students are endowed with greater intelligence, guiding them to acquire moral thinking and behaviors cannot be predicated upon blind imitation or plain obedience. Teaching the gifted moral theories or to follow rules will not suffice either. The teacher must first seek sources of moral motivation (Schulman 2002) and share these with the gifted students. Knowledge of the reasons why human beings need to be good is an example: that we live in a highly interconnected world breathing the same air, drinking the same water and eating the same foods, fearing the same nuclear catastrophe, and that it is only when our fellow beings are safe and prosperous that we will be safe and well. When gifted students are inspired, they become truly concerned about the well-being of others, and are more convinced to act in praiseworthy ways. Positive actions are taken only when people know the importance and urgency of the consequences of non-action and evil deeds.

Gifted students also need to be educated on those deeds, which lead to loftiness or lowliness, to glory or abasement. This serves as a deterrent to committing crimes. How often is an eminent personality like a politician removed from the position of power and admiration when the immoral acts he committed were made known to the public? Knowledge of the consequences of good and evil deeds creates awareness for choice or volition. That is, all human beings could choose to act in a morally proper or improper manner. A person must accept personal responsibility for the consequences of his or her choices. No one is responsible for the choices made by another person. Gifted students, with so much intelligence, must be taught to make responsible choices based on conscious knowledge so that their intelligence may become wisdom.

Moral choice is predicated upon two polarities. One may choose to do good or otherwise. Human beings have both capacities. We have a higher, moral or spiritual nature identified by selflessness, and a lower, immoral or animalistic/instinctive nature characterized by self-centeredness or selfishness. A person may make a conscious choice between either the "good" or the "bad"; this is his or her volition, will or moral choice. Gifted children could, for instance, choose to be truthful or to lie, to complete their homework or not.

Parents and teachers are the prime persons in contact with gifted children and they play an important and crucial role in guiding their decision-making. Helping gifted students to exercise their volition often occurs during teachable moments or incidents of moral crisis. The adult, be it a teacher or parent, needs to guide the gifted students to develop moral reasoning, and to encourage them to put in effort when facing moral dilemmas. Moral reasoning involves thinking, appreciating the law of causality, namely, that every effect has a cause. With practice, moral capacities will be strengthened in due course. The development of a moral character is not a random or chance phenomenon. The person, in this case the gifted pupil, must first possess conscious knowledge of what constitutes "goodness" and the lack thereof. S/he then makes a choice, and executes the decision in terms of actions. The practice of good deeds is first based on the principle of "to know" and then "to do" (Teo 2002). The authors propose that gifted children be taught to develop their moral capacities based on the knowledge, volition and action framework. The process of the betterment of the world will be hastened if gifted children constantly acquire moral education as they become contributing adults.

References

Confucius. (2005). The analects of confucius: Confucius modernized—thus spoke the master (X. Y. Z., Trans.). [Chinese–English ed.]. Beijing, China: Higher Education Press. (Original work published after 479 BC)

Kamdi, W. (2004). *Kelas akselerasi dan diskriminasi anak* (Acceleration class and children discrimination). Indonesia: Kompas cyber media.

Ministry of education. (2004). *20 years of gifted education: From promise to flow*. Singapore: ministry of education.

Ministry of education, Singapore. (2008). Desired outcomes of education. Retrieved August 17, 2008, from http://www.moe.edu.sg/education/desired-outcomes/

Runco, M. A. (2007). *Creativity: Theories and themes: Research, development, and practice*. Boston, MA: Elsevier Academic Press.

Schulman, M. (2002). How we become moral: The sources of moral motivation. In C. R. Snyder & S. J. Lopez (Eds.), *Handbook of Positive Psychology* (pp. 499–512). New York: Oxford University Press.

Teo, C. T. (2002). Building character in school children in the new millennium. In A. Tan & L. Law (Eds.), *Psychology in Contexts: A Perspective from the South East Asian Societies* (pp. 122–144). Singapore: Lingzi Media.

Teo, C. T., & Cheng Y. S. (2008, November). *Moral attributes of students in China and Singapore: A comparative study*. Paper presented at the APERA Conference 2008, Singapore.

Thailand education system and policy handbook. (2008). Washington, DC: International business publications.

We do not need magic to change the world. (2008, June 22). *The Straits Times*, p. 30.

Chapter 19
Giftedness and Moral Promise

Annemarie Roeper and Linda Kreger Silverman

Abstract The relationship between giftedness and moral development is complex. One does not have to be gifted to be moral, and the gifted are capable of incredibly destructive, immoral behavior. However, many have observed that gifted children express moral concerns at a younger age and in a more intensified manner than their age peers, and some theorists suggest that moral sensitivity increases with intelligence. From our experience, which spans more than 5 decades, we contend that gifted children are *at promise* for high moral development in adult life. Their ethical sensitivity stems from their heightened cognitive awareness, keen sense of justice, emotional sensitivity, empathy, insightfulness, powers of observation, knowledge of consequences, questioning of the morality of the culture, and their ability to imagine alternatives. Moral promise comes to fruition within a nurturing environment. Self-regulation – the ability to put the needs of one's community before one's own desires – develops through the establishment of emotional bonds with caring adults who honor one's inner world.

Keywords Attachment · Awareness · Bond · Community · Complexity · Conscience · Ethical · Empathy · Honesty · Interdependence · Justice · Leader · Moral judgment · Moral promise · Psyche · Self-protection · Sensitivity · Values

What is morality and what prompts us to be moral? To a great extent, our concepts of right and wrong are culturally determined. A guard at a Nazi concentration camp rescued a 3-year old boy and then put him back into a gas chamber because her conscience bothered her. She thought that she was being moral by adhering to the dictates of her regime. Hitler was clearly a genius who understood the German

A. Roeper (✉)
2089 Tapscott Ave., El Cerrito, CA 94530, USA
e-mail: AMRoeper@aol.com

L.K. Silverman
Gifted Development Center, 1452 Marion Center, Denver, CO 80218, USA
e-mail: lindafay@nilenet.com

D. Ambrose, T. Cross (eds.), *Morality, Ethics, and Gifted Minds*,
DOI: 10.1007/978-0-387-89368-6_19,
© Springer Science+Business Media LLC 2009

mind during a period of great suffering and was able to use it in the service of his own hunger for power. He had the ability to manipulate people's minds, twisting their normal conscience, so that they no longer knew the difference between good and evil.

Unfortunately, Hitler is only one of many individuals who used their great intelligence in destructive ways. Throughout history, gifted people who lacked morality have created havoc. By the same token, gifted people such as Rosa Parks, Nelson Mandela, Martin Luther King, Jr., Albert Schweitzer, and Gandhi have been moral beacons. As examples exist at both extremes of the continuum, is there a correlation between high intelligence and morality?

The relationship between giftedness and moral development is complex. We have a tendency to confuse giftedness with goodness. Not all gifted people behave morally, and one does not have to be highly intelligent to act with conscience. Yet, high intelligence appears to be a requisite for leadership. "No one has ever advocated stupidity as a qualification for a leader" (Hollingworth 1939, p. 575). Moral leaders are usually gifted (Brennan 1987; Brennan and Piechowski 1991; Grant 1990; Piechowski 1978, 1990, 1992). Some theorists even suggest that moral sensitivity is essential to the preservation of the species and increases with higher intelligence (Csikszentmihalyi 1993; Loye 1990). Loye (1990) asserted that moral sensitivity is biologically based and governed by the frontal lobes. It appears to increase in species with higher intelligence. In *The Evolving Self*, Csikszentmihalyi (1993) contended that there is an evolutionary thrust of moral concern related to the complexity of the organism.

> The final principle of evolution is: (7) Harmony is usually achieved by evolutionary changes involving an increase in an organism's complexity, that is, an increase in both differentiation and integration. (p. 156, italics in original)

In our combined experience we have seen more gifted children with exquisite moral sensitivity than bright children who lack that sensitivity. This trait appears to be born from a keen sense of justice. "Concerned with justice, fairness" is one of 25 qualities in the *Characteristics of Giftedness Scale* (Silverman 1993a), which has been used as a screening tool at the Gifted Development Center for the last 30 years. In the Annemarie Roeper Method of Qualitative Assessment (Roeper 2003), examiners are trained to look for "an enormous sense of justice" as a strong attribute of giftedness (Roeper 1988). Lewis Terman (1925) and Leta Hollingworth (1942), early leaders in gifted education, noted the moral sensitivity of this population; it has been a common theme in the writings of those who followed. Gifted children repeatedly have been found to demonstrate moral concerns at an earlier age and in a more intensified manner than their peers (see Boehm 1962; Clark and Hankins 1985; Drews 1972; Galbraith 1985; Gross 1993; Janos et al. 1989; Karnes and Brown 1981; Martinson 1961; Passow 1988; Simmons and Zumpf 1986; Vare 1979).

In this chapter, we will attempt to glean insights into the nature of the relationship between giftedness and moral promise, and provide examples from our practices of children who demonstrate high degrees of moral sensitivity. The material that follows is derived directly from our many years of intimate experience with gifted children. We depart somewhat from an academic tone and use more evocative accounts to help readers experience the depth of moral awareness exhibited by our clients.

Gifted children show early promise of becoming morally responsible adults. Promise is potential, and, like all other aspects of giftedness, moral promise does not come to fruition in a vacuum. It can be dampened by neglect or disfigured by ridicule. Full realization requires early attachment to primary caretakers and a nourishing environment.

19.1 The Development of a Moral Sense

A child is born with her eyes closed; otherwise the impact of the outside world would be too overwhelming. Her emerging psyche cannot face this world by itself. Relationship is the essential ingredient in healthy development – the foundation of moral connection to the community. An invisible replacement for the umbilical cord, the relationship to the mother or caretaker is the child's lifeline. All future relationships are modeled after this primary one.

For a child to learn to care about others, she must feel loved and safe. The infant begins her journey toward developing trust that her needs will be fulfilled, needs that are enormously strong during this time of total dependency. The original bond with the parent becomes the protective hallway of growth. There is a delicate balance between the inner and the outer world, which is mediated by empathic interactions with the primary caretaker. The health of this original relationship, therefore, is of crucial importance. The primary bond expands to others in the environment, and to the family unit, the first community that becomes the prototype for future communities.

Moral reasoning originates with the development of the conscience. The newborn does not have a concept of morality. At first the child wants to still his hunger and meet his own needs. There is no morality, just the basic need for survival. The newborn has a sense of entitlement – he feels entitled to the nurturing, to the food. In order for a moral sense to emerge, the baby needs to have internalized the idea of being an independent human being. The infant at the mother's breast does not see himself as separate from the mother. The breast is a part of him. The child cannot develop a sense of morality until he has a sense of self and a sense of separateness – of "I."

Once the child develops a sense of her own existence separate from the mother, she begins to explore her personal power. That is when the concept of right and wrong enters the child's awareness. Reactions of her primary caretakers are the basis of this developing conception. The sense of right and wrong is outside the self. Then there comes a moment when it is incorporated into her sense of self. Her inner agenda grows and develops as she learns to increasingly differentiate and recognize her own environment. In the beginning, the child's conscience is totally dependent on the approval or disapproval of those who are closest to her. Through the bond of trust that develops with her caretakers, gradually she begins to learn some inner control.

Children who believe that their needs will be taken care of develop power and control while learning to adapt and to submit. If postponement is learned safely, children accept adult power as supporting them. They learn inner control when they begin to realize that postponement means soon – not never (Roeper 2007). As time goes on, they learn to regulate between their own needs and the needs of the outside world. They start to understand that time and attention must be shared. If a trust relationship has been established with parents, children learn the give and take of living harmoniously with others.

On the other hand, if primary relationships are flawed or the outside demands are too great, panic sets in. This makes it more difficult to develop the inner structure of control and mastery – to put the needs of others before the needs of the self. For example, two young children are scheduled to have an operation. One parent arranges to stay in the hospital with her son, even though she must occasionally leave to take care of other responsibilities. The relationship is an open, honest and secure one for the child. He has been told the truth about the operation and is prepared for what will happen. The relationship is emotionally uncluttered. The other child has had a conflicted relationship with the parent. She has been deceived about the severity of the operation and is left alone in the hospital. The feeling of abandonment overcomes her. She feels she was a bad girl and is being punished. There is intense panic; she feels terribly threatened. She cannot control her anger and anxiety (Roeper 2007). In the first scenario, the child feels protected, and in the second, the child feels abandoned. These early experiences set the stage for moral development.

The child's unconscious hope is unconditional acceptance and love from the all-powerful parent, gradually expanding to the world as an extension of the parent. Realistically, this is impossible for the parent, who has other obligations that go beyond the child. The parent's own conscious and unconscious needs have an impact on the vital bond with the child. However, the more uncluttered the parent-child relationship remains, the easier it is for the child's moral sense to blossom.

The normal reaction of young children is to take what they desire, but at the same time, they have a sense of community. Is this a built-in sense of identifying with others' feelings or simply the function of what they learn? There is so much moral judgment that surrounds a child from the day he is born. This makes it difficult to discriminate in-born traits from learned behavior. Lois' grandmother had a cookie jar on a shelf in the cupboard that her grandchildren could reach. She made batches of freshly baked cookies and placed them in the cookie jar. Her grandchildren were expected not to eat all the cookies, but to leave some to share with others. And the grandchildren responded to this expectation. Children who take all the cookies for themselves and leave none for others have not developed a sense of community.

Morality, in its original essence, is self-protection. The psyche's first task is to protect itself, to remain a unit, to feel this inner unit as unity, rather than be torn apart. This need for survival, self-protection, is the overriding motivation for all actions. "Do unto others as you want others to do unto you" is actually a self-protective statement. As the growing self goes on its journey, it encounters the needs, world-views, and agendas of other psyches. In an optimal environment, the psyche comes to recognize the principle of reciprocity: kindness to others is likely to result in kindness in return.

19.2   Children at Promise for Moral Development

In general, as well as in specific cases, morality is almost always a silent partner in our process of experiencing the soul of the gifted child. Many gifted children have an unerring sense of morality that begins rather early in life (Gross 1993). It stems from their great cognitive ability, their powers of observation, their sensitivity and their intuition. Insightfulness, empathy, cognitive understanding, sense of justice, knowledge of consequences, questioning the morality of the culture, the ability to understand that there are alternatives, all play a part in moral judgment. Because the gifted have these characteristics, they are at promise for high levels of moral development. This does not imply, however, that children who are not gifted are less moral.

Deeply interwoven with the concept of morality is the enormous sense of justice so many gifted children seem to experience at the center of their emotional lives.

> One of the well known characteristics of the gifted is their acute sense of justice. Gifted children are questioners, keen observers, logical thinkers. They will notice inequities, unfairness, double standards, and will question instances and experiences of that sort with passion. Often they feel helpless and powerless to make an impact, and they suffer deeply from this. They worry about the injustices of the world. They worry about peace, about the bomb, about their futures, about the environment, about all the problems that they encounter. (Roeper 1988, p. 12)

A sense of justice and of fairness (which are not necessarily synonymous) grows directly out of the deep insights of the gifted child. For example, even a very young gifted child will notice when parental expectations vary among siblings.

An infant with greater cognitive awareness develops an understanding of cause and effect early in life. With this understanding comes a greater knowledge of consequences. Gifted children do not need as many repetitions to learn consequences. Average children usually learn by trial and error, whereas gifted children often will have the forethought to solve problems without trial and error. For example, if an average toddler were to reach the top of a staircase unsupervised, there would be a great chance that this child would fall down the stairs head first. However, if a gifted toddler reached the top of a staircase unsupervised, the child would be more likely to back away to keep from being hurt, or problem solve another way to negotiate the stairs that would be safer, such as turning around and going down the stairs backward.

During the time she was Head of the Nursery School at The Roeper School, Annemarie was watching two boys, Joe and Hal, who were not yet 3 years old. They were fighting over a toy. Joe wrested the toy from Hal, and Hal angrily picked up a block and aimed it at Joe's head. There was no one close enough to him to intervene. He stopped himself with the block in mid-air and put the block back down. Something inside of him prevented him from hurting Joe. Had he learned at such a young age that hurting someone would bring punishment from adults? Or was his restraint motivated by an inner sense of compassion?

One can't fool really gifted children (much as many adults try). They will cut through all attempts at deceiving them and come directly to the truth. It is impressive how decisive they are, and how they apply this knowledge to their daily lives. They are offended by the deception of adults, and find it immoral. No amount of trying to disguise one's shortcomings will prevent a child from seeing through falsehood. Loving adults often try to protect children from the vicissitudes of life, and try to present conflict to them in a simplified and mostly positive way. However, honesty is a better policy than protection.

> The result [of protecting the child] is almost a conspiracy of silence which is reciprocated by children. It is as though a mutual agreement exists that certain things, even though obvious to all, simply have not occurred. This means that we may believe we have succeeded in keeping certain realities from children, while, in actuality, they have successfully kept their concerns from us. The consequence is that they are forced to deal with difficult problems by themselves and are left to face questions without help, for which they are neither emotionally nor intellectually equipped. (Roeper 2004, p. 5)

Gifted children actually develop a sense of personal power earlier than their age-mates, and, therefore, develop a conscience earlier. One gifted infant, within a few hours of birth, screamed until all the other children in the nursery were crying, and then would be quiet to listen to them. As soon as they quieted down, he would start again. In the crib, gifted babies often move objects to see what they will do, recognizing that it is within their power to make these objects move. This sense of personal power, combined with their sensitivity and awareness, and their early development of conscience, may lead to feelings of omnipotence.

> In the more average child, the feeling of omnipotence is limited by reality before the conscience develops. ... Feelings of omnipotence make children believe that there is no limit to their abilities, while the newly developed conscience forces them to act with moral perfection. In other words, they feel that their ability to achieve has no limitation and that it is their duty to live up to this unlimited capacity. Imagine the burdens these children take upon themselves, feeling responsible for everything and feeling guilty every time they fail to live up their responsibility. (Roeper 1982, p. 22)

Several years ago, a 5-year-old child came to Annemarie all bent over. She said to him, "You look like you are carrying the world on your shoulders." He responded, "Oh, but I am!" He had a 7-year-old sister who had a chronic illness. He felt that if he wasn't at home to take care of things, it would be disastrous.

Most gifted children have a greater sense of guilt than other children the same age, because they are more aware of the consequences of their behavior. Because of their sense of morality, (which, again, is because of their knowledge), they feel an obligation to behave in a certain way, and also to make the world a better place. They fail themselves in both these aspects, very often, which is why it is essential for gifted children to be involved in good deeds.

Gifted children often become outspoken leaders within a school community. This happens because they develop a greater awareness of everything around them and either a conscious or unconscious realization about the connection of everyone in the world in general, and specifically among members of a school community. Their moral attitudes often become a major factor in our understanding them, as well as in our desire to help them be a part of the whole fabric of life and education.

Gifted children are more likely than others to understand the interdependence of all life on the planet. This awareness has an increasing impact on their perceptions of moral concern and responsibility. "Am I my brother's keeper?" has expanded meaning in a global society. In the disappearing world of little fiefdoms, we believed we had a choice. We felt morally obligated to certain people and not to others. In an interdependent society, there is no choice, for we see how we depend on each other. If we mistreat each other, mistreatment becomes acceptable behavior and our own safety is threatened. Every action on our part creates a multitude of reactions in others, which results again in multitudes of actions by others.

Interdependence applies not only to people but also to our environment. Once we thought the world's resources would last forever and that we could use them as we wished, but we are quickly coming to the realization that we are morally responsible even to the air we breathe. If our actions destroy the ecosystem, we will endanger our lives and all future life. In this manner, morality is actually self-preservation. Self-preservation involves the preservation of others as well as the self and also preservation of the planet.

Gifted individuals have the intellectual capacity to understand the intricacies of an interdependent world. Even as young children, they can envision "what would happen if..." we polluted all the lakes and rivers, cut down all the trees, lost all the polar bears, and so on. While other children are absorbed with what is happening in this moment of their lives, gifted children are more aware of what is happening in other parts of the world and worry about the future of the planet. Greater cognitive complexity and greater awareness make gifted children more likely to take on the weight of the world, to feel personally responsible for leaving this world a better place than they found it.

Research on gifted children's moral development echoes our observations. Eighty percent of the 400+ gifted children whom Galbraith (1985) polled reported that they worry a great deal more about world problems than their peers – problems such as world hunger, nuclear war, pollution and international relations. Clark and Hankins (1985) conducted a comparative study of gifted and average children. They found that young gifted students read the newspapers more often than nongifted students, paid more attention to world news items and were more concerned about war. Rogers (1986) asked parents of gifted and average third graders to rate their children's concerns about morality and justice on a 5 point scale, from "always" to "never." While 36% of the gifted children were described as having deep concerns about morality and justice, only 8% of the average children were characterized in this manner. Janos et al. (1989) found accelerated gifted adolescents to be advanced in moral reasoning on Rest's (1979) *Defining Issues Test*, attaining levels similar to those achieved by graduate students.

19.3 Examples of Moral Sensitivity in Gifted Children

Over the last several decades, we both have encountered countless morally advanced gifted children. They protect those whom they feel are more vulnerable: babies, disabled people, the elderly, the outcasts. They stand up to bullies, overcoming their own fears, in the name of justice. If a classmate is humiliated, they become terribly upset, and may even challenge the instructor. For example, a teacher destroyed the artwork of a student because he didn't draw a figure the way she wanted him to, whereupon an unusually shy and withdrawn boy, who never spoke up in class, shouted, "That's not fair!"

When parents are asked to describe their gifted children, "sensitive" appears more frequently than any other trait (Silverman 1983). The following description is typical of the children brought to the Gifted Development Center for assessment:

> P is quite sensitive to the feelings of others and has a well developed sense of justice. She befriends the outcasts in her class and will not tolerate cruelty from other children. She comments to me if she feels her teacher is not treating children consistently. (Silverman 1994, p. 111)

Another parent described her 9-year-old daughter as sensitive to the feelings of others "to a degree that almost defied belief." Kay can't be convinced "to do anything she perceives as wrong, unsafe, or boring." From an early age, Kay "exhibited an unusually keen awareness of the world around her, particularly as it relates to the feelings and needs of others." She often seemed "burdened by the weight of knowledge she has not had the emotional maturity to deal with" (Silverman 1993b, p. 63).

With a deep understanding of the importance of conserving resources, gifted children are the ones who initiate ecological campaigns in their schools and communities. Some become vegetarians in meat-eating families as young as 5, because of their revulsion to the idea of killing animals for food. We often hear stories of young gifted children crying at the slapstick violence in cartoons and being unable to bear the cruelty depicted in Disney movies. Some refuse to fight back when attacked because they consider all forms of violence – including self-defense – morally wrong. We've read poems of anguish and letters to Presidents begging them to stop wars. Gifted children are not easily comforted by the knowledge of their own safety when they know children in other parts of the world are dying.

Empathy is often the basis of moral sensitivity in the gifted. A 4-year-old boy who was assessed at the Gifted Development Center was described by his father as an "incredible peacemaker," able to keep harmony in groups as large as 19 of all different ages:

> A is an exceptionally gentle and kind boy. I have never seen him hit or push and, in fact, have had to teach him that it is not good to let his little brother hit him.... He is extremely loving (e.g., he sings, 'I'm so glad when Daddy comes home' every day to me). He daily praises my wife and me for taking care of his baby brother. He has an intense love of games and frequently seeks out adults to play with him. When he plays with his friends, he will help them find the best move in a game and deliberately lose – all the while telling his friends how good *they* are at the game.... He is easily upset if he believes someone else has been treated unfairly (e.g., was sobbing because someone had taken his friend's toy – the friend was not crying). (Silverman 1993b, p. 63)

Children like this one are "emotionally gifted" (Roeper 1982). Their compassion is remarkable, more advanced than most adults who have learned to conform to the expectations of society. A classic example of emotional giftedness is John, a brilliant chess player, who was obviously winning a chess tournament, when suddenly he began to make careless mistakes, and purposely lost the game.

> When asked why, he replied, *'I noticed my opponent had tears in his eyes. I could not concentrate and lost my desire to win.'* John's empathy was greater than his ambition. Many adults, especially those who supported John, were disappointed. Yet, one could argue that his reaction was a more mature one than theirs for his self-esteem did not depend on his winning the competition. (Roeper 1982, p. 24)

When Sara Jane was 2 years old, she saw a television report of an earthquake that hit Russia, leaving countless people homeless. With tears in her eyes, she brought her piggy bank to her mother and said, "Mama, send my money." The following Christmas, at the age of 3, Sara Jane requested that her presents be given to needy children: "I have everything I need. I wish you would give my presents to some little girl or boy who won't get any" (Silverman 1993c, p. 313). At age 6, Sara Jane contacted a nearby soup kitchen to find out what was needed right before Christmas and wrote a letter to her school community requesting donations of specific foods, soap, toothbrushes, shampoo, and gifts for poor children:

> If you can earn the money to donate a gift for a poor child, think of how many children will be happy on this holiday. Please try to bring in a small gift that is wrapped and please put a tag on the gift telling exactly what the present is so they will know who should get this gift.
>
> You can help make a child's holiday much happier. Please bring food and a small gift by December 15. (Silverman 1994, p. 112)

At the age of 9, Mark picked fruits and vegetables one summer to sell in his neighborhood so that he could earn money to donate to the homeless. This was his own idea, not inspired by teachers or parents. Jason Crowe began his peace crusade when he was 9. Devastated by the death of his grandmother, Jason turned to Jim Delisle, who suggested that reaching out to help others is sometimes the best cure. So Jason published a newspaper, and donated the proceeds to the American Cancer Society.

> Four months after starting my "By-Kids-For-Kids" newspaper, another awesome friend, Laura Whaley from the Center for Gifted Studies at WKU, sent me an article to read about a cellist in Bosnia who witnessed the massacre of 22 of his friends and reacted by playing the cello for 22 days amidst sniper fire. To me, his musical harmony represented social harmony, and I immediately knew that I had to keep his message alive. Thus, at age 10, I became a peace activist.
>
> Besides organizing local events, I decided to commission a peace statue to be sent to Bosnia from the kids of the world. I wrote to President Clinton and received an encouraging reply, got endorsements from Joan Baez, Pete Seeger, Yo-Yo Ma, U2's Bono, and also received a thumbs-up from statesmen, businessmen, and educators. I found a sculptor and commissioned The Children's International Peace-and-Harmony Statue. (Crowe 2001, p. 3)

We have found that the higher the child's IQ, the earlier moral concerns develop and the more profound effect they have on the child (Silverman 1994). But it usually takes maturity before the child can translate moral sensitivity into consistent moral action.

This is not to say that all gifted children are morally advanced. There are some children who have been emotionally damaged by neglect, abuse, insensitivity or lack of understanding. An emotionally damaged gifted youth may be of greater danger to society than a young person with less ability, because this individual has a greater intellectual capacity to put in the service of antisocial behavior. There are also gifted children who are one-sided in their development, who have been allowed to develop their specific talents without equal attention to their social and emotional development (Silverman 1994). According to Lovecky (1994):

> My own work with gifted children also suggests unusual moral and social concerns. Both boys and girls worry about war, the environment, the homeless, poverty, crime and drugs. And yet, for many gifted boys, there is also a fascination with violence.... In fact, many of the gifted boys I have questioned see violence as the only solution to interpersonal conflicts.
>
> Both the influence of peers and of the media around them appear to place gifted children, particularly boys, in conflict with their innermost feelings and judgments. To continue with the generous, compassionate and altruistic responses of early childhood places many gifted boys at considerable risk for peer rejection and ridicule. They are too vulnerable this way, so they often conceal the moral side of themselves behind the same invulnerability modeled for them by others; that is, they wall off and deny compassionate responses to others. (p. 3)

While moral sensitivity appears to be correlated with giftedness in early childhood, it is in danger of being snuffed out or buried through environmental exposure, especially exposure to the inexorable media blitz, which glorifies violence. By the middle grades, morally aware children, especially boys, seem to face two choices: become victims or "prove" themselves by repressing their moral sensitivity to gain acceptance (Silverman 1994).

19.4   Recommendations for Encouraging Moral Development in Gifted Children

We recommend the following activities to enable gifted children to fulfill their moral promise:

1. Provide opportunities for gifted children to internalize caring values by making community service a part of their curriculum or extra-curricular activities (e.g., in hospitals, day care centers, nursing homes). Allow them to select their own service projects.
2. Support their courage to stand up for their convictions, despite the blows to self-esteem they might sustain from others.
3. Introduce students to Barbara Lewis' books (e.g., *The Kids' Guide to Social Action* [1991, 1998], *The Kid's Guide to Service Projects* [1995], *What Do You Stand For?* [1998]). (Additional books are listed in the references). Lewis highlights projects initiated by children to help others, and provides wonderful ideas for community service projects for children of all ages.
4. Give them books to read and films to watch to familiarize themselves with moral leaders, so that they have appropriate role models (Hollingworth 1942). Explore with them humanitarian values and the lives of individuals dedicated to service.

5. Assist them in designing projects related to social and moral issues: (for example, writing research papers; developing films, videotapes or plays; conducting panel discussions; using an art medium, such as painting or sculpting, to represent a contemporary social ill; planning strategies for raising the consciousness of their community with respect to a particular concern) (Weber 1981).

6. Help them critically examine the historical development of philosophies and the effects of these values on the development of societies.

7. Introduce them to the contributions of the inconspicuous and unsung who show admirable qualities and lead worthwhile lives (e.g., parents who sacrifice for their children; handicapped individuals who lead productive lives; VISA and Peace Corps volunteers who leave comfort and security in order to help others).

8. Examine with them moral issues shown on television, seen in the newspapers, or found in the community (Drews 1972).

9. Employ simulations, role play, or perspective-taking exercises. Focus on different viewpoints in everyday interactions; have the teacher and students share their feelings about interactions, events, or activities (Hensel 1991).

10. Involve them in group dynamics activities, in which children learn to interact cooperatively with each other, respect each others' rights and gain a sense of social responsibility (Sisk 1982).

11. Have students establish their own code of rules for behavior (Leroux 1986).

12. Have students participate on an equal footing with faculty members in decision making (Roeper 1990).

13. Model caring behaviors (Roeper 1991).

14. Help students become activists by engaging in the study and solution of real life problems confronting society (Passow 1988). Encourage them to attempt to share these alternatives with civic leaders (Weber 1981).

15. Encourage students to read the newspapers so that they can begin to see how they and their communities are not isolated from the outside world; provide opportunities for them to share their perceptions and questions with others on a regular basis (Clark and Hankins 1985).

16. Encourage gifted students to think about the moral and ethical dimensions of the subjects they study and to raise questions of conscience regarding content (Passow 1988).

17. Give students opportunities to think about their role in the world. For example:

What impact could they make? What impact do they want to make? What impact does the world have on their lives? They need the tools to make an impact on their own destiny and the ever expanding inter-relatedness of the destiny of everybody on the planet. (Roeper 1988, p. 12)

19.5 Conclusion

Some researchers have suggested that the unique ethical sensitivity of the gifted indicates a special potential for high moral development (Drews 1972; Vare 1979). We call this potential *moral promise*; it is probably due to the complexity of moral

262 A. Roeper and L.K. Silverman

issues and the intellectual demands involved in ethical judgments. However, this potential needs support. Without prior training, the gifted are not any better equipped to grapple with the value dimensions of their studies than they are to solve problems in non-Euclidean geometry (Tannenbaum 1972). Rarely has the moral awareness or promise of the gifted been used as a basis for program planning or counseling.

Honesty, fairness, moral issues, global concerns, and sensitivity to others are common themes in the lives of gifted children. If we want moral leaders, we need to understand and nurture the inner world of the gifted – the rich, deep internal milieu from which moral sensitivity emerges (Silverman 1994). We cannot educate the mind and forget the *Self* of the child (Roeper 1990). Gifted children need relationships with people who care about who they are, not just what they can do. And they need opportunities to develop and express their emerging moral awareness. With nurturing, their moral promise will be fulfilled.

References

Boehm, L. (1962). The development of conscience: A comparison of American children of different mental and socioeconomic levels. *Child Development, 33*, 575–590.
Brennan, T. P. (1987). *Case studies of multilevel development.* Unpublished doctoral dissertation, Northwestern University, Evanston, IL.
Brennan, T. P., & Piechowski, M. M. (1991). The developmental framework for self-actualization: Evidence from case studies. *Journal of Humanistic Psychology, 31*(3), 43–64.
Clark, W. H., & Hankins, N. E. (1985). *Giftedness and conflict.* Roeper Review, 8, 50–53.
Crowe, J. (2001, Winter). The odd-isy. *Global Connections, 7*(2), 3.
Csikszentmihalyi, M. (1993). *The evolving self: A psychology for the third millennium.* New York: HarperCollins.
Drews, E. M. (1972). *Learning together.* Englewood Cliffs, NJ: Prentice-Hall.
Galbraith, J. (1985). The eight great gripes of gifted kids: Responding to special needs. *Roeper Review, 8*, 15–18.
Grant, B. (1990). Moral development: Theories and lives. *Advanced Development, 2*, 85–91.
Gross, M. U. M. (1993). *Exceptionally gifted children.* London: Routledge.
Hensel, N. H. (1991). Social leadership skills in young children. *Roeper Review, 14*, 4–6.
Hollingworth, L. S. (1939). What we know about the early selection and training of leaders. *Teachers College Record, 40*, 575–592.
Hollingworth, L. S. (1942). *Children above 180 IQ Stanford-Binet: Origin and development.* Yonkers-on-Hudson, NY: World Book.
Janos, P. M., Robinson, N. M., & Lunneborg, C. E. (1989). Markedly early entrance to college: A multi-year comparative study of academic performance and psychological adjustment. *Journal of Higher Education, 60*, 496–518.
Karnes, F. A., & Brown, K. E. (1981). Moral development and the gifted: An initial investigation. *Roeper Review, 3*, 8–10.
Leroux, J. A. (1986). Making theory real: Developmental theory and implications for education of gifted adolescents. *Roeper Review, 9*, 72–77.
Lewis, B. A. (1991, 1998). *The kids' guide to social action: How to solve the social problems you choose—and turn creative thinking into positive action.* Minneapolis, MN: Free Spirit.
Lewis, B. A. (1995). *The kid's guide to service projects: Over 500 service ideas for young people who want to make a difference.* Minneapolis, UT: Free Spirit.

Lewis, B. A. (1998). *What do you stand for? A kid's guide to building character*. Minneapolis, UT: Free Spirit.

Lewis, B. A. (2000). *Being your best: Character building for kids 7–10*. Minneapolis, UT: Free Spirit.

Lovecky, D. V. (1994). The moral child in a violent world. *Understanding Our Gifted, 6*(3), 3.

Loye, D. (1990). Moral sensitivity and the evolution of higher mind. *World Futures: The Journal of General Evolution, 30*, 1–2, 41–52.

Martinson, R. A. (1961). *Educational programs for gifted pupils*. Sacramento, CA: California State Department of Education.

Passow, A. H. (1988). Educating gifted persons who are caring and concerned. *Roeper Review, 11*, 13–15.

Piechowski, M. M. (1978). Self-actualization as a developmental structure: A profile of Antoine de Saint-Exupery. *Genetic Psychology Monographs, 97*, 181–242.

Piechowski, M. M. (1990). Inner growth and transformation in the life of Eleanor Roosevelt. *Advanced Development, 2*, 35–53.

Piechowski, M. M. (1992). Giftedness for all seasons: Inner peace in a time of war. In N. Colangelo, S. G. Assouline, & D. L. Ambroson (Eds.), *Talent development* (pp. 180–203). Proceedings of the Henry B. and Jocelyn Wallace National Research Symposium on Talent Development. Unionville, NY: Trillium Press.

Rest, J. (1979). Development in judging moral issues. Minneapolis, MN: University of Minnesota Press.

Roeper, A. (1982). How the gifted cope with their emotions. *Roeper Review, 5*, 21–24.

Roeper, A. (1988). Should educators of the gifted and talented be more concerned with world issues? *Roeper Review, 11*, 12–13.

Roeper, A. (1990). *Educating children for life: The modern learning community*. Monroe, NY: Trillium.

Roeper, A. (1991). Gifted adults: Their characteristics and emotions. *Advanced Development, 3*, 85–98.

Roeper, A. (2003). *Annemarie Roeper method of qualitative assessment of giftedness: Certification program*. El Cerrito, CA: Roeper Consultation Service.

Roeper, A. (2004). *My life experiences with children: Selected writings and speeches*. Denver, CO: DeLeon.

Roeper, A., with A. Higgins. (2007). *The "I" of the beholder: A guided journey to the essence of the child*. Scottsdale, AZ: Great Potential Press.

Rogers, M. (1986). *A comparative study of developmental traits of gifted and average children*. Unpublished doctoral dissertation, University of Denver, Denver, CO.

Silverman, L. K. (1983). Personality development: The pursuit of excellence. *Journal for the Education of the Gifted, 6*, 5–19.

Silverman, L. K. (1993a). *Characteristics of giftedness scale*. Denver, CO: Gifted Development Center.

Silverman, L. K. (1993b). A developmental model for counseling the gifted. In L. K. Silverman (Ed.), *Counseling the gifted and talented* (pp. 51–78). Denver, CO: Love.

Silverman, L. K. (1993c). Social development, leadership, and gender issues. In L. K. Silverman (Ed.), *Counseling the gifted and talented* (pp. 291–327). Denver, CO: Love.

Silverman, L. K. (1994). The moral sensitivity of gifted children and the evolution of society. *Roeper Review, 17*, 110–116.

Simmons, C. H., & Zumpf, C. (1986). The gifted child: Perceived competence, prosocial moral reasoning, and charitable donations. *The Journal of Genetic Psychology, 147*(1), 97–105.

Sisk, D. A. (1982). Caring and sharing: Moral development of gifted students. *Elementary School Journal, 82*, 221–229.

Tannenbaum, A. J. (1972). A backward and forward glance at the gifted. *National Elementary Principal, 51*(5), 14–23.

Terman, L. M. (1925). *Genetic studies of genius: Vol. 1. Mental and physical traits of a thousand gifted children.* Stanford, CA: Stanford University Press.

Vare, J. V. (1979). Moral education for the gifted: A confluent model. *The Gifted Child Quarterly, 24,* 63–71.

Weber, J. (1981). Moral dilemmas in the classroom. *Roeper Review, 3,* 11–13.

Chapter 20
Self-Actualization and Morality of the Gifted: Environmental, Familial, and Personal Factors

Deborah Ruf

Abstract How family, school, and social background contribute to the self-identity and subsequent self-concept and self-esteem of highly gifted individuals may be related to whether or not they eventually self-actualize. The author examined factors that possibly relate to the development of individuals who are self-actualized; and which, if any of these factors, are predictors of highly principled moral reasoning development. Forty-one case studies were analyzed using characteristics of emotional and moral reasoning stages outlined by Erikson, Maslow, Dabrowski, Kohlberg, and Rest. Findings indicate that self-actualization that follows inner transformation is highly correlated with advanced levels of moral reasoning. Such people are not necessarily happier or more successful in careers than subjects who attain lower emotional and moral reasoning growth. There was a significant correlation between scores on Rest's *Defining Issues Test* (DIT) and Dabrowski's and Kohlberg's stages of development. New terms for the study, Searcher and Nonsearcher, appeared to correlate with developmental levels, with Searchers being more likely to eventually self-actualize. Evidence exists that people can become Searchers. Emotional, physical, or sexual abuse in childhood was highly related to both lower and higher DIT scores and Dabrowski levels among highly gifted adults. Those who overcame persistent bitterness over abuse were more likely to become Searchers and eventually self-actualize. Those who do not experience inner transformation but are "good people" and career self-actualizers are generally in the Conventional (Kohlberg) or Stereotypical (Dabrowski) levels of development. Finally, subjects' perceptions that someone significant to them cared about them or respected them emerged as a significant positive factor in those who eventually self-actualized.

Keywords Abuse · Career self-actualization · Dabrowski, K. · Defining Issues Test (DIT) · Emotional development · Erikson, E. · Highly gifted adults · Kohlberg, L. · Maslow, A. · Moral development · Rest, J. · Self-actualization

D. Ruf
Educational Options, 4500 Heathbrooke Circle, Golden Valley, MN 55422, USA
e-mail: dr.ruf@educationaloptions.com

D. Ambrose, T. Cross (eds.), *Morality, Ethics, and Gifted Minds*,
DOI: 10.1007/978-0-387-89368-6_20,

Does being smart necessarily lead to being emotionally mature and wise? This chapter describes an investigation of the possible connections between high intelligence and advanced emotional and moral development. By exploring environmental effects, we can consider how family, school and social background may contribute to growth toward self-actualization and advanced moral reasoning in gifted individuals.

The gifted tend to reach higher levels of moral reasoning at younger ages (Boehm 1962; Gross 1993; Janos et al. 1989; Kohlberg 1984). Does this early advantage translate into higher levels in gifted adults than average adults? Is high intelligence a conditional but not necessarily sufficient factor for higher level moral reasoning? Do some highly intelligent adults remain at a fairly low level of moral reasoning, and, if so, can we identify environmental, familial, or other personal factors associated with this outcome? Results clearly support the conclusions that high intelligence is no guarantee of advanced emotional and moral development, but when compared to typical adults, the highly intelligent reach both advanced emotional development (e.g., self-actualization) and advanced levels of moral reasoning (Ruf 1998).

20.1 Background to the Inquiry

The backgrounds of 41 highly gifted adults were explored in case studies through analysis of self-reported, anonymous questionnaire responses. The purpose was to gain a better understanding of how the treatment and attitude of highly gifted children by home, school, and community influence overall developmental outcomes. Individuals learn about themselves and their value, and develop their self-concept, through comparisons of themselves to others and from the feedback and nurturing they receive from others (Erikson 1968; Falk and Miller 1998; Festinger 1954; Greenspon 1998; Maslow 1970; Piechowski 1989).

The investigation centered on the subjects' perceptions of the *relevance* of background experiences related to their own sense of accomplishment, fulfillment and satisfaction with their adult lives. Themes emerged and formed a theoretical framework during the course of the data analysis. Common markers among subjects that might connect specific childhood circumstances to specific adult outcomes were tabulated.

20.2 Description of Subjects

A reasonable question arises: how representative of highly gifted people was the study's sample? It was clear from the case studies that the group represented considerable diversity of family composition, parenting styles, parental socio-economic background, educational type and quality, and adult career fields. The subjects originated from all over the United States, attended public and private rural, suburban, and city schools, and came from families who had very little money or education to those who had much of both. All subjects were of western, middle, or eastern European, Caucasian ancestry, and two identified themselves as Jewish. The most consistent factor in the background of the subjects involved their educational experiences. The educational experiences did not appear to vary by geographic location; in fact, the biggest difference between rural and suburban schools was the degree to which the neighborhoods and communities knew the students and teachers.

Factors of age, intelligence and education were substantially reduced by the subject selection process. Though not required for inclusion, all subjects had at least undergraduate college degrees, and nearly all continued their intellectual stimulation through careers, continuing education, and reading. Nearly every subject listed reading first as a favorite pastime in both childhood and adulthood.

The subjects' career experiences varied considerably. Specifically, only one person had never done paid work outside the home; and there were two medical doctors, one small film maker, numerous university professors, psychologists, psychotherapists, attorneys, and engineers, several small business owners, two major business CEOs, and a number of social workers, writers, and classroom teachers. A great many of the subjects did much of their work alone. Interestingly, none of the subjects claimed management level work, although some were their own bosses.

Although 183 subjects volunteered to participate, the final selected participants were all within the 40- to 60-year-old age range to minimize generational cohort effects (Strauss and Howe 1991). The final subjects were not a randomized sample, and from the pool with completed author-designed inventories, an even number of males and females, and one transgendered subject, were selected. The case study content was not considered prior to selection. The self-reported IQ levels of the subjects – at least one 99th percentile score on a recognized nationally standardized test of ability – are equivalent to or higher than the mean of people in the professions. For elaboration on the subjects, the case studies and the methodology, see *Environmental, Familial, and Personal Factors That Affect the Self-Actualization of Highly Gifted Adults: Case Studies* (Ruf 1998). These data are derived from this study.

20.3   Brief Review of Self-actualization and Moral Development

Self-actualization basically means living up to one's potential. Although this research began with the view that "living up to one's potential" means that persons have achieved intellectual and career success while also achieving inner satisfaction and emotional well-being, it became apparent that some achieve inner satisfaction and a sense of emotional well-being *without* achieving overt career or financial success. Some attain career, intellectual, or financial success but never find a sense of inner satisfaction and emotional well-being.

Self-actualization is "high levels of responsibility, authenticity, reflective judgment, empathy for others, autonomy of thought and action, and self-awareness" (Nelson 1989, p. 8). Here, a distinction is made between two types:

1. Identity formation without going through a developmental crisis. "Successful" people – those who fulfill the role of good, law-abiding, and socially responsible members of their society – meet the traditional description of self-actualized individuals (Peck and Havighurst 1960; Piechowski 1989).
2. Those people who experience inner transformation after undergoing one or more developmental crises, "personal growth guided by powerful ideals ... moral questioning, existential concerns ... process by which a person finds an inner direction to his or her life and deliberately takes up the work of inner transformation" (Piechowski 1989, p. 89). They may or may not appear to be "successful" in a career or monetary sense.

Maslow (1970) emphasized the role of an individual's own *perceptions* of the world and society. His theory focused on the emergence of self, the search for identity, and the individual's relationships with others throughout life. "The highest and most evolved motive is self-actualization, a healthy desire to be the best one can be ... [the most self-actualized] were intent upon doing things to make a better world, they volunteered, tutored, and gave of themselves without much concern for financial gain" (Hall and Hansen 1997, p. 24). The following is a listing of Maslow's characteristics of self-actualizers (derived from Turner and Helms 1986):

1. More efficient perception of reality
2. Acceptance of self and others
3. Spontaneity
4. Problem centering
5. Detachment
6. Autonomy
7. Continued freshness of appreciation
8. The mystic experience
9. Gemeinschaftsgefuhl, (sympathy, compassion, identification with others)
10. Unique interpersonal relations
11. Democratic character structure
12. Discrimination between means and ends
13. Philosophical, unhostile sense of humor
14. Creativeness
15. Resistance to enculturation

An expansion on Erikson's work pointed out that adolescents face four possible alternatives when solving the crisis of "who am I?" (Marcia, as cited in Woolfolk 1995; Scheidel and Marcia 1985):

> The first is identity achievement. This means that after considering the realistic options, the individual has made choices and is pursuing them. It appears that few students achieve this status by the end of high school. Most are not firm in their choices for several more years; students who attend college may take a bit longer to decide (Archer 1982). Identity foreclosure describes the situation of adolescents who do not experiment with different identities or consider a range of options, but simply commit themselves to the goals, values, and lifestyles of others, usually their parents. Identity diffusion, on the other hand, occurs when individuals reach no conclusions about who they are or what they want to do with their lives; they have no firm direction. (p. 70)

Table 20.1 Erikson's developmental crises (From Lefton, 1994)

1. Basic trust versus mistrust	Birth to 12–18 months	Feeding	The infant must form a first, loving relationship with the caregiver or develop a sense of mistrust.
2. Autonomy versus shame/doubt	18 months to 3 years	Toilet training	The child's energies are directed toward the development of physical skills, including walking, grasping, controlling the sphincter. The child learns control but may develop doubt and shame if not handled well.
3. Initiative versus guilt	3–6 years	Independence	The child continues to become more assertive and to take more initiative but may be too forceful, which can lead to guilt feelings.
4. Industry versus inferiority	6–12 years	School	The child must deal with demands to learn new skills or risk a sense of inferiority, failure, and incompetence.
5. Identity versus role confusion	Adolescence	Peer relationships	The teenager must achieve identity in occupation, gender roles, politics, and religion.
6. Intimacy versus isolation	Young adulthood	Love relationships	The young adult must develop intimate relationships or suffer feelings of isolation.
7. Generativity versus stagnation	Middle adulthood	Parenting	Each adult must find some way to satisfy and support the next generation.
8. Ego integrity versus despair	Late adulthood	Reflection on and acceptance of one's life	The culmination is a sense of acceptance of oneself as one is and a sense of fulfillment.

Some people reach an alternative, moratorium, a form of break from the task of deciding who one really is and what one ought to do.

Table 20.1 lists Erikson's series of eight interdependent developmental crises that all individuals face. It provided a structure for evaluating what the subjects wrote in their author-designed Childhood and Adult Inventories. How each crisis is resolved has lasting effect on the person's self-image and view of society.

Further investigative structure is provided by the inclusion of Dabrowski's levels of emotional development. Although Dabrowski's levels are arranged hierarchically as an emotional maturity progression, results indicate that low, medium, or high levels, *per se*, are not necessarily good or bad, better or worse. Dabrowski searched for the "authentically real, saturated with immutable values, those who represented 'what ought to be' against 'what is'" (Dabrowski, as cited in Piechowski 1975, p. 234). He believed that some individuals are born with a higher ability to transcend life's difficulties and evolve into mature, wise, "evolved" human beings than other people. Some people,

> ...could not reconcile themselves to concrete reality; instead, they clung to their creative visions of what ought to be. They searched for "a reality of a higher level. And often they were able to find it unaided" (Dabrowski, in Piechowski, p. 236). These clients experienced intense inner conflict, self-criticism, anxiety, and feelings of inferiority toward their own ideals... Dabrowski saw these ... symptoms as an inseparable part of the quest for higher level development. He fervently desired to convince the [medical] profession that inner conflict is a developmental rather than degenerative sign. (Silverman 1993, p. 11)

Dabrowski's theory of positive disintegration proposed that advanced development requires a breakdown of existing psychological structures in order to form higher, more evolved structures (Silverman 1993, p. 11). In simpler terms, the house of cards that we build up during our youth to help us explain life no longer works for us. Some idea enters our consciousness and throws off all that we have believed. As we struggle with this new concept we can feel as though nothing makes sense anymore, and it can lead to a sense of helplessness or despair. That's the *disintegration* part. The reason it is called *positive* is because it is actually a step toward maturity and a greater understanding of the world and our place in it. Dabrowski listed five fairly distinctive levels of emotional development. Table 20.2 describes characteristics and motivations of people at each level of emotional development. Theoretically, emotional growth beyond Level II is uncommon. Evidence exists that the advanced growth described by Dabrowski is probably not found in identity foreclosure or diffusion, is experienced only briefly in pre-mid-life identity achievement, and is probably present during a mid-life moratorium-type crisis. It is likely that few people experience their day-to-day lives in a fashion described by Dabrowski's Levels III, IV, and V (Josselson 1991; Levinson 1978; Ruf 1998; Sheehy 1974).

"Dabrowski observed that the most gifted and creative individuals with whom he worked seemed to exhibit higher levels of empathy, sensitivity, moral responsibility, self-reflection, and autonomy of thought than the general population" (Nelson 1989, p. 5). Although the study results indicate that subjects exhibited a wide range of emotional maturity, almost all subjects in the study exhibited the majority of these qualities. One quality was more commonly exhibited by subjects in Dabrowski's "advanced" levels of emotional maturity (See Table 20.2): autonomy of thought.

Until the late twentieth century, most considered moral reasoning a function of socialization rather than cognition. Many assumed "moral development was a matter of learning the norms of one's culture, of accepting and internalizing them, and of behaving in conformity with them" (Rest and Narvaez 1994, p. 2). Kohlberg argued that conformity to social norms is sometimes morally wrong, as when dutiful soldiers commit atrocities.

Table 20.2 Moral and emotional development schemes

Kohlberg's levels of moral development	Approximate moral development levels by DIT P-score[a]	Dabrowski's levels of emotional development[b]
Preconventional: (typically attainable between ages 7–11+) Stage 1 – Fear of punishment Stage 2 – Self-aggrandizement	Low: Subjects who are described as fitting the study's first levels of emotional development generally scored below 40 (the average score for American adults) on the DIT P-score. Table 20.5 details the stage scores attained by each subject on the DIT.	Level I: Self-interest, self-preservation (characterized by egocentrism, desire for material gains, goals of success, power, fame, competitive with others, external conflicts, little self-reflection, lack of empathy, rigid psychological structure.)
Conventional: (typically attainable between ages 11 to adult) Stage 3 – Desire for approval Stage 4 – Maintains social order	Medium: Scores between 40–65 were found among subjects who fit the study's description of conventional or stereotypical normal adult development. (57.67 is the average for the current study's subjects).	Level II: Stereotypical roles (highly influence by others, values introjected from parents, church, etc., relativistic, situational values, conflicted feelings, contradictory actions, desire for acceptance, feelings of inadequacy compared to others, lack of hierarchy of values.)
Postconventional (ages 21+, not typically attained by most adults) Stage 5 – Democratic values Stage 6 – Universal ethics	High: Scores of approximately 65 (the average score for moral philosophy and political science students is 65.2) and higher coincided with the study subjects whose viewpoints, as found in case study writing, corresponded most with high scorers on the DIT, moral philosophers.	Level III: Personality transformation (inner conflict, hierarchy of values, positive maladjustments, inferiority toward one's ideals, feelings of guilt and shame, independent thinker, moral framework believed but inconsistently applied.) Level IV: Self-actualization (conscious direction of development, commitment to one's values, acceptance, objectivity, responsibility and service to others, philosophical, unhostile sense of humor.)
Stage 7 – Cosmic consciousness	Theoretically, scores would close in on 100.	Level V: Attainment of the personality ideal (inner peace and harmony, altruism, universal compassion, devotion to service).

[a]Norms from Rest and Narvaez 1994.
[b]From Piechowski and Silverman 1993.

Kohlberg focused on cognition – "the thinking process and the representations by which people construct reality and meaning" (Rest and Narvaez 1994, p. 3). He developed a stage theory that included preconventional, conventional, and post-conventional thinking (See Table 20.2). Kohlberg's interest was to uncover major markers in life-span development. He assumed any measurement device would be accurate if people scored higher as they matured.

In early results from his assessment instrument, more men reached high conventional levels than women, and his longitudinal study involved only men. Gilligan (1982) interpreted the findings as indicative of a primary difference between the reasoning of men and women. She argued that Kohlberg's higher levels depicted a progressive separation of the individual from other people, and that women come from an ethic of care, move from a focus on self-interests to a commitment to specific individuals and relationships, and then to the highest level of morality based on the principles of responsibility and care for all people.

"The stages do not depict the progressive separation and isolation of individuals from each other (as Gilligan said), but rather how each individual can become interconnected with other individuals" (Rest and Narvaez 1994, p. 8). Over time, research with Kohlberg's theory shows women as a group score slightly higher than men on Kohlberg's Moral Judgment Interview (Colby and Kohlberg 1987; Narvaez 1993). They also score higher on Rest's *Defining Issues Test* (Rest 1986), a machine-scorable inventory based on Kohlberg's moral reasoning stages.

The *Defining Issues Test* (DIT) was completed by all subjects in the Ruf (1998) study. Its *P*-score, for "principled" thinking, emerged as an important indicator of potential for more abstract, complex emotional reasoning. Use of the terms emotional growth and maturity does not imply good or bad, but instead indicates a propensity or openness to change, particularly *inner* change. Table 20.2 places Kohlberg's moral development stages alongside Dabrowski's emotional development levels. As the data analysis evolved, DIT scores were placed between the two other theorists, Kohlberg and Dabrowski, because it became clear they were all related. Subjects did not fall as perfectly into the depicted DIT score ranges and Dabrowski levels as the three column Table 20.3 would suggest; however, there were always at least some characteristics of the associated Dabrowski level that lined up next to the DIT score range.

Tables 20.3 and 20.4 add perspective to the discussions of DIT scores in relation to emotional change potential. Table 20.3 details the study group results. Table 20.4 lists specific group averages for the DIT accumulated from previous studies.

It is difficult to adequately define and describe the post-conventional levels of Kohlberg's stages 5 and 6 because most people never attain that level of reasoning themselves. Research generally supports an assumption that the stages comprise a hierarchical structure where higher is better (Rest and Narvaez 1994; Rest et al. 1969; Walker et al. 1984). The tasks in these studies of the DIT involve asking subjects to paraphrase arguments from each of the stages. Subjects are always able to paraphrase levels lower but not above their own. Also, subjects can describe moral reasoning lower than their own level as immature, the way they once were, or simple-minded. The validity of a progressive stage theory is tested through

Table 20.3 Highly gifted study DIT summary (Derived from Ruf 1998)

Score statistics		Women's results	Men's results
Range	30–83.3	6 scored below the mean	13 scored below mean
Mean	57.67	13 scored above the mean	6 scored above the mean
Median	56.7		
Standard Deviation	13.78		

39 of 41 subjects had valid DIT P−scores ($P = principled$).

1 transgender male to female scored above the sample mean.

5 subjects scored below 40, the population average P−score for American adults (Rest and Narvaez 1994).

Table 20.4 Norms for selected groups on the DIT P-scores (Derived from Rest and Narvaez 1994)

65.2	Moral philosophy and political science graduate students
59.8	Liberal Protestant seminarians
52.2	Law students
50.2	Medical students
49.1	Practicing physicians
47.6	Dental students
46.3	Staff nurses
42.8	Graduate students in business
40.2	College senior business and education majors
41.6	Navy enlisted men
40.0	Adults in general
31.8	Senior high school students
23.5	Prison inmates
21.9	Junior high school students
18.9	Institutionalized delinquents

a series of tasks with volunteers who were asked to "fake bad" and "fake good" on the MJI or DIT. Subjects are able to fake bad because they understand the thinking that they have outgrown. They were unable to fake good (McGeorge 1975).

Past research on the Defining Issues Test has indicated that adults with low scores—or scores that do not continue to climb with age – lack intellectual stimulation in their lives. The factor most consistently found to correlate with DIT scores is years of education (Rest 1979). Nonetheless, a study on high achieving eighth graders (Narvaez 1993), showed that high achievement scores were necessary but not sufficient for high scores on the DIT. None of the low achievement scores were related to high DIT P-scores, but only some of the high achievement scores were. In other words, high ability to achieve in school is necessary but not enough for high DIT scores. Narvaez compared the eighth grade scores to college scores collected from a previous study and found that the highest DIT scores came from the identified high achievers from the eighth grade group, although the college men had the highest score average, followed by female eighth graders, then female college, and finally eighth grade males. The selection of highly gifted, well-educated, middle-aged adults was purposeful for the Ruf study in that factors other than educational level might be more easily identified as contributors to moral reasoning growth.

Many agree that high giftedness manifests itself as a personality characteristic as much as it does a learning ability. Highly gifted people think more complexly, learn new material faster, and are generally more successful at training for and maintaining successful careers. Their high intelligence, however, does not make all gifted people more able than nongifted to solve their own emotional and social problems, as is amply borne out by analysis of this subject population. Furthermore, highly gifted people often experience considerable difficulty during their childhoods in finding compatible friendships and in developing a clear sense of who they are and how they fit in.

According to Rest (1986),

> people who develop in moral judgment are those who love to learn, who seek new challenges, who enjoy intellectually stimulating environments, who are reflective ..., who take responsibility for themselves and their environs ... they have an advantage in receiving encouragement to continue their education and their development ... they profit from stimulating and challenging environments, and from social milieus that support their work, interest them, and reward their accomplishments ... are more fulfilled in their career aspirations, ... take more interest in the larger societal issues. This pattern is one of general social/cognitive development. (p. 57)

20.4 Data Analysis: Primary Sorting Categories and Terminology

Categories that helped explain levels of adult success, happiness, satisfaction, and levels of inner development and were used as the primary sorting categories in the analysis of case study data are:

- Childhood abuse
- Tone
- Searcher, Nonsearcher, Neutral
- Counseling or therapy
- DIT P-score

Significant life issues such as childhood emotional or physical abuse, adult subject's religiosity, suicide, marriage, divorce, and sexual preference were compared to the subjects' levels of emotional development. There appeared to be a relationship between these encounters and factors with their eventual moral and emotional growth. Related to this is the analysis of subjects' perceptions of themselves based on feedback from other people. Themes emerged of confusing or hurtful feedback received during their school years, feedback related to their differentness as highly gifted, in developing their own sense of who they are and how they fit into the world.

It was initially theorized that subjects who experienced abuse would have more difficulty self-actualizing. Abuse refers to any treatment, as perceived and reported by the study participants, which led them to be to feel unloved, or unworthy of love, respect, or admiration. Although some abuse is intentional, it need not be intentional to cause harm. The following description of abuse was used for case study analysis:

1. Physical – excessive punishment or rough physical treatment
2. Emotional – excessive criticism, lack of approval, parental temper tantrums or addiction problems, or words or behaviors that suggest the child is unliked or unwanted
3. Sexual – incest, rape, or exposing child to sex inappropriately
4. Spiritual – frightening or threatening God's disapproval or punishment
5. Neglect – basic physical, emotional or attention needs not met
6. Ignorance – poor parental treatment due to lack of correct information

It became apparent that categorizing the case studies based on emotionally and sexually abusive versus nonabusive backgrounds still did not explain apparent differences in adult level happiness or self-actualization. Abuse also was not verifiable by the written case study approach, since some subjects described abusive circumstances but denied that they were abused. Other subjects realized their treatment was not optimal but did not feel damaged because they always felt loved and supported. Consequently, abuse as a category was assigned only when the subject stated clearly that he or she felt abused.

As it became evident that attitude might be more significant than actual presence or absence of abuse, a new sorting category was developed called Tone, "A particular mental state or disposition; spirit, character or tenor" (*Random House Unabridged Dictionary* 1987, p. 1994). The term conveys the presence or absence of satisfaction and contentment in each subject's life. The following list explains how Tone Scores were assigned to the case study subjects:

- Tone 1: Subjects wrote that they are happy, content, satisfied; have a positive outlook.
- Tone 2: Same as Tone 1 but also revealed some sadness or disappointment.
- Tone 3: Not possible to discern subject's tone or the subject seemed to be in emotional limbo, neither content nor particularly discontent.
- Tone 4: Wrote statements that they were not at all happy or content; filled with many unresolved feelings.
- Tone 5: Subjects wrote that they were very angry or resentful.

The next analysis stage was based on whether or not subjects mentioned receiving psychological therapy; it was possible that both DIT and Tone scores could be influenced by therapy. The data indicated that although counseling was associated with higher DIT scores, it did not seem to be associated with adult happiness to any strong degree. It became clear that the search for precursors to inner growth was not the same as the search for happy adults. When it became clear that abuse and therapy still did not identify the people whose complexity of viewpoint was higher level reasoning, an additional sorting category was invented and added: Searcher. Dabrowski's description of "positive disintegration" was viewed as an indication of Searcher behavior.

- Searcher. Searchers are still actively deciding who they are and who they want to be; they tend to see many sides to many issues. Searchers examine and re-examine themselves, others, and issues and are open to changing their views if new, convincing information becomes available. Searchers may or may not be self-actualized in either their careers or intrapersonal (inner) lives. They may go through periods of emotional turmoil – "positive disintegrations" – as they strive, consciously or unconsciously, to reach their personality ideal, their best overall selves. (See Silverman 1989).
- Nonsearcher. Subjects do not report identity exploration as an active concern. Nonsearchers give evidence of either identity foreclosure or identity achieve-ment, as described by Erikson (1968). Some nonsearchers are people who may be self-actualized in a career sense in that they are productive people who live and work at a high level, presumably up to their potential. This is not the same as the inner emotional maturity achieved after extensive identity exploration and adaptations. Other subjects described as nonsearchers say they are underachiev-ing but accept the status quo.
- Neutral. Someone who is neither clearly a Searcher nor a Nonsearcher.

The final sorting category was the DIT P-score itself. It was initially assumed that all of the highly gifted subjects would score well above the population average of the DIT. As is evident from Table 20.5, the subjects' score range was quite wide despite their uniformly high intellectual and educational levels. Results showed a steady progression of DIT scores corresponding to the advancing complexity lev-els of moral and emotional reasoning of Kohlberg and Dabrowski. When case file analysis yielded a result that was out of synch with this fairly linear progression, the file was reviewed again to see if it was the DIT that missed the expected emo-tional level or the researcher. The difficulty was always related to the definition of the term Searcher. A final terminology distinction for clarifying this last issue was incorporated into the definition. Apparently "searching for answers" is not the same as being open to new information that can totally transform one's viewpoint. A Searcher continues to be open; someone who is not a Searcher will stop being open when the "answer" is found.

Subjects who gave evidence of being Searchers or Nonsearchers provided the most conspicuous factor for separating high emotional reasoning levels from the low. Positive disintegrations proved to be more difficult to count or verify; and there were some subjects who gave no detail describing positive disintegration-type episodes but who were still categorized at high emotional levels.

It appears that a DIT score below 65 indicates a person who is probably not a Searcher, although some scores above that level could only be categorized as Neutral. In line with the finding that Searchers are open to inner change, all of the subjects categorized as Searchers are placed at Dabrowski Level III or higher. There is also a consistent pattern in the DIT scores with low to high scores coin-ciding with the emotional development levels. The lowest DIT score received by a Searcher is 67.8.

All of the subjects who were categorized as Nonsearchers were placed in Levels I and II of Dabrowski's Levels of Emotional Development, and the highest DIT score

Table 20.5 Highly gifted subjects and factors related to emotional growth

Subject	Age	Dabrowski level	DIT	Tone	Abuse/therapy	Searcher
41F	58	I	*	4	Yes/yes	Non
12M	52	I	*	3	No/no	Non
26F	46	I	30.0	5	Yes/no	Non
30F	47	I	33.3	4	Yes/no	Non
10M	51	I	43.3	1	No/no	Non
27M	54	II	38.3	5	Yes/no	Non
14M	48	II	40.0	3	No/no	Non
28M	57	II	40.0	5	Yes/no	Non
13M	47	II	41.7	4	No/no	Non
31F	51	II	43.3	3	Yes/no	Non
11M	56	II	45.0	4	No/no	Non
29F	48	II	46.7	3	Yes/no	Non
15F	50	II	55.9	1	No/no	Non
25M	43	II	46.7	3	Yes/no	Neutral
22M	45	II	46.7	1	Yes/no	Neutral
6M	42	II	51.7	3	No/no	Neutral
8M	54	II	51.7	3	No/no	Neutral
9M	57	II	56.0	2	No/no	Neutral
23M	51	II	56.7	3	Yes/no	Neutral
39F	45	II	56.7	2	Yes/yes	Neutral
20M	54	II	58.3	4	Yes/no	Neutral
2F	44	II	61.7	1	No/no	Neutral
40F	46	II	61.7	3	Yes/yes	Neutral
3F	43	II	65.0	1	No/no	Neutral
21F	50	II/III	55.0	3	Yes/no	Neutral
37M	40	II/III	59.6	4	Yes/yes	Neutral
38F	49	II/III	64.4	4	Yes/yes	Neutral
1F	43	II/III	65.0	3	No/no	Neutral
36M	47	III	48.3	3	Yes/yes	Neutral
24M	46	III	70.0	4	Yes/no	Neutral
4M	47	III	75.0	4	No/no	Yes
18F	40	III	67.8	2	No/yes	Yes
7F	60	III/IV	65.0	4	No/no	Neutral
5M	46	III/IV	73.3	3	No/no	Yes
16M	40	III/IV	74.0	3	No/yes	Yes
32F	52	III/IV	70.0	1	Yes/yes	Yes
17F	44	IV	74.5	1	No/yes	Yes
35F	47	IV	71.7	2	Yes/yes	Yes
33F	45	IV/V	80.0	2	Yes/yes	Yes
19F	42	IV/V	82.0	1	Yes/no	Yes
34F/M	42	IV/V	83.3	1	Yes/yes	Yes

∗ stands for DIT results that were not considered valid (according to the scoring rules in the Manual).

among Nonsearchers was 55.9. There appeared to be two types of Nonsearchers. One type gave evidence of trying hard to be a good person by being hard-working, responsible, and nice. They generally sounded optimistic and earned Tone scores of 1, 2, and 3. They often stated directly or indirectly that they hoped their behaviors and attitudes and accomplishments would change those around them to be more accepting of and loving toward them. It was common for them to work hard on finding meaning and value in their lives through avenues others would find accept-able. The motivation seemed to come from a desire for love and approval. This first type of Nonsearcher often discovered fairly early in life how to formulate and meet goals, and once successful at meeting those goals, stayed with the original plan. Additionally, this first type of Nonsearcher usually found career and financial success.

The second type of Nonsearcher was the person who stated that life is the way it is, fine or otherwise, and there is no point in trying to change anything. These were the subjects who always had someone else or some circumstance to blame for their own short-comings or underachievement. Rather than being highly encour-aged, motivated, or guided by outside people or institutions as described in Level II's stereotypical roles, these subjects already had all their own answers. This second type of Nonsearcher sounded angry, cynical, or negative and earned Tone scores of 3, 4, and 5. Deeper case study analysis indicated that people who hold on firmly to resentments and their own way of viewing life, whether it makes them happy or not, are highly resistant to positive disintegrations.

Table 20.5 lists the subjects by ascending DIT scores, apparent Dabrowski level, age at the time of DIT completion, Tone score, and whether or not they reported they were abused or received therapy. The right column lists whether the subjects ap-peared from their questionnaire responses to be Searchers, Neutral, or Nonsearchers.

20.5 Conclusions and Implications

20.5.1 Who Becomes Self-actualized?

The DIT was significantly correlated with Dabrowski levels in the study subjects at $r = 0.851$. Fully 44% of the subjects gave evidence that they had moved at least somewhat past the conventional developmental stage, the stage that is typical for most American adults. The corresponding DIT score was above 60 compared to the American adult average of 40, and well beyond where Maslow and Dabrowski pro-posed most people achieve. The attainment of self-actualization levels by nine of the study subjects, 22%, was above the average for an unselected, random population, and indicates that highly gifted, highly educated adults *do* more often reach higher levels of emotional and moral development than adults in general.

A subtle distinction between good behavior motivated by a need for approval and recognition and that which is intrinsically motivated was largely identifiable by DIT score ranges. The *career* self-actualizers had a number of identifiable characteristics: products and accomplishments, awards and busy schedules. Career actualizers without inner transformation – the hallmark of higher, more open and complex, emotional levels – generally scored lower than the study group average, below about 60, on the DIT; and they also tended to be at the conventional or stereotypical stages of development. Their approach to making life choices and problem solving in general was captured by the terms "Nonsearcher" and "Neutral." They wrote that they found satisfaction and happiness in their accomplishments and tended to recognize their worth as achievers and doers. A large number of subjects at this level of development received Tone scores of 1 and 2 and led very stable lives. So, even without inner transformation, these were people who appeared to "live up to their potential."

Self-actualizers who have experienced inner, emotional growth tended to score higher than the study group average on the DIT. The case studies of the most satisfied and secure members gave descriptions of Dabrowski Levels IV or V thinking. All wrote they had not always been satisfied and secure, but that it was something they developed. High scores, generally scores over 65 on the DIT, appear to indicate a strong potential for the highest Dabrowski levels; high DIT scorers fit the category of Searchers. When unhappiness and depression were present in high DIT scorers, it generally indicated the subject had not achieved inner, emotional self-actualization but was actively struggling with it.

20.5.2 School and Community Environment

Of the three main topics investigated, school experiences were the most similar among subjects. Subjects who described problems with other students in school came from homes that were described as neglectful, hostile or rejecting. Several people described very negative experiences at school, but only one man and one woman wrote that they internalized the negative treatment and felt very bad about themselves. Both came from very negative home environments. The woman, #35F, eventually progressed emotionally away from the pain and bitterness of her past; the man, #27M, still had not. Not all students from troubled homes experienced difficulty with school friendships, however. Two subjects who came from rather positive homes, #3F and #5M, did well with other children but had some problems with teachers, both related to circumstances where the teachers apparently resented the student.

20.5.3 Family Environment

Although 56% of the subjects describe their own experiences in their childhood homes as emotionally abusive, only one subject reported that the abuse in her home drew attention from the authorities. Several cases included physical abuse.

The environmental and familial factors strongly affected the subjects' sense of self-worth and general happiness in their early years. The subjects who entered their middle years as the most emotionally miserable generally came from strongly emotionally abusive backgrounds where one or both parents were hostile and rejecting. Several subjects, most notably #16M and #18F, struggled with existentialist questions on their own despite generally supportive household environments. Of the subjects who eventually advanced to high emotional development levels, even those with background abuse, most could name at least one person who cared about them. Although a caring person from the past did not guarantee advanced emotional development, the *lack* of the subject's perception of a caring person was a common factor among all subjects who exhibited great hostility and received low Tone scores. Few subjects gave specific credit to any one person, group of people, or circumstances that gave them their sense of worth or happiness, although numerous people were credited with making the subject feel they must be worth *something*.

20.5.4 Personal Factors

The data in the study support a theory that there are both internal and external factors that lead to advanced levels of emotional and moral reasoning. Subjects who grew emotionally beyond the normal, conventional levels of most American adults described disappointment and confusion as precursors to their inner changes. Not all advanced emotional and moral reasoners experienced encouragement, and apparently part of their "Personality Transformation" included a new perspective on other people. Nearly all subjects described at Dabrowski Levels III/IV and above indicated good social/emotional intelligence that was deliberately and often painstakingly acquired later in life. One can argue that the self-actualized person exhibits the characteristic strengths and tendencies *after* achieving advanced emotional growth.

20.5.5 Career Success

The study subjects were selected for their intellectual level and age cohort rather than any personal eminence or unusual achievement. All younger than 60 years old, eminence could still be in the future for some. A definitive assessment of subjects "living up to their potential" was assessed primarily by whether or not the subjects themselves felt they were successful. Subjects who experienced educational and career success came from every type of parenting and every type of school and also fell into all levels of emotional development. To summarize, a career choice need not preclude inner growth, and a nurturing positive childhood does not appear to guarantee eventual inner growth.

Although all subjects in the present study who had *not* reached a recognizable degree of career success came from abusive backgrounds, there were many subjects categorized as abused who achieved career success. Subjects who fell into the low career success description were found at all emotional development levels. In other words, there were some formerly abused subjects who managed to grow and develop to higher emotional levels but who still were not obvious career achievers. From these particular examples, it can be concluded that career success and inner self-actualization are not highly related, yet neither are they exclusive to one another.

20.6 Some Limitations

A number of issues limit the general usefulness of the current study. Included among them are the imprecision of the case study analysis approach, the lack of agreement in the wider community regarding what constitutes giftedness, the snapshot approach to the subjects' assessments, the self-selection inherent in research with volunteer subjects, and lack of more than one rater for a number of highly subjective evaluations.

20.7 Why Inner Growth Matters: A Discussion

Two considerations stand out as important when one evaluates emotional self-actualization. First, people who have reached levels of self-actualization feel good about themselves, their lives, and the world around them. They are generally hopeful and have positive attitudes toward others. They are not generally depressed and they have a natural drive to contribute through their efforts.

As the analysis of the case study material progressed, it became evident that there is reason to consider advanced emotional and moral reasoning levels not necessarily better or desirable for everyone. Stage theory suggests that higher is better, but judging from the kinds of lives the different subjects are leading, and the happiness and contentment often reported by subjects at lower levels, it is important to keep an open mind about what advanced level emotional growth is and is not.

Only through future research can it be determined what personal, perhaps inherent, factors may contribute to eventual self-actualization in individual people. It is clear that there are identifiable characteristics present in people at different levels of development. How early they reach a level, and whether or not they will continue to progress to the highest stages, cannot be concluded from this study. Only one subject showed attitudes and behavior that differed significantly from his DIT results, subject #36M. He took a 2-year break before finishing the study and reported that he underwent significant internal changes. The questionnaire dealing with his childhood was completed at the same time as his first DIT, on which he received a 48.3.[1] His clear change from probable Nonsearcher to Searcher by the time he completed the adult level inventory indicated that there are self-actualizers who did not begin life as natural Searchers. If they did not begin life, or even their adulthoods, as Searchers, that means something can happen to turn a person into a Searcher and increase the likelihood of self-actualization. What that something is did not become clear in this study.

In conclusion, the very nature of self-actualized growth and advanced moral reasoning may preclude either concept being understood well enough for teaching to children, young parents, or even teachers. Perhaps what parents, teachers, and children need to know is that there is the possibility of an emotional journey and it involves feelings of instability and struggle along the way. They can be taught what the typical milestones are, what their life goals may be, and the reasons for establishing those goals.

References

Boehm, L. (1962). The development of conscience: A comparison of American children of different mental and socioeconomic levels. *Child Development, 33*, 575–590.

Colby, A., and Kohlberg, L. (1987). *The measurement of moral judgment:* Vol. I, *Theoretical foundations and research validation.* New York: Cambridge University Press.

Erikson, E. (1968). *Identity, youth, and crisis.* New York: Norton.

Falk, R. F., and Miller, N. B. (1998). The reflexive self: A sociological perspective. *Roeper Review, 20*(3), 150–153.

Festinger, L. (1954). A theory of social comparison processes. *Human Relations, 7*, 117–140.

Flexner, S. B. (Ed.). (1987). *The random house dictionary of the English language* (2nd ed.). New York: Random House.

Gilligan, C. (1982). *In a different voice.* Cambridge, MA: Harvard University Press.

Greenspon, T. (1998). The gifted self: Its role in development and emotional health. *Roeper Review, 20(3)*, 162–167.

Gross, M. U. M. (1993). *Exceptionally gifted children.* London: Routledge.

Hall, E. G., and Hansen, J. B. (1997). Self-actualizing men and women: A comparison study. *Roeper Review, 20(1)*, 22–27.

Janos, P. M., Robinson, N. M., and Lunneborg, C. E. (1989). Markedly early entrance to college: A multi-year comparative study of academic performance and psychological adjustment. *Journal of Higher Education, 60*, 496–518.

Josselson, R. (1991). *Finding herself: Pathways to identity development in women.* San Francisco, CA: Jossey-Bass.

Kohlberg, L. (1984). *The psychology of moral development* (Vol. 2). San Francisco, CA: Harper & Row.

Lefton, L. A. (1994). *Psychology* (5th ed.). Boston, MA: Allen & Bacon.

Levinson, D. J. (1978). *The seasons of a man's life.* New York: Ballentine Books.

Maslow, A. H. (1970). *Motivation and personality* (2nd ed.). New York: Harper & Row.

---

[1] Subject #36M retook the *DIT* nearly 4 years after taking it the first time and after the body of this paper was completed. He scored 83.3.

McGeorge, C. (1975). The susceptibility to faking of the defining issues test of moral development. *Developmental Psychology, 44*, 116–122.

Narvaez, D. (1993). High achieving students and moral judgment. *Journal for the Education of the Gifted, 16*(3), 268–279.

Nelson, K. C. (1989). Dabrowski's theory of positive disintegration. *Advanced development: A Journal on Adult Giftedness, 1*, 1–14.

Peck, R. F., and Havighurst, R. J. (1960). *The psychology of character development.* New York: Wiley.

Piechowski, M. M. (1975). A theoretical and empirical approach to the study of development. *Genetic Psychology Monographs, 92*, 231–297.

Piechowski, M. M. (1986). *Defining issues test, manual.* Minneapolis, MN: Center for Ethical Development, University of Minnesota.

Piechowski, M. M. (1989). Developmental potential and the growth of self. In J. L. VanTassel-Baska and P. Olszewski-Kubilius (Eds.), *Patterns of influence on gifted learners: The home, the school, and the self* (pp. 87–101). New York: Teachers College Press.

Piechowski, M. M., and Silverman, L. K. (1993, July). *Dabrowski's levels of emotional development.* Paper presented at the Lake Geneva Dabrowski Conference, Geneva, WI.

Rest, J. R. (1979). *Development in judging moral issues.* Minneapolis, MN: University of Minnesota Press.

Rest, J. R., Turiel, E., and Kohlberg, L. (1969). Level of moral judgment as determinant of preference and comprehension made by others. *Journal of Personality, 37*, 225–252.

Rest, J. R. (1986). *Defining issues test, manual.* minneapolis: Center for Ethical Development, University of Minnesota.

Rest, J. R. and Narvaez, D. (1994) (Eds.) *Moral developement in the professions.* Hillsdale, NJ: Lawrence Erlbaum.

Ruf, D. L. (1998). *Environmental, familial, and personal factors that affect the self-actualization of highly gifted adults*: Case studies. Unpublished dissertation: University of Minnesota.

Scheidel, D., and Marcia, J. (1985). Ego integrity, intimacy, sex role orientation, and gender. *Developmental Psychology, 21*, 149–160.

Sheehy, G. (1974). *Passages: Predictable crises of adult life.* New York: E. P. Dutton.

Silverman, L. K. and Kearney K. (1989). *Parents of the extraordinarily gifted.* In advanced development: A journal on adult giftedness, *1*(1), 41–56.

Silverman, L. K. (Ed.) (1993). *Counseling the gifted & talented.* Denver, CO: Love.

Strauss, W., and Howe, N. (1991). *Generations: The history of America's future.* New York: William Morrow.

Turner, J.S., and Helms, D. (1986). *Contemporary adulthood* (4th ed.). Chicago, IL: Harcourt College Publishers.

Walker, L., deVries, B., and Bichard, S. L. (1984). The hierarchical nature of stages of moral development. *Developmental Psychology, 20*, 960–966.

Woolfolk, A. E. (1995). *Educational psychology* (6th ed.). Needham Heights, MA: Allyn & Bacon.

Chapter 21
Teaching for Intellectual and Emotional Learning (TIEL): Bringing Thinking and Moral-Ethical Learning into Classrooms

Christy Folsom

Abstract Teaching in ways that promote the moral development of students is a daunting task for teachers in gifted programs and in general education classrooms. While time and curriculum requirements are often a factor, teacher preparation programs do not adequately prepare teachers to address the moral-ethical aspects of learning. Additionally, the voluminous terminology that refers to moral development can be confusing. Often overlooked is the relationship between the intellect and the moral aspect of learning for gifted students. When intellectual needs are not addressed in school, moral development can suffer. The TIEL Curriculum Design Wheel brings these important intellectual and emotional components together forming a framework that guides teachers in developing curriculum that includes the teaching of thinking processes as well as social emotional learning.

Keywords Affective · Anti-intellectualism · Cognitive · Curriculum · Dewey · Empowerment · Emotional · Guilford · Intellectual · Moral-ethical · School · Teaching

Helping students develop morally and ethically is a daunting task for teachers. In general education classrooms, where most gifted students spend the majority of their time, mandated curriculum, pacing charts, and standardized testing have priority and consume the majority of classroom time. In gifted programs, where teachers have limited time with their students and the focus is more often on creativity, thinking skills, and problem-solving, not necessarily related to academic content (Borland 1997), the moral-ethical aspects of learning are often neglected.

In addition, teaching for moral-ethical learning can be a confusing enterprise. Little in teacher education prepares teachers with the knowledge of the intellectual or emotional components necessary to consciously design curriculum and establish

C. Folsom
Department of Early Childhood and Childhood Education, B-43 Carman Hall, Lehman College, City University of New York, Bronx, NY 10468, USA
e-mail: christy@gfolsom.com

D. Ambrose, T. Cross (eds.), *Morality, Ethics, and Gifted Minds*,
DOI: 10.1007/978-0-387-89368-6_21,
© Springer Science+Business Media LLC 2009

environments that help students develop moral-ethical principles. Teacher education programs provide even less information about advanced learners and how to accommodate their needs in the classroom.

The purpose of this chapter is to present Teaching for Intellectual and Emotional Learning (TIEL), a model that I developed to help teachers bring the moral-ethical aspect of education into programs for the gifted as well as general education classrooms. The TIEL Curriculum Design model (Folsom 1998) connects cognitive and affective components of learning and provides a valuable tool that helps teachers develop curriculum that includes the teaching of thinking and moral/ethical learning. Four questions will be addressed in the chapter. What terms address the concept of moral or morality? What does moral education mean in school? What is the experience of gifted students in school? How can the TIEL Curriculum Design model help teachers address the intellectual and emotional learning needs of gifted students, as well as improve learning opportunities for all students?

21.1 Meaning of Moral and Morality

In describing critical thinking, itself an important component of moral development (Kwak 2008; Paul 1995), Cuban said, "defining thinking skills, reasoning, critical thought and problem solving [is] a conceptual swamp" (as cited in Lewis and Smith 1993, p. 131). Defining the terms moral and ethical is a similarly confusing task. Character, communication, reflection, interactions, relationships, competency, ethical reasoning, wisdom, social and emotional development, and feelings are all used to discuss the moral dimension of learning (Folsom 2009; Gilligan 1993; Hoffman 2000; Kramer 1990). In addition, discipline, knowledge, understanding, empathy, moral emotion, motivation, caring, justice, and moral judgment (Durkheim 1961; Hoffman 2000; Noddings 1984; Sternberg 2000) are all terms that add to the meaning of moral behavior.

While many terms refer to the social emotional or affective aspects of moral development, intellect also plays an important role. Kohlberg's (1978) cognitive-developmental approach to moral education has a logical hierarchical orientation. Kohlberg describes stage six, within the post-conventional level, as the highest form of moral development. Concerned by the narrow focus of Kohlberg's theory tested only on men, Gilligan (1993) replicated his study with boys, girls, and women. She found that relationships, responsibility, and care for others, more common in women's way of thinking, were missing in Kohlberg's theory. According to Gilligan, "empathy, listening, courage, and emotional stamina" (p. xix) are characteristics of a moral person.

Purpose and context are important in determining what is moral (Frankena 1970; Whiteley 1970). Ambrose (2003) drew from ethical philosophy to add to the meaning of morality. Aspiration and capacity development are "two interactive dimensions" of self-fulfillment, which "signifies the highest development of the individual" and includes moral concern for others (p. 283). Yet, Ambrose points out that both aspiration and capacity development are related to opportunities made available by race, class, gender, ethnicity, and socioeconomic circumstances. Altruism is also heavily reliant on context, but in a different way. Monroe (1996) states that altruism extends morality in that it requires a significant self-sacrifice that can include risk to life.

Wisdom and spiritual intelligence add further dimension to the concepts of moral development. Some see wisdom as a component of moral development (Howley et al. 1995), while others see wisdom as sharing many characteristics of moral development (Kramer 1990; Labouvie-Vief 1990; Sternberg 2000). Spiritual intelligence, the use of "multiple modalities to access one's inner knowledge" (Sisk 2008, p. 24), includes the characteristics of "compassion, honesty, fairness, responsibility, and respect" (Kidder, as cited by Sisk, p. 27), all terms found in discussions of moral development and wisdom.

21.2 Moral Development and School

While there are many definitions, points of view, and increasing research on moral development, teaching in ways that promote moral development for all students remains a difficult and often contentious enterprise. Few disagree that we need moral education, yet finding a suitable way to do it has been somewhat of a Goldilocks affair. Three major methods of moral education used over the last 40 years, have all been found wanting. The values clarification programs of the 1970s were found to be too relativistic. Character education programs, often referred to as the "bag of virtues" approach, are considered by many educators to be too didactic and only minimally effective. Others find that Kohlberg's cognitive-moral approach relies too much on logical thinking and too little on caring and relationships.

Ultimately, children learn care for others by example. Morley (1979), an assistant superintendent for instruction in St. Louis, put it simply, "When I speak of moral dimensions, I am referring to continuums in human growth and development in which youngsters move in positive directions toward adulthood" (p. 594). Given the amount of time children spend in school, Morley emphasized the important role of teachers in helping their students develop morally. Noddings (2005) concurs, pointing out that teachers need to develop relationships with their students and model empathic behavior in order to support students' moral-ethical development.

Such teachers contribute to school as Maslow (1971) described. He writes that schools should be places where students learn to know themselves, discover their vocations, become aware of the "beauty and wonder of life" (p. 183). School should be a place to feel accomplishment; a place to learn that "life is precious" (p. 180). School should be a place where teachers and students should have peak experiences that support the project of self-actualization. Unfortunately, Maslow saw that school is too often "an extremely effective instrument for crushing peak experiences and forbidding their possibility" (p. 181).

21.2.1 Gifted Students and School Experience

Cross (2005) pointed out the difficulty that many gifted students have in school. In the anti-intellectual environment (Howley et al. 1995) of school, gifted children often experience misunderstanding, misteaching, and, at times, outright hostility. Many gifted students manifest behaviors such as boredom, lethargy, depression, hyperactivity, misbehavior, or the catch-all of underachievement. In an anti-intellectual environment where little is expected in the way of deep thinking or feeling, many students remain below the radar, achieving enough to get by, but far below their innate capacities. For others, gifts and talents go unrecognized because little in the classroom experience has required their utilization.

Many gifted students feel anger and rage about their experiences in school (Cross 2005; Kanevsky and Keighley 2003). In their study of ten underachieving high school students, Kanevsky and Keighley found that the students refused to do unchallenging class work or did not come to class at all. While these students understood the challenge teachers had in meeting the needs of all their students, they felt strongly about their right to learn at an appropriate level and pace. They made a moral decision not to do work in which they saw little value and which demonstrated a lack of respect for their abilities.

School is seldom a friendly place for those who are different in any way. Many gifted students feel the sting of hurtful messages that say they are "physically weak, socially inadequate, and not interesting people" (Cross 2005, p. 114). Gifted students also receive what Cross referred to as "not too" (p. 115) messages, meaning that you can be smart, but "not too" smart. You can be interested in your school work, but "not too" interested. Inversely, underachieving students hear that they must not be gifted or they would spend more time on their school work and get better grades (Cross).

21.2.2 Intellectual Aspect of Moral Education

The intellectual components and the moral-ethical, social emotional, affective, or conscience components of education are intertwined, complementary, and reciprocal (Howley et al. 1995; Kramer 1990; Labouvie-Vief 1990; Tannenbaum 1975; Vare 1979). While clearly students need a moral education that attends to their emotional needs and their feelings for others, they need an intellectual and academic education as well. Cross (2005) found that most of the students served by a school psychology clinic are there because they are not being challenged in school. The presence or absence of challenging work affects them emotionally which in turn affects their moral development.

The anti-intellectualism of schooling prevents the moral learning that all students need. Howley et al. (1995) stated that "a true education is one that develops the intellect of students, particularly with respect to considering the enduring dilemma of the human condition" (p. 182). Any student or adult who fails to respect those perceived to be different from themselves also needs an education that fosters reflection, empathy, and ethical reasoning.

According to Howley et al. (1995), "schooling must nurture intellect above all else" (p. 184). If we are to transform schools into emotionally safe places where all students have a chance to develop both their intellectual and moral potential, teachers and administrators must take up their "stewardship of the intellect" (p. xi). They need to show care of the intellect by consciously including both intellectual and social-emotional components that are important to moral development in their teaching, curriculum planning, and administrative management. In so doing, educators will be empowered to "create learning environments in which gifted students feel fully accepted" and develop "sophisticated approaches to teaching that help students develop their talents" (Cross 2005, p. 36).

21.3   Teaching for Intellectual and Emotional Learning (TIEL)

Teachers need to develop curriculum and instruction that helps students develop both intellectually and emotionally. *Teaching for Intellectual and Emotional Learning* (TIEL) is a framework that helps teachers create accepting environments and sophisticated approaches to teaching and learning (Folsom 2009). The TIEL Curriculum Design Model, also referred to as the TIEL model, is based on the work of J. P. Guilford (1977) and John Dewey (1964). The TIEL model connects and codifies fundamental intellectual and social-emotional processes that are necessary in the complex teaching and learning that lead to moral-ethical development (Cross 2005; Darling-Hammond 1997; Dewey 1964; Doddington 2008; Folsom 2004; Kramer 1990). The TIEL model provides an accessible tool for educators to use in designing curriculum, instruction, and a learning environment that helps students develop both cognitively and affectively.

21.4   The TIEL Curriculum Design Wheel

Teaching for Intellectual and Emotional Learning is graphically represented by the TIEL Curriculum Design Wheel (Fig. 21.1), a color-coded graphic that is also called the TIEL Wheel. The five thinking operations in the lower portion of the TIEL Wheel originate in the Structure of Intellect theory developed by Guilford (1977). The thinking operations are *cognition, memory, evaluation, convergent production*, and *divergent production*. The five social-emotional aspects of teaching and learning found in the upper portion of the TIEL Wheel are adapted from Dewey's (1964) writings. The qualities of character include *reflection, empathy, ethical reasoning, mastery*, and *appreciation*.

In addition to the work of Guilford and Dewey, I also used the work of Meeker (1979) to create the TIEL Curriculum Design Wheel. When Meeker adapted

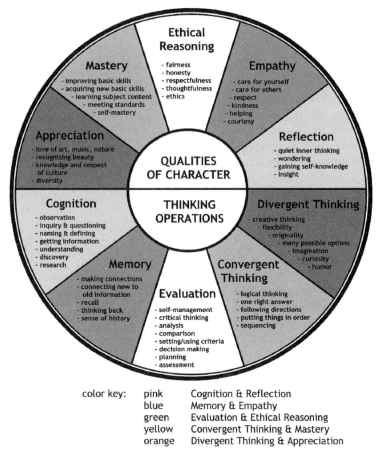

Fig. 21.1 TIEL curriculum design wheel (Folsom 2008, reprinted with permission from: Folsom, C. 2009)

Guilford's model to educational uses, she assigned colors to each of the five operations. The colors play an important part in the TIEL Wheel by visually scaffolding the concepts represented in the wheel. They connect each thinking operation to the corresponding quality of character; highlight the relationships between thinking operations and qualities of character; and make the model visually accessible to teachers and their students. A more detailed description of the TIEL model can be found in Folsom (2008).

21.4.1 Cognitive and Affective Teaching

According to Kramer (1990), "one cannot have cognition without affect or affect without cognition. The two systems … are inherently interrelated" (p. 291). By bringing these two functions together, TIEL helps teachers address both the intellectual and moral needs of gifted students in general education classrooms where they often have less than optimal learning experiences. TIEL also helps teachers address intellectual and moral development in programs and special classes for the gifted where students spend limited time. At the same time, TIEL helps teachers improve instruction for all their students.

In the following sections, each of the components of the TIEL model is described in more detail, and the relationship between each intellectual component and the corresponding quality of character or social-emotional component is explained. In addition, questions are given that can assist teachers in planning curriculum that supports moral development.

21.4.2 Cognition and Reflection

Reflection goes hand in hand with *cognition*. Dewey (1964) connected the intellectual skill of observation to reflection. He stated that "there can not be observation in the best sense of the word without reflection, nor can reflection fail to be an effective preparation for observation" (p. 196).

21.4.2.1 Cognition

Cognition, the process of getting information, includes the skills of observation, research, discovery, knowing, and understanding (Guilford 1977). Meeker (1979) added "awareness, rediscovery, recognition of information in various forms, and comprehension" to the definition (p. 14). Children need to observe, research, discover, and understand content found in the disciplines of math, literature, science, social studies, music, and art.

Doddington (2008) emphasized the importance of gathering information through a "primordial relationship" that requires manipulation of real objects. She shared Heidegger's thoughts on gaining knowledge in ways that involve the corporeality of thinking or using one's hands to make discoveries and comprehend rather than through observation removed from the object. Doddington's point is especially important at this time in education, when corporeality of thinking is being sacrificed for published test preparation booklets and the standardized tests that follow.

In the TIEL Design Wheel (Fig. 21.1), the operation, *cognition* helps teachers think in new ways about how students can acquire information. How can teachers plan for students to learn through using their hands? How can teachers, as Maslow (1971) suggests, use art, music, drama, or dance in ways that help children acquire information about the content they are learning? How can teachers encourage children to ask questions about the people and the topics they are studying?

21.4.2.2   Reflection

Reflection is the act of wondering; questioning or accepting; gaining insight and self-knowledge. Dewey (1991) said that reflective thinking is "troublesome." It requires "overcoming the inertia that inclines one to accept suggestions at their face value" (p. 13). Reflection helps one "be in touch with one's feelings, needs, and expectations" (Kramer 1990, p. 286), important in the development of wisdom. When teachers are reflective, they think holistically. They go beyond rational problem solving (Zeichner and Liston 1996) to seek solutions through intuition, emotion, and passion (Greene as cited in Zeichner and Liston 1996; Doddington 2008; Labouvie-Vief 1990). Reflection helps you learn about yourself as you are learning about your teaching.

Reflection does not stop with the teacher. The TIEL Wheel visually reminds teachers to plan opportunities for their students to reflect on their learning. How can teachers use quiet time, soothing music, purposeful writing, and thoughtful sharing to help students learn to reflect on the concepts they are learning? How can teachers help students to learn about themselves through the content they are learning? How can teachers help students reflect on the intellectual and social-emotional processes used in learning? How can teachers help their students develop the capacity to wonder?

21.4.3   Memory and Empathy

Empathy emerges from *memory*. To feel compassion for another means that "one must draw upon one's own capacity ... one's own experience" (Jersild 1955, p. 127). It is through remembering experiences of caring, either in reality, or sometimes vicariously through observing the experiences of others, that we ourselves learn to be caring individuals.

21.4.3.1   Memory

Memory is the glue that allows us to use our experiences to learn. Through use of memory we are able to recall, memorize, and make connections, combine information, and recognize relationships (Bloom 1956; Guilford 1977; Sternberg 1985). While recall can be considered a "lower order use of the mind" (Paul 1995, p. 55), the storage function of memory allows us to make connections that are important in learning new information and higher level thinking.

TIEL helps teachers recognize that *memory* goes well beyond the recall of information and encourages a broader range of questions for teachers to consider as they plan for their students. How can teachers help students connect concepts to something that is familiar to the students? How can teachers help students develop their memory skills within a content area? How can teachers help students make connections between concepts and thinking processes across multiple subject areas? How can teachers help students make connections between intellectual and social emotional processes involved in their learning?

21.4.3.2 Empathy

Dewey (1964) stated that the development of human sympathy, or *empathy* and caring, is an important "aim of education" (p. 197). While memory serves us academically, it is also the foundation of caring in each of us. We draw on our own experiences in order to feel compassion for others. Cross (2005) points out that to "know and understand another's experiences, we must live them ourselves" (p. 101). Yet, while there are limitations to "truly being empathic," these gaps in experience can be filled by "compassion and respect" (p. 101).

Hoffman (2000) defined empathy "as an affective response more appropriate to another's situation than one's own" (p. 4). As we empathize with others, the connecting cues to our own experiences are strengthened and our capacity for empathy increases (Hoffman 1991). Cross (2005) pointed out the importance of teaching empathy since "some gifted children have an abundance of empathy, while others need to be taught" (p. 76). As gifted students move into adulthood and assume responsibility for various kinds of policy making, it is important that they have cultivated empathy to prepare them to make decisions based on the common good.

As teachers plan, they need to ask themselves questions about how to teach empathy. What experiences have students had that will help them develop empathy for others and for themselves? How can teachers help students develop empathy during this study? How can teachers make sure that all students, including the gifted students in the class, have work they can care deeply about? How might we incorporate service to others into our project?

21.4.4 Evaluation and Ethical Reasoning

Evaluation and *ethical reasoning* hold a central position in the complex teaching and learning that encourage moral development. Ethical reasoning involves the same evaluative skills of setting criteria, weighing options, and self-evaluation, yet it is anchored by consideration for others.

21.4.4.1 Evaluation

Evaluation includes the critical thinking and self-organization skills involved in comparing, judging, and decision making using sound criteria (Doll 1993; Guilford 1977; Paul 1995) that is commonly termed higher-order thinking. The opportunity to choose motivates, opens opportunity for exploring options, and promotes self-directed learning. Many have written about the critical thinking skills included in *evaluation*. Marzano (1993) stated that the processes of decision making, planning, and self-evaluation "render any activity more thoughtful and more effective" (p. 158).

It is difficult to overstate the importance of choice in both cognitive and moral development. Jonas, the protagonist in The Giver (Lowry 1993), speaks passionately for all human beings when he says, "I want to wake up in the morning and *decide* [original emphasis] things!" (p. 97). Those with limited opportunities for self-fulfillment have had limited choices in their lives, while those with optimal opportunities for self-fulfillment more commonly have had the resources that provide an array of choices (Ambrose 2003). Yet, while choice is essential to moral development, learning how to manage those choices must occur simultaneously.

The TIEL model makes visible the self-management skills of decision making, planning, and self-evaluation that are often expected, but infrequently taught in any explicit way. As they plan, teachers can ask questions about how to teach self-management skills. Where can students make decisions within this content study? How can teachers teach students to set criteria that will help them evaluate their work? What projects will provide an opportunity for teaching students how to plan? How can teachers help students understand that learning to manage their own learning will lead to more opportunities?

21.4.4.2   Ethical Reasoning

Ethical reasoning, or to use Dewey's (1964) term, "unswerving moral rectitude," (p. 197), is evaluation anchored by qualities of character. Making ethical decisions requires the same evaluative skills of setting criteria, weighing options, planning, or self-evaluating. Yet, for reasoning to be ethical, it must be combined with qualities of character that include reflection, empathy and appreciation. Moral autonomy, necessary to ethical reasoning, relies on "productive thinking in the form of decision-making, moral reasoning and ethical principles" (Vare 1979, p. 494). Vare pointed out that persons with moral autonomy display the characteristics of "self-initiated [and] self-directed behavior … [they are] self-reliant, inner-directed, responsible, [and] have the capacity for self-criticism and evaluation" (p. 494).

The TIEL framework can guide teachers in planning learning experiences that promote moral reasoning. As they plan, teachers can ask themselves the following questions. In the course of this study, where can children become aware of decisions based on honesty, respect, and fairness? What eminent people can we study who demonstrate moral-ethical reasoning and focus on the common good of all humanity? How can teachers use group project work to help students develop capacity for ethical reasoning? Where in this study can students learn tolerance for the ideas and beliefs of others?

21.4.5 *Convergent Production and Mastery*

Convergent production is focused on the one right answer. Convergent production and mastery are related in a number of ways that include emphasis on the mastery of information that calls for one answer; the effect on self-esteem and character development when mastery is not attained; and intellectual and emotional self-mastery that support moral development.

21.4.5.1 Convergent Production

Convergent production is the focused production of information and "retrieval of items of information from memory" (Guilford 1977, p. 109) in order to answer questions or solve problems that have one answer. Logical and deductive thinking, important to critical thinking (Paul 1995), are also included in convergent thinking.

Many gifted students have difficulty with the linear sequential thinking focused on one right answer that dominates our school system. Much of a student's day is filled with work that requires correct answers in math, spelling, and reading. When such work is inappropriate for a student's learning level, anger, frustration, boredom, and non-achievement can be the result. The current emphasis on standardized testing adds to the amount of time spent on convergent thinking.

Nevertheless, when students have the opportunity to work at their own learning level and pace, the skills associated with convergent thinking and production are important to learn. Several questions can help teachers consider the multiple aspects of convergent production. Where can students practice sequencing and organizational skills in this study? How can teachers help students develop logical thinking skills? How can concepts be taught in a manner appropriate for the gifted students in the class? How can assignments be modified for the advanced learners?

21.4.5.2 Mastery

Mastery, found within the qualities of character, is linked to convergent production. Because assignments, assessments, and standardized testing require right answers, mastery is most often associated with convergent production in school. Mastery in school is usually perceived as meeting externally imposed requirements. Kanevsky and Keighley (2003) subjects felt strongly about the external standards imposed upon them. They wanted to feel control over their own learning, make choices, and be challenged with complex projects. Without these elements, school was the anti-intellectual place described by Howley and colleagues (1995).

Teachers need to consider the relationship between mastery in school and the development of social-emotional characteristics that are an integral part of self-fulfillment, self-actualization, and moral-ethical development. While some students need more challenge in school, other students experience repeated failure and come to believe they cannot learn. Interestingly, these two groups of students with different capacities for mastery can share similar feelings of confusion, frustration, and defeat that can contribute to a loss of confidence in themselves (Cross 2005; Weiner 1998), none of which support self-actualization or self-esteem.

Yet, teachers cannot bestow self-esteem upon students. Students build self-esteem when they feel empowered. Giving unfounded positive feedback for work that is too easy or not understood does not help students develop the self-empowerment that comes from understanding their own thinking, organizing their own learning, and the opportunity to develop creative and critical thinking skills. Paul (1995) asked,

> What good is education for "self-esteem" if it is based on the false assumption that we can "give" students self-esteem by continually giving them positive feedback—while we ignore the skills and abilities the possession of which gives them a real sense of empowerment? (p. 44)

Teachers need to be conscious of helping students develop social-emotional self-mastery as well as academic mastery. Emotional self-mastery comes through the same skills and abilities needed to feel empowered as a learner. When students experience the power of planning and using carefully considered criteria to evaluate their own work, they develop emotional self-mastery as well as make academic progress. When students overcome their perfectionism and persevere in their assignments and projects without giving up (Dweck 2007), they are developing emotional self-mastery. Teaching students the skills and abilities that match their learning levels strengthens both their academic and emotional mastery.

Teachers who are conscious of the multiple meanings of mastery ask the following questions. How can teachers help each student develop mastery in academic skills at his or her learning level? How can teachers plan learning experiences that will help students develop self-confidence as a learner? How can teachers teach students the skills they need to feel empowered? How can teachers encourage students not to give up? How can teachers support students' development of personal mastery in the area of social-emotional qualities?

21.4.6 Divergent Production and Appreciation

Divergent production is connected to *appreciation* through creativity. Experiencing creativity leads to an increase in feeling comfortable with difference, whether it is a difference in cultures, people, or the natural world around us. It is through these two components that Maslow (1971) saw the possibility of creating,

> …a new kind of human being who is comfortable with change, who enjoys change, who is able to improvise, who is able to face with confidence, strength, and courage a situation of which he has absolutely no forewarning. (p. 56)

21.4.6.1 Divergent Production

Divergent production involves the production of information that results in generating alternatives with an "emphasis on variety and quality of output" (Meeker 1979, p. 20) and "inventing, designing, contriving, composing" (Guilford 1968, p. 78). Divergent production includes creative thinking and risk-taking. It is the kind of fluent, flexible, imaginative thinking that students need to succeed in our complex world and to change it.

Divergent thinking and production are necessary for complex learning to take place. Creative project work provides opportunities to develop both intellectual skills and social-emotional processes. When students create a project, they are involved in research, decision making, planning, and self-evaluation. Collaboration skills are learned when a group works together on a creative project. Creative projects encourage the use of imagination to see alternatives in solving problems. Students learn in a real situation what it means to be flexible and make fair and ethical decisions.

Teachers need to ask themselves how they can help students develop the divergent thinking ability to "seek alternative ways of being, to look for openings…to discover new possibilities" (Greene 1988, p. 2). How can teachers plan for students to use their creativity within this content area? Where can teachers teach students how to think flexibly and take risks within this study? How can teachers provide a space for students to explore their imaginations? How can teachers design assessment that takes into account divergent thinking and production? How can teachers group students so that high-ability students can work together on specified projects?

21.4.6.2 Appreciation

Appreciation and *divergent production* have a reciprocal relationship. Opportunities for divergent thinking help students acquire flexibility, risk-taking, and imagination. An ability to think openly and imaginatively helps students develop appreciation for a world of difference. Dewey described this quality as developing a love of beauty in nature and art. The TIEL Wheel expands this description to include cultures and circumstances of others that are different from what we know. In a test-saturated school system where too few schools place priority on art, music, and drama, the TIEL model reminds educators of the importance of helping students develop aesthetic appreciation. (McNamee et al. 2008).

Teachers need to ask themselves how they can plan opportunities for students to learn appreciation. How can this study help students develop an appreciation for differences and diversity? How can teachers help students develop an appreciation for their own differences? How can art, music, and drama support the learning of content while, at the same time, help students develop a deep appreciation for the arts?

21.5 Conclusion

The TIEL Curriculum Design Model can help teachers become aware of the possibilities for moral development and provide them with tools needed to include this important component in their teaching. First, terminology that refers to moral-ethical development, spiritual intelligence, and wisdom requires clarification. Teachers need to understand fundamental intellectual and social-emotional characteristics that are common among all three concepts in order to support moral development in their classrooms.

Second, schools need to become intellectually and emotionally safe places for all children to learn. Teachers need to understand the cognitive and affective needs of students, including those identified as gifted, and use this knowledge to uncover students' talents and abilities that have been hidden. The TIEL Curriculum Design Model helps teachers integrate intellectual and emotional/affective processes into their planning of classroom curriculum in ways that make peak experiences possible for each student.

Third, the TIEL model reminds teachers of what they intuitively know, but have received little instruction to carry out. It helps them develop confidence in their abilities to teach the intellectual and social emotional processes that lie at the heart of moral development. The TIEL model can help assure teachers that they *can* take on the intellectual stewardship required to help students develop both intellectually and morally.

References

Ambrose, D. (2003). Barriers to aspiration development and self-fulfillment: Interdisciplinary insights for talent discovery. *Gifted Child Quarterly, 47*(4), 282–294.

Bloom, B. (1956). *Taxonomy of educational objectives: The classification of educational goals.* New York: D. McKay.

Borland, J. H. (1997). The construct of giftedness. *Peabody Journal of Education, 72*(3–4), 6–20.

Cross, T. L. (2005). *The social and emotional lives of gifted kids: Understanding and guiding their development.* Waco, TX: Prufrock Press.

Darling-Hammond, L. (1997). *The right to learn: A blueprint for creating schools that work.* San Francisco, CA: Jossey-Bass.

Dewey, J. (1964). *John Dewey on education: Selected writings* (R. D. Archambault, Ed.). Chicago, IL: University of Chicago Press.

Dewey, J. (1991). *How we think.* Buffalo, NY: Prometheus Books.

Doddington, C. (2008). Critical thinking as a source of respect for persons: A critique. In M. Mason (Ed.), *Critical thinking and learning* (pp. 109–119). Richmond, Victoria, Australia: Blackwell.

Doll, W. E., Jr. (1993). *A post-modern perspective on curriculum.* New York: Teachers College Press.

Durkheim, E. (1961). *Moral education: A study in the theory and application of the sociology of education.* New York: Free Press.

Dweck, C. S. (2007). *Mindset: The new psychology of success.* New York: Ballantine Books.

Folsom, C. (1998). From a distance: Joining the mind and moral character. *Roeper Review, 20*(4), 260–270.

Folsom, C. (2004). Complex teaching and learning: Connecting teacher education to student performance. In E. Guyton (Ed.), *Association of teacher educators yearbook* (Vol. XII, pp. 205–231). Reston, VA: ATE.

Folsom, C. (2008). Teaching for intellectual and emotional learning (TIEL): A model for creating powerful curriculum. Lanham, MD: Rowman & Littlefield.

Folsom, C. (2009). *Teaching for intellectual and emotional learning (TIEL): A model for creating powerful curriculum.* Lanham, MD: Rowman & Littlefield Education.

Frankena, W. K. (1970). The concept of morality. In G. Wallace & A. D. M. Walker (Eds.), *The definition of morality* (pp. 146–173). London: Camelot Press.

Gilligan, C. (1993). *In a different voice: Psychological theory and women's development.* Cambridge, MA: Harvard University Press.

Greene, M. (1988). *The dialectic of freedom.* New York: Teachers College Press.

Guilford, J. P. (1968). *Intelligence, creativity, and their educational implications.* San Diego, CA: Robert R. Knapp.

Guilford, J. P. (1977). *Way beyond the IQ.* Buffalo, NY: Creative Education Foundation.

Hoffman, M. L. (1991). Empathy, social cognition, and moral action. In W. M. Kurtines & J. L. Gewirtz (Eds.), *Handbook of moral behavior and development* (Vol. 1: Theory, pp. 275–301). Hillsdale, NJ: Lawrence Erlbaum.

Hoffman, M. L. (2000). *Empathy and moral development: Implications for caring and justice.* New York: Cambridge University Press.

Howley, C. B., Howley, A., & Pendarvis, E. D. (1995). *Out of our minds: Anti-intellectualism and talent development in American schooling.* New York: Teachers College Press.

Jersild, A. T. (1955). *When teachers face themselves.* New York: Teachers College Press.

Kanevsky, L., & Keighley, T. (2003). To produce or not to produce? Understanding boredom and the honor in underachievement. *Roeper Review, 26*(1), 20–28.

Kohlberg, L. (1978). The cognitive developmental approach to moral education. In P. Scharf (Ed.), *Readings in moral education* (pp. 36–51). Minneapolis, MN: Winston Press.

Kramer, D. A. (1990). Conceptualizing wisdom: The primacy of affect-cognition relations. In R. J. Sternberg (Ed.), Wisdom: Its nature, origins, and development (pp. 279–313). New York: Cambridge University Press.

Kwak, D. (2008). Re-conceptualizing critical thinking for moral education in culturally plural societies. In M. Mason (Ed.), Critical thinking and learning (pp. 120–130). Richmond, Victoria, Australia: Blackwell.

Labouvie-Vief, G. (1990). Wisdom as integrated thought: Historical and developmental perspectives. In R. J. Sternberg (Ed.), *Wisdom: Its nature, origins, and development* (pp. 52–83). New York: Cambridge University Press.

Lewis, A., & Smith, D. (1993). Defining higher order thinking. *Theory into Practice, 32*(3), 131–137.

Lowry, L. (1993). *The giver.* New York: Bantam Doubleday Dell Books for Young Readers.

Marzano, R. J. (1993). How classroom teachers approach the teaching of thinking. *Theory into Practice, 32*(3), 154–160.

Maslow, A. H. (1971). *The farther reaches of human nature.* Oxford, UK: Viking.

McNamee, A. S., Zakin, A., Saravia-Shore, M., Ross, A. L., Peloso, J.M., Dubetz, N.E., Folsom, C., Mercurio, M., Morales-Flores, J., Fairbank, H., & Iurato, J. P. (2008). A renaissance of the arts in classrooms: A collaboration between a college, a public school and an arts institution. In C. J. Craig & L. F. Deretchin (Eds.), *Imagining a renaissance in teacher education. Teacher education yearbook* (Vol. 16, pp. 328–347). Lanham, MD: Rowman & Littlefield Education.

Meeker, M. (1979). *A structure of intellect.* El Segundo, CA: SOI Institute.

Monroe, K. R. (1996). *The heart of altruism: Perceptions of a common humanity.* Princeton, NJ: Princeton University Press.

Morley, F. P. (1979). The essence of personalized teaching and learning. *Educational Leadership, 36*(8), 590–594.

Noddings, N. (1984). *Caring: A feminine approach to ethics & moral education.* Berkeley, CA: University of California Press.

Noddings, N. (2005). Caring in education. *The encyclopedia of informal education*. Retrieved July 12, 2008, from www.infed.org/biblio/noddings_caring_in_education.htm.

Paul, R. (1995). *Critical thinking: How to prepare students for a rapidly changing world*. Santa Rosa, CA: Foundation for Critical Thinking.

Sisk, D. (2008). Engaging the spiritual intelligence of gifted students to build global awareness in the classroom. *Roeper Review, 30*(1), 24–30.

Sternberg, R. J. (1985). *Beyond IQ: A triarchic theory of human intelligence*. New York: Cambridge University Press.

Sternberg, R. J. (2000). Wisdom as a form of giftedness. *Gifted Child Quarterly, 4*(4), 252–260.

Tannenbaum, A. J. (1975). A backward and forward glance at the gifted. In W. B. Barbe & J. S. Renzulli (Eds.), *Psychology and education of the gifted* (pp. 21–31). New York: Irvington.

Vare, J. W. (1979). Moral education for the gifted: A confluent model. *Gifted Child Quarterly, 22*(3), 487–499.

Weiner, L. (1998). *Urban teaching: The essentials*. New York: Teachers College Press.

Whiteley, C. H. (1970). On defining 'moral.' In G. Wallace & A. D. M. Walker (Eds.), *The definition of morality* (pp. 21–25). London: Camelot Press.

Zeichner, K. M., & Liston, D. P. (1996). *Reflective teaching: An introduction*. Hillsdale, NJ: Lawrence Erlbaum.

Chapter 22
Moral Development in Preparing Gifted Students for Global Citizenship

Kay L. Gibson and Marjorie Landwehr-Brown

Abstract Gifted students have the potential to become tomorrow's world leaders with a strong grasp of the ethics and morality of issues related to global politics, economics, health, religions, and the environment. The heightened sensitivity of the gifted to justice, fairness, honesty, and a sense of responsibility to act on such ideals, accelerates the development of knowledge, attitudes and skills needed for global citizenship in the twenty-first century. If gifted students are provided with an appropriately challenging and respectful global curriculum, we can help them prepare to do good works with global impact. This chapter examines ways that global learning experiences in schools can encourage the gifted to adopt high ethical standards, moral behavior, and attitudes in order to lead our interconnected, interdependent, globalized world.

Keywords Altruism · Ethics · Giftedness · Global citizenship · Global learning · International education · Moral sensitivities · Morality · Universal consciousness · Values

> The next generation will be the stewards of our communities, nation and planet in extraordinarily critical times. In such times, the well-being of our society requires an involved, caring citizenry with good moral character.
>
> The Aspen Declaration (1992)
> Josephson Institute: Center for Youth Ethics

Since the time of Socrates, Plato, and Aristotle, education as a perpetuator of societal culture has included moral and ethical development in some form such as Socratic questioning, religious instruction, character education, values clarification, role-play activities, and moral dilemmas. At the same time, the teaching of ethics and morality

K.L. Gibson (✉)
Wichita State University, 1845 Fairmount, Wichita, KS 67260-0028, USA
e-mail: kay.gibson@wichita.edu

M. Landwehr-Brown
Douglass Public Schools, USD, 396 921 E. 1st St., Douglass, KS 67039
e-mail: mlb@usd396.net

D. Ambrose, T. Cross (eds.), *Morality, Ethics, and Gifted Minds*,
DOI: 10.1007/978-0-387-89368-6_22,
© Springer Science+Business Media LLC 2009

301

is not without conflict as evidenced by the execution of Socrates. Today, debate continues on four questions about teaching morality: Is it the responsibility of the education system to teach ethics? If so, how should it be taught? If one can teach ethics and morality, which values will be taught? Are there values that transcend cultural boundaries to a universal, active global conscience?

In the late twentieth century, rapid social and technological change, and multiple global crises changed the context of ethical decision-making and moral action (Ambrose 2007). The challenge in the twenty-first century is to develop a mindset which includes ethics and moral behavior needed for global citizenship. If people feel disenfranchised from the global community, then many immoral behaviors occur such as terrorism, international corporate fraud, and environmental plundering.

Families have traditionally been a main source for the development of ethics and morality in the individual (Josephson Institute: Center for Youth Ethics 1992). The primary role of schools has been "...to prepare the young to take their responsible place in and for the community...." (Starratt 1991, p. 191) including the propagation of cultural values. During the last 5 decades, the traditional family unit has been dramatically evolving in response to a rapidly changing world. The family has been redefined in such terms as membership, gender roles, transient lifestyles, and a shift from rural to urban communities. As the family unit has changed, society has come to depend more on schools to perpetuate values and social norms in the next generation.

Modes of communication for human interaction have also evolved in the same time period faster than ever before (Adams and Carfagna 2006). New communication technologies, particularly the Internet, have had an enormous influence on the way students socialize, communicate, and internalize ethics and moral behavior. Human interactions have been reduced in this virtual world, thus decreasing traditional opportunities for cultural transmission. In turn, students' sense of belonging to the community can be weakened and an associated lack of commitment to other members of the community may be created. Gifted students with their heightened sensitivities to moral issues such as justice, fairness, honesty and a sense of moral responsibility (Lovecky 1997; Piechowski 1986, 1991) are more vulnerable to feelings of alienation, despair and cynicism (Sword 2002) in a world where modern technologies continue to restructure human interactions.

As the twenty-first century globalized community advances, a need for ethical and moral leaders is paramount for dealing with global challenges. Marland's (1972) definition of gifted children provides six areas, including leadership, in which gifted children may demonstrate achievement and/or potential ability. "Gifted persons have a moral duty to be morally developed, to refine their leadership skills and to make an especial contribution to society and the solution of social problems" (Jewell 2001). Hence, we as educators must develop in gifted students, the potential leaders of tomorrow, an active universal consciousness with a sense of empowerment and connection to humanity that is needed to achieve good works as integral to global citizenship.

Ethics and morality are inexorably linked to a universal consciousness. Definitions of ethics and morality and their relationship have been debated since the mid-1900s. Originally, Kohlberg's (1969) book *Development of Moral Thought and Action* treated the two as one by virtue of his use of moral dilemmas in which objective reasoning was to be used to obtain an ethical decision. In later life, Kohlberg (1981) acknowledged that moral questions could not be answered without considering 'reasons of the heart' and talked of a higher final stage in his theory which encompassed moral questions that required affective as well as cognitive responses (Hague 1998).

Today, scholars usually make a distinction between ethics and morality, saying that one should make ethical decisions and then put those decisions into moral practice. As a proponent of this view, Hague (1998) recommended going beyond intellectualizing morals to moral behavior, asserting that Kohlberg restricted morality to the cognitive domain and "failed to touch the full scope of human qualities" (p. 170). When one consistently puts into practice ethical decisions, one is considered to be living a moral life (Hague). To further clarify the distinction, Ambrose (2007) compared ethics and morality to theory and practice. Hague alluded to this idea of two concepts referring to two aspects of morality, judgment and action. Jewell (2001) defined morality simply as "choosing to behave in appropriate ways towards others" (p. 3), while Hague called morality "a holistic response to life" (p. 17). In general, the literature views ethics as making decisions based on a value system, while morality is seen as transferring those decisions into action.

Ambrose (2007) discussed another type of altruism that does "not come from rational calculation but instead happen(s) naturally, reflexively.... The identity of self as naturally intertwined with humanity seems to drive the altruist's actions" (p. 5). This is the altruism that defines a person with a fully developed consciousness. Gewirth (1998) called this universalist morality in which a person's identity is based on their perception of being interconnected to the whole of humanity, not as an individual or member of a selective group. Such a person views their actions, values, and life as a part of the whole of humanity, interconnected and interdependent with one another (Bahá'í 1993; Frey 2003).

This morality should not be confused with rational choice theory where the individual does good work so that the recipient will be indebted to the provider, creating a repayment type of morality known as reciprocal altruism (Ambrose 2007). Although some universal good may randomly occur with this type of morality, there is a concern that if a person does not see any individual benefit, moral behavior will be less likely to occur. Ambrose emphasizes that a requisite of true altruistic behavior is feeling a connectedness, a oneness with humanity, which is the antithesis of individualistic morality.

22.1 Teaching Ethics

Ambrose (2007) posed the question: "Is it possible to teach young people to behave in morally responsible ways?" (p. 12). Assuming educators do have the ability to teach morality, and that the twenty-first century global society requires graduates who possess a global consciousness, schools must examine effective strategies by which the values, skills and attributes associated with morality can be transmitted.

22.1.1 Kohlberg's Moral Development Model

Kohlberg's Moral Development model has long been the educational cornerstone for the creation of curriculum involving ethics and morality. However, his moral dilemmas are incomplete in their scope and fall short of putting ethical decisions into moral actions (Hague 1998; Jewell 2001). The moral dilemmas limit the development of moral role models and leadership (Hague).

Another concern is that Kohlberg's (1981) moral dilemmas are hypothetical as opposed to real world (Jewell 2001). If a person provides a morally correct response to a hypothetical dilemma, there is no guarantee of translation to moral action. "It is fascinating to entertain moral dilemmas: it is challenging to advance to moral action. It is even more challenging to follow through with a consistent theme of a moral life" (Hague 1998, p. 170). A strong correlation between ethical decision making and moral actions is lacking in Kohlberg's dilemmas (Jewell). Performance on the moral dilemma level does not reflect real life responses.

22.1.2 Dabrowski's Theory of Positive Disintegration

Dabrowski's Theory of Positive Disintegration holds promise as a more comprehensive approach when developing ethics and morality instruction (Hague 1998; Piechowski 1979; Piirto 2005; Sword 2002). Dabrowski's theory states that when normal expectations are challenged, internally and/or externally, then a positive disintegration can occur, resulting in a progression to a higher level of psychological development, at varying rate, depending on developmental potential. Three factors determine the developmental potential to which an individual can progress after the positive disintegration: natural and physical characteristics, social influences, and the individual's psychological development (Mika 2005). The third factor, named "active conscience," is the foundation that guides moral behavior, leading one to accept responses that are aligned with personal values and rejecting unacceptable choices.

The specific Dabrowski levels IV: Organized Multilevel Disintegration, and V: Secondary Integration are the most relevant to the development of moral behavior and an active universal conscience. Level IV details internal personal growth and behavior consisting of service to others, previously identified as an element of altruism. Level V apexes when "selflessness and a sense of universal unity prevail" (Piirto 2005, p. 107), resulting in a universal consciousness. When Dabrowski's theory is used to guide the teaching of ethics and morality, the question for educators should be, "Does the instruction require students to develop this altruistic behavior required of Dabrowski's levels IV and V?"

22.1.3 Maslow's Hierarchy of Needs

Another approach worth consideration when planning ethics and morality instruction for gifted students would be Maslow's Hierarchy of Needs. Maslow and Lowery (1998) identified Level 8 Self-Transcendence, the level of personal development in his *Hierarchy of Needs* that is similar to Dabrowski's level V (Piirto 2005). Self-transcendence relates to the interconnectedness of humanity as the highest level of an individual's development. Maslow concluded that as one transcends ego, one develops wisdom and thus moral behavior becomes an unconscious act (Huitt 2004). Moral characteristics in Dabrowski's Levels IV and V and Maslow's Level 8 are linked to emotional aspects of human development which ultimately result in high levels of moral sensitivity.

22.2 Gifted Characteristics

Giftedness is most often associated with a high cognitive ability. Yet, when considering global events and societal injustices, gifted children often demonstrate high levels of idealism and moral sensitivities, such as truthfulness and fair play (Lee and Olszewski-Kubilius 2006; Piechowski 1991; Sword 2002; Terman 1925). The dichotomy of "what is" versus "what should be" is deeply troublesome for many gifted children (Webb et al. 2007). These concerns with social justice and truth are desirable in an increasingly interconnected, global world where being "...actively concerned ... is the only true moral state..." (Hague 1998, p. 171). However, such sensitivities can cause a sense of hopelessness and cynicism in gifted children living in an individualistic society rather than an altruistic society built on collaboration and collectivism (Ambrose 2007; Sword 2002).

Inclusion of nonintellectual characteristics extends the concept of giftedness beyond academic potential to encompass such characteristics "... as emotional, moral, or ethical sensitivity and leadership ability..." (Lee and Olszewski-Kubilius 2006, p. 29). Piechowski (1991) pointed out that moral characteristics are critical to the growth and maturation of high levels of moral sensitivity. With the successful integration of high cognitive ability, creativity, and heightened sensitivities, comes wise leaders who capably choose short term and long term goals for the common good, balancing the interest of themselves and others, in a variety of settings (Craft et al. 2008; Sternberg 2007). "If ... (gifted children) ... are to be our future leaders ... the values they hold are important because they will influence ... future decisions and actions" needed to do good works of global importance (Piirto 2005, p. 116).

Should there be a higher moral responsibility for ethical thought and behavior from gifted people? Gifted people have a duty, a noble obligation, to develop their moral sensitivities and leadership skills for the good of humanity, "...to make an especial contribution to society and the solution of social problems" (Jewell 2001, p. 3). A student in Shi-Shi #1 High School, Chengdu, China, demonstrated his sense of noble obligation in a conversation discussing the topic of holding the same expectations for all students. He likened this perspective to climbing a hill: "Everyone gets a chance to climb. Those of us who can reach the top have the responsibility to make life better for those who cannot climb the hill for whatever reason" (M. Landwehr-Brown personal communication, June, 2005).

22.3 Global Citizenship

Citizenship suggests intrinsically based motivation in support of an organization that goes beyond a self-serving orientation (Frey 2003). The term "global citizen" holds a variety of meanings depending on the perceptions and beliefs of a person. The literature provides no consistent definition, but some aspects of world or global citizenship are repeatedly described.

A basic premise of global citizenship is the understanding of the interconnectedness and interdependence of humanity and an acceptance of universal responsibility leading to global consciousness (Bahá'í 1993; Frey 2003). A global perspective is necessary for the achievement of "a common (sustainable) future and for solving our common problems" (Osler and Vincent 2002, p. 125). Without a sense of belonging as a citizen in the global community, an individual's contributions of global significance are unlikely (Osler and Vincent).

Other aspects of global citizenship from the literature include a "shared vision of basic values to provide an ethical foundation for the emerging world community" (Earth Charter 2000, n.p.), an appreciation of diversity (James, 2005; Osler and Vincent 2002; Oxfam 2006), an imperative for social and economic justice (Bahá'í 1993; Earth Charter; Oxfam) sacrifice for the common good (Bahá'í), and an active community involvement at the local, national, and global levels (Bahá'í; Osler and Vincent; Oxfam). Global citizenship, in a general sense, implies a stewardship towards humanity and the environment.

Some have objections to the concept of global citizenship, fearing the "... abandonment of legitimate loyalties, the suppression of cultural diversity, the abolition of national autonomy, ... (and) the imposition of uniformity" (Bahá'í 1993). These fears are created by a lack of understanding. Global citizenship does not imply a world government or the decline of rational allegiance to a nation or a single global culture. Global citizenship does not replace national citizenship; rather it is an extension of citizenship to the global level. Global citizens have "a sense of universal responsibility, identifying ... with the whole Earth community as well as ... local communities. We are at once citizens of different nations and of one world in which the local and global are linked" (Earth Charter 2000, n.p.).

Table 22.1 Details of the knowledge, attitudes and skills of a global citizen

Global citizen aspect	Details
Knowledge	Understanding of culture, awareness of the interconnectedness and interdependence of humanity and the world, peace and conflict, nature and environment, and possible future scenarios for an equitable and sustainable world
Attitudes and values	Appreciation of human dignity, respecting diversity with empathy toward other cultures and perspectives, caring, tolerance, compassion, valuing justice, trustworthiness, fairness, curiosity about global issues and conditions, willingness to sacrifice for the common good, and a sense of universal responsibility
Skills	Research and inquiry skills, interpersonal skills, intrapersonal skills, non-adversarial decision-making, conflict resolution, collaboration, theory testing, leadership, critical thinking skills, communication skills and political skills essential for civic engagement

The knowledge, skills, and attitudes of a global citizen are essential for creating viable solutions to global concerns that now confront us such as political conflicts, environmental destruction, economic disparity, terrorism, accessibility of natural resources, and violation of human rights (Merryfield 2002; Noddings 2005). What are the knowledge, skills, and attitudes requisite for a global citizen?

Table 22.1 is an elaboration from Gibson et al. 2008) based on the work of Fisher and Hicks (1985) and Oxfam (2006). Further descriptions of a global citizen's knowledge, skills and attitudes were included from Bahá'í (1993), Earth Charter (2000), James (2005), and Josephson Institute (1992).

Taking action as a responsible global citizen (see Table 22.1), places us in a situation where it is necessary to have knowledge and understanding of others' cultures and perspectives. Geographical, and historical knowledge, particularly concerned with environmental and peace issues, is required to create and implement future scenarios for an equitable and sustainable world. In addition, a global citizen needs knowledge of the political, religious, and economic forces in order to establish a peaceful co-existence in a globalized world.

To utilize this knowledge productively, global citizens "need a shared vision of basic values to provide an ethical foundation for the emerging world community" (Earth Charter 2000, n.p.). As an understanding of the interconnectedness and interdependence of the world is developed, values such as compassion, tolerance, trustworthiness, fairness, respect for diversity, as well as appreciation of human dignity, promote a sense of universal responsibility.

With recognition of basic global citizenship values comes responsibility to advance the common good. Such universal responsibility depends on interpersonal skills such as communication, collaboration, leadership in addition to nonadversarial decision making and conflict resolution. Other fundamental abilities of a global citizen include research and inquiry skills to provide the foundation for global change.

22.4 Global Learning

"Teachers ... face the challenge of teaching for equity, justice and solidarity in contexts where their students are all too aware of inequality and injustice..." (Osler and Vincent 2002, p. 1). Although gifted people may possess high cognitive ability, it is not safe to assume that they also possess the knowledge, attitudes and skills of a moral, global citizen. A global citizen's active universal consciousness leads to the achievement of an equitable and sustainable world through good works. Hence, educators must develop in gifted students a sense of empowerment, leadership, and connection to the global community; and a commitment to the ideals of noble obligation and global citizenship. Global learning is an effective method for teaching gifted students the ethical and moral behaviors required for the twenty-first century global citizen.

Global learning has aspects of multicultural education, character education, global education, international education, and moral development education. All of these educational approaches foster the development of similar knowledge, attitudes and skills within a multi-cultural context with the goal of ethical and moral communities (Banks and Banks 1995; Husén and Postlethwaite 1985 cited in James 2005; Josephson Institute 1992). However, global learning expands the goal beyond national boundaries by focusing on global issues instead of local, through student-to-student relationships. Students are connected through modern communication technologies such as email, podcasting, wikis, and videoconferencing to work in intercultural teams on authentic, real-world problems or tasks. Through global learning experiences, students develop multiple perspectives and the moral behaviors of a global citizen with a universal consciousness.

22.5 The Global Learning Curriculum Development Model

Global citizenship knowledge, attitudes, and skills are essential for the development of a sustainable, equitable world (Merryfield 2002; Noddings 2005). Moral behavior cannot be developed by reading or discussing scenarios such as Kohlberg's (1981) moral dilemmas. Ethical decision making does not necessarily translate into moral behavior and ultimately, universal consciousness (Hague 1998). Educators need direction in guiding gifted students as they develop into global citizens with the knowledge, attitudes, and skills necessary for a moral life. The Global Learning Curriculum Development Model (GL-CDM) provides a comprehensive approach for designing global learning opportunities.

Global learning curriculum provides educational settings in which students use modern communication technologies to interact across cultures with diverse populations to acquire multiple perspectives and develop the knowledge, attitudes, and skills of a global citizen (see Table 22.1). Design conditions for global learning indicated in the GL-CDM include the degrees of cultural contrast, availability of communication technologies, and a purposeful and authentic goal that can only be achieved through collaborative, intercultural teams.

Figure 22.1 shows the processes and attributes used in global learning. It is assumed that learners have a basic level of the attributes and prior experiences in

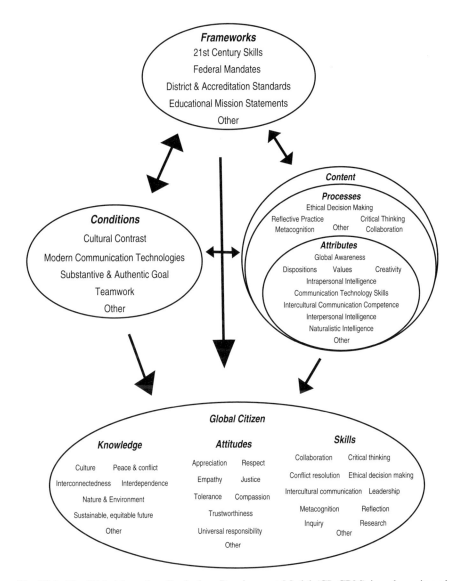

Fig. 22.1 The Global Learning Curriculum Development Model (GL-CDM) is a dynamic and interactive approach to designing global learning opportunities that result in students who are twenty-first century global citizens. Curriculum planners consider the frameworks and conditions as parameters for the project that is to be developed. As well, the processes and attributes related to learner outcomes are identified. The three elements of frameworks, conditions, and processes and attributes are examined in relation to one another and to the ultimate outcome of each student as a global citizen to ensure a successful global learning experience for the learners

using the processes identified in the GL-CDM. The symbiotic interactions between the processes and attributes stimulate the growth of both. For example, it is impossible to collaborate (process) without some degree of intercultural communication and interpersonal intelligence (attributes). The attributes and processes cultivated in global learning are integral to the development of the knowledge, attitudes, and skills of a global citizen. Each additional global learning experience increases the student's mastery level of the processes and attributes related to global citizenship and a universal consciousness.

22.6 Conclusion

Ethics and morality have been taught using a variety of methods since the time of Socrates, but never in the context of a globalized world that now confronts educators. The rapid advancement of communication technology has forever altered human interactions and relationships while changes in the traditional family unit have placed greater responsibility for the teaching of ethics and morality on education systems.

The educational challenge in the twenty-first century is to develop in students the ethics and moral behavior needed for global citizenship. Gifted students' heightened sensitivity to universal responsibility accelerates the acquisition of knowledge, attitudes, and skills needed by a global citizen.

To develop ethics and morality, educators in the past have relied on such approaches as character education, role-playing and Kohlberg's (1981) moral dilemmas. But working with hypothetical situations lacks the essential transfer of ethical thought to moral action leading to automaticity of behavior.

Global learning holds promise as an educational approach to nurture students for their role as future global citizens by fostering the knowledge, attitudes and skills necessary to take on the responsibilities of a moral life. Through modern communication technologies, students have opportunities in global learning to build intercultural relationships across cultures based on shared ideals and goals and an acceptance of differences. This "unity in diversity" (Bahá'í 1993, n.p.) promotes a sense of belonging to the global community as well as the altruistic desire to sacrifice for the common good.

Global learning projects require the participation and collaboration of intercultural teams in order to make ethical decisions that take into account the circumstances of all stakeholders in addition to the interdependence and interconnectedness of the world. The process of completing an authentic, substantive task within a global learning project requires students to put these decisions into practice. Global learning projects, therefore, require students to go beyond the moral intellectualizing found in Kohlberg's (1981) dilemmas to practice and internalize behaviors of Hague's (1998) moral life.

Using the Global Learning Curriculum Development Model (GL-CDM), educators can create intercultural opportunities for gifted minds that facilitate achievement of an attitude of selflessness (Dabrowski 1967) and transcendence beyond one's ego (Maslow and Lowery 1998) to a universal consciousness. Global learning experiences increase participants' understanding of the interconnectedness and interdependence of the world, appreciation of life and human dignity, and a sense of responsibility towards humanity and the environment. The knowledge, skills, and attitudes acquired in global learning are the foundation for the responsible, moral actions of a global citizen.

> We stand at a critical moment in Earth's history, a time when humanity must choose its future. As the world becomes increasingly interdependent and fragile, the future at once holds great peril and great promise. To move forward we must recognize that in the midst of a magnificent diversity of cultures and life forms we are one human family and one Earth community with a common destiny. We must join together to bring forth a sustainable global society founded on respect for nature, universal human rights, economic justice, and a culture of peace. Towards this end, it is imperative that we, the peoples of Earth, declare our responsibility to one another, to the greater community of life, and to future generations. (Earth Charter 2000, n.p.)

At no time in history has the need for ethical decision making and moral behavior been more critical to the survival of not only humanity, but also the entire world. Global learning programs can help to meet the challenge of developing twenty-first century citizens who appreciate the diversity of cultures, yet who understand the interconnectedness and interdependence of the world. Citizens who value human dignity and justice, and possess a sense of universal responsibility; and who have attained skills such as leadership, communication, critical thinking and collaboration necessary to practice moral behavior in order to ensure an equitable, sustainable future – true global citizens for the twenty-first century.

References

Adams, J. M., & Carfagna, A. (2006). *Coming of age in a globalized world: The next generation.* Bloomfield, CT: Kumarian Press.

Ambrose, D. (2007, November). *Morality and giftedness: From pure altruism to malevolence.* Paper presented at the annual meeting of the National Association for Gifted Children, Minneapolis, MN.

Bahá'í International Community Statement Library. (1993). *World citizenship: A global ethic for sustainable development.* Retrieved June 16, 2008 from http://www.bic-un.bahai.org/93–0614.htm

Banks, J. A., & Banks, C. A. M. (Eds). (1995). *Handbook of research on multicultural education.* New York: Macmillan

Craft, A., Gardner, H., & Claxton, G. (Eds.). (2008). *Creativity, wisdom, and trusteeship: Exploring the role of education.* Thousand Oaks, CA: Corwin Press.

Dabrowski, K. (1967). *Personality shaping through positive disintegration.* Boston, MA: Little Brown.

Earth Charter. (2000). *Earth Charter Preamble.* Retrieved February 2, 2008 from http://www.earthcharterus.org/about-earth-charter/the-earth-charter/the-earth-charter.html

Fisher, S., & Hicks, D. (1985). *World studies 8–13: A teacher's handbook.* London: Oliver & Boyd.

Frey, B. S. (2003). Flexible citizenship for a global society. *Politics, Philosophy & Economics, 2*(1), 93–114.

Gewirth, A. (1998). *Self-fulfillment.* Princeton, NJ: Princeton University Press.

Gibson, K. L., Rimmington, G. M., & Landwehr-Brown, M. (2008). Developing global awareness and responsible world citizenship with global learning. *Roeper Review, 30*(1), 11–23.

Hague, W. J. (1998). Is there moral giftedness? *Gifted Education International, 12*(3), 170–174.

Huitt, W. (2004). Maslow's hierarchy of needs. *Educational Psychology Interactive.* Valdosta, GA: Valdosta State University. Retrieved June 16, 2008 from http://chiron.valdosta.edu/whuitt/col/regsys/maslow.html

James, K. (2005). International education: The concept, and its relationship to intercultural education. *Journal of Research in International Education, 4*(3), 313–332.

Jewell, P. (2001). *Measuring moral development: Feeling, thinking, and doing.* Adelaide, Australia: The Flinders University of South Australia. (ERIC Document Reproduction Service No. 457646).

Josephson Institute: Center for Youth Ethics. (1992). *The Aspen Declaration.* Retrieved June 13, 2008 from http://charactercounts.org/overview/aspen.html

Kohlberg, L. (1969). *Stages in the development of moral thought and action.* New York: Holt, Rinehart & Winston.

Kohlberg, L. (1981). *Philosophy of moral development: Moral stages and the idea of justice.* San Francisco, CA: Harper & Row.

Lee, S.-Y., & Olszewski-Kubilius, P. (2006). The emotional intelligence, moral judgment, and leadership of academically gifted adolescents. Journal for the *Education of the Gifted, 30*(1), 29–67.

Lovecky, D. V. (1997). Identity development in gifted children: Moral sensitivity. *Roeper Review, 20*(2), 90–94.

Marland, S. P., Jr. (1972). *Education of the gifted and talented, Volume 1. Report to the Congress of the United States by the U.S. Commissioner of Education.* Washington, DC: U.S. Government Printing Office.

Maslow, A., & Lowery, R. (Ed.). (1998). *Toward a psychology of being* (3rd ed.). New York: Wiley.

Merryfield, M. M. (2002). The difference a global educator can make. *Educational Leadership, 60*(2), 18–21.

Mika, E. (2005). Theory of positive disintegration as a model of personality development for exceptional individuals. *Perspectives in gifted education: Complexities of emotional development, spirituality and hope, 3,* 1–2. Retrieved June 15, 2008 from http://talentdevelop.com/articles/TOPDAAM2.html

Noddings, N. (Ed). (2005). *Educating citizens for global awareness.* New York: Teachers College Press.

Osler, A., & Vincent, K. (2002). *Citizenship and the challenge of global education.* Wiltshire, UK: Cromwell Press.

Oxfam. (2006). *Education for global citizenship: A guide for schools.* Retrieved January 24, 2008 from www.oxfam.org.uk/coolplanet/teachers/globciti/wholeschool/getstarted.htm

Piechowski, M. M. (1979). Developmental potential. In N. Colangelo & R. T. Zaffrann (Eds.), *New voices in counseling the gifted* (pp. 25–57). Dubuque, IA: Kendall/Hunt.

Piechowski, M. M. (1986). The concept of developmental potential. *Roeper Review, 8,* 190–197.

Piechowski, M. M. (1991). Emotional development and emotional giftedness. In N. Colangelo & G. Davis (Eds.), *Handbook of gifted education* (pp. 285–306). Boston, MA: Allyn & Bacon.

Piirto, J. (2005). I live in my own bubble: The values of talented adolescents. *Journal of Secondary Gifted Education, 16*(2–3), 106–118.

Starratt, R. J. (1991). Building an ethical school: A theory for practice in educational leadership. *Education Administration Quarterly, 27*(2), 185–202.

Sternberg, R. J. (2007). A systems model of leadership. *American Psychologist, 62*(1), 34–42.

Sword, L. (2002). *Gifted children: Emotionally immature or emotionally intense.* Retrieved March 10, 2008 from http://www.giftedservices.com.au

Terman, L. M. (1925). *Genetic studies of genius: Mental and physical traits of a thousand gifted children.* Stanford, CA: Stanford University Press.

Webb, J. T., Gore, J. L., Amend, E. R., & DeVries, A. R. (2007). *A parent's guide to gifted children.* Scottsdale, AZ: Great Potential Press.

Chapter 23
Growing Up Smart and Criminal

Maureen Neihart

Abstract Criminals don't just show up, they grow up. The precursors to adult criminal activity can be observed in some children as early as the preschool years and some authorities believe that antisocial patterns of behavior are established by age 10. In many cases, the developing criminal mind is evident by mid to late adolescence. What does it look like and what can we do to intervene when we recognize it? A national spotlight on bright minds that act violently against others contributes to the popular notion that a latent vulnerability lies in some gifted children. Is there any empirical evidence to support this idea? These are the questions this chapter attempts to answer, first by summarizing what we know about the prevalence of antisocial behavior among gifted youth and about the development of antisocial behavior in children in general, and then by describing a cognitive model that has been effective in preventing and reducing antisocial behavior in children and adolescents of wide ranging ability levels.

Keywords Antisocial adolescent · Conduct disorder · Criminal · Criminal logic · Delinquent · Empathy · Gifted · Moral · Thinking errors

Syllogistically, it has been argued and implied that a gifted child's sensitivities, heightened arousal, intelligence, and need for connection and challenge may lay a foundation for pathology if the child is placed in a rejecting or marginalizing environment. It's argued that years of covert and overt social rejection, benign neglect, or even ridicule and humiliation may push some children to greater identification with out-groups as a way to meet their basic human needs for belonging and empowerment (Mahoney 1980; Seeley 1993; Mahoney and Seeley 1982). There is no systematic research to support this proposition. The broad research on the development of antisocial behavior consistently finds significantly higher rates of *lower than average* verbal intelligence among antisocial children, youth, and adults. It also

M. Neihart
Psychological Studies Academic Group, Blk 2 Level 3 Room 78, National Institute of Education, 1 Nanyang Walk, Singapore 637616
e-mail: maureenneihart@gmail.com; maureen.neihart@nie.edu.sg

D. Ambrose, T. Cross (eds.), *Morality, Ethics, and Gifted Minds*,
DOI: 10.1007/978-0-387-89368-6_23,
© Springer Science+Business Media LLC 2009

observes that high verbal ability is *negatively correlated* with the development of antisocial behavior (Bassarath 2001; Caplan and Powell 1964; Farrington 1989; Garland and Ziegler 1999; Gath and Tennet 1972; Mahoney 1980; Neihart 2002; West and Farrington 1973; Young 1999). In addition, broader studies of problem behavior among high ability children have consistently reported rates of maladjustment that are either similar or lower than what is reported in the general child and adolescent population (Garland and Ziegler 1999; Neihart et al. 2002). A few studies have observed a higher than expected incidence of high practical intelligence (Seeley 1993), and patterns of twice exceptionality (e.g. high Performance IQ with lower Verbal IQ) in juvenile delinquents (Gath et al. 1971; Mahoney and Seeley 1982; Seeley 1984).

Theoretically, it makes sense that gifted children would have a lower risk for antisocial behavior given that they are often characterized as demonstrating advanced moral reasoning and a great capacity for empathy (see chapters by Lovecky, Silverman, or Piechowski in this volume, for example). However, it is important to note that the available research is very limited because it relies on traditionally narrow definitions of intelligence and giftedness and often fails to investigate broader, more contemporary conceptions of either.

The most reasonable conclusions we can draw from the literature for now are that antisocial behavior seems to be less prevalent among youth with high verbal ability and that we know almost nothing about the relationship between the development of antisocial behavior and other kinds of superior abilities. We do, however, know quite a bit about the developmental trajectories of antisocial behavior in children and its prevention and effective intervention.

23.1 Characteristics of Antisocial Youth

Antisocial individuals of any age are those who persistently break the rules and violate the norms of accepted social behavior. They seem to have little concern for the needs or wishes of others unless they can manipulate them to get something they want. Various estimates suggest that anywhere from 2–16% of children and adolescents exhibit antisocial tendencies (American Psychological Association 1994; Samenow 1998). However, crime statistics, especially among juveniles, are confounded by inconsistency in terminology. Clinically, antisocial children are said to have a *conduct disorder.* Legally, they are said to be *delinquent.* Both are characterized by persistent rule breaking behavior, but *delinquent* is the term used for minors who have been criminally charged for their rule breaking behavior while *conduct disordered* is the diagnostic term used to describe children who have engaged in serious aggressive behaviors such as stealing, fighting, firesetting, or forced sexual activity (American Psychological Association 1994). Clearly, some conduct-disordered youth will be charged for their offenses, but many will not. Similarly, a subset of delinquents will be diagnosed with a conduct disorder, but many will not. Such distinctions make accurate estimates of antisocial behavior among young people nearly impossible.

Antisocial children are often described as having several or all of the following characteristics (Rutter et al. 1998; Samenow 1998; Young 1999).

A Sense of Entitlement:

- Tries to control others to enhance his own sense of power
- Argues for the sake of arguing
- Capitalizes on the weaknesses of others
- A loner
- Associates with people but doesn't really let anyone know him
- Skilled at telling people what they want to hear
- Rarely tells the whole story
- Acts prosocially when he stands to benefit
- Doesn't care what others think

Unrealistic expectations of self:

- Thinks great things should happen to him just because he showed up
- Doesn't cope well with or anticipate daily frustrations and setbacks
- Thinks he should succeed with minimal effort

Fearless:

- Engages in thrill-seeking behavior
- Reckless
- Manipulative

May look good:

- Can be charming and intelligent
- May appear conscientious and helpful
- Can change from anger to tears in a second
- Wins the trust and confidence of others and then preys upon them
- Regards himself to be a good, moral person
- Has just enough conscience to be dangerous
- Believes there are things he wouldn't do

How does it happen that some children grow up to persistently break the rules and violate the norms of acceptable social behavior? When does it begin and how is it maintained? Given the high rates of crime and violence in America, it's no surprise that considerable research has been devoted to understanding the nature of criminal thinking and behavior (Barriga and Gibbs 1996; Barriga et al. 2000; Beck 1999; Dodge et al. 1990; Eron et al. 1994; Farrington 1989; Holcomb and Kashani 1991; Keenan et al. 1999; Neihart 1999; Rutter et al. 1998; Seeley 1984; Tisak and Jankowski 1996; Yochelson and Samenow 1995). Most of this research is found in the fields of sociology, psychology, and criminal justice and is focused either on the developmental trajectories of antisocial behavior or the patterns of cognitive distortion in antisocial individuals. The research is clear that there are multiple pathways to antisocial behavior and that no single set of risk factors contributes. Rather, multiple factors contribute differentially to such outcomes and their contributions are offset by protective factors.

Strongly predictive risk factors include:

- A history of rule breaking behavior (the single best predictor of future rule break-ing behavior)
- Antisocial friends
- Passive leisure activities (e.g., computer games, hanging out at the mall)
- Weak social connections
- Substance use
- Gender (males are higher risk)
- Antisocial parents (whether the contribution is genetic or social learning is not clear)

Moderately predictive risk factors include:

- Early aggressive behavior
- Low socioeconomic status
- Harsh and inconsistent parental discipline and weak supervision
- Low school achievement and negative academic attitudes
- Low average IQ

However, it is important to note that most children growing up with multiple risk factors do not develop antisocial behaviors and attitudes, pointing to the power of protective factors – circumstances or characteristics that mitigate the impact of risk factors. Among these protective factors are being female, having a high verbal IQ, strong relationships with caring adults, involvement in extracurricular activities, and having a talent or skill (Bassarath 2001). It's also noteworthy that factors often perceived to contribute to the development of antisocial attitudes and behavior, such as parental abuse, divorce, family stress or conflict contribute negligibly or not at all (Bassarath).

Delayed or arrested moral and empathy development is an identified precursor to antisocial behavior in children (Keenan et al. 1999). Kohlberg's theory of moral reasoning development (1984) is the conceptual basis for understanding this delay. According to Kohlberg's theory, an individual's motivation for decisions about right and wrong behavior may be based on:

- Pursuing pleasure and avoiding pain
- An understanding of giving something to get something
- Getting someone's approval
- Respect for the rules or law
- Consideration of what is best for society
- Concern for justice and equality, ethical principles and conscience

When we're young, we make decisions about right and wrong behavior based largely on avoiding pain and pursuing pleasure, the lowest level of moral decision-making. It's simple and self-centered thinking. A common scenario illustrates this age-appropriate stage of moral reasoning.

Imagine that you are the parent of a 3 year old and you are baking chocolate chip cookies. When the oven timer goes off, you remove the tray of cookies and set it on the counter to cool. Your child, drawn by the tantalizing aroma, begs for a cookie. You explain that they are too hot to eat and ask your child to wait a few minutes. He is unhappy. Moments later you leave the room for a couple of minutes. What happens?

If the child can manage it, he will try to take a cookie. Small children often break the rules if doing so will gratify their immediate desires and if they believe they can get away with it. They comply with rules when they perceive the risk is high for disapproval or painful consequences if they do not.

Most children grow out of this stage quickly and begin to make decisions based on mutual reciprocity – the understanding that there are personal benefits for doing something for someone else. By adolescence, most have reached the stage at which decisions about right and wrong behavior are based on adhering to rules or societal norms. But some don't. Some children get stuck at the very lowest level, and live their adult lives making decisions based on avoiding pain and pursuing pleasure.

Imagine what life looks like for those who operate at this level of moral reasoning. How do they spend their day? What are their relationships like? How do they manage their obligations? People who make decisions about right and wrong behavior from the lowest developmental levels of moral reasoning frequently have poor educational and work histories. They perform poorly; drop out of school; and change jobs frequently. Their relationships are usually dysfunctional and they manage their obligations inconsistently at best. They are typically viewed by others to be irresponsible or self-absorbed.

Many antisocial individuals reach the second level of Kohlberg's stages of moral reasoning. They live by the motto, "I'll do this for you if you do this for me." This forms the basis of much group antisocial activity.

We witness the strengths and weaknesses of this level of moral reasoning when we observe the friendships of third graders. This is often the age at which children first encounter the pleasures and pains of having a best friend. They may be inseparable at school and very generous and protective of one another. But should a bad turn come about – in a moment of envy, greed or anger – and one child does something hurtful to his friend, the result is retaliation. The problem at this stage of moral development is that revenge is justified. One bad turn deserves another and retaliations can escalate until an adult intervenes. Many criminals operate at this stage of moral development. It is popularly referred to as the "criminal code." They make decisions about right and wrong behavior based on pursuing pleasure, avoiding pain, and doing something to get something.

23.2 How Can We Prevent Antisocial Behavior in Children?

The starting point for preventing antisocial behavior is to recognize it when it appears and hold children accountable. We need to resist our tendencies to make excuses for it. Samenow (1998) specifically identifies seven common errors adults make when working with antisocial children:

- They deny there's a problem
- They fail to be consistent and firm with their expectations and don't use their leverage to motivate change
- They let the child play one authority against another (e.g., school vs. home)
- They blame themselves for the child's problems
- They don't demand trustworthiness and accountability
- They allow excuses
- They persist in looking for explanations for the child's behavior

Most people who choose to work with children or adolescents do so because they genuinely care about their well-being. They are compassionate, concerned adults who are willing to set aside their own needs and interests in order to make the world a better place for a child. No one wants to think the worst about a child, especially an exceptionally intelligent, charming, or talented child, but it is precisely this tendency to look for explanations in the unfortunate circumstances of a child's family life or history that often prevents those closest to a child from intervening early when he or she begins to show signs of criminal thinking. If adults are naive or in denial about the realities of developing antisocial behavior in young people, they can make things worse by rationalizing or justifying their wrong behavior.

Let's take as an example an 11-year-old boy with superior intelligence and a charming personality. He is well liked by peers and adults. Imagine that he comes from a family where the parents are recently divorced and there is a history of substance abuse by the father and perhaps a moderate level of emotional neglect by the mother who is overwhelmed with demands since the divorce. And although he's been a relatively good student until now, he has let his work slip since he got into the sixth grade. He has some history of stealing: two episodes of shoplifting in the previous year, several questionable episodes of taking things from the drawers and pockets of his parents, and one incident 2 years ago where he "borrowed" a bike from a neighbor's garage. An additional concern of teachers is that he has a habit of not telling the whole story. He doesn't really tell lies, he just doesn't bother to tell, period.

Given just these facts alone, it's easy to see how caring parents and teachers might ignore his developing antisocial behavior. The parents feel guilty and responsible. They may blame themselves and the negative impact of the divorce for his problems. The teachers enjoy him; he is bright, charming and attractive. It doesn't even cross their minds that a serious problem may be developing. They don't see the problem lying with him, they see the problem lying with his life circumstances. Never mind that thousands of families go through the same life events every year and the children in those families don't choose to lie and steal. Never mind that this child has both and older and younger siblings who do not demonstrate these antisocial behaviors. Parents and school put the blame on external factors. If they do not recognize his developing antisocial thinking and intervene, it will continue. To change these harmful thinking patterns, the adults in this child's life must do two things together: hold him accountable, and help him to change.

It won't be easy. Antisocial children require a close eye and considerably more confrontation. There are likely to be more conflicts with them than with other children, and at the same time they give less back. It is hard work to be firm consistently and to follow through with consequences for all misbehavior, but essential to the child's future well-being is being held accountable and forced to accept the consequences of his or her wrong decisions. Adults must form a unified front, otherwise the smart manipulative child will play one adult against another. When one teacher holds him accountable, he may go to another and play the victim. When teachers confront him, he may say to the counselor, "You're the only one I can trust. You're the only person I feel safe with." What he means is that she's the one person left he can fool.

Bright, antisocial children can read others extremely well. They are on the lookout for vulnerable people from whom they can get something. If they find a weak spot in someone, they are likely to exploit it for their own gain if they think they will benefit. This is why antisocial children commonly pick friends who are vulnerable or weaker than them in some way. It gives them leverage and control and makes them look good to others.

They may also become especially adept at convincing others that their problems lie in external factors. The problem is that their parents don't understand. The problem is the stress they are under. It's their depression, the divorce. They learn what moves adults. Their ability to turn on the tears or to appear sincere in their concern heightens their effectiveness at not taking responsibility for their behavior.

Increasingly, the public is calling for holding adolescents accountable for their antisocial activity, but there is little mention outside of clinical psychology and criminal justice about what works to change their behavior. Some might think this is because no one is certain what would make a difference, but there is a considerable body of literature, spanning at least 3 decades, about what is effective in changing antisocial behavior. It begins with understanding criminal logic.

23.3 What Is Criminal Logic?

It's difficult for responsible, prosocial individuals to understand how the antisocial person thinks, because most of us assume others think like we do. "How can she do that?" we wonder when we hear about someone doing something unthinkable. Why do convicted criminals serve time in prison and upon release commit more crimes and get caught again? How can an intelligent child be caught red handed, confronted with the evidence, and remain steadfast in his lies that he was not the culprit? If we understood criminal logic, or the cognitive deficits that drive antisocial behavior, we would understand that antisocial people *think differently*. They manifest a particular kind of moral reasoning that allows them to violate the rights of others *and to feel justified* in doing so (Dodge et al. 1990; Kazdin 1994). This thinking is sometimes called *criminal logic*. Effective intervention appreciates this unique thinking style and attempts to change it.

Robust empirical evidence and wide consensus says that what drives antisocial behavior is faulty cognition, or *thinking errors* (Barriga et al. 2000; Bassarath

Table 23.1 Common thinking errors and some examples

Error	Explanation	Example
Blaming	Saying someone or something else is responsible for one's actions	"It's not my fault!" "She started it."
Making excuses	Justifying behavior	"I was abused." "My parents are getting divorced."
Denial	Refusing to acknowledge any truth about the situation	"I don't have a drug problem." "There's nothing wrong."
Minimizing	Avoiding full responsibility by making one's behavior seem smaller or less important	"I only touched him." "I just drink socially."
Playing the victim	Insisting that you're the one who's hurt rather than someone else	"No one's helping me." "I don't know how to do it."
Assuming	Taking it for granted that something is true rather than getting the facts	"She's racist." "He's sexist."
Changing the subject	Avoiding responsibility by diverting the conversation	"I don't know if anyone's told you, but my parents are getting divorced."

2001; Frey and Epkins 2002; Liau et al. 1998; Samenow 1998; Yochelson and Samenow 1995). These are inaccuracies that skew the truth about a situation, thus allowing a person to believe they are justified in their wrong behavior. Everyone makes thinking errors some of the time, but they are common and pervasive in antisocial individuals. Table 23.1 lists some of the most common thinking errors with examples.

A slightly different framework based on the same concept of faulty thinking and arrested moral development is used in corrections and law enforcement to explain antisocial motivation (National Institute of Corrections 1996; see Fig. 23.1).

This framework says that antisocial individuals are motivated by one or more of five needs: to look good, be in control, feel good, be right, and have power. These needs motivate their behavior to dehumanize or put others down and to engage in frequent power struggles. This perspective maintains that in nearly everything they do, their aim is to feel powerful (Samenow 1998). They want to be in control and have things go their way. This is why they argue for the sake of arguing; ignore the rights and needs of others; and exploit the vulnerabilities of others who care about them. They are pathologically self-centered.

The antisocial individual violates the rules and expected norms of behavior to meet these needs, and also to justify his behavior. As a result, he is often engaged in power struggles with others, especially authority. Samenow (1998, p. 45) argues that it is possible to make a distinction between this kind of antisocial self-absorption and the normal, developmental self -focus of some periods of childhood.

Although at times moody, demanding, and inconsiderate, teenagers as a group are concerned with fairness, they are often amazingly sensitive to others' feelings, they manifest a streak of idealism, they ponder life's purpose, and they are

LEARNING THE REWARDS OF CRIMINAL THINKING

Fig. 23.1 Learning the rewards of criminal thinking

immersed in accomplishing something worthwhile at school, in sports, or in social and community organizations. Despite intense disagreements with adults, adolescents generally accept their guidance and live within the limits that are imposed.

As Fig. 23.1 illustrates, no matter what the outcome of the power struggle, the person's criminal logic is reinforced. If the child wins the power struggle, he thinks he's right, in control, and powerful. If the child loses the power struggle, his needs to look good, be right and be in control have been threatened and he feels victimized. He does not say, "Oh, I made a mistake. I'll change my behavior." He says to himself (or to your face) "This guy's a jerk. He's picking on me. I'll show him." Once he feels victimized and angry, he believes he's justified to break more rules, so he commits another crime, or violence, or acts irresponsibly, and the cycle continues. Therefore, a first step in changing criminal thinking is to avoid power struggles. Criminal logic explains the repeating cycle of offending, consequences, and re-offending that characterizes many people who persist in antisocial activity. It helps us to understand why consequences are not sufficient to change the behavior of antisocial youth. They need effective intervention that targets their cognitive deficits and arrested moral development.

Grounded in broad research, several curricula have been developed, tested and demonstrated to be effective in correcting the faulty thinking and arrested moral development of youth with antisocial tendencies (Gibbs et al. 1996; Goldstein and Glick 1994; Goldstein et al. 1998; Little and Robinson 1993, 1995) All have similar components and include exercises that challenge thinking errors, practice social-problem-solving skills, and target moral reasoning. The exercises progress from simple to increasingly complex tasks. Participants do not advance to higher levels until they have demonstrated mastery of the lower level objectives. Using a group format and a highly structured and sequenced series of activities, they help young people to learn positive social behaviors and to make decisions about right and wrong behavior from a higher level of moral judgment. Most of these curricula have been demonstrated to be effective in significantly decreasing rule-breaking behavior among both juvenile and adult offenders (Kazdin 1994; Leeman et al. 1993; Liau et al. 2004). As a result, they are widely used in institutional and community-based correctional programs across the country and in recent years have been instituted in public school systems to effectively reduce rule-breaking behavior.

23.4   What About Prosocial Gifted Children Who Commit Heinous Acts of Violence?

When bright young people do unspeakable things, society tends to look for the reasons outside the individual. Parental abuse, bullying in the schools, the home environment, emotional disturbance, or drug abuse is blamed. So prevalent and pervasive is this trend of excusing behavior that even the lawyers for Aaron McKinney, one of Matthew Shephard's killers, opted to go to trial with the defense that Aaron participated in the murder only because he was "suffering" from a combination of a methamphetamine hangover and homosexual panic triggered by a sexual abuse memory. They were apparently hopeful that these excuses might mitigate the homicide in the eyes of the jury, and that he would get a lighter sentence.

There is no direct empirical evidence to suggest that there are conditions or characteristics of gifted people that raise their vulnerability for antisocial behavior, but this author has previously proposed a dynamic which may explain some of the most shocking acts of violence committed by gifted persons (Neihart 1999, 2002).

Episodic dyscontrol (Ewing 1990; King 1975) is an alleged, rare psychological condition in which individuals with arrested or poorly integrated ego development are suddenly so overwhelmed with feeling that they lose impulse control. They are said to be in diminished capacity and unable to stop themselves from doing things that ordinarily they would never do. I have postulated elsewhere (Neihart 2002) that on rare occasions, gifted children's capacity to modulate their impulses and emotions may fail to develop adequately as a result of precocious cognitive ability and a too early mastery and reliance on intellectualization as a defense mechanism. Over time, these unusual children may fail to integrate a healthy capacity to modulate strong affect because they consistently think away, avoid, or distract themselves from intense, negative feelings. In some cases, circumstances may arise in which the child's brittle or fragmented defenses are overwhelmed and their negative feelings erupt violently. The eruption can take the form of violent behavior, psychosis, or an emotional breakdown. Though unproven, this theory does seem to fit well the rare instances in which a gifted person with no history of antisocial or aggressive behavior "loses it" and commits a single shocking offense. Close examination of the histories of high profile, bright violent offenders, however, typically reveals some history of antisocial behavior (e.g. A & E Television Networks 2007).

23.5   Conclusion

The patterns of thinking and behavior that characterize adult criminals have been noted by many leading authorities and are recognizable in varying degrees among juveniles (Bassarath 2001; Caplan and Powell 1964; Farrington 1989; Garland and Ziegler 1999; Gath and Tennet 1972; West and Farrington 1973; Samenow 1998; Yochelson and Samenow 1995; Young 1999). The very limited empirical research suggests that high verbal ability may protect against the development of antisocial cognition, perhaps by mediating the accelerated development of prosocial moral reasoning. It further suggests that high practical intelligence, in combination with lower than average verbal ability may be overrepresented among adult and juvenile offenders in detention facilities.

Antisocial individuals are not a homogenous group, however. A thorough analysis of developmental trajectories for adult antisocial behavior must consider multiple risk and protective factors. Recognizing developing antisocial patterns in children and adolescents enables parents, teachers, pastors, and counselors to intervene effectively early on, before a child launches a career of criminal activity.

We know a lot about the ways in which antisocial individuals make decisions about right and wrong behavior. The evidence is clear that faulty cognition plays a powerful role in the emergence and persistence of rule-breaking behavior. Also well supported in the literature is the finding that it's possible to moderate and correct such thinking through a group intervention focused on cognitive retraining, moral reasoning practice, and social- problem-solving skills training. The fact that the developmental precursors for antisocial behavior are evident as early as the preschool years implies that the age of assessment and intervention should be during early childhood. Since symptoms tend to be stable once they emerge (Keenan et al. 1999), intervention efforts should be targeted to the primary school years. Further, research indicates that interventions that target the development of empathy, guilt, and emotional responsiveness should be the focus of our efforts. In addition, given that some risk factors appear to play a stronger role across different developmental periods (e.g., family conflict) it may be that there are developmental periods when children's risk is heightened. As research continues, we may be able to develop customized interventions that have even greater impact.

Intense media scrutiny of brilliant individuals who commit heinous acts of violence prompts people to ask how something so terrible could be committed by someone so full of promise. The answer for now seems to be the same cognitive deficits and arrested moral development that underlie most antisocial acts.

References

A & E Television Networks (2007). Eric Harris Biography. Retrieved from http://www. biography.com/search/article.do?id = 235982 on August 20, 2008.

American Psychological Association (1994). *Diagnostic and statistical manual of mental disorders.* Washington, DC: Author.

Barriga, A. Q. & Gibbs, J. C. (1996). Measuring cognitive distortion in antisocial youth: Development and validation of the "How I Think" questionnaire. *Aggressive Behavior, 22,* 333–343.

Barriga, A. Q., Landau, J. R., Stinson, B., Liau, A., & Gibbs, J. C. (2000). Cognitive distortion and problem behaviors in adolescents. *Criminal Justice and Behavior, 27,* 36–56.

Bassarath, L. (2001). Conduct disorder: A biopsychosocial review. *Canadian Journal of Psychiatry, 46,* 609–616.

Beck, A. (1999). *Prisoners of hate: The cognitive basis of anger, hostility, and violence.* New York: HarperCollins.

Caplan, N. S. & Powell, M. (1964). A cross comparison of average and superior IQ delinquents. *The Journal of Psychology, 57,* 307–318.

Dodge, K. A., Price, J. M., Bachorowski, J., & Newman, J. P. (1990). Hostile attributional biases in severely aggressive adolescents. *Journal of Abnormal Psychology, 99,* 385–392.

Eron, L. D., Gentry, J. H., & Schlegel, P. (Eds.) (1994). *Reason to hope: A psychosocial perspective on violence and youth.* Washington, DC: American Psychological Association.

Ewing, C. (1990). *When children kill: The dynamics of juvenile homicide.* Lexington, MA: Lexington Books.

Farrington, D. P. (1989). Early predictors of adolescent aggression and adult violence. *Violence and Victims, 4,* 79–100.

Frey, E. D. & Epkins, C. C. (2002). Examining cognitive models of externalizing and internalizing problems in subgroups of juvenile delinquents. *Journal of Clinical Child and Adolescent Psychology, 31,* 556–566.

Garland, A. F. & Ziegler, E. (1999). Emotional and behavioral problems among highly intellectually gifted youth. *Roeper Review, 22,* 41–44.

Gath, D. & Tennet, G. (1972). High intelligence and delinquency: A review. *The British Journal of Criminology, 12,* 174–181.

Gath, D., Tennet, G., & Pidduck, R. (1971). Criminological characteristics of bright delinquents. *British Journal of Criminology, 11,* 275–279.

Gibbs, J. C., Potter, G. B., Barriga, A. Q., & Liau, A. (1996). Developing the helping skills and prosocial motivation of aggressive adolescents in peer group programs. *Aggression and Violent Behavior, 1,* 283–305.

Goldstein, A. P. & Glick, B. (1994). Aggression replacement training: Curriculum and evaluation. *Simulation and Gaming, 25,* 9–26.

Goldstein, A. P., Glick, B., & Gibbs, J. C. (1998). *Aggression replacement training: A comprehensive intervention for aggressive youth.* Champaign, IL: Research Press.

Holcomb, W. R. & Kashani, J. H. (1991). Personality characteristics of a community sample of adolescents with conduct disorders. *Adolescence, 26,* 579–587.

Kazdin, A. E. (1994). Interventions for aggressive and antisocial children. In L.D. Eron, J.H. Gentry, and P. Schlegel (Eds.). *Reason to hope: A psychosocial perspective on violence and youth* (pp. 341–382). Washington, DC: American Psychological Association.

Keenan, K., Loeber, R., & Green, S. (1999). Conduct disorder in girls: A review of the literature. *Clinical Child and Family Psychology Review, 2*, 3–19.

King, C. H. (1975). The ego and the integration of homicidal youth. American *Journal of Orthopsychiatry, 45*, 134–145.

Kohlberg, L. (1984). *The psychology of moral development*. New York: Harper & Row.

Leeman, L. W., Gibbs, J. C., & Fuller, D. (1993). Evaluation of a multi-component group treatment program for juvenile delinquents. *Aggressive Behavior, 19*, 281–292.

Liau, A., Barriga, A. Q., & Gibbs, J. C. (1998). Relations between self-serving cognitive distortions and overt vs. Covert antisocial behavior in adolescents. *Aggressive Behavior, 24*, 335–346.

Liau, A., Shively, R., Horn, M., Landau, J., Barriga, A., & Gibbs, J. C. (2004). Effects of psychoeducation for offenders in a community correctional facility. *Journal of Community Psychology, 32*, 543–558.

Little, G. & Robinson, K. (1993). *Juvenile MRT: How to escape your prison*. Memphis, TN: Eagle Books.

Little, G. & Robinson, K. (1995). *Discovering life and liberty in the pursuit of happiness*. Memphis, TN: Eagle Books.

Mahoney, A. R. (1980). Gifted delinquents: What do we know about them? *Children and Youth Services Review, 2*, 315–330.

Mahoney, A. R. & Seeley, K. R. (1982). *A study of juveniles in a suburban court. Technical Report*. Washington, DC: U.S. Department of Justice, OJDPP.

National Institute of Corrections (1996). *Criminal logic*. Workshop presented at Parole Board Orientation Training. Longmont, CO.

Neihart, M. (1999). The treatment of juvenile homicide offenders. *Psychotherapy, 36*, 36–46.

Neihart, M. (2002). Delinquency and gifted children. In M. Neihart, S. Reis, N. Robinson, & S. Moon (Eds.). *The social and emotional development of gifted children: What do we know?* (pp. 103–111). Waco, TX: Prufrock Press.

Neihart, M., Reis, S., Robinson, N., & Moon, S. (Eds.) (2002). *The social and emotional development of gifted children: What do we know?* Waco, TX: Prufrock Press.

Rutter, M., Giller, H., & Hagell, A. (1998). *Antisocial behavior by young people*. New York: Cambridge University Press.

Samenow, S. E. (1998). *Before it's too late: Why some kids get into trouble and what parents can do about it*. New York: Random House.

Seeley, K. R. (1984). Giftedness and juvenile delinquency in perspective. *Journal for the Education of the Gifted, 8*, 59–72.

Seeley, K. R. (1993). Gifted students at risk. In L. Silverman (Ed.). *Counseling the gifted and talented* (pp. 263–275). Denver: Love Publishing.

Tisak, M. S. & Jankowski, A. M. (1996). Societal rule evaluations: Adolescent offenders' reasoning about moral, convention, and personal rules. *Aggressive Behavior, 22*, 195–207.

West, D. J. & Farrington, D. P. (1973). *Who becomes delinquent?* London: Heinemann\ Educational Books.

Yochelson, S. & Samenow, S. (1995). *The criminal personality, Volume 1: A profile for change*. Northvale, NJ: Jason Aaronson.

Young, D. (1999). Wayward kids: Understanding and treating antisocial youth. New Jersey: Jason Aaronson.

Chapter 24
Character Problems: Justifications of Character Education Programs, Compulsory Schooling, and Gifted Education

Barry Grant

Abstract Proponents of character education (CE) efforts neglect an essential aspect of any CE program: *justifications* of their implementation in compulsory public schools. This chapter defends two claims: Justifications for CE programs should, but do not, demonstrate consistency between the moral values stated or implied in the justification and the moral values taught and embodied in the program should, but do not, address the compulsory nature of public schooling. The chapter argues that the only justifiable form of CE in public schools is one that teaches compliance with the values and beliefs of the adults with the power to define the content of public schools. Educators of the gifted ought to be especially concerned about the soundness of justifications for CE programs. Gifted students are special targets of CE interventions and may be especially vulnerable to ill-conceived CE interventions. The chapter concludes with a call for gifted educators interested in CE to think beyond compulsory schooling.

Keywords Character education · Compulsory schooling · Gifted education · Justification · Moral justification

Educators of the gifted have been concerned with the character development of gifted youth since the beginnings of gifted education. Hollingworth, one of the field's pioneers, called for the "emotional education" of gifted children. This included "developing leadership abilities," learning to conform to rules and expectations, "avoiding the formation of habits of extreme chicanery," and "not becoming negativistic toward authority" (Silverman 1990, p. 172). Tannenbaum (2001) argued that giftedness can be used for great good or great evil and made a plea to "make moral education an integral part of enrichment for the gifted" (p. 115). More recently, the Spring 2002 and Fall 2003 issues of the National Association for Gifted Children *Conceptual Foundations Newsletter* contained articles on gifted character education.

B. Grant
328 S. Third W. Missoula, MT 59801, USA
e-mail: bgrant@runbox.com

D. Ambrose, T. Cross (eds.), *Morality, Ethics, and Gifted Minds*,
DOI: 10.1007/978-0-387-89368-6_24,
© Springer Science+Business Media LLC 2009

There are few gifted education textbooks that do not address how schools can foster, and indeed, have the obligation to foster the development of the character of gifted children. In this regard, gifted education is of a piece with the probable history of our species, the history of public school education in the United States, and current trends in public school education. Since the dawn of *homo sapiens*, people have been concerned with shaping their young so that they reach adulthood as proper members of their group (cf. Berkowitz et al. 2006). American public schools were developed to shape the character of students (Glenn 2002; Purpel 1997; Spring 1994). Horace Mann, the Father of the American Public School, wrote that "no idea can be more erroneous than that children go to school to learn the rudiments of knowledge only, and not to form character" (cited in Goldberg 1996, p. 85).

The idea that schools should develop students' character may seem to some to be about as contentious as the claim that parents have a responsibility to care for their kids. Schools are *in loco parentis*: they are supposed to help kids grow up to be decent people and good citizens. But character education (CE) is controversial. Every aspect of CE programs is contested. Glenn's (2002) examination of the history of state education in the United States shows that questions about who should teach morality and shape the character of youth and how this should be done have long been part of the debate about education in the United States. Here I mention but a handful of recent criticisms. Nash (1997) scathingly characterized much character education as,

> unnecessarily apocalyptic and narrow in its cultural criticism, inherently authoritarian in its convictions, excessively nostalgic and premodern in its understanding of virtue, too closely aligned with a reactionary (or radical) politics, anti-intellectual in its curricular initiatives, hyperbolic in its moral claims, dangerously anti-democratic, and overly simplistic in its contention that training and imitation alone are sufficient for instilling moral character. (p. 10)

Purpel (1997) deplored the "naiveté or disengeousness of the [CE] discourse and … the inadequacies of its political and social assumptions" (p. 140). Kohn (1997b) criticized both the means and ends of certain character education efforts. Mendus (1998) argued that state schools should teach the skills of citizenship, not moral values. For all the controversy about CE programs and the potential impact of such programs, proponents of CE have given little thought to one essential aspect of any CE program: *justifications* of their implementation in compulsory public schools. I have not encountered a single writer who addresses the morality of shaping the character and moral developmental of subjects who are compelled by law to have their character shaped. This chapter defends two claims: Justifications for CE programs (a) should, but do not, demonstrate consistency between the moral values stated or implied in the justification and the moral values taught and embodied in the program and (b) should, but do not, address the compulsory nature of public schooling.

Most critiques of CE programs judge a program or program rationale in light of moral values other than those propounded by the program under review. Nash opposed the traditional virtues promoted by Kilpatrick (1992) and Bennett (1993, 1995) and argued that students should learn "certain postmodern virtues" in order to develop "democratic dispositions" (p. 11). Helwig et al. (1997) believe that "character based conceptions of virtue must be embedded within a larger frame-work of morality as justice or fairness" (6th para from end). Purpel (1997) opposed the teaching of Puritan values of "obedience, hierarchy, and hard work" and, in-stead, wants schools to participate in creating a "just and loving society and culture of fulfillment for all" (p. 152). Kohn (1997a) wants a more participatory and re-flective approach to teaching values than traditional character education allows. Schultz (2002) opposed coercing students "to display orthodox attitudes" and wants education to be "a system of personal growth" (p. 11). The dialogue over who gets to control how school children are shaped continues with passion and conviction on all sides.

My critique of CE justifications is *internal*. It addresses the logic, factual ba-sis, and moral coherence of justifications for CE programs. I examine writers in and out of the field of gifted education, focusing on what is often called *traditional* character education (e.g., Kilpatrick 1992; Lickona 1991; Wynne and Ryan 1993), the dominant type of CE in the United States (Glanzer and Milson 2006). There is no agreed upon meaning to terms such as *character education* or *moral educa-tion* (Berkowitz and Grych 2000). I use "CE" as a shorthand for any school-based intervention that aims at moral change of students. These include developmental (Nucci 2006) or rational (Narvaez 2006) moral education, efforts to address "posi-tive youth development" (Berkowitz et al. 2006), citizenship education (Althof and Berkowitz 2006), and attempts to encourage a positive perception of school, emo-tional literacy, and social justice activism (Benninga et al. 2006). The differences among these approaches, while important to the proponents of these approaches, make no difference to my argument.

The literature I survey is far from comprehensive, but it is extensive enough to show that gifted CE has a character problem that mirrors that of public school CE in general. Every justification I examine shows an inconsistency between the moral values it promotes and the compulsory setting and other means by which the pro-gram is implemented. I conclude that the only form of character education that can be justified in public schools is one that teaches compliance with the values and beliefs of the adults with the power to define the content of public schools.

Educators of the gifted ought to be especially concerned about the soundness of justifications for CE programs. There is a literature arguing that gifted stu-dents have heightened moral sensitivity and a great potential to be moral leaders (Lovecky 1997; Maker 1982; Piechowski 2006; Tannenbaum 2001) yet are also vulnerable to uncongenial educational environments (Piechowski 2006; Silverman 1994). Gifted students are special targets of CE interventions (e.g., Leigh 2002) and may be especially vulnerable to ill-conceived CE interventions.

Five sections follow. The first argues that CE programs are moral enterprises re-quiring moral justifications. The second advances criteria for a sound justification. The third examines inadequate CE justifications. The fourth describes how sound justifications should address compulsory schooling. The fifth concludes the chap-ter with a call for gifted educators interested in CE to think beyond compulsory schooling.

24.1 Moral Enterprises, Moral Justifications, and Character Education Programs

A moral enterprise is a purposeful undertaking implicitly or explicitly based on moral values (Grant 2005). That CE programs are moral enterprises is obvious and recognized by their proponents. All CE programs seek to change students' attitudes, beliefs, values, habits, dispositions and behavior in purportedly morally good ways (cf. Davis 2003). Wiley (2002) claimed that "character education is a form of moral education" (p. 17) that "describes and prescribes what is meant by right and wrong" (p. 18). Kilpatrick (1992) wrote of a "crisis in moral education" (p. 14) and believes "the core problem facing our schools is a moral one. ... all the various attempts at school reform are unlikely to succeed unless character education is placed at the top of the agenda" (p. 225). Noddings (1995) argued in defense of CE programs that "our main educational aim should be to encourage the growth of competent, caring, loving, and lovable people" (p. 366). Lickona (1991) described moral education as an approach that "seeks to develop full moral character – its cognitive, emotional, and behavioral aspects. ... through the total moral life of the school" (p. 46) Hoge (2002) defined character education as "any conscious or overt effort to influence the development of desirable individual qualities or traits" (Rebirth section, para 1). CE programs, in short, aim at shaping fundamental aspects of the personhood of children – how they treat others, how they regard themselves, how they conceive of right and wrong, and so forth.

Moral enterprises require moral justifications. They require reasons why the enterprise is good or obligatory in the light of the moral views that found and guide the enterprise. The requirement to justify a moral enterprise arises from two sources: from "within" the enterprise itself as a matter of being true to, integral with, the values the enterprise serves and expresses; from "without," as a matter of honoring standards of public discussion on matters of public concern. Delattre and Russell's (1993) claim that "as rational beings, persons owe and are owed a reasoned account of the actions they perform or that affect them. ... we ought to behave in ways that can be justified" (Schooling, para 12) neatly sums up both requirements. Justice to one's moral beliefs requires that one be able to state why an action or an extended and complicated series of actions that constitute a program is obligatory or good in light of one's moral beliefs. The conventions of rational public discourse require that one not simply issue assertions but attempt to articulate sound reasons *why* an action or program is permissible or an evil. What are the requirements for an adequate justification? My answer relies on the notion of integrity, with its intimations of wholeness, harmony, consistency, and soundness.

24.1.1 Criteria for a Sound Justification of a Character Education Program

Human enterprises and actions show their character as much by the reasons offered in their support as in the actual work they entail and goals they serve. The reasons show if the enterprise is soundly conceived, if due respect is paid to objections, if factual and causal claims are supported with evidence, if facts are treated fairly, and if basic canons of rational argument are followed. We may sum all this up in a single word – integrity. A good justification for an action or enterprise has integrity.

We can admire justifications with integrity even if we disagree with their basic premises, moral positions, and reading of evidence. We respect those who propose them because we see that they are committed to a rational search for truth and respect their conversational partners and audiences by attempting to do the hard work of making good arguments for their positions. We scorn justifications that lack integrity. We judge those who propose them as unskilled, lazy, or deceptive.

We can see the importance of an integral justification in current events. Recently, the *reasons* for waging war against Iraq have become a topic for public debate. Questions have been raised about the quality of empirical evidence for the claim that Iraq had "weapons of mass destruction," assumptions of the merits of defeating "terrorists" in Iraq so they don't come to the US, and so forth. Even some of those who supported the war doubt the soundness of the reasons offered by the Executive Branch in its support of the war.

An integral justification or argument for a CE program articulates the guiding moral values of the proposed program and reasons for granting them merit. It shows how the means by which the program is implemented are consistent with the values founding the program and how the ends serve to realize these values. It follows basic standards of reason and evidence. It shows why the program is right or good in light of the values promoted in the program. Such a justification has moral consistency. It hangs together as a whole. It shows that the program "walks its talk," and demonstrates "the moral ideal of acting both self-consistently and in accordance with one's principles" (Nesteruk 2004, p. 69). It takes a firm stand on certain moral values and show how the program adheres to the values in every respect. These criteria require proponents of CE programs to ask themselves: Are we clear about what we think is right or good? Are our moral ideas compatible with the setting in which the program takes place? Do we make a solid case for the program? Is our evidence sound? Our reasoning logical? Are the means and the goals of our program consistent with our view of what is right?

The criteria say that you should teach the value of respect for others in a way that respects those you are teaching. They say one cannot justify teaching love of one's neighbors through the use of violence and force, because violence and love are incompatible. They say that violence and hatred can be taught through violence and hatred, because they are compatible. They say that if you justify teaching certain values on the grounds that society is deteriorating and schools must teach certain values in order to restore society, as some in CE claim (e.g., Lickona 1997; Wynne 1989), you must also say clearly what you mean by "deteriorate," give evidence that society is deteriorating, and give evidence and reason to believe that your program will improve society. They say that claims such as "schools have a responsibility to shape the character of students" and "schools have always been concerned with character" and "in order to maintain a democratic society we must teach children democratic values" and "there will be chaos if we don't teach children values" are the beginnings of arguments, not the conclusions of them.

My critique primarily addresses one element of an adequate justification: Whether the justification shows that the program means and ends are consistent with the values and moral concepts the program upholds. This is the key element of an integral justification. The absence of consistency between program means and moral values indicates that the moral vision of a program's proponents is incomplete, fragmented. The proponents advance a program that teaches and promotes values that they have not thought through sufficiently to justify teaching. A program that teaches values it does not itself enact is hypocritical, even dangerous, as the proponents do not understand their own moral positions well enough to see the limits it imposes on their actions. We see this clearly in the lives of individuals. One of the characteristics of moral exemplars is that they enact their moral views in ways that are consistent with their views. Gandhi campaigned for social justice peacefully and respectfully of the oppressors he opposed. Had he used violence, he would not be the admired moral leader he is. We would consider him a revolutionary or terrorist.

24.1.2 Inadequate Justifications for CE Programs

My review of the CE literature illustrates five forms of inadequate justifications for CE programs: instrumental, essentialist, moralist, historical, and universalistic. This taxonomy is not exhaustive, merely illustrative. It offers a way to easily identify flawed rationales and serves to organize my discussion. These rationales alone or in combination fail to meet the criterion of moral consistency outlined above.

24.1.2.1 Instrumental, or Means Justify Ends

This type of justification gives as a fundamental reason for a CE program that it fixes problems in school or society or prepares students for life in a democracy. This is the most common justification in the field. At its root is the belief that an important purpose of schools is to fix ills of the world, create a just society, and suchlike. Those who offer such justifications do not state how their moral values place limits on the means the program may use. Nor, and more importantly, do they teach "means justify ends" in their program. Indeed, the values taught in their programs are not compatible with such thinking. No one seems to think good character employs "means justify ends" as a fundamental concept in moral reasoning. Wiley (2002), for example, canvased lists of "universal values," from respect and responsibility to honesty, integrity, and justice. "Means justify ends" is not on her or any other list of virtues or values. Instrumental thinking is implicitly the privilege of adults whose position of power frees them from having to live the values they teach.

Instrumental justifications get whatever force they have from the merits of their argument that a program actually will improve society or school or learning or whatever. Such arguments have little merit. Minchew (2002), for example, stated that the "need" for CE programs is shown by the increase in the teenage crime rate. She cites no evidence to support the claim of an increase in teen crime, nor argument in support of the crime-reducing effect of CE programs. Wynne (1989) claimed that society must transmit "proper values" to the young in order to survive. What, according to Wynne, are the proper values upon which the survival of society depends? His answer is the "work ethic and obedience to legitimate authority and the important nonreligious themes articulated in the Ten Commandments" (p. 19). What is the evidence that our society cannot survive without these values? Wynne does not say. Nor, does he define what he means for a society to survive and so is open to the charge of advancing a circular argument: A society that is based on Wynne's "proper values" can only survive as that particular type of society as long as it holds to "proper values."

That our society has strayed from these values can be seen, Wynne claims, in increased youth homicide, suicide, and illegitimate birth rates since the 1930s and 1940s, and increased marijuana use among youth. Wynne does not attempt to show that these behaviors are associated with declines in the transmission of proper values, nor how they indicate that society is having survival problems, nor how these and other "youth disorders" *are* disorders in light of "proper values" (cf. Purpel 1997; Helwig et al. 1997). Killing is addressed in the Ten Commandments. But out-of wedlock birth and marijuana use?

In a later work co-authored with Ryan (Wynne and Ryan 1993), Wynne offered more extensive data on societal decline and a more elaborate discussion of the meaning of his data. Wynne and Ryan wrote that "there is no explicit tie between these data and school policy. However it seems reasonable to believe that the widespread and remarkable trends. ... are probably partly due to deficient school policies" (p. 9). How "reasonable" this interpretation may be is brought into doubt by the authors themselves. Later, referring to declines in test scores, increases in drug use and sex and other conduct "problems" among youth, they write, "no one knows definitively why these many unfortunate changes in conduct and learning have occurred in our young. ... a vast number of economic and social changes have occurred over many years. In many ways, these changes have helped generate disorder in schools" (pp. 14–15). They also refer to work showing that Americans value individual fulfillment and equality more than any other nation and note that "the research clearly did not clearly show long term trends" and had nothing to do with "youth unrest" (p. 14). Yet, they are unwilling to abandon their "reasonable" interpretation: the "statistics about youth disorder suggest that the moral instruction of young American have been receiving is less adequate than previously" (p. 36). Clearly, any claim about the causes of "youth disorder" and societal decline based on the evidence presented in the text is rank speculation (cf. Nash 1997; Purpel 1997).

Gifted educators also use instrumental justifications. Renzulli (2002b) claimed that gifted and creative individuals are most responsible for the forward movement of culture and history. This, he believes, is sufficient reason for providing special resources to gifted and potentially gifted students. This argument is open to several challenges: *are* gifted and creative people the main movers of history? This is a truism in the field of gifted. Whether it is actually true is an entirely other matter.

Even assuming it is true, it carries little force as a reason for state-funded schools to intervene in the movement of history. Gifted people have acted for millennia without the help of public schools. Why do they *now* need special programs in public schools in order to continue to drive history?

Renzulli's Operation Houndstooth (Renzulli 2002a, b; Renzulli et al. 2006) refers to programs that encourage the development of "co-cognitive factors" (optimism, energy, romance with a discipline, sense of destiny, courage, and sensitivity to human concerns) associated with "socially constructive giftedness" and the creation of social capital. Renzulli doesn't show how any of the values his Operation Houndstooth promotes are consistent with using compulsory schooling to move history forward. He quoted Margaret Mead – "Never doubt that a small group of thoughtful, committed citizens can change the world ... indeed, it is the only thing that ever does." – but doesn't recognize that there is a world of moral difference between a group of people getting together to change the world and a group of people getting together to get school children to change the world.

Renzulli (2002a) envisions a world in which more people and more gifted people contribute to the well-being of the nation and world. This is an ambitious vision, and Renzulli sees it doesn't fit in schools as they are: "It would be naive to think that a redirection of education goals can take place without a commitment at all levels to examine the purposes of education in democracy" (p. 5). But he does make specific recommendations for how schools now can facilitate development of the Houndstooth factors.

Renzulli argues that Houndstooth-related programs should be voluntary and optional. He doesn't argue this because he believes that schools value freedom of choice and respect for the self-determination of students. They don't, and he doesn't seem to either, at least he doesn't say he does. He argues it because he believes that requiring participation in the programs *doesn't work*: "Direct teaching about [the Houndstooth factors] through prescriptive lessons simply doesn't work – you can't teach or preach vision or sense of destiny. We should avoid *requiring* students to participate in programs and projects designed to promote [Houndstooth characteristics]" (p. 4). Renzulli justifies a program to make the world a better place solely on the basis of means justifying ends set by authorities, not on the basis of moral argument. He judges approaches to helping students internalize Houndstooth factors by their degree of effectiveness (Renzulli et al. 2006). He doesn't see that the values he wants to promote set limits on how he can enact the values. There's nothing in his Houndstooth factors or his notion of social good that says mean justify ends. By implication, if requiring participation in Houndstooth programs did work, Renzulli would support participation.

Sternberg's (2002) notion of teaching for wisdom developed out of his thinking on "whether our conventional conceptions of what giftedness is and of how to develop gifts. ... are adequate to the demands of society" (p. 9). Sternberg's thinking runs along the tracks of means justifying ends thinking: He wants to retool conceptions of giftedness and gifted programs to better serve "the demands of society." Wisdom, as the "application of one's successful intelligence to a common good" (p. 9) is, he argues, well-suited to this task. His thinking stays on an instrumental track into his account of the implementation of a pilot Wisdom program that "infuses" wisdom training into an American history course and through the rest of the paper. He wrote, the "seeds of wisdom can be planted early. . . . If we do not start early in teaching children to think about others, by the time we get around to it, it may be too late. . . . We thus believe that teaching for wisdom *should* [my emphasis] start early" (pp. 9–10). Here Sternberg appeals to pragmatics, not "wise" principles or values.

He also did this in his book on WICS – wisdom, intelligence, creativity synthesized (Sternberg 2003). There he gave four reasons for including wisdom in the school curriculum: wisdom seems to be a good vehicle for achieving happiness; wisdom promotes mindfulness; wisdom is an avenue for creating a better world; students who learn wisdom will benefit their communities. These are instrumental justifications that rest on empirical claims, the merits of which depend only on the values and judgments of the readers of his book.

A program that aims to improve the world by teaching kids to think wisely should consider the question of how to implement wisdom, teaching programs in public schools in a way that is consistent with the wisdom it teaches. Wisdom, as Sternberg (2005) characterizes it, is a form of practical reasoning that seeks to balance relevant interests and short- and long-term consequences in making decisions that are good for all. What is a wise implementation of teaching for wisdom? Sternberg doesn't address the question, here or in another paper on wisdom (Sternberg 2000). Is "infusing" wisdom thinking into an American history class, as he describes, wise? He does not address any connection between the goal of wisdom, wise thinking, and the means by which wisdom teaching is implemented in schools.

24.1.2.2 Essentialist

The essentialist argument is that teaching and schooling by their very nature shape character, and CE programs simply organize and focus a process that happens anyway. It is a commonplace that schools transmit moral messages to students (see Damon 2005; Hansen 1995; Noddings 1997). Rusnak (1998), for example, claimed that "teaching is driven by goals, and values are an intrinsic part of goals. . . . Teachers are always influencing the character of each student. Try as we might, teaching cannot be extracted from the building of character. It is the nature of teaching" (p. 2).

There are three flaws in the essentialist argument. First, *if* teachers and others in authority shape behavior and advocate values, it does not follow that they thereby shape character (habits) and not merely encourage and gain compliance. They may well do so, but evidence is required to establish this. Second, if schools *do* shape character in all sorts of incidental ways, it does not follow that school *should* undertake organized programs of CE. Whether schools should institute CE program is an entirely separate matter from whether they in fact shape character. We can see this clearly when we look at life in a civil society. Our behavior is shaped and regulated by many, many laws. It may be the case that these laws shape our character. But even if they do, it doesn't follow that they should be written with the goal of shaping a specific character. Effects on character can be regarded as incidental to the goal of gaining compliance. Third, the essentialist argument provides no justification for any *particular* CE program or any *particular* values. The fact, if it is a fact, that schools by their nature teach values and shape character is completely irrelevant to a justification of a particular CE program.

We can see the latter point in Rusnak (1998). After arguing that building of character is intrinsic to teaching, invoking Horace Mann and John Dewey, and claiming that CE has always been at the heart of "school success," he introduced certain virtues and values without any argument as to why schools should teach these and not others. He says that "always buried in [curriculum] content are lessons of responsibility, respect, cooperation, hope, and determination – the essence of good character" (p. 4). Are these values *really* always there? And, more importantly, if they are there, why *should* they be taught at all or as part of a CE program, and can they be rightly taught in a compulsory setting?

24.1.2.3 Historical

The historical justification is that a CE program is justified by virtue of it fulfilling the historical mission of schools. Laud (1997), for example, made this argument. He wrote that the teaching of moral values was at the core of American education for two centuries. The values of Franklin, Mann, and others that once informed schooling should do so again because, he implied, these values are necessary to a "successful democracy." He did not argue for the merits of these historic values; he simply assumed they are good and true. The irrationality of this argument is obvious: That something has been done for a long time is no reason for continuing to do it. The argument devolves into a moralist justification: We should teach certain values in the way we once taught them simply because the values are true.

24.1.2.4 Moralist

The argument of the type of justification, usually implicit, is that the right and wrong upon which a CE program or CE programs in general are based are obvious and should be taught. Sommers (1993) offered a pure example of a moralist position. She has no doubt that right and wrong exist and that she knows what they are. "It is wrong to mistreat a child, to humiliate someone, to torment an animal. ... It is right to be considerate and respectful of others" (p. 35). She didn't give reasons why these are moral truths or how one is to know moral truth. She admitted that not everyone would agree with her about these moral claims, but that, nevertheless, "right and wrong do exist. This should be laid down as uncontroversial" (p. 35). But of what value is the claim that there are moral truths unless one can produce at least one demonstrable truth? And, if one is to give a sound justification for teaching moral truths to school children, one must also show that teaching the truth in compulsory public schools is consistent with the truth. Sommers did not attempt to show this.

She returned to the issue of moral truth later in the essay: "Is there really such a thing as moral *knowledge*? The answer to that is an emphatic *yes*" (p. 36). She suggested that the past few thousand years have taught us that "gratuitous cruelty and political repression are wrong, that kindness and political freedom are right and good" (p. 36). Of course history does not deliver tidy lessons, and Sommers found in the history what she already believes. She asked: "why should we be the first society in history that finds itself hamstrung in the vital task of passing along its moral tradition to the next generation?" (p. 36). "Society," of course, can pass its values along in many ways other than CE programs in compulsory public schools. Sommers advocated very fine sentiments that many of her readers will agree with, but she was merely asserting her claims.

24.1.2.5 Universalist

Closely related to the moralist position, the universalist justification argues that some values are universal and the universal nature of these values provides a justification for CE programs to teach these values. "Universal" is a charmed word in character and moral education. Claiming that one is teaching universal values has considerable rhetorical force, but it has little rational force and does nothing to justify a CE program.

The idea of *teaching* universal values seems absurd on the surface. If the values are universal, why do we need to teach them in schools? Won't people pick them up or find them within themselves just as they have everywhere for millennia? How can a value be universal and yet need to be taught in what in the context of human history are very eccentric and very recent venues – compulsory public schools in the United States and within them, CE programs?

Almost no one who uses *universal values* or related concepts provides adequate evidence for their claims. (Kohlberg (1984) is an exception, but he used the phrase differently than CE exponents do. In his theory, universal values cannot be taught directly but only realized through life experiences that spark what he believed to be a universal process of moral development). For example, Sternberg (2002) named "honesty with others, respect toward others, treating others as you would want to be treated by them, and recognition of the need to hear all sides of an argument" (p. 11) as the values on which the United States is founded. He didn't offer any evidence for this claim. In what sense are these values the foundation of our country or of any other country? What does this mean? The values aren't in the U.S. Constitution or Bill of Rights. They are not shown in the words or deeds of our leaders. They are not evident in the actions of most persons reported in newspapers and magazines. One is lucky to have a mate or friend who consistently lives these values. Maybe Sternberg meant that these are some sort of glue that holds the country together and without some minimum amount of it, society would become unglued. Or, they are some sort of logically necessary foundation to our laws and practices. In the absence of explication, one can only guess.

Some see life as the prime candidate for a universal value. By seeing how this is not a universal value, we can see how the notion of a universal value has little credibility. Reimer et al. (1983) drawing on Kohlberg's work argued that "all cultures share a common concern with preserving human life" (p. 84). A universal value is not a value held by everyone, but by every "culture." Proponents of universal values have to argue something like this because individuals believe and do all sorts of things. Every culture, the argument goes, values life, even though members of the culture murder one another, wage war on other cultures, sacrifice virgins, kill infant female babies, and leave the old and weak behind to die. This is a very peculiar universality. That Reimer et al. can hold to the idea that life is a universal value in the face of this evidence is puzzling. They argue that a culture "may disagree on the criteria for choosing whom to sacrifice, but that disagreement would presuppose a common adherence to the *basic* value of human life" (p. 84). But it does not. It shows that life is not a *basic* value, but one value among others used to make decisions, and not always the most important one. Israelis at Masada, for example, went to their demise rather than face enslavement. A more accurate statement is that all cultures believe some lives are more important than others. This is shown every day in our country. The lives of the poor and powerless are less important than those of the rich and powerful. The lives of darker-skinned people are less important than those of lighter-skinned people. Lives of people far away, such as in Palestine and Afghanistan, are less important than those nearby. The "universality" of the value of life is certainly of a very peculiar sort. It is the universality of a subject matter or a topic, like cleanliness or child-rearing. Every culture has something to say about them, but they say very different things.

Delattre and Russell (1993) admirably saw the value of providing a moral justification for CE programs. The gist of their argument was that "schools have a duty to stand for genuinely moral standards, moral standards such as justice that are universal. … justice as impartiality, fairness, and reciprocity" (Schooling, para 17). They claimed not to offer a proof of the universality of moral standards, but what they did argue shows the great difficulty in offering such a proof. Not everyone has moral standards, they said – some people use others as they please. So "universal" doesn't mean "held by everyone." Gang members and others "who twist moral standards and principles to suit their own motives" (Schooling, para 9) also don't count. "People who are downtrodden, including children who are taught they are inferior to others, often don't learn about justice" (Schooling, para 3). They don't count either. This leaves "universal" to refer to "every individual and society that is serious about moral life" (Schooling, para 2). Everyone in this category "relies on a standard of justice." But this claim is either circular or highly dubious and unsupported. It is circular if "serious about moral life" refers only to people and groups that hold standards of justice described in their paper. The claim that "virtually everyone" fits in this category is an empirical claim for which no evidence is offered. The number of people who hold the Kohlbergian notion of justice they describe can't be very many. So "universal" roughly means "held by an unknown number of people who have moral beliefs similar to ours."

In entertaining the possibility that we may disagree about fundamental moral standards, Delattre and Russell introduce another meaning of "universal." "Disagreement would not show that no standards hold for everyone" (Schooling, para 11) because the existence of universal moral truths is like the shape of the earth. Just as the earth is round regardless of what we think about its shape, so moral truths are true regardless of what we think about them. Well, of course, the proof is in showing the earth has a certain shape. Delattre and Russell cannot provide an analogous proof in ethics.

Even if "universal value" could be given a meaning and determination, it still would not provide a sufficient basis for action. Simply because everyone has a value, it does not mean it is good that everyone has it. The question of the universality of a value is logically independent of the questions Is the value good? and Can its promotion in schools be justified? Every moral value has to pay its own way, with reason and evidence.

24.2 Compulsory Schooling and the Justification of CE Programs

The second claim I argue, that sound justifications should address the compulsory nature of public schooling, is actually an implication of the criterion of consistency. Insofar as a CE effort occurs in a compulsory setting, the program should show how the moral values it promotes are consistent with students being compelled to be exposed to and taught the values. Pubic school students are a captive audience. They are required by law to attend school or risk bringing the police and legal systems upon themselves or their parents. This aspect of public education is not addressed by anyone in CE I have read. Once one notices this absence, even among thoughtful and philosophically-minded CE proponents (e.g., Noddings 2005; Purpel 1997, 2005), it becomes quite puzzling.

Those who argue and debate and maneuver to be able to influence the character development of children seem blind to the fact that the children are forced to be the objects of their ministrations. They make no effort to show how their CE programs are justified in settings in which students are compelled to receive them. Purpel (1997) wrote that we "simply cannot allow those in the [traditional] character education movement to monopolize and control the moral discourse of education" (p. 151). But at issue is not control of discourse, but control of children. The discourse matters only insofar as it determines who gets their views into schools. With approximately two-thirds of the states requiring schools to implement CE programs (Traub 2005), there are many opportunities to get one's ideas into play. That there are laws requiring CE programs in school is not in itself justification for a CE program. Each program must show that its values are consistent with laws compelling students to attend school and to participate in a CE program.

The values of freedom and personal responsibility, for example, are not compatible with the setting of compulsory schooling, because force and freedom are not consistent. The "universal characteristics of a morally mature person" posited by Ryan (1989) – respect for human dignity, care for the welfare of others, seeking peaceful resolution of conflict, being able to reflect on moral choices, integration of individual interests and social responsibility, and demonstration of integrity – cannot be taught in schools that do not enact or allow the exercise of these values. Cooperation cannot be taught in an environment that establishes winners and losers and rewards winners. Noddings (1995) argued that "our main educational aim should be to encourage the growth of competent, caring, loving, and lovable people" (p. 366). How is this consistent with compulsory schooling? The question has particular force for Noddings, who objects to liberal education because it is based on "an ideology of control" (p. 366).

Leigh (2002), writing in gifted education, and Wynne and Ryan (1993), traditional character educators, have views about CE that are consistent with compulsory schooling. The reason is simply that they teach compliance, which is consistent with compulsory education. Leigh serves as an example.

Leigh described an example of CE as compliance education or pacification that will "satisfy the needs of both gifted children and society" (p. 14). She claimed that CE must temporally and logically precede education, for without CE there can be no other education. Without, for example, "sharing, taking turns, and listening skills," kids can't learn the alphabet (p. 14). She argued that "desirable social characteristics" must be inculcated in students so that education can occur. Once an effective CE program is in place, students can then "learn more about more esoteric matters – like algebra, sentence structure and why college is important" (p. 18). "Inculcating desirable social characteristics" is indeed as Leigh said, "a tricky business" (p. 14). The trick is to effectively manipulate students according to their abilities and characteristics into receiving school:

> Animals and a few low-functioning deficient persons must be trained in socially acceptable behavior with a system of rewards and perhaps occasional aversive consequences.... Children of normal intelligence are able to comprehend rules... and the consequences of breaking those rules. Gifted children... have unique characteristics which give them little tolerance for unexplained rules and glib platitudes. (p. 14)

While Leigh may be right that students must have certain "desirable social characteristics" in order to do American compulsory public education, she offered no reason for thinking that these characteristics have merit outside of the special circumstance of school and no moral argument in support of the characteristics or means of teaching them. Indeed, she did not advance any particular moral concepts or principles, only moral rules, such as "help others not to feel embarrassed or unhappy" and be courteous. She claimed that appropriate CE programs will "avoid repeating the sad history of too many gifted leaders whose principles made them great villains" (p. 14). She provided no evidence for this claim, and it's hard to see how learning compliance and receptivity to school will create leaders.

The only type of CE program that can be justified in compulsory schools is compliance education. All other types require for their justification an unsustainable distinction between those, older, who can teach and promote values they do not wholly follow and those, younger, who must submit to the teachings. This distinction, while perhaps necessary in parent-child relationships, supports state control of children when applied in public schools. Questions of wisdom, maturity, and culture that are largely begged in parent-child relationships are unavoidable and unsolvable in state-child relationships. Parents, within broad limits, may be happily left to help their children carry on the culture they inherited. When the state attempts to pass on a culture, the question of which culture to pass on and how to pass it on are impassable blocks. Noddings (2005) claimed that CE works best when there is general agreement on values among community members. Indeed, if there is general agreement on values, the field of CE would not exist in anything like its current form. Schools would teach the values of the community with nary any debate, much as occurs in homogenous cultures. It's because we don't agree on values that we debate which ones should be taught. The distinction between the older and wiser and younger and needing-to-be-molded can be supported in private schools. Private schools can be communities of like-minded persons.

Aren't I being too fussy, too all-or-nothing, in my standards? Must we choose between compliance education and private schools? As Purpel (2005) wrote, "life is extremely complicated, contradictory, and messy" (p. 363). Many situations call for practical reasoning, the conclusions of which can't be deduced from one or two concepts. Isn't it better to have what one thinks is the best possible influence on students, even though one is caught in a contradiction? Perhaps, but one has to argue for this: and, more importantly – argue and teach that moral consistency (dare I say, integrity?) has only relative value. Teach students how and when to compromise themselves and consort with institutions, persons, and situations that contradict their deepest held beliefs.

24.3   Conclusion: Gifted Education and Character Education

Educators who follow my arguments have two choices: promote compliance education programs or turn their attention away from compulsory schools and start thinking about and creating forms of schooling that don't rely on force. I have argued elsewhere (Grant 2005) that gifted education is ripe for articulating and enacting educational visions that reject compulsion. Roeper's (1990) Education for Life, Schultz's and Delisle's (1997) work on the relationships among curricula, self, and visions of the good life, Heng's (2003) call to serve children's search for meaning, Cooper's (1998) "curriculum of conscience," Schultz's (2002) character education as community building, Sternberg's (2002) teaching for wisdom, Folsom's (1998) teaching that integrates mind and character, and other views on education that serve students' personal growth and honor the autonomy and dignity of students do not jibe with compulsory schooling. A look at Schultz's (2002) view of CE serves as an example of this point.

Schultz (2002) defined CE as "a process where adults, adolescents, and others engage in the development of community" (p. 10). It is a "democratic process necessitating the conscious involvement of students and teachers to construct a community of trust and respect" (p. 11). He wants education to be a "system of personal growth rather than a means to economic potential" (p. 11). He envisions teachers and students working as equals to build all aspects of the school community – rules, curriculum, place of spiritual values, and so forth. "The boundary between teacher and learner is blurred in favor of liberty and learning" (p. 11).

Schultz presented a vision of a democratic school that serves personal growth, but he doesn't show how his vision of CE view is compatible with compulsory education. Indeed it isn't, and he *almost* said this. He saw, of course that his vision of education is a challenge to the status quo. He questioned whether "mandates for basic proficiency" align with CE as a responsibility of schools. He asked, "in school, where adults represent conformity and authority, how does community building occur? Where do trust and respect develop?" (p. 10), but he didn't take the final step in his thinking and conclude that students and teachers cannot meet as equals when students are compelled by law to attend school. Schultz and others in gifted education cannot do justice to their views by promoting them as options in compulsory schools. Gifted educators have long pushed against the walls of public schools to try to make better spaces for gifted students. They have rarely questioned the legitimacy of the walls, only the limits of the opportunities they afford. They owe it to themselves and to the children they wish to inspire to begin developing alternative venues for their ideas.

References

Althof, W. & Berkowitz, M. (2006). Moral education and character education: Their relationship and roles in citizenship education. *Journal of Moral Education*, 35(4), 495–518.

Bennett, W. (1993). *The book of virtues*. New York: Simon & Schuster.

Bennett, W. (1995). *The moral compass: Stories for a life's journey*. New York: Simon & Schuster.

Benninga, J. S., Berkowitz, M. W., Kuehn, P., & Smith, K. (2006, February). Character and academics: What good schools do. *Phi Delta Kappan*. Retrieved April 1, 2007 from Expanded Academic ASAP.

Berkowitz, M. & Grych, J. (2000). *Early character development and education*. Early Education & Development, 11(1), 55–72.

Berkowitz, M., Sherblom, S., Bier, M., & Battistich, V. (2006). Educating for positive youth development. In M. Killen & J. Smetana (Eds.) *Handbook of moral development* (pp. 683–701). Mahwah, NJ: Lawrence Erlbaum.

Cooper, C. (1998). For the good of humankind: Matching the budding talent with a curriculum of conscience. *Gifted Child Quarterly*, 42, 238–244.

Damon, W. (2005, Spring). Good, bad, or none of the above? The time-honored mandate to teach character. *Education Next*, 20–27.

Davis, M. (2003). What's wrong with character education? *American Journal of Education*, 110(1), 32–57.

Delattre, E. & Russell, W. (1993). Schooling, moral principles, and the development of character. *Journal of Education*, 175(2), 23–45.

Folsom, C. (1998). From a distance: Joining the mind and moral character. *Roeper Review* 20(4), 265–270. Retrieved April 4, 2007 from Expanded Academic ASAP.

Glanzer, P. & Milson, A. (2006). Legislating the good: A survey and evaluation of character education laws in the United States. *Educational Policy*, 20(3), 525–550.

Glenn, C. (2002). *The myth of the common school*. Oakland, CA: ICS Press.

Goldberg, B. (1996). *Why schools fail*. Washington, DC: Cato Institute.

Grant, B. (2005). Education without compulsion: Towards new visions of gifted education. *Journal for the Education of the Gifted*, 29(5), 161–186.

Hansen, D. (1995). Teaching and the moral life of classrooms. *Journal for a Just and Caring Education*, 2, 59–74. Retrieved May 5, 2003 from http://tigger.uic.edu/~lnucci/MoralEd/articles/hanson.html

Helwig, C., Turiel, E., & Nucci, L. (1997). Character education after the bandwagon has gone. Paper presented in L. Nucci (chair), Developmental perspectives and approaches to character education. Symposium conducted at the meeting of the American Education Research Association, Chicago, March 1997. Retrieved May 5, 2003 from http://tigger.uic.edu/~lnucci/MoralEd/articles/helwig.html

Heng, M. (2003). Beyond school: In search of meaning. In J. Borland (Ed.) *Rethinking gifted education* (pp. 46–60). New York: Teachers College Press.

Hoge, J. (2002). Character education, citizenship education, and the social studies. *Social Studies*, 93(3), 103–108. Retrieved September 5, 2002 from Academic Search Elite.

Kilpatrick, W. K. (1992). *Why Johnny can't tell right from wrong*. New York: Simon & Schuster.

Kohlberg, L. (1984). *The psychology of moral development*. New York: Harper & Row.

Kohn, A. (1997a, February). How not to teach values: A critical look at character education. *Phi Delta Kappan*, 429–439 Retrieved June 5, 2007 from http://www.alfiekohn.org/articles.htm#null

Kohn, A. (1997b). The trouble with character education. In A. Molnar (Ed.) *The construction of children's character: Ninety-sixth yearbook of the National Society for the Study of Education, Part II* (pp. 154–162). Chicago, IL: NSSE.

Laud, L. (1997). Moral education in America: 1600s–1800s. *Journal of Education*, 179(2), 1–10.

Leigh, M. (2002). Six principles of gifted character education. *Conceptual Foundations: Newsletter of the Conceptual Foundations Division of the National Association for Gifted Children*, 10(1), 14–18.

Lickona, T. (1991). *Educating for character: How our school can teach for respect and responsibility*. New York: Bantam.

Lickona, T. (1997). In A. Molnar (Ed.) *The construction of children's character: Ninety-sixth yearbook of the National Society for the Study of Education, Part II* (pp. 45–62). Chicago, IL: NSSE.

Lovecky, D. (1997). Identity development in gifted children: Moral sensitivity. *Roeper Review*, 20(2), 90–94.

Maker, C. J. (1982). *Teaching models in the education of the gifted*. Rockville, MY: Aspen Systems.

Mendus, S. (1998). Teaching morality in a plural society. *Government and Opposition*, 33(3), 355–363.

Minchew, S. (2002). Teaching character through sports literature. *The Clearing House*, 75(3), 137–142. Retrieved September 6, 2002 from InfoTrac OneFile.

Narvaez, D. (2006). Integrative ethical education. In M. Killen & J. Smetana (Eds.) *Handbook of moral development* (pp. 703–734). Mahwah, NJ: Lawrence Erlbaum.

Nash, R. (1997). Answering the "virtuecrats": A moral conversation on character education. New York: Teachers College Press.

Nesteruk, J. (2004). Liberal education as moral education. *National Civic Review*, 93(1), 68–72.

Noddings, N. (1995, January). A morally defensible mission for schools in the 21st century. *Phi Delta Kappan*, 365–368.

Noddings, N. (1997). Character education and community. In A. Molnar (Ed.) *The construction of children's character: Ninety-sixth yearbook of the National Society for the Study of Education, Part II* (pp. 1–16). Chicago, IL: NSSE.

Noddings, N. (2005). Care and moral education. In H. Shapiro & D. Purpel (Eds.) *Critical issues in American education: Democracy and meaning in a globalizing world* (3rd ed., pp. 297–308). Mahwah, NJ: Lawrence Erlbaum.

Nucci, L. (2006). Education for moral development. In M. Killen & J. Smetana (Eds.) *Handbook of moral development* (pp. 657–682). Mahwah, NJ: Lawrence Erlbaum.

Piechowski, M. (2006). *"Mellow out" they say. If only I could: Intensities and sensitivities of the young and bright*. Madison, WI: Yunasa Books.

Purpel, D. (1997). The politics of character education. In A. Molnar (Ed.) *The construction of children's character: Ninety-sixth yearbook of the National Society for the Study of Education, Part II* (pp. 140–153). Chicago, IL: NSSE.

Purpel, D. (2005). Social justice, curriculum, and spirituality. In H. Shapiro & D. Purpel (Eds.) *Critical issues in American education: Democracy and meaning in a globalizing world* (3rd ed., pp. 349–366). Mahwah, NJ: Lawrence Erlbaum.

Reimer, J., Pritchard, P., & Hersh, R. (1983). *Promoting moral growth: From Piaget to Kohlberg* (2nd ed.). Long Grove, IL: Waveland.

Renzulli, J. S. (2002a). Co-cognitive components underlying socially constructive giftedness. *Conceptual Foundations: Newsletter of the Conceptual Foundations Division of the National Association for Gifted Children*, 10(1), 1–7.

Renzulli, J. S. (2002b). Expanding the conception of giftedness to include co-cognitive traits and to promote social capital. *Phi Delta Kappan*, 84(1), 33–58. Retrieved on June 8, 2007 from http://www.gifted.uconn.edu/sem/expandgt.html

Renzulli, J. S., Koehler, J., & Fogarty, E. (2006). Operation Houndstooth intervention theory: Social capital in today's schools. *Gifted Child Today*, 29(1), 14–24. Retrieved on June 8, 2007 from www.prufrock.com/client/client_pages/GCT_articles/Operation_Houndstooth/ Operation_Houndstooth.cfm

Roeper, A. (1990). *Educating children for life*: The modern learning community. Monroe, NY: Trillium.

Rusnak, T. (1998). Introduction: The six principles of integrated character education. In T. Rusnak (Ed.) *An integrated approach to character education*. Thousand Oaks, CA: Corwin.

Ryan, K. (1989). In defense of character education. In Nucci, L. (Ed.) *Moral development and character education: A dialogue* (pp. 3–17). Berkley, CA: McCutchan.

Schultz, R. (2002). Passionate hopefulness. *Conceptual Foundations: Newsletter of the Conceptual Foundations Division of the National Association for Gifted Children*, 10(1), 10–14.

Schultz, R. A. & Delisle, J. R. (1997). School, curriculum, and the good life: Knowing the self. *Roeper Review*, 20, 99–104.

Silverman, L. (1990). Social and emotional education of the gifted: The discoveries of Leta Hollingworth. *Roeper Review*, 12(3), 171–178.

Silverman, L. (1994). The moral sensitivity of gifted children and the evolution of society. *Roeper Review*, 17, 110–116.

Sommers, C. (1993, December 13). How to teach right & wrong: A blueprint for moral education in a pluralistic age. *Christianity Today*, 37(15), 33–37.

Spring, J. (1994). *The American school*, 1642–1993 (3rd ed.). New York: McGraw-Hill.

Sternberg, R. (2000). Wisdom as a form of giftedness. *Gifted Child Quarterly*, 44(4), 252–260.

Sternberg, R. (2002). What to do with gifted children? Teaching for wisdom. *Conceptual Foundation: Newsletter of the Conceptual Foundations Division of the National Association for Gifted Children*, 10(1), 8–10.

Sternberg, R. (2003). *Wisdom, intelligence and creativity synthesized*. New York: Cambridge University Press.

Sternberg, R. (2005). A model of educational leadership: Wisdom, intelligence, and creativity synthesized. *International Journal of Leadership in Education*, 8(4), 347–364.

Tannenbaum, A. (2001). Giftedness: The ultimate instrument for good and evil. In N. Colangelo & S. Assouline (Eds.) *Talent development: Proceedings of the 1998 Henry B. and Jocelyn Wallace national research symposium on talent development* (pp. 89–120). Scottsdale, AZ: Great Potential Press.

Traub, J. (2005, Winter). The moral imperative. *Education Next*, 23–33.

Wiley, L. (2002). *Comprehensive character building classroom: A handbook for teachers*. De Bary, FL: Longword Communications.

Wynne, E. A. (1989). Transmitting values in contemporary schools. In L. Nucci (Ed.) *Moral development and character education: A dialogue* (pp. 19–36). Berkeley, CA: McCutchan.

Wynne, E. A. & Ryan, K. (1993). *Reclaiming our schools: A handbook on teaching, character, academics, and discipline*. New York: Merrill.

Part VI
Where We've Been and Where We're Going

Chapter 25
Capitalizing on Cognitive Diversity in Explorations of Ethical High Ability

Don Ambrose

Abstract The attempt made in this book to build cognitive bridges between the complex bodies of work on ethics and high ability requires a big-picture assessment. Cognitive diversity, a construct from recent investigations in complexity theory, serves as a framework for analysis of the breadth of scope needed in such a project. In addition, the architectural metaphor of desire lines assists in clarification of the processes and benefits of interdisciplinary collaboration in this project and in future, similar work. Large-scale patterns in the collective insights generated by the contributing authors also are developed. Themes derived from the patterns include panoramic visions enabling perception of creative intelligence and escape from dogma, the dynamics of identity formation, and bridge building across interdisciplinary and sociocultural chasms.

This has been a long, exciting journey with many interdisciplinary twists and turns. Our authors have shown us political and economic influences on bright, young minds; neurophysiological dynamics of those minds and some concomitant cognitive processes; the inner, emotional aspects of ethics; the nature and limitations of educational interventions aimed at strengthening moral imagination and values; and the dynamics of identity formation, among other phenomena. Where do we begin an assessment of the worthiness of such a broad-scope, collaborative endeavor? First, it is helpful to consider just how broadly we did scan the intellectual terrain for gems of insight. Employing a construct from complexity theory helps with that. Second, we draw some comparisons and interconnections among some of the discoveries our authors made. Third, we suggest some directions for future investigation of this intriguing topic.

D. Ambrose
Editor, Roeper Review, Graduate Department, School of Education, College of Liberal Arts, Education, and Sciences, Rider University, 2083 Lawrenceville Road, Lawrenceville, NJ, 08648-3099, USA
e-mail: ambrose@rider.edu

D. Ambrose, T. Cross (eds.), *Morality, Ethics, and Gifted Minds*,
DOI: 10.1007/978-0-387-89368-6_25,
© Springer Science+Business Media LLC 2009

Keywords Altruism · Cognitive diversity · Cognitive science · Complexity theory · Continuum of visibility · Continuum of consent · Dialectical synthesis · Ethics · Gifted · Interdisciplinary · Morality · Sociopolitical contexts

25.1 Generating Cognitive Diversity Along Interdisciplinary Desire Lines

Consider an unusual metaphor for understanding the moral dimensions of giftedness, talent, intelligence, and creativity. Imagine that ethical high ability is a large, intriguing, complex, ill-defined mass resting somewhere out on the lawn of a large university. It is late evening and the campus is dimly lit. An experimental psychologist exits his building, which is northeast of the mass, and shines a brilliant but narrowly focused quantitative–empirical, methodological flashlight on the object thereby gaining some understanding of it from that perspective. The flashlight enables him to grasp some important insights about the mass, but if he is satisfied with that unidirectional understanding, he misses many important nuances on the other sides of the object. Now imagine that a moral philosopher exits her building, which is west of the mass, and uses a conceptual–analytic lantern to illuminate it from that angle, giving us a very different view, which adds to the experimental psychologist's findings. Together, these two glimpses provide a more complete, but still inadequate, picture of the mass. Still other investigators emerge from the sociology building, the natural–science complex, the cultural–anthropology annex, and other locations on campus. Each provides another perspective on the ethical high ability mass. All of the investigators share their discoveries with one another, strengthening and clarifying their collective understanding but likely never reaching completion.

25.1.1 The Benefits of Cognitive Diversity

Only a collection of views from all directions, plus some deep probing into the mass itself, can reveal most of the phenomena of interest. Taken together, these differing perspectives and approaches to understanding represent the productive results of cognitive diversity: a construct articulated by Page (2007), a complexity theorist who has synthesized much interdisciplinary research and theory on complex, collaborative problem solving. Cognitive diversity exists if a group encompasses diverse perspectives or interpretations, diverse heuristics, and diverse predictive models. Diverse perspectives or interpretations correspond to varied ways of viewing, representing, categorizing, or framing problems or issues. Diverse heuristics imply varied methods of problem solving. Diverse predictive models represent varied ways of inferring cause and effect.

Page analyzed discoveries about the problem-solving capacities of groups engaged in various endeavors ranging from the work of interdisciplinary teams, to the dynamics of organizations, markets, and democratic processes at the national level. His summary of findings indicated that cognitive diversity is at least as important as intelligence for dealing with complex, multidimensional issues. A cognitively diverse team, undistinguished in terms of measured intelligence, is likely to be as effective as, or even superior to, a team of gifted but like-minded people who share a single perspective or problem-solving approach. Of course a team combining intellectual power with cognitive diversity will be stronger yet. These insights apply only to the study and solution of complex problems. Cognitive diversity can be ineffective or even counterproductive when dealing with simple problems requiring algorithmic approaches.

25.1.2 Cognitive Diversity and Interdisciplinary Inquiry

Given the complexity of ethical high ability, even if the experimental psychologist on the northeast side of the nebulous object on the campus green is a MacArthur genius, a Nobel laureate, or the most intelligent investigator on earth, his findings from a solitary, disciplinary perspective will be inadequate in comparison with the insights provided by the team of investigators who collectively viewed the mass from all angles. The same problem would exist if a team of exceptionally bright but like-minded investigators from a single discipline scrutinized the mass from the same northeastern angle, missing the other perspectives. They would gain a number of brilliant, probing insights about one side only and lack the big picture.

The importance of cognitive diversity magnifies the value of interdisciplinary work. In Page's (2007) words,

> [Findings about the efficacy of cognitive diversity] can and should be read as supportive of interdisciplinary research. People with different disciplinary training naturally bring diverse understandings and tools to problems. That diversity of tools can lead to breakthroughs that would not occur, or would occur more slowly without interdisciplinary research (p. 16).

Applying these insights to our inquiry in this volume illuminates the importance of interdisciplinary investigations of ethics, giftedness, talent development, intelligence, and creativity. Studying ethical high ability from the viewpoint of a single discipline or field, using a single, preferred methodology, is analogous to viewing the mass on the imaginary campus green with a single methodological flashlight from only one direction. The mass is very complex and multidimensional so, according to Page's findings, its investigation requires much cognitive diversity. Fortunately, we amassed a considerable amount of it in the collective works of the authors who contributed to this volume.

25.1.2.1 Meeting on Interdisciplinary Desire Lines

Garber (2001), a scholar of English Studies, also recognized that some of the most unyielding, complex problems transcend disciplinary boundaries and require multiple interpretations. Consequently, she employed the architectural metaphor of *desire lines* to grapple with the difficulties that attend interdisciplinary work. Desire lines are the footpaths that emerge in the well-trod grass on the lawn between buildings in a multi-building complex such as a university campus. Facilities planners use these emerging paths as guidance for decisions about where to put permanent sidewalks. In Garber's metaphor, the university is the sum of academic knowledge; the individual buildings on the campus are the separate academic disciplines; and the intersections on the desire lines in the grass are promising points of contact for interdisciplinary collaboration on difficult, complex problems of common interest.

A group of investigators from a single discipline or field studying a complex phenomenon, such as scholars of gifted education studying the nature of ethical high ability, will produce some varied insights but these will be confined by the specialized inquiry tools and epistemological conventions employed in the particular building that houses them on Garber's imaginary campus. Applying Garber's metaphor to the example of research on giftedness, the vibrant gifted-education community works in a small building that sits in the shadows among larger structures such as the stark, metal-sheathed psychology building, the ostentatious, modernist business school, and the stuffy, old, vine-covered, graystone philosophy building decorated with metaphysical gargoyles.

The gifted-education group benefits from some unity within the walls of its building but suffers from some parochialism, which foments a distinct lack of broad vision. They have more cognitive diversity than most fields because their small building houses empirical psychologists, counseling psychologists, curriculum theorists, and subject-matter specialists, among others. They even include the odd importer of philosophical constructs such as postmodernism applied to curriculum theory (Piirto 1999), tenets of moral philosophy (e.g., Ambrose 2003a; White 2003) and phenomenological inquiry methods (e.g., Cross et al. 2003; Schultz 2002).

The related field of creative studies enjoys a little more cognitive diversity. While dominated by psychologists, from diverse subfields, its primary journals (e.g., *Creativity Research Journal, Journal of Creative Behavior*) include occasional contributions from management theorists, educational researchers, economists, and theoretical physicists, among others.

Although the high-ability fields of gifted education and creative studies have this cognitive diversity, they need even more when investigating the ethics-high ability nexus because the relevant phenomena are more complex than most objects under investigation in Garber's metaphorical university. For example, such inquiry requires broad, interdisciplinary searches for theories and research findings from multiple levels of analysis to ensure scrutiny of constructs revealing (a) the nuances of broad, sociopolitical, economic, and cultural influences on ethical high ability, (b) the structure and dynamics of brain subsystems and neural networks, (c) genetic influences on intelligence, and even (d) possibilities that quantum paradoxes at the subatomic level could influence dynamics in microstructures of the brain (for additional justification of interdisciplinary work at multiple levels of analysis see Ambrose 2005; Nicolescu 1996).

Astonishingly, even this wide-ranging list of relevant realms of inquiry may be insufficient. Only very broad, interdisciplinary searches can provide the cognitive diversity needed to encompass these dimensions of ethical high ability along with others we have not yet considered. The scope of the search for relevant theories and research findings must be extremely broad, approximating or even going beyond a recent exploration of creative intelligence encompassing 87 theories and research findings from 26 academic fields (see Ambrose in press). This exploration revealed the surprising extent to which constructs from very diverse fields can apply to high ability. In one example derived from this collection, contextual cognitive scientists (e.g., Descombes 2001; Wang 1995) can make us think twice about our entrapment within *psychophysiological parallelism*, which is the portrayal of cognition as strictly derived from inside-the-cranium electrochemical processes. Instead, contextual cognitive scientists highlight ways in which cognition derives largely from interaction with others and with the larger historical and cultural context, making the mind context-embedded and constructed instead of assembled solely from hard wiring inside the skull of an atomistic individual.

In a more developed example, borrowing one of the 87 insights from the collection can generate the following scenario. If Larry Coleman and Tracy Cross walked out of the gifted-education building and bumped into ethical philosopher Gail Presbey on a desire-line intersection on the metaphorical campus green, they could collaborate in the synthesis of their *continuum of visibility* (Coleman and Cross 1988, 2005) with the philosophical *continuum of consent* (Presbey 1997). Borrowing constructs from the eminent philosopher Hannah Arendt, Presbey argued that power relationships in families, communities, and nations range on a five-level continuum. Level one generates the most freedom and self-actualization for individuals while level five generates the most pernicious and confining conditions. The Presbey–Arendt continuum is explained in more detail in Chapter 4.

Coleman, Cross, and Presbey could combine this continuum of consent with the continuum of visibility, which portrays gifted children as behaving in ways that (a) maximize their visibility to others, or (b) enable them to become less visible by blending in among their peers, or (c) make them even more invisible because they *disidentify* with giftedness. The interdisciplinary innovation here would be application of the continuum of visibility to the work of adult expert professionals in various sociopolitical contexts. For example, the synthesis of the two continua could lead to predictions about the behavior of gifted, expert professional scientists and writers. These professionals likely would be inclined to maximize their visibility, celebrating their giftedness in a society at level one of the continuum of consent. The informed reason and level playing field for professional discourse in such a society, absent manipulation, propaganda, coercion, and violence, would pose little threat to their professional and personal lives. On the other hand, scientists and writers who live under the thumb of regimes operating at the lowest levels of the Presbey–Arendt continuum, which employ manipulation, coercion, and violence, likely would be more inclined to hide their abilities, approximating the disidentification of some gifted children, because intellectuals in totalitarian regimes are targeted for persecution and even extermination. For example, only about 300 of 380,000 intellectuals and artists survived the Cambodian Pol Pot regime (Jacobson 1997).

In societies somewhere between vibrant democracy and totalitarianism, scholars can face career-threatening suppression instead of life-threatening violence. For example, many scientists who have disagreed with the Bush administration's ideological reinterpretations of science, which often advance corporate policies at the expense of scientific truth, have been marginalized when their findings and theories have run counter to the administration's policies on political and economic issues (Herrera 2004). Overall, the influences of sociopolitical contexts on adult expert professionals might approximate the influences of democratic or autocratic classroom environments on bright children. The interconnections between the philosophical Presbey–Arendt continuum and the continuum of visibility from gifted education reveal some ethical implications that emerge from even mildly oppressive sociopolitical contexts. Consequently, interdisciplinary meetings at the intersection of desire lines on Garber's metaphorical campus can prove their worth in studies of ethics.

25.1.2.2 Some Possible Disciplinary Contributions to Cognitive Diversity

In a cognitively diverse, interdisciplinary team, social science and humanities disciplines such as anthropology, history, archaeology, economics, sociology, political science, and ethical philosophy can reveal insights about the large-scale and long-range contextual dimensions of ethics. For example, anthropology can highlight diverse cultural shaping influences on moral behavior while history and archaeology can reveal transitory preferences for certain moral codes from one era to another. Economics can illustrate ways in which contextual pressures to channel giftedness, talent, or creativity into pursuit of materialistic ends, possibly at the expense of ethics, can vary from one nation to the next. Sociology, political science, and ethical philosophy can reveal the sociocontextual influences of power and domination that support or warp the manifestation of ethical behavior in particular sociopolitical contexts.

The natural sciences and professions can make their contributions as well. Biology can postulate and clarify genetic, evolutionary, or neurobiological bases for altruism. Legal theory can reveal the rights, obligations, and principles of justice that shape moral decision making in particular societies. Educational research can articulate the nuances of instructional practices that promote collaboration, empathy, and broader awareness of the issues requiring ethical thought and moral action.

25.1.2.3 Examples of Fields that Benefit from Cognitive Diversity

Some highly complex areas of study benefit from extensive cognitive diversity. The interdisciplinary field of cognitive science collectively generates a set of very divergent perspectives on cognitive processes by embracing energetic dialogue and debates among linguists, psychologists, neuroscientists, philosophers, artificial intelligence researchers, anthropologists, and others (see Baumgartner and Payr 1995; Descombes 2001). The equally vibrant, interdisciplinary field of complexity theory, which entails the study of complex adaptive systems, enjoys similar dialogic processes and interdisciplinary borrowing among economists, political scientists, biologists, physicists, chemists, and mathematicians, among others (see Kauffman 2002; Miller and Page 2007; Morowitz 2004). It is difficult to argue that ethical issues are not as complex as these areas of study and that we would not benefit from similar cognitive diversity in projects such as this book.

25.1.2.4 Benefiting from Dialectical Synthesis

There may be one other benefit of interdisciplinary, cognitive diversity applied to ethics. Collaborative, interdisciplinary sharing can bring conflicting perspectives into a common forum and provide opportunities for revision and refinement of important constructs along with productive syntheses of ideas. Conflicting viewpoints can generate dialectical processes in which the dynamic tensions between opposing positions can create a productive new synthesis (Ambrose 2003; Sternberg 1999, 2001; Yan and Arlin 1999). In an example of dynamic tension from another domain of investigation, a productive dialog between Paul Ricoeur, a leading holistic philosopher, and Jean-Pierre Changeux, an eminent reductive neuroscientist, appeared in a high-profile academic publication (Changeux and Ricoeur 2000). On the surface, the perspectives of a phenomenological philosopher of mind and a mechanistic analyst of brain structure and function appeared to be irreconcilable. Nevertheless, each scholar's key ideas served as reflective mirrors for his opponent clarifying the relative merits and flaws of each position and even revealing some promising correspondences such as the importance of the mind's aesthetic characteristics.

25.2 Some Patterns and Interconnections in Our Cognitively Diverse Collection of Insights

Some themes recur throughout this volume. They are worthy of some attention because they emerge from such diverse sources. When leading minds in diverse disciplines discover similar motifs they might be following productive investigative paths. Some of these commonalties are explored briefly here, along with some interesting creative associations between specific insights. In addition, the potential embedded in intellectual discord, and some ideas for future investigations are reviewed.

25.2.1 Patterns Emerging from the Insights

Consistent with the ideal of cognitive diversity, our contributors addressed multiple dimensions of the ethics-high ability nexus. The mind map in Fig. 25.1 provides a brief and admittedly incomplete overview of some patterns in the contributors' discussions. Ideally, the map would include much more detail, hundreds more nodes, which, unfortunately, would make it too unwieldy for inclusion here. Nevertheless, this abbreviated map provides some grasp of the ethical terrain covered and the integrative possibilities in such a cognitively diverse collection of theories and findings about ethical high ability.

The major themes in the map include some constructs and general frameworks that repeat throughout many of the chapters. For example, the larger theme, *panoramic visions*, represents insights that expand awareness about important dimensions of ethics. The subcategory, *escaping dogma*, includes phenomena that keep large numbers of people in the dark about important ethical issues: ideological or economic dogmatism and metaphorical entrapment for example. The panoramic vision theme also includes aspects of high ability and thought processes that can enable bright individuals to see farther than peers of lesser creative intelligence. The theme *identity dynamics* captures constructs that reveal ways in which individuals of high ability can develop either very deep intrapersonal, or expansive, external, context-situated senses of self that enable them to act in altruistic ways. The theme *bridge building* addresses ways to overcome sociocultural insularity so bright individuals can strengthen tenuous bonds between diverse groups, or establish these bonds where they've been absent, it also addresses ways that disciplinary insularity can be transcended for the strengthening of cognitive diversity and the concomitant advanced discoveries about ethical high ability.

25.2.2 Sample Interconnections

The dotted arrows in Fig. 25.1 represent a few of many possible interconnections that can be made between insights in this volume. Analyses of all possible connections would require messy cluttering of the map with arrows and likely another book to describe their details. The few examples here provide a brief glimpse into the integrative possibilities encompassed by a cognitively diverse collection of insights about ethical high ability. Interdisciplinary connections can reveal some dimensions of ethics not normally considered. Moreover, they can serve as examples for use with gifted young people themselves. For instance, an educator or mentor can select two chapters from this volume and share them with gifted students, asking them to make creative associations between the works of two authors.

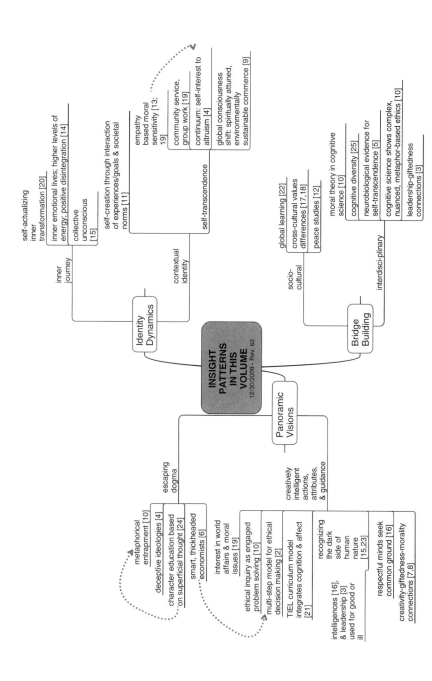

Fig. 25.1 Patterns in the explorations in this volume (Numbers in parentheses designate chapters in the book where the insights on the map can be found)

25.2.2.1 Dogmatic Economists and Elements of Ethical Decision Making

For example, the gifted group might decide that there are informative connections between psychologist, Robert Sternberg's model of ethical decision making in Chapter 2, and economist, Tom Green's portrayal of the dogmatic insularity embedded in mainstream economic theory in chapter 6. Green argues that bright economists inhibit their own intelligence by rigidly narrowing their focus to the tenets of neoclassical economic theory. One result is excessive trust in market dynamics, which marginalize ethical considerations and remove the long-term costs of actions from economic calculation. Several of Sternberg's steps in his multi-step model of ethical behavior seem to be violated by such economic decision making. Steps two and three seem especially transgressed.

Step two requires thinkers to define the event as having an ethical dimension. Economists seem to have ignored Sternberg's second step of ethical decision making when they posit the legitimacy of letting the market dictate that steel be used in the manufacture CO_2-emitting Hummers instead of the construction of wind-powered irrigation pumps in impoverished third-world nations (see this and other examples in Chapter 6). Mainstream economists simply don't recognize that ethics should come into play when resources are lavished on the frivolous wants of the affluent at the expense of the desperate needs of the deprived.

Step three requires thinkers to decide that the ethical dimension is significant. As Green's example of the disappearing Pacific island nation of Kiribati suggests, mainstream economists are trapped in a form of short-range vision that obscures considerations of long-term, large-scale disasters such as global warming. Using this creative association, a group of gifted young people could modify their own taken-for-granted perceptions of the economy and the market while working to build awareness in others of less-expansive intellects.

25.2.2.2 Empathic, Gifted Children and Self-transcendent, Altruistic, Adult Rescuers

Another intriguing creative association comes from connecting the inclination of many gifted children toward empathy based moral sensitivity (see analyses by Deirdre Lovecky, Michael Piechowski, Deborah Ruf, and Annemarie Roeper and Linda Silverman in chapters 13, 14, 20, and 19 respectively) and studies of self-transcendence detailed by Adam Martin and Kristen Monroe in Chapter 5. The self-transcendent rescuing behaviors shown by Monroe's subjects, which were elucidated by qualitative interviews and connected with neurobiological findings, could represent the highest levels of moral giftedness even though many of these impressive people never would be selected for gifted programs, which employ measures of academic-oriented intellectual aptitude in screening processes. Those who score well in measures of the linear–sequential, verbal, symbolic cognitive processing often overemphasized in the screening processes that select gifted students for special attention might show up anywhere on Monroe's self-centered through altruistic continuum; however, the rescuers she identified cluster at the self-transcending altruistic end. Martin and Monroe's evidence for rare, impressive moral behavior, derived from political psychology and neuroscience, provides strong reasons for giving ethics a more prominent place in conceptions of high ability.

25.2.2.3 Metaphorical Ethics Refining Character Education

An additional, promising creative association could emerge from considering Barry Grant's concerns about superficial thought underpinning character education (CE) programs (see chapter 24) and then connecting them with Mark Johnson's illumination of the nuanced, metaphorical nature of ethical thinking (see chapter 10), which emerges from developments in cognitive science. Among other points, Grant argues that justifications for CE programs in schools must include clarity about fundamental assumptions such as the nature of right and wrong or the dangers in society that CE programs can address or correct. Policy makers contemplating the development and implementation of CE programs could benefit from Johnson's insights about the deep, shaping influences of metaphor. With their newfound sensitivity to the power of metaphor, they might use Lakoff's (2002) analysis of the ways in which conservatives and liberals differ on the basis of conflicting family metaphors for society. The strict-father metaphor framing conservative thought portrays human nature as inherently negative and human interaction as a competitive struggle for survival. Consequently, character requires strength and obedience to hierarchical authority. In contrast, the nurturing-parent metaphor framing liberal thought portrays human nature as essentially good and human interaction as a process of democratic negotiation. Character within this framework would include an open-minded willingness to compromise. With the benefit of metaphorical awareness, the policy makers could understand and explain the deep foundations of their CE programs. Moreover, they could assess the worthiness of their fundamental assumptions. Such assessment would make them less likely to remain trapped mindlessly within a dogmatic framework.

These sample interconnections are suggestive. Many more can be found, and we encourage you to make your own integrative discoveries.

25.2.3   Possible Disagreements: Kindling for Dialectical Synthesis

Recall that disagreements can be starting points for productive dialogue and possibly, eventually, the generation of productive dialectical syntheses. One deeply rooted conflict embedded in the work of most contributors is the dynamic tension between mechanistic and organismic–contextualist world-view conceptions of phenomena relevant to ethical high ability.

Several philosophical world views implicitly guide scholars' beliefs about the nature of the phenomena they study and about the efficacy of various investigative methodologies (Overton 1984; Pepper 1942). These deeply rooted world views include mechanism, contextualism, organicism, and formism, the first three of which are addressed here. Investigation from within a single world view cannot provide an adequate representation of highly complex phenomena; however, when insights from two or more world views are considered together they can provide broad and deep understandings. The more complex the phenomena under investigation, the more necessary it is to consider contributions from multiple world views.

A mechanistic thinker metaphorically views the world as machine-like, predictable, and reducible to component parts. A contextualist thinker perceives the world through the metaphorical lens of an ongoing event within its context, thereby focusing on the unpredictably evolving, contextually shaped nature of events. An organicist thinker is guided by the metaphor of a living entity and appreciates the coherence, integration, and totality of systems, and how different properties emerge at higher levels of development as the system evolves. Philosophical insularity arises within and between disciplines when scholars and professionals adhere strongly to competing metaphorical world views and ignore or denigrate the viewpoints of colleagues whose world views differ from their own. World-view analyses have been applied to cognitive science (Gillespie 1992), and to scholarship in high-ability fields (Ambrose 1996,1998a, b, 2000).

Metaphorical world-view conflicts aren't at the forefront of our contributors' arguments. In fact, most of the authors were invited on the basis of their resistance to excessively mechanistic emphases in their disciplines. Consequently, their insights collectively contribute to the dynamic tension between the mechanistic thought that dominates most disciplines and the blend of contextualism and organicism that provides alternative viewpoints. Although different world views are incommensurable, lacking common standards for comparison and agreement on terminology (Overton 1984), bringing conflicting root-metaphorical paradigms together in a field can set the stage for dialectical synthesis.

Examples of insights from this volume that align with the world views include the following.

- Arguments against the dominance of rational-choice theory (see Chapters 5 and 6); which portrays individuals as perfectly informed actors who make calculated, rational decisions for personal benefit; are contextualist–organicist because they resist the mechanistic reduction of the individual to an atomistic, mechanized calculator.
- The TIEL curriculum model (Chapter 21) is organicist because it promotes the integration of the cognitive and affective subsystems within the individual.
- Engaging bright young people in experiences such as community service (Chapter 16) and global learning (Chapter 22) is contextualist–organicist because it promotes the unpredictable emergence of novelty within real-world contexts while integrating the gifted with the larger sociocultural context.
- Synthesizing neurobiological findings (derived from mechanistic research) with qualitative (organicist) research on altruistic rescuers (see Chapter 5) represents a promising blend of world views.

Many other examples are embedded in the chapters. Considering the ways in which they are framed by deep-level metaphorical assumptions can set the stage for some movement toward productive dialectical syntheses.

25.3 An Interdisciplinary Mosaic of Ethical High Ability

Imagine that we could employ the insights provided by the contributing authors in this volume to manufacture ideal, creatively intelligent individuals of strong ethical fiber. Considering these insights, along with some integrative patterns that show up throughout the book, we can speculate about the nature and dispositions of individuals who combine ethics with high ability. They may approximate the following description.

Emotion is as important as rational calculation to their ethical decision making. Both heart and mind are necessary. Reason provides direction for action. Passion provides the motivation for decision making and action. In addition, their reason must not be clouded by self-deception or the mass deception that prevails in the sociocultural, economic, and ideological environment. If they fall prey to manipulation and propaganda, their emotions can be swayed toward malevolent ends. Consequently, they must acquire incisive critical thinking skills, which are developed by grappling with real issues in real-world contexts that expose them to diverse cultures and to peers who adhere to differing values. Through such exposure, they will develop the interpersonal; and intrapersonal skills necessary for dealing with difference. Accordingly, they may come to identify with a nationality, ethnicity, and a creed but these elements of personal identity formation will not override a larger sense of universal connectedness with humanity and with the ecosystem itself. Their wants and the wants of their friends and relatives will not override the needs of outsiders. This speculative depiction is incomplete but it is a starting point for further analyses.

25.4 Ideal Search Conditions for Future Explorations

The cognitive diversity represented in this volume could be stronger if our authorship included some representatives of disciplines beyond those incorporated here: disciplines such as archaeology, cultural anthropology, feminist theory, history, indigenous studies, journalism, the history and philosophy of science, sociology, the arts, and theology. Nevertheless, our scope is impressive. Our authors include leading psychologists, political theorists, philosophers, critical theorists, scholars of creative studies, critical thinking specialists, a legal theorist, a theoretical physicist, and a variety of educational researchers with empirical, practical, and theoretical investigative agendas. We add more cognitive diversity, albeit in abbreviated form, by providing short depictions of other scholars' potential contributions to conceptions of ethical high ability.

In essence, one key to gaining the benefits of cognitive diversity is to vigorously search for inspiration from interdisciplinary sources. We can find this inspiration by searching for the nebulous mass of ethical high ability at the interdisciplinary intersections in the desire lines on Garber's imaginary campus. The best way to find these intersections is to consider driving questions that diverse scholars are likely to follow out of their parochial disciplinary buildings onto the interdisciplinary lawn. For example, one such promising question is "Why do some gifted people engage in altruistic acts that entail personal sacrifice or danger while others do not?" This question can entice ethical philosophers, evolutionary psychologists, cultural anthropologists, political theorists, and educators of the gifted to meet out on the interdisciplinary lawn to share, argue, and synthesize ideas. Another promising interdisciplinary question is "How does exceptional moral leadership emerge in our cultures?" This question can draw scholars of indigenous studies, organizational development, feminist theory, sociology, and creative studies or gifted education out onto meeting places on Garber's lawn. Other driving questions appear in the introductory chapter of this volume. Until we strengthen our interdisciplinary exploration and collaboration, limited perspectives on the complex phenomenon of ethical high ability will continue to confine us.

References

Ambrose, D. (1996). Unifying theories of creativity: Metaphorical thought and the unification process. *New Ideas in Psychology, 14*, 257–267.

Ambrose, D. (1998a). A model for clarification and expansion of conceptual foundations. *Gifted Child Quarterly, 42*, 77–86.

Ambrose, D. (1998b). Comprehensiveness of conceptual foundations for gifted education: A world-view analysis. *Journal for the Education of the Gifted, 21*, 452–470.

Ambrose, D. (2000). World-view entrapment: Moral-ethical implications for gifted education. *Journal for the Education of the Gifted, 23*, 159–186.

Ambrose, D. (2003a). Barriers to aspiration development and self-fulfillment: Interdisciplinary insights for talent discovery. *Gifted Child Quarterly, 47*, 282–294.

Ambrose, D. (2003b). Theoretic scope, dynamic tensions, and dialectical processes: A model for discovery of creative intelligence. In D. Ambrose, L. M. Cohen & A. J. Tannenbaum (Eds.), *Creative Intelligence: Toward Theoretic Integration* (pp. 325–345). Cresskill, NJ: Hampton Press.

Ambrose, D. (2005). Interdisciplinary expansion of conceptual foundations: Insights from beyond our field. *Roeper Review, 27*, 137–143.

Ambrose, D. (in press). *Expanding visions of creative intelligence: Interdisciplinary perspectives.* Cresskill, NJ: Hampton Press.

Baumgartner, P., & Payr, S. (Eds.). (1995). *Speaking minds: Interviews with twenty eminent cognitive scientists.* Princeton, NJ: Princeton University Press.

Changeux, J. P., & Ricoeur, P. (2000). *What makes us think?* (M. B. DeBevoise, Trans.). Princeton, NJ: Princeton University Press.

Coleman, L. J., & Cross, T. L. (1988). Is being gifted a social handicap? *Journal for the Education of the Gifted, 11*, 41–56.

Coleman, L. J., & Cross, T. L. (2005). *Being gifted in school* (2nd ed.). Waco, TX: Prufrock Press.

Cross, T. L., Stewart, R. A., & Coleman, L. J. (2003). Phenomenology and its implications for gifted studies research: Investigating the lebenswelt of academically gifted students attending an elementary magnet school. *Journal for the Education of the Gifted, 26*, 201–220.

Descombes, V. (2001). *The mind's provisions*: A critique of cognitivism (S. A. Schwartz, Trans.). Princeton, NJ: Princeton University Press.

Garber, M. (2001). *Academic instincts*. Princeton, NJ: Princeton University Press.

Gillespie, D. (1992). *The mind's we: Contextualism in cognitive psychology*. Carbondale, IL: Southern Illinois University Press.

Herrera, S. (2004). Echo chamber of secrets: How science policy is being made by politicized science. *Acumen Journal of Life Sciences, 11*, 118–123.

Jacobson, M. (1997, September). For whom the gong tolls. *Natural History, 106*, 72–75.

Kauffman, S. A. (2002). *Investigations*. New York: Oxford University Press.

Lakoff, G. (2002). *Moral politics: How liberals and conservatives think* (2nd ed.). Chicago, IL: University of Chicago Press.

Miller, J. H., & Page, S. E. (2007). *Complex adaptive systems: An introduction to computational models of social life*. Princeton, NJ: Princeton University Press.

Morowitz, H. J. (2004). *The emergence of everything: How the world became complex*. New York: Oxford University Press.

Nicolescu, B. (1996). Levels of complexity and levels of reality: Nature as trans-nature. In B. Pullman (Ed.), *The emergence of complexity in mathematics, physics, chemistry, and biology* (pp. 393–417). Vatican City: Pontifical Academy of Sciences.

Overton, W. F. (1984). World views and their influence on psychological thoughts and research: Khun-Lakatos-Laudan. In H. W. Reese (Ed.), *Advances in child development and behavior* (Vol. 18, pp. 91–226). New York: Academic.

Page, S. E. (2007). *The difference: How the power of diversity creates better groups, firms, schools, and societies*. Princeton, NJ: Princeton University Press.

Pepper, S. C. (1942). *World hypotheses*. Berkeley, CA: University of California Press.

Piirto, J. (1999). Implications of postmodern curriculum theory for the education of the talented. *Journal for the Education of the Gifted, 22*, 324–353.

Presbey, G. M. (1997). Hannah Arendt on power. In L. D. Kaplan & L. F. Bove (Eds.), *Philosophical perspectives on power and domination* (pp. 29–40). Amsterdam: Rodopi.

Schultz, R. A. (2002). Illuminating realities: A phenomenological view from two underachieving gifted learners. *Roeper Review, 24*, 203–212.

Sternberg, R. J. (1999). A dialectical basis for understanding the study of cognition. In R. J. Sternberg (Ed.), *The nature of cognition* (pp. 51–78). Cambridge, MA: MIT Press.

Sternberg, R. J. (2001). What is the common thread of creativity? Its dialectical relation to intelligence and wisdom. *American Psychologist, 56*, 360–362.

Wang, H. (1995). On 'computabilism' and physicalism: Some subproblems. In J. Cornwell (Ed.), *Nature's imagination: The frontiers of scientific vision* (pp. 161–189). Oxford, UK: Oxford University Press.

White, D. A. (2003). Philosophy and theory in the study of gifted children. *Roeper Review, 26*, 16–19.

Yan, B., & Arlin, P. (1999). Dialectical thinking: Implications for creative thinking. In M. A. Runco & S. R. Pritzker (Eds.), *Encyclopedia of creativity* (Vol. 1, pp. 547–552). New York: Academic.

Author Index

Subject Index

Printed in the United States of America